Stories Matter

Stories Matter

The Complexity of Cultural Authenticity in Children's Literature

Edited by

Dana L. Fox
Georgia State University

Kathy G. Short
University of Arizona

National Council of Teachers of English
1111 W. Kenyon Road, Urbana, Illinois 61801-1096

Staff Editors: Tom Tiller and Bonny Graham

Interior Design: Doug Burnett

Cover Design: Pat Mayer

NCTE Stock Number: 47445-3050

Cover Art: From *My Daughter, My Son, the Eagle, the Dove/Mi Hija, Mi Hijo, el Aguila, la Paloma* illustrated by Susan Guevara. Illustrations copyright © 2000 by Susan Guevara. Used with permission of the Author and BookStop Literary Agency. All rights reserved.

Library of Congress Cataloging-in-Publication Data

Stories matter : the complexity of cultural authenticity in children's literature/ edited by Dana L. Fox, Kathy G. Short.
    p. cm.
  Includes bibliographical references and index.
  ISBN 0-8141-4744-5 (pbk.)
    1. Children's literature, American—History and criticism—Theory, etc. 2. Children's literature, English—History and criticism—Theory, etc. 3. Children—Books and reading—English-speaking countries. 4. Children—Books and reading—United States. 5. Multiculturalism in literature. 6. Storytelling in literature. 7. Culture in literature. I. Fox, Dana L. II. Short, Kathy Gnagey.

PS490.S74 2003
813.009'9282—dc21

2003012055

About the Cover

The cover illustration by Susan Guevara comes from *My Daughter, My Son, the Eagle, the Dove/Mi hija, mi hijo, el aguila, la paloma,* written by Ana Castillo (Dutton, 2000). We chose this illustration for the cover of *Stories Matter* because it so powerfully conveys the primary theme of this book—children's need for stories in their lives that authentically convey their own and others' cultures. Stories *do* matter to children. They influence the ways in which children think about themselves and their place in the world as well as the ways in which they think about other cultural perspectives and peoples. As this illustration indicates, these influences come both from ancient traditions and wisdom and from interacting with stories alongside significant adults in a child's world. In this case, the grandmother is sharing a story with her granddaughter, which reflects the importance of story being passed from one generation to another through personal interactions with those who matter in a child's life. The Aztec symbols connect this Latina grandmother and granddaughter to their own heritage in the ancient land now known as Mexico. It is fitting that this book is rooted in the ancient chants that were recited as a rite of passage by a parent or wise elder for a child on her way to adulthood. The combination of ancient traditions and contemporary images reflects the ways in which stories continue to weave particular cultural traditions and values from one generation to the next and the importance of those stories in authentically reflecting both the past and present of those cultures.

Susan's process of creating this illustration reflects her careful attention to authenticity as she drew from her own personal and cultural experiences as well as engaged in extensive research on Aztec daily life and their use of glyphs or "picture writing." She includes two levels of story in this illustration, showing both a contemporary story of a grandmother and granddaughter and a metaphoric story related to the glyphs. The two glyphs above the heads of the girl and her grandmother are their name glyphs, and the glyphs below symbolize their missions and journeys. Susan's careful research and her strong connection to this chant unite accuracy of cultural fact with the authenticity of cultural values in order to create a powerful image that visually introduces many of the issues addressed by authors of the chapters in *Stories Matter.*

—Kathy G. Short and Dana L. Fox

The ideographic language of the pre-Hispanic peoples is an important part of my Mesoamerican heritage. It is important not solely because of my obvious genealogical connection but also because I am a picture maker. I describe the world around me, the worlds of specific stories I am illustrating, in pictures. Picture making is how I retell the feeling of being in a certain world at a certain time. I am closely aligned to the "image" as a way of communicating, just as children first draw pictures to make sense of and relate to their world. It is no coincidence that I make pictures for children's books.

This Mesoamerican picture language has the power to relate whole concepts of feeling and existence. Studying it as part of my research for *My Daughter, My Son, the Eagle, the Dove*, even as a layperson, has enriched my life. My liberal attempt to use this language within the contemporary illustrations for that book has been an attempt to share this richness with my readers. It is my hope that I have communicated even the smallest aspect of this poetic expression and given voice to that which has no words.

—Susan Guevara

Contents

Acknowledgments

Our sincere appreciation goes to all of the contributors, who have written so thoughtfully and provocatively about issues related to cultural authenticity in children's literature. As we state in our opening chapter, we began our work with many of these authors during the time when the two of us worked together as colleagues at the University of Arizona, where we were coeditors for five years of *The New Advocate,* a journal for those involved with young people and their literature. Our dialogues with the contributors over time, whether in print or in person, have been extremely productive and have raised for us a number of theoretical and practical issues related to the role of culturally authentic literature in the lives of educators and those of the children and adolescents with whom they work. We would particularly like to recognize children's book illustrator Susan Guevara, who graciously gave us permission to feature one of her paintings from *My Daughter, My Son, the Eagle, the Dove: An Aztec Chant* (Castillo, 2000) on the book cover.

We thank Kurt Austin, managing editor for books and acquisitions editor for the National Council of Teachers of English, as well as the members of the NCTE Editorial Board and the anonymous field reviewers for their insightful readings and constructive suggestions on both the early drafts and later versions of our work. NCTE staff editors Tom Tiller and Bonny Graham provided helpful editing, excellent questions, and tremendous support to us during the production of this book. We would also like to recognize the editorial assistance of Shannon Smith, Terri Kotlar, and Donna Taylor of Georgia State University, and Lupita Romero of the University of Arizona, who tracked down references in the library, proofread pages, and performed other important tasks.

Finally, our love and gratitude go to our families, particularly our husbands, David Wigley and Jerry Short, who offer their continuing support of our work and who help make life so meaningful.

—Dana L. Fox and Kathy G. Short

I The Sociopolitical Contexts of Cultural Authenticity

1 The Complexity of Cultural Authenticity in Children's Literature: Why the Debates Really Matter

Kathy G. Short and Dana L. Fox

Cultural authenticity in children's literature is one of those contentious issues that seems to resurface continuously, always eliciting strong emotions and a wide range of perspectives. Authors, illustrators, editors, publishers, educators, librarians, and scholars all have different points of view about authenticity that they each feel strongly about based on their own sociocultural experiences and philosophical views. But do these debates about cultural authenticity really matter?

We first became closely involved with these issues when we were editors of *The New Advocate*, a professional journal for those involved with young people and their literature, where we published a number of articles on cultural authenticity. The controversy and debates intrigued us, so we read everything we could locate on the topic. We were impressed by the complexity of the issues being discussed, but we were also concerned about how often the debates quickly moved to simplistic insider/outsider distinctions, specifically whether whites should write books about people of color. We found that no one article dealt with the complexities of the debates about cultural authenticity, and we realized that, given the nature of the issues, no one article ever could reflect this complexity and range of viewpoints. That is when the idea of this edited collection came into being.

Often, publishers discourage edited collections, believing that they have less coherence and appeal for readers, but in this case we believed that cultural authenticity *needed* to be addressed through a collection of differing voices and perspectives. We knew from our own explorations that these voices are passionate and strong, and that the arguments are not merely academic but reflect deeply held beliefs at the heart of each person's work in creating literature for young people and using these books with children. It was the complexity and intensity of the debates about cultural authenticity that we found provocative, and that complexity demanded an edited book to highlight the range of multiple perspectives, viewpoints, and voices.

We were also concerned, however, by how often the debates seemed to swirl back to dichotomies and simplistic outsider/insider distinctions. One of our goals in pulling together this edited collection was to invite new conversations, questions, and critiques about cultural authenticity, but we knew that those conversations had to be based in thoughtful and thorough understandings of what had already been discussed. We believe that this edited collection on cultural authenticity does just that through a range of voices that provide a sense of history, a broad understanding of the current issues and debates, and a glimpse of possible new conversations and questions.

A unique feature of this book is the continual interaction between authors, as writers refer across their pieces and positions to the texts, ideas, and stances of others in the volume. Thus, the book itself becomes one whole, seamless experience for readers rather than a collection of discrete essays or chapters. Although edited collections are often approached by reading individual chapters separately from others, this volume is indeed a complex conversation about cultural authenticity, and we believe the conversation is much more powerful if the book is read as a whole.

Readers of this book will not only find a rich overview and background, but they will also be invited to consider new directions for the field as they reflect on topics such as the social responsibility of authors, the role of imagination and experience in writing for young people, cultural sensitivity and values, authenticity of content and images, and authorial freedom. Importantly, in exploring cultural authenticity in children's literature, each chapter author cites specific children's books from a wide variety of cultural groups, including African American, American Indian, Asian American, Canadian, Chinese, Latino/Latina, and West African cultures.

Since this is a book about cultural authenticity, we knew that we would be expected to provide a foundational definition of cultural authenticity to frame the book. This undertaking seemed appropriate and important to us, until we attempted to draft a definition. We then realized why so many authors and educators who discuss cultural authenticity are reluctant to define it in formulaic or prescriptive terms. We found ourselves agreeing with Rudine Sims Bishop, who argues that cultural authenticity cannot be defined, although "you know it when you see it" as an insider reading a book about your own culture. In defining cultural authenticity, Howard (1991) states that we cannot ignore what the book does to the reader, and she argues that we know a book is "true" because we feel it deep down, saying, "Yes, that's how it is." The reader's sense of truth in how a specific cultural experience has been represented within a book, particularly when the reader is an insider to the culture portrayed in that book, is probably the most common understanding of cultural authenticity.

Howard (1991) argues that an authentic book is one in which a universality of experience permeates a story that is set within the particularity of characters and setting. The universal and specific come together to create a book in which "readers from the culture will know that it is true, will identify, and be affirmed, and readers from another culture will feel that it is true, will identify, and learn something of value, sometimes merely that there are more similarities than differences among us" (p. 92). Given that each reading of a book is a unique transaction which results in different interpretations (Rosenblatt, 1938/1995), and given the range of experiences within any cultural group, this definition of cultural authenticity immediately hints at why there are so many debates about the authenticity of a particular book. Weimin Mo and Wenju Shen argue, however, that even though there are always differences within a cultural group, cultural authenticity can be defined as whether or not a book reflects those values, facts, and attitudes that members of a culture as a whole consider worthy of acceptance or belief. Rudine Sims Bishop defines cultural authenticity as the extent to which a book reflects the worldview of a specific cultural group and the authenticating details of language and everyday life for members of that cultural group. She notes that while there will be no one image of life within a specific cultural context, there are themes, textual features, and underlying ideologies for each cultural group that can be used to determine cultural authenticity.

Although these understandings about cultural authenticity serve as the basis for the chapters in this book, we decided not to offer one specific definition of cultural authenticity. In fact, one of the key issues under debate *is* the definition of cultural authenticity. Instead, the authors of each chapter offer their own perspectives related to how cultural authenticity should or should not be defined. Because there are no easy answers to the questions of cultural authenticity in children's literature, we hope that this book will provide readers with an opportunity to engage in productive discussions about a range of issues.

In the remainder of this chapter, we provide important background and contextual discussions on cultural authenticity to introduce and frame the chapters in this book. Before we can move into the complexities of this issue, however, we begin with a broader discussion of the central role that literature plays in an education that is multicultural. An understanding of the role of culture in our lives and the lives of the young people with whom we work is essential as we look at more complex issues of cultural authenticity in literature and its usefulness in multicultural education. Next, we explore several complex issues of cultural authenticity that emerge from the various chapters in this book and discuss how each chapter author characterizes this concept. Finally, we turn our attention to the most significant audience of culturally authentic literature for young people—the children and adolescents with whom we work—and conclude with a discussion of the implications of these complex issues for those who create, publish, and teach children's literature.

The Sociopolitical Nature of Multicultural Education

Central to these debates about cultural authenticity are definitions of culture and multiculturalism. Although culture and multiculturalism are sometimes defined superficially only in terms of the awareness and appreciation of the traditions, artifacts, and ways of life of particular groups of people, the authors in this book base their discussions in more complex understandings of culture and the goals of multiculturalism.

Culture can be understood as all the ways in which people live and think in the world. Geertz (1973) defines culture as "the shared patterns that set the tone, character, and quality of people's lives" (p. 216). These patterns include race, ethnicity, gender, social class, language, religion, age, sexual orientation, nationality, geographical regions, and so forth. Banks (2001) states that most social scientists define culture as primarily consisting of the symbolic, ideational, and intangible aspects of society—the values, symbols, interpretations, and perspectives that distinguish one group of people from another. He also argues that cultures are always dynamic, complex, and changing and must be viewed as wholes, rather than as composed of discrete parts. Weimin Mo and Wenju Shen agree, characterizing culture as a seamless significant experience shared by a group of people that influences the way they view themselves, society, and human relationships, including what they value and believe to be true. Florio-Ruane (2001) stresses the notion of agency, stating that culture is "both meaning and the process of making meaning," an idea fundamental to the process of education. "As both the web and the weaving," Florio-Ruane argues, "we all make local cultural meaning," and we also connect our webs to "a much more complex network of webs linking human beings over time and across distance and difference" (p. 27).

Multiculturalism is often viewed as a curriculum reform movement that involves changing the curriculum to include more content and children's books about ethnic groups, women, and other cultural groups. This view limits multicultural education to lessons on human relations and sensitivity training along with units on ethnic festivals, foods, folklore, and fashions (Nieto, 2002). Mingshui Cai points out that this practice conflicts with the goals of multicultural education, which have never been just to appreciate cultural differences, but to transform society and to ensure greater voice, power, equity, and social justice for marginalized cultures. Similarly, Ladson-Billings (1994) proposes that a "culturally relevant" pedagogy is built on the cultures of students to maintain those cultures and to "transcend the negative effects of the dominant culture" (p. 17).

Both Banks (2001) and Nieto (2002) note that while the specific definition and list of qualities for multiculturalism may vary, there is consistency across major theorists on the goals and purposes of multicultural education. Those goals emphasize the sociopolitical nature of education through challenging and rejecting racism and discrimination and affirming pluralism, particularly for individuals and groups considered outside the cultural mainstream of society. They argue that, from the beginning, multicultural education has had reforming education as its goal, so that students from diverse racial, ethnic, and social class groups can experience educational equality. Issues of inequality, discrimination, and oppression cannot be excluded from multiculturalism without changing its very nature. Sleeter (1991) writes that "multicultural educators give voice and substance to struggles against oppression and develop the vision and the power of our future citizens to forge a more just society" (p. 22).

Underlying this focus on sociopolitical goals is the belief that multiculturalism is not a special unit or piece of literature, but a perspective that is part of all education. Sleeter and Grant (1987) argue for the use of the phrase "an education that is multicultural" to indicate that multiculturalism is an orientation that should pervade the curriculum.

These understandings about the underlying sociopolitical nature of multicultural education provide an important backdrop for many of the debates about children's literature and cultural authenticity. One controversy addressed by Joel Taxel, Kathryn Lasky, Violet Harris, and Hazel Rochman is that multiculturalism and cultural authenticity are often dismissed as "political correctness," a movement characterized by the popular press as the suppression of statements (or books) deemed offensive to women, blacks, or other groups. Kathryn Lasky, for example, views cultural authenticity as political correctness, a fanaticism which has led to "self-styled militias of cultural diversity" who dictate who can create books about specific cultural groups. Hazel Rochman believes that concerns about authenticity have sometimes led to "politically correct bullies" who use pretentious jargon to preach mindless conformity.

Joel Taxel, in contrast, believes that the labeling of multicultural education as "political correctness" is a backlash against the goals of multiculturalism. He argues that cries of "political correctness" ignore the history of racist representations in children's books and the lack of equal access to publishing. Violet Harris points out that this lack of access continues today, with the field of children's book publishing and the academic study of children's literature remaining overwhelmingly in the control of whites. Joel Taxel believes that the term "political correctness" has been used to denigrate those who raise questions about the cultural content of children's books and question white privilege.

Although multicultural literature is typically defined as books about specific cultural groups, either people of color or people who are members of groups considered to be outside of the dominant sociopolitical culture, Rudine Sims Bishop, Mingshui Cai, Joel Taxel, and Laura Smolkin and Joseph Suina all point out that the definition of multicultural literature has more to do with its ultimate purpose than with its literary characteristics. They state that multicultural literature is a pedagogical construct that has the goal of challenging the existing canon by including literature from a variety of cultural groups. Debates about multicultural literature and cultural authenticity, therefore, are not so much about the nature of the literature itself, but about the function of literature in schools and in the lives of readers.

If "multicultural literature" is a pedagogical term rather than a literary term, then the issues of cultural authenticity take on significance related to the role of literature in children's lives, specifically in the power of literature to change the world. Viewed in this way, literature serves a crucial role in multicultural education, social justice, and reform. Cai and Bishop (1994) argue that multicultural literature "opens the group's heart to the reading public, showing their joy and grief, love and hatred, hope and despair, expectations and frustrations, and perhaps most importantly, the effects of living in a racist society" (p. 68). As Rosenblatt (1938/1995) reminds us, literature has the potential to be a powerful educational force, fostering the kind of sensitivity and imagination needed in a democracy. This potent force, combined with dynamic and informed teaching, can enable young people to empathize with others, develop moral attitudes, make sound choices, think critically about emotionally charged issues, and understand the consequences of their actions. All literature may be read as "voices from the heart" that, "once heard, can change other hearts" (Cai & Bishop, 1994, p. 68).

Given these understandings about multicultural education and the role of children's literature within an education that is multicultural, the debates about definitions and issues of cultural authenticity included in this book are not just ivory tower bickering. As Mingshui Cai points out, different definitions reflect different stances and different courses of actions that change what happens in classrooms and in children's lives.

The Complexity of Debates about Cultural Authenticity

Each of the chapter authors in this book adds another layer of complexity to identifying and interpreting cultural authenticity. These layers relate to their differing perspectives as authors, editors, and scholars and to their various sociopolitical experiences and beliefs as members of a range of cultural groups. A quick overview of some of the words and phrases used by chapter authors hints at the diversity of their ideas about cultural authenticity:

- Authenticity is the success with which a writer is able to reflect the cultural perspectives of the people whom he or she is writing about, and make readers from the inside group believe that he or she "knows what's going on." (Rudine Sims Bishop)

- This movement isn't about white people; it's about people of color. We want the chance to tell our stories, to tell them honestly and openly. (Jacqueline Woodson)

- Although authenticity is often based in personal relationships, negative intercultural experiences can also play an important role in heightening awareness of our prejudices. (W. Nikola-Lisa)

- An authentic work is a work that feels alive—something true from the culture exists there and creates a connection between its creator and its reader. (Susan Guevara)

- When an author who has written a book from outside his or her own culture shows up at a school for an author visit, students should be surprised to learn that the author isn't a member of the culture depicted in the book. (Judi Moreillon)

- Our world is not made up of separate cultures who have *a* view that belongs to *a* people, but instead is the "mess of stories" that we receive and write. (Marc Aronson)

- The first criteria for publication should always be that the book is good literature. Aesthetic heat is not the product of ethnicity, but of the artist's craft. (Kathryn Lasky)

- What better way to control the images of "otherness" than to define the cultural discourse by representing everyone yourself and silencing those who demand the right to represent themselves. (Thelma Seto)

- Authenticity matters, but there is no formula for how you acquire it. The only way to combat inaccuracy is with accuracy—not with pedigrees. (Hazel Rochman)

- The important question is not authorial freedom, but the arrogance of authors who demand the freedom to write about any culture without subjecting their work to critical scrutiny. (Violet Harris)

- [O]ur histories, individual and collective, do affect what we wish to write and what we are able to write. But that relation is never one of fixed determinism. No human culture is inaccessible to someone who makes the effort to understand, to learn, to inhabit another world. (Henry Louis Gates Jr.)

- The attacks on cultural authenticity as "political correctness" are a backlash against those who have demanded long-overdue changes in children's literature and throughout society. (Joel Taxel)

- The crux of the issue is not the relationship between an author's ethnic background and literary creation, but the relationship between imagination and experience. (Mingshui Cai)

- Writers and illustrators have a responsibility to ensure that they are providing accurate information and authentic cultural images. (Elizabeth Noll)

- Cultural authenticity is not just accuracy or the avoidance of stereotypes, but involves cultural values, facts, and attitudes that members of the culture as a whole consider worthy of acceptance and belief. (Weimin Mo and Wenju Shen)

- No culture is monolithic, so no single member of a culture can issue a final assessment of the cultural authenticity of a text. (Laura Smolkin and Joseph Suina)

- Postcolonial theory provides a framework through which scholars can identify and resist subtle and blatant social injustices that privilege Western cultural practices. (Vivian Yenika-Agbaw)

- Secondary language elements can evoke powerful bilingual images, but the actual words incorporated into a book and the specific methods for integrating them determine authenticity. (Rosalinda Barrera and Ruth Quiroa)

- The debate over definition is not just bickering over terminology in the ivory tower of academia, but rather is concerned with fundamental sociopolitical issues. (Mingshui Cai)
- The discourses of power and dominance that are written into literature are sustained when readers are not encouraged to engage in a critical reading of these books. (Zhihui Fang, Danling Fu, and Linda Lamme)
- The role of the teacher is not to represent identities but to create a space where students can represent themselves and see themselves represented within the books in our classrooms. (Curt Dudley-Marling)

In the paragraphs that follow, we identify what appear to be the key debates that occur across the chapters through a series of interrelated questions about cultural authenticity.

Can Outsiders Write Authentically about Another Culture?

As we noted earlier, the outside/insider distinction is probably the most frequently, and endlessly, debated issue in discussions of cultural authenticity. The question is often asked and answered from oppositional positions, with both sides vehemently arguing their perspective. Some children's authors, such as Kathryn Lasky, see this question as a form of censorship and an attempt to restrict an author's freedom to write. From this perspective, cultural authenticity seems to be a personal attack on an author's ability as a writer.

Other children's authors, such as Jacqueline Woodson, argue that the question reflects larger issues of power structures and a history of negative misrepresentations of people of color. Violet Harris and Rudine Sims Bishop agree, pointing out that this question often ignores the historical context of racist stereotypes and misrepresentations of people of color in children's books by white authors, as well as the desire of people of color for their children to see themselves more positively portrayed within literature.

The majority of authors in this book note that this question is simplistic and sets up a dichotomy that overlooks the broader sociopolitical issues. They provide a variety of discussions about ways to problematize this question. Jacqueline Woodson finds it troubling that this question is typically posed by whites to authors of color and argues for changing the question to examine "why others would want to try to tell my story." Hazel Rochman and Violet Harris note that publishers often limit the creative choices of authors of color by asking them to write books featuring only their own specific ethnic group. Violet Harris argues that authors of color are often viewed as representative of their racial identity and not allowed to assume multiple perspectives, while white authors are allowed to do so because they are seen as the norm.

Susan Guevara believes that consideration of the question of authenticity needs to address the complexity of those who create children's books. Speaking from a biracial perspective, she argues against definitions that establish rigid boundaries based on appearances and experiences. She believes that valuing the complexity in what is "true" makes literature and life rich and varied. Questioning the simplicity of the insider/outsider debates, Henry Louis Gates Jr. suggests that authors' social identities do indeed matter and that their personal and collective histories affect what they wish to write and what they are able to write. However, he also believes that all cultures are accessible to those who make a thoughtful and careful attempt to understand and learn about those cultures.

These discussions of how various assumptions reflect broader issues of power structures and white privilege lead to questions about the social responsibilities of authors.

Does an Author Have a Social Responsibility, and, If So, How Does That Responsibility Relate to Authorial Freedom?

Violet Harris points out that many children's authors see authenticity as standing in opposition to authorial freedom—the freedom of authors to use their creative imaginations and literary skills to tell a powerful story. Kathryn Lasky argues that it is this freedom that is at the heart of great literature and is endangered by the call for cultural authenticity. Joel Taxel maintains that this debate is really about social responsibility and that authors have both a social and artistic responsibility to be thoughtful and cautious when they write about characters, plots, and themes related to specific cultural groups, whether they are insiders or outsiders to that culture. Rosenblatt (2002) maintains that social responsibility does not stand in opposition to freedom, because while authors need freedom to determine their own writing, their work has social origins and effects that also need to be examined and critiqued.

Another related issue is whether authors have a social responsibility to provide multicultural characters that are role models. Violet Harris argues that these stories and characters should provide role models who either inspire readers or correct stereotypes. Hazel Rochman notes, however, that stories can be too reverential and that they need to provide a complex picture of individuals, showing both their faults and their courage.

Violet Harris and Joel Taxel believe that the real issue is the contrast between authorial freedom and authorial arrogance, or the belief that an author should be able to write without subjecting his or her work to critical scrutiny. Rudine Sims Bishop connects authorial arrogance with white privilege, noting that whites have been socialized into a racialized society which gives them particular privileges and statuses that are not available to people of color and that are not acknowledged but simply taken for granted as the way life is for everyone. Without critical scrutiny, white authors are often unable to transcend their positions of privilege when writing books about people from marginalized cultures and thus perpetuate subtle forms of racism, even when the more blatant racism and misrepresentations of the past have been eliminated from their writing. This cultural arrogance is based in the unconscious assumption by many members of mainstream society that what they value is universally valued by other cultures (Nodelman, 1988) and in what Morrison (1992) calls the "willed scholarly indifference" of those who fail to recognize the blatant and subtle presence of racism, sexism, and prejudice in literature.

Thelma Seto states that it is arrogant for whites to assume that they can represent everyone themselves. She believes that this arrogance silences those who demand the right to represent themselves. Jacqueline Woodson argues that the issue is not whether white people should be prevented from writing certain stories, but the rights of people of color to tell their own stories. Woodson feels that the focus on authorial freedom for white writers keeps whites in a position of power and ignores the more complex aspects of cultural authenticity. Rudine Sims Bishop agrees that the real issue is the desire of members of a particular culture to tell their own stories as a way to pass on their culture, and that this desire is not the same as restricting the freedom of authors to choose their own topics.

Questions about authorial freedom and how that freedom relates to an author's social responsibility are intimately connected to exploring the relationship of literary excellence and authenticity in evaluating children's books.

How Do Criteria for Cultural Authenticity Relate to Literary Excellence in Evaluating a Book?

Most of the chapters in this book address some variation on the question of what criteria should be used to evaluate children's books, specifically the use of cultural authenticity as a criterion when the book reflects the experiences of a specific cultural group. While everyone agrees that children's books should always be evaluated according to standards of literary excellence, most believe that cultural authenticity should also be an essential criterion. Some see this view as problematic and believe that literary excellence should stand alone as the primary criterion for evaluating a book. Marc Aronson is concerned that authenticity involves judging a book only by the ancestry of the author and so does not reflect the complexity of culture with conflicting values and points of view. He discusses the cultural crossing that occurs continuously in music and argues that multiculturalism is the "mess of stories" that we all receive and write. He believes in demanding high standards of artistry rather than trying to assess the author's cultural qualifications. Kathryn Lasky agrees that authenticity often leads to prejudging a book based on authorship, instead of allowing a book to stand or fall based on its own literary merits and ability to generate "aesthetic heat" through the artist's craft.

Many of the chapter authors, however, take the stance of Mingshui Cai that literary excellence and cultural authenticity are not in opposition and are both essential. He notes that a book is always evaluated for both content and writing style and that cultural authenticity focuses on content while criteria of literary excellence focus on writing. He argues that there is no dichotomy between a good story and an authentic story. The majority of chapter authors agree that the debate is not whether or not cultural authenticity should be a criterion for evaluating a book, but what kind of criteria and understandings should be used, particularly when the book is created by a cultural outsider. The development of criteria that can be used to evaluate authenticity has been discussed in a range of other sources including Harris (1993, 1997), Slapin and Seale (1998), IRA Notable Books for a Global Society Committee (2002), the Council on Interracial Books for Children (1980), and Yokota (1993). Yokota, for example, argues that cultural authenticity can be evaluated through criteria such as richness of cultural details, authentic dialogue and relationships, in-depth treatment of cultural issues, and the inclusion of members of minority groups for a purpose.

The belief that cultural authenticity should be a criterion for critiquing children's books brings us back to the issue of the essence of cultural authenticity and raises another group of questions. One such question connects to the definition of cultural authenticity as the reader's sense of truth in how a particular cultural experience has been represented within a book (Howard, 1991), particularly when an author is writing outside of his or her own cultural experience.

What Kinds of Experiences Matter for Authors in Writing Culturally Authentic Books?

The questions of how "experience" is characterized and what types of experiences authors and illustrators need in order to write with genuineness as a cultural outsider are raised by many of the chapter authors. Mingshui Cai directly addresses this issue through his discussion of the relationship between imagination and experience. He notes that imagination is needed for a book to have literary excellence but that too much imagination without experience leads to inaccuracies and bias and defeats the purpose of multicultural literature to liberate readers from stereotypes. The chapter authors seem to agree that specific authors have successfully crossed cultural gaps to write outside their own experiences and do not argue that only insiders can write about a particular culture; however, most believe that it is very difficult and requires extreme diligence by authors to gain the experiences necessary to write authentically within another culture. There is disagreement, however, on what counts as the experience needed to cross a cultural gap as an outsider.

Thelma Seto believes that it is morally wrong for whites to write about other cultures unless they have direct, personal experiences that lead to understanding a particular culture within their hearts. Jacqueline Woodson uses the metaphor of sitting around a dinner table to argue that an author must experience another's world through personal experiences and/or significant personal relationships in order to write with truth about that world. She makes it clear that she is not arguing that authors can only write semi-autobiographical literature, but that the experiences must be deep and significant. W. Nikola-Lisa notes the increasing diversity of those who sit around our tables and the multiracial nature of communities, families, and individuals. He argues that there are other kinds of experiences beyond personal relationships that count, including negative intercultural experiences and an awareness of one's own prejudices.

Reese and Caldwell-Wood (1997) point out that non-native authors often "rely on their own perceptions of what it means to be an 'Indian,' rather than on careful research or spending long periods of time with the tribe about whom they write" (p. 159). They are thus more likely to portray American Indians as heroic or mystical rather than to capture the authenticity of their emotions and lives as real people. Mingshui Cai agrees, stating that most authors who successfully write outside their own culture have had significant in-depth experiences over many years within the culture they portray and have engaged in careful and thorough research.

Judi Moreillon provides insights into the strategies she used as an author writing outside her own culture, including consulting a range of information sources, asking for responses to her text from an insider who also had expertise in the study of that culture, and hiring an insider illustrator for the text. She also shares the ways in which readers from a range of cultural backgrounds have responded to her book, reflecting the notion that cultural authenticity relates to readers' interactions with books.

Susan Guevara believes that all authors create from their own experiences, intuition, and research, so there can never be a simplistic scale for evaluating authenticity based on appearance or experience. As an illustrator, she reads a story from the perspective of whether or not the story moves her, whether she experiences the world of the story, not whether or not the text seems "authentic." If she is able to experience the world of the story, she knows she will be able to draw from her own experiences, relationships, and multiple identities to illustrate the book; what she is unable to envision through experience, she researches. If she does not feel a sense of intuitive connection, she chooses not to illustrate that text.

Rudine Sims Bishop argues that authors should be explicit about the difficulties inherent in writing outside their own culture and indicate how they have worked to gain the "real" experiences needed to write a particular book. Evaluating authenticity could thus involve an author's note or some other indication of the process by which a book was created. Susan Guevara also discusses her concern about so much emphasis being placed on the product, divorced from the complex process of thinking and research that went into creating that product.

The types of experiences necessary to write a particular book relate to the author's intentions for that book. Bishop (1992) has noted that children's books that are multicultural are both specific and universal in that they reflect difference by portraying a culturally specific experience as well as commonality through universal themes. Some authors write generic books that are based only in universal themes and experiences. The intentions of these authors is not to portray a specific cultural experience, so the ethnicity of the characters may only be apparent by skin color, not in the character's actions, dialogue, relationships, or ways of thinking. Bishop believes that an author who intends to write a generic book does not need the same depth of experience as an author who intends to write a culturally specific book. These generic books can be evaluated on literary criteria, but not for authenticity, since a specific cultural experience has not been portrayed.

Vivian Yenika-Agbaw, however, argues that these universal or generic books are problematic because they are based on the assumption that a unitary and homogeneous human nature exists. This focus on "universal" themes, separate from a specific cultural experience, maintains the superiority of the dominant culture and so marginalizes and excludes oppressed cultures. Her discussion of this issue connects to the concerns of other chapter authors about cultural arrogance and white privilege wherein the dominant worldview is accepted as the "normal" one.

Many of the chapter authors draw from the framework created by Sims (1982) for examining the distinguishing characteristics of African American books. She identified a category of culturally conscious books that place a child of color within the context of families and neighborhoods, tell the story from that child's perspective, and indicate through text and illustrations that this is a story about a child of color. Elizabeth Noll suggests that authors need to write with cultural consciousness to accurately portray the cultural traditions, behaviors, and language of a specific cultural group while also drawing on human universals. Authors write, however, not only out of experiences but also out of particular intentions, which leads to the next question.

What Are an Author's Intentions for Writing a Particular Book?

Violet Harris, Jacqueline Woodson, Thelma Seto, and Rudine Sims Bishop suggest that authors should ask themselves *why* they want to write a particular book. When authors make their intentions and ideologies explicit, this disclosure influences the evaluation of their writing for its cultural authenticity. This process also engages authors in clarifying what kind of story they are really seeking to write and in examining critically whether or not to write outside their own cultures. These chapter authors point out that authors of color often write within their own cultures with the intention of enhancing the self-concept of children of color, challenging existing stereotypes and dominant culture assumptions, and passing on the central values and stories of their own cultures to their children. Authors writing outside their own cultures often intend to build awareness of cultural differences and improve intercultural relationships. These differing intentions result in different stories for different audiences and, thus, different evaluations of authenticity.

Several chapter authors point out the problematic nature of the intentions of authors who write outside their own culture for monetary gain. Thelma Seto believes that writers who do not have direct, personal experiences with the culture they are writing about are engaging in cultural thievery. Laura Smolkin and Joseph Suina label these intentions as cultural exploitation where property and possessions are taken from the culture for the financial benefit of the author.

Questions of authorial freedom, social responsibility, and intentions are perspectives that authors consider in selecting and creating a piece of literature. Once the literary work has been created, however, other questions need to be asked to evaluate the cultural authenticity of the product.

What Are the Criteria beyond Accuracy for Evaluating the Cultural Authenticity of the Content and Images of a Book?

The first types of criteria that are typically considered in evaluating the content of a book are the accuracy of the details included within the book and the lack of stereotyping and misrepresentation. As Mingshui Cai notes, authors cannot ignore cultural facts, which include the accurate representation of both the visible facts of external reality and the invisible facts of internal reality.

Elizabeth Noll provides criteria related to recognizing culturally offensive images and raises the issue of historical literature where there is a necessity to provide accurate perspectives without perpetuating negative images. She discusses the need to portray accurately the prevailing views of a particular historical time period while also presenting alternative views.

Laura Smolkin and Joseph Suina argue that simply locating inaccuracies is not enough to determine authenticity. They use the term "cultural sensitivity" to determine whether or not a book is sensitive to the concerns of the culture that is portrayed. Mingshui Cai refers to this cultural sensitivity as an ethnic perspective, the worldview of a specific cultural group that has been shaped in part by ideological difference from the majority view. He is most concerned that authors who write outside their own culture often do not take on this "ethnic perspective" and instead may unconsciously impose their own perspective onto the depicted culture with an attitude of cultural arrogance.

Weimin Mo and Wenju Shen agree that authenticity not only requires accuracy or the avoidance of stereotyping but also involves the cultural values and practices that are accepted as norms within that social group. They argue that accuracy focuses on cultural facts while authenticity focuses on cultural values. Evaluations of accuracy can therefore indicate whether or not the facts in a story believably exist in a culture but not whether those facts actually represent the values held by most of the people in that group. From their perspective, a story can be accurate but not authentic by portraying cultural practices that exist but are not part of the central code of a culture. This central code relates to the range of values acceptable within a social group and also recognizes the conflicts and changes in beliefs within a culture. However, they also argue that there are certain values that are appropriate to all cultures and that authenticity does not provide the right to introduce values in violation of basic human rights. They further complicate authenticity by discussing issues involved in value conflicts between the culture from which a story is taken and the culture for whom the book is intended and the need to consider both cultures in determining authenticity.

Illustrations provide the basis for additional criteria for authenticity. Weimin Mo and Wenju Shen indicate that authenticity is based on whether the art form serves its purpose in relation to the story, but they also argue that an authentic art form does not have to be rigidly interpreted as the typical traditional style. They value the creative process that leads to art that is part of the story to create an authentic whole. Laura Smolkin and Joseph Suina note, however, that the role of art differs across cultures and that mainstream traditions of graphic experimentation with art elements can change or confuse meanings for members of that culture when that experimentation contradicts specific cultural traditions.

Rosalinda Barrera and Ruth Quiroa state that another factor to consider is the use of particular words and phrases from a specific culture within an English-language book. The issue is not so much accurate translations of how words are used, but rather whether the words are added stereotypically for cultural flavor. These words should be used strategically and skillfully with cultural sensitivity to create powerful bilingual images of characters, settings, and themes. Not only must these phrases and words enhance the literary merits of the book, but they must also make the story comprehensible and engaging to both monolingual and bilingual readers without slighting the language or literary experience of either. The tendency to stay with formulaic and safe uses of the language of a specific culture and to translate these words literally in order to cater to the needs of monolingual readers often results in culturally inauthentic texts for bilingual readers and poor literary quality for all readers.

Although many of the chapter authors write about cultural authenticity within books reflecting specific cultural traditions within North American society, Weimin Mo and Wenju Shen and Vivian Yenika-

Agbaw extend this frame to international literature, arguing that the same issues of cultural facts and values are relevant in international contexts. Vivian Yenika-Agbaw adds a postcolonial theoretical perspective to a consideration of authenticity in particular international contexts. She argues that postcolonialism is essential in deconstructing colonial ideologies of power that privilege Western cultural practices, challenging the history of colonized groups, and giving voice to those who have been marginalized by colonization. She extends the notions of domination and unequal power distribution to nations rather than only to specific cultural groups within a nation. She also points out that there is no one outsider or insider perspective. The issue of insider perspectives leads to a final question that further complicates the criteria for cultural authenticity.

What Is an "Insider" Perspective on Cultural Authenticity?

Several chapter authors provide powerful demonstrations that there is no one insider perspective that can be used to evaluate cultural authenticity. Laura Smolkin and Joseph Suina document how variations within a particular culture lead to completely different evaluations of the authenticity of a book by readers from different groups of insiders. Vivian Yenika-Agbaw shares examples of books where insiders inadvertently perpetuate stereotypes of their own culture. In addition to showing how insiders vary in their views of their own culture, she also examines how outsiders create different types of stereotypes and images, based on their own intentions and ethnic perspectives.

Recognizing the complexity of both insider and outsider perspectives adds another layer to all of the issues that have been previously raised, including cultural facts and values and what is considered "truth" about a particular cultural experience. Rudine Sims Bishop argues that because variance always exists within a specific culture, no one set of definitive criteria can ever be created to evaluate books about that culture. However, she also points out that scholars can create a set of criteria that show the range of themes and ideologies at the core of a particular culture through a serious scholarly study of the body of books published by insiders.

So Why Does Cultural Authenticity Matter?

An entire book on the issues of cultural authenticity might be viewed by some as simply pedantic academic debates that are insignificant in the lives of children, parents, and educators. As Mingshui Cai points out, however, those definitions determine the actions we take in class-rooms and the ways in which children approach the reading of a book. Joel Taxel, Violet Harris, and others argue that cultural authenticity matters because all children have the right to see themselves within a book, to find within a book the truth of their own experiences instead of stereotypes and misrepresentations. Several of the chapter authors, including Jacqueline Woodson and Rudine Sims Bishop, extend this argument to assert the right of authors of color to tell the stories that are used within a particular cultural group to pass on their cultural identity to children within that culture. Repeatedly, the authors of these chapters contend that literature is one of the significant ways that children learn about themselves and others; therefore, those literary images should not be distorted or inauthentic.

Curt Dudley-Marling points out that culturally authentic books are more engaging for children from the culture portrayed and also serve as a source of intercultural understandings. In addition, these books provide children with insights into power and sociopolitical issues while also serving to challenge the dominant, monocultural perspective that characterizes most schooling. While he argues convincingly for the necessity of making a wide range of culturally authentic books available for children, he also points out the dangers of teachers assuming that they should match their perceptions of children's cultural identities with specific books. The teacher's role instead is to make available authentic texts reflecting diverse cultural and ethnic images and to create a space where students can represent themselves and find themselves represented within books.

Laura Smolkin and Joseph Suina and Vivian Yenika-Agbaw argue that evaluations of the cultural authenticity of a book are not designed to lead to censorship. Instead they want to engage children in reading these books critically and learning to question the meanings embedded in texts from dominant cultural perspectives. Mingshui Cai points out that since the goal of multicultural education is to work for equity and social justice, children need to be able to tackle issues of cultural difference, equity, and assumptions about race, class, and gender as they read literature. Thus, the criteria for evaluating cultural authenticity and for raising complex issues are not merely of concern for those who create or choose books for children, but criteria that children themselves need to understand and employ as critical readers.

Zhihui Fang, Danling Fu, and Linda Lamme document how the dominant cultural code tends to get reinforced and sustained throughout the entire process of writing and reading a book when there is no attention to the discourses of power and dominance. They document the misuse of books about specific cultural groups within classrooms where students are taught to look at culture through categories such as food and holidays that actually reinforce stereotypes and mainstream domination. These chapter authors argue that children and teachers need to learn how to take negotiated and oppositional positions in their interpretations of literature and to analyze the authenticity of a book and the perspectives it presents to the reader.

Stories Matter

Taken as a whole, these discussions about cultural authenticity provide much more complex understandings than simply judging whether or not the author is an insider or outsider to the culture depicted in a book. We believe that these discussions invite the field into new conversations and questions about cultural authenticity instead of continuing to repeat the old conversations. At the heart of these new conversations is the powerful role that literature can play in an education and a society that are truly multicultural.

Stories *do* matter, particularly in this troubling time when the constraints of scripted reading programs, mandated high-stakes testing, and monocultural standards often relegate literature and multicultural concerns to the fringes of classroom life. The recent changes in the creation and publishing of children's literature are also disturbing, particularly the acquisitions of publishing companies by huge entertainment conglomerates. This consolidation of control has led to less diversity in what and who are being published.

We must ensure that young people have regular, meaningful engagements with high-quality children's books that are culturally authentic and accurate. "From the standpoint of multicultural education," write Barrera, Liguori, and Salas (1993), "authenticity of content and images in children's literature is essential because inauthentic representation subverts the very cultural awareness and understanding that such literature can build" (p. 212). Because children's literature has the potential to play such a central role in an education that is multicultural and focused on social justice, all young readers should have access to culturally authentic literature. We should also take an active role in enabling students to "read multiculturally" (Hade, 1997) and in helping them explore, create, and use criteria for evaluating cultural authenticity in the books they read.

Above all, we must hold fast to our belief that literature and democracy are intertwined, and that the thoughtful use of literature can "enhance the education of people for a democratic way of life" (Rosenblatt, 1938/1995, p. xx). Democracy highlights the value of individual beliefs within the context of considering the consequences those values may have for others and of maintaining an open mind to other points of view. The debates about cultural authenticity in children's literature matter because they foster the dialogue that is essential to democracy and to the struggle for social justice.

References

Banks, J. (2001). *Cultural diversity and education* (4th edition). Boston: Allyn and Bacon.

Barrera, R. B., Liguori, O., & Salas, L. (1993). Ideas a literature can grow on: Key insights for enriching and expanding children's literature about the Mexican-American experience. In V. J. Harris (Ed.), *Teaching multicultural literature in grades K–8* (pp. 203–41). Norwood, MA: Christopher-Gordon.

Bishop, R. S. (1992). Multicultural literature for children: Making informed choices. In V. J. Harris (Ed.), *Teaching multicultural literature in grades K–8* (pp. 37–53). Norwood, MA: Christopher-Gordon.

Cai, M., & Bishop, R. S. (1994). Multicultural literature for children: Toward a clarification of the concept. In A. H. Dyson & C. Genishi (Eds.), *The need for story: Cultural diversity in classroom and community* (pp. 57–71). Urbana, IL: National Council of Teachers of English.

Council on Interracial Books for Children. (1980). *Guidelines for selecting bias-free textbooks and storybooks.* New York: Author.

Florio-Ruane, S., with deTar, J. (2001). *Teacher education and the cultural imagination: Autobiography, conversation, and narrative.* Mahwah, NJ: Lawrence Erlbaum.

Geertz, C. (1973). *The interpretation of cultures.* New York: Basic Books.

Hade, D. D. (1997). Reading multiculturally. In V. Harris (Ed.), *Using multiethnic literature in the K–8 classroom* (pp. 233–56). Norwood, MA: Christopher-Gordon.

Harris, V. J. (Ed.). (1993). *Teaching multicultural literature in grades K–8.* Norwood, MA: Christopher-Gordon.

Harris, V. J. (Ed.). (1997). *Using multiethnic literature in the K–8 classroom.* Norwood, MA: Christopher-Gordon.

Howard, E. F. (1991). Authentic multicultural literature for children: An author's perspective. In M. V. Lindgren (Ed.), *The multicolored mirror: Cultural substance in literature for children and young adults* (pp. 91–99). Fort Atkinson, WI: Highsmith.

IRA Notable Books for a Global Society Committee. (2002, October/November). Books promote global understanding. *Reading Today,* 15.

Ladson-Billings, G. (1994). *The dreamkeepers: Successful teachers of African American children*. San Francisco: Jossey-Bass.

Morrison, T. (1992). *Playing in the dark: Whiteness and the literary imagination*. Cambridge, MA: Harvard University Press.

Nieto, S. (2002). *Language, culture, and teaching: Critical perspectives for a new century*. Mahwah, NJ: Lawrence Erlbaum.

Nodelman, P. (1988). Cultural arrogance and realism in Judy Blume's *Superfudge*. *Children's Literature in Education, 19*(4), 230–41.

Reese, D., & Caldwell-Wood, N. (1997). Native Americans in children's literature. In V. J. Harris (Ed.), *Using multiethnic literature in the K–8 classroom* (pp. 155–87). Norwood, MA: Christopher-Gordon.

Rosenblatt, L. M. (1995). *Literature as exploration* (5th ed.). Chicago: Modern Language Association (Original work published 1938).

Rosenblatt, L. M. (2002, November). A pragmatist theoretician looks at research: Implications and questions calling for answers. Special Research Session, National Reading Conference, Miami, FL.

Sims, R. (1982). *Shadow and substance: Afro-American experience in contemporary children's fiction*. Urbana, IL: National Council of Teachers of English.

Slapin, B., & Seale, D. (Eds.). (1998). *Through Indian eyes: The native experience in books for children*. Berkeley, CA: American Indian Studies Center, University of California.

Sleeter, C. E. (1991). Multicultural education and empowerment. In C. E. Sleeter (Ed.), *Empowerment through multicultural education* (pp. 1–23). Albany: SUNY Press.

Sleeter, C. E., & Grant, C. (1987). An analysis of multicultural education in the United States. *Harvard Educational Review, 57,* 421–44.

Yokota, J. (1993). Issues in selecting multicultural children's literature. *Language Arts, 70,* 156–66.

2 Reframing the Debate about Cultural Authenticity

Rudine Sims Bishop

My work, as a novelist, a biographer, and a creator and compiler of stories, has been to portray the essence of a people who are a parallel culture community in America.

Virginia Hamilton, Laura Ingalls Wilder Award Acceptance Speech

The issue of cultural authenticity in children's literature apparently strikes an exposed nerve. It is a topic that generates much heat, brings out deeply felt emotions, and raises questions that are not easily answered: What does it take to "portray the essence of a people?" Can it be done by writers who are not *of* those people? It is a political issue, and touches on matters having to do with economics, cultural appropriation, ethnic pride, and the desire of ethnic/cultural groups to transmit to the young, through story, a sense of what it means to be a member of their group. Across ethnic, racial, cultural, and national boundaries, and across time, children's literature has long been considered a vehicle for transmitting moral and cultural values as well as entertaining. When a group has been marginalized and oppressed, the cultural functions of story can take on even greater significance because storytelling can be seen as a means to counter the effects of that marginalization and oppression on children.

Ninety-year-old Cousin Seatta (Yarbrough, 1989) asserts, "A people's story is the anchor dat keeps um from driftin', it's the compass to show the way to go, and it's a sail dat holds the power dat takes um forward" (p. 21). Given such a perspective on the significance of a group's history and literature, it should not be surprising that people from parallel cultural groups insist on the right to tell their own stories, and to be critical of work that does not seem to them to ring true. Nevertheless, the topic is controversial and the debate has been long-standing. What follows are the reflections of one who has been a part of the conversation for a number of years. Although the issue arises across the spectrum of multicultural literature, I am most knowledgeable about African American children's literature, which will therefore serve as my exemplar. Given what appears to me to be a predominantly ahistorical approach to the topic, I believe it is useful to begin by reviewing the historical context out of which the controversy over cultural authenticity in African American children's literature arose.

The Historical Context of Debates about Cultural Authenticity

For the first two-thirds of the twentieth century, African American characters were almost nonexistent in mainstream American children's literature, which was generally created by White authors. Those that did appear were, with a few notable exceptions, either comic relief or objects of ridicule, created for the amusement of White readers. This situation spurred some exceptional African American writers and activists to produce or foster, over a number of decades, children's literature intended to counter the prevailing literary representations. In January 1920, W. E. B. Du Bois (1919) launched a magazine for "the children of the sun." Along with entertainment, its first explicitly stated goal was to make "colored children realize that being 'colored' is a normal beautiful thing" (p. 285), a strong indictment of then-popular misconceptions about African Americans. Early in the next decade, the poet Langston Hughes (1932) urged adults to take responsibility for creating books that would boost the self-concept of African American children: "Faced too often by the segregation and scorn of a surrounding white world, America's Negro children are in pressing need of books that will give them back their own souls. They do not know the beauty they possess" (p. 110). By the 1940s prominent African American librarians, such as Charlemae Hill Rollins and Augusta Baker, had begun to publish lists of criteria by which to assess and select books about African Americans. Rollins (1941) noted in the introduction to the bibliography *We Build Together* (1941) that "there are many books of high literary quality which do not present a true picture of the Negro" (p. 4). This early framing of the authenticity issue assumed a distinction between "high literary quality" and "a true picture," a difference that would become relevant in criticisms of later award-winning but controversial books such as *Sounder* (Armstrong, 1969). Rollins edited two more versions of the bibliography, in 1948 and 1967. In spite of years of criticisms and exhortations, however, the problem has been long lasting. For instance, an apparently popular book about the comical pickaninny Little Brown Koko and his stereotypical "nice, good, ole, big, fat, black Mammy" was being published as late as the early 1950s (Hunt, 1951). The copy I own was checked out of an Ohio school library as late as 1970, almost forty years after Hughes's statement and thirty years after Rollins's first edition.

With the turbulent sixties came the Elementary and Secondary Education Act, with its injection of book-purchasing money into schools and libraries, and demands for educational equity, curriculum reform, and the desegregation of the "all-white world of children's books" (Larrick, 1965). Although a number of prominent African American writers and artists, such as Lucille Clifton, Walter Dean Myers, Tom Feelings, Virginia Hamilton, and Eloise Greenfield, began publishing in the late 1960s and early 1970s, the majority of books about African Americans published during that time period were created by White authors. Urban upheavals, school and neighborhood desegregation battles, and the dream of an integrated, homogeneous society seem to have significantly influenced the themes and topics of many of the books that these authors produced. Although a number of such books were well written and satisfying in the sense that their portrayals of African Americans were appealing and positive, some were criticized for their lack of authenticity.

Even then, defining authenticity was a complicated issue. For some, it is one of those terms that they cannot define verbally, but they "know it when they see it." In terms of African American children's literature, some critics implicitly defined authenticity in terms of whether a text ignored or downplayed cultural differences, rather than acknowledging and reflecting the distinctiveness of the culture being represented. The best-known example may be Ray Shepard's (1971) critical commentary on the contrast between Ezra Jack Keats's *The Snowy Day* (1962) and John Steptoe's *Stevie* (1969). Shepard asserted that Keats's characters merely *look* Black, while Steptoe's "know what is going on" (p. 30). Shepard also made the point that, because Keats's Black characters seemed exactly like Whites, they were accepted by mainstream critics as "universal." In his view, this brand of universality stripped the characters of their identity as African Americans.

In my own early work (Sims, 1982), I implicitly defined authenticity in relation to two dimensions. The first had to do with which aspects of the cultural, physical, or social environment the authors chose to emphasize, for example whether the ghetto was "a place of sudden violence, sordid poverty, and crime" (Etter, 1969) or simply "home" as Lucille Clifton (1987) characterized the "inner city" in one of her poems. Noting the elements of the environment emphasized by the text provided an indication of the extent to which the work reflected the cultural perspective or worldview of the people whose lives are reflected in the work or that of someone passing through and projecting their own sensibilities onto the book.

The second dimension was the accuracy of what I called "authenticating details." It was my contention that such details as the grammatical and lexical accuracy of the characters' dialect, and taken-for-granted information possessed by members of a cultural group, help to determine authenticity. For example, some authors tried to represent Black vernacular by seemingly sprinkling "be" constructions or expressions such as "I is" randomly throughout the dialogue. One book described an African Methodist Episcopal (A.M.E.) church service in a way that was inaccurate and offensive, indicating both an ignorance of the facts and an insensitivity to the meanings that the service holds for church members. I described the differences as those between writing as an "insider" or as an "outsider" to the cultural environment in which the story was set. That description was not original with me (e.g., Shepard used the terms in his 1971 article), but the "insider/outsider" dichotomy is still at the core of arguments over cultural authenticity.

The insider/outsider distinction in the 1982 study was simultaneously a Black author/White author distinction, which further complicated and fueled the debate by positioning it within a racialized social context (i.e., one in which race carries great social significance). Twenty years later, the racialized nature of the social context has not changed and the debate continues. It appears that non–African American writers continue to produce the majority of children's books about African Americans. Horning, Kruse, and Schliesman (2002) document 201 newly published books by or about "African or African American history, culture and/or peoples" issued in 2001, 99 of which—less than half—had been created by "Black authors or illustrators" (p .9). That figure suggests that non–African American writers and artists continue to be drawn to writing about African Americans and topics related to African American history and culture. Thus the stage is set for continuing the debates about who has the right to tell "the African American story" (which is also a great number of individual stories), and whether what is produced by an "outsider" can be considered authentic. Over time, the question has come to be framed frequently in terms of whether White writers, acculturated into a racialized society that grants them certain status and privilege denied to parallel culture groups, are capable of transcending their acculturation to represent an "insider's" perspective on the lives of people from marginalized groups.

This framing of the issue has sometimes been reduced to absurd arguments about whether skin color or an author's ethnicity is the determinant of authenticity. In fact, much of the authenticity debate seems to be oversimplified, ignoring or downplaying both history and the complexities of the ways race, power, and privilege operate in this society and in the field of children's literature. Too often it becomes simply fodder for provocative journal articles that generate much heat and little light.

Toward a Reconsideration of Cultural Authenticity

This volume provides an opportunity to reconsider the issue, to think about reframing the debate in a way that respects the intelligence of the debaters, acknowledges their stake in the argument, and possibly helps us move forward. What follows are my personal thoughts about four aspects of the issue that might benefit from further contemplation.

Rethinking the Meaning of Cultural Authenticity

For one thing, it would be useful to rethink the ways we attempt to define or determine what we mean by "cultural authenticity." It is an elusive term that carries a number of different connotations. In some sense it has to do with the success with which a writer is able to reflect the cultural perspectives of the people about whom he or she is writing, and make readers from inside the group believe that the writer "knows what's going on." In my view, one productive strategy for understanding those perspectives would be to devote serious and informed critical attention to the literature produced by writers from parallel culture groups. A substantial body of African American children's literature exists, for example, produced over the last three and a half decades by well-known, highly respected, and highly skilled African American writers and artists, such as Patricia McKissack, Christopher Paul Curtis, Mildred Taylor, Jerry Pinkney, Nikki Grimes, and Angela Johnson, to name just a few. Close readings of that literature can provide a vision of how African American writers have set about to "portray the essence of a people who are a parallel culture community in America" (Hamilton, 1995), and how that essence is manifested through the body of work produced by those writers. Harvard literary scholar Henry Louis Gates Jr. (1988) contends, for example, that "the blackness of black American literature can be discerned only through close readings. By 'blackness' here I mean specific uses of literary language that are shared, repeated, critiqued, and revised" (p. 121).

Close critical examination of the work can reveal the distinctive features of a body of literature and thereby provide some sense of what "culturally authentic" literature from a particular group looks like. At the same time, it could reveal the ways in which the literature of a group also comes to represent "the experience of humankind" (Hamilton, 1975). A story that captures the specifics and peculiarities of a people's experience also captures something of the human experience, and thereby becomes "universal." This use of the term contrasts with a definition—typical of students in my children's literature courses—that eschews difference and equates "universal" with "White middle-class American." This sense of the universal as drawn from the particulars of life within a specific cultural context is part of the argument of African American writers who are not interested in being identified primarily as *African American* writers, or creators of *African American* children's literature. They prefer to be seen as American writers, and insist that, although they write about African Americans and African American experiences, because the African American story is a vital component of the American story, they are creating American children's literature for any and *all* children to read. They do not wish to be set aside as "other."

Clearly then, no formula or prescription for culturally authentic African American or other parallel-culture children's literature would emerge from the study of the works of writers from those cultures. For all the common cultural experiences and sensibilities shared by a group, there is still much within-group diversity, which also will be reflected in the literature. Nevertheless, my own in-progress examination of the development of African American children's literature reveals certain recurring themes, textual features, and underlying ideologies that justify identifying the body of that literature as a distinctive component of American children's literature. Likely the same is true of other parallel-culture children's literature, and understandings derived from serious scholarly attention to that literature could inform the study and criticism of literature about parallel-culture people produced by outsiders.

Accepting the Validity of Various Kinds of Criticism

Secondly, it might turn down the heat if writers acknowledged and accepted the existence and validity of various kinds of criticism. In recent years, when the work of White writers has been criticized, some have been quick to hurl the dismissive charge of "PC"—political correctness—at the critics. They apparently question the legitimacy of criticism based on criteria other than those they consider "literary" or aesthetic, such as the art and craft of the writing and the structure of the text. Nevertheless, at this point in time, texts of all kinds are being subjected to a variety of readings from a range of critical/theoretical perspectives. Soter (1999) discusses a number of poststructural perspectives from which texts are currently being viewed by critics and theorists. Of particular interest are those that incorporate current ideas about the importance of the cultural perspectives that inform, shape, and perhaps drive, writers, texts and readers. Soter states that cultural studies critics, for example, see "texts, writers, and readers embedded in cultural contexts that frame their creation and interpretation" (p. 8). In another example, she describes ethnic/postcolonial criticism as arguing that "works representative of other cultures must be culturally situated, as must critical practice, in order to appropriately evaluate them" (p. 8). In today's critical climate, it is possible to have more than one valid reading of a text. It should not be surprising that critics who read a text from within one cultural context might discover that, from their perspective, that cultural context is misrepresented in the text. That is not a matter of political correctness, it is a matter of bringing differing perspectives to both the reading and writing of the text.

Acknowledging the Difficulties of Writing outside One's Culture

Third, writers who attempt to write across cultures within American society need to acknowledge the difficulties inherent in the task. Most are quick to recognize the difficulties and challenges inherent in writing about the distant past, or about life in a foreign country where they have not spent considerable time. When it comes to writing about American parallel cultures, however, some writers believe that, because Americans share a social and cultural context, it takes only imagination, craft, and possibly some research into factual information.

In that regard, I was intrigued by a White writer's discussion of the challenges he faced in writing books that incorporate an African American perspective. W. Nikola-Lisa (2002) describes the process of creating his Christmas book *Hallelujah! A Christmas Celebration* (2000), which portrays the infant Jesus and the Holy Family as Black. Initially he set the book in the context of a Black church service, with a Black minister telling the Christmas story and the congregation joining in through a call-and-response pattern of discourse. When he shared his manuscript-in-progress with a predominantly African American audience, some responded negatively to the text. The article explores possible reasons for the negative response. I applaud his willingness to acknowledge some of his mistakes, to be self-critical, and to include a portion of the quite problematic early draft of the book manuscript in his article. He admits that his attempt to use a call-and-response technique was doomed by his "having no first-hand experience of the Black church" (p. 139). He also acknowledges that his attempt to represent a Southern Black dialect resulted in stereotyped and inaccurate language, such as "Now I knows you know . . . I'm gonna tells you again" (p. 138). Although he considers himself "steeped in the language and culture of African American writers" (p. 135), he discovered that his "various readings about the Black church was not an adequate substitute for the real experience" (p. 139).

It is this lack of "real experience" that makes such a difference. Nikola-Lisa eventually decided to abandon the idea of the Black minister and congregation. Clearly the combination of research and imagination were not adequate preparation for representing a cultural experience that was outside his own. He acknowledges that, even if he had visited a Black church, it might not have been enough, since all Black churches are not alike. Furthermore, the perspective of a visitor is different from that of a person for whom the event in question is part of their ongoing lived experience. My point is that there is a certain arrogance in assuming that one can incorporate into a work a cultural perspective that is only superficially familiar, and that writers who attempt to do so should understand the difficulties and the risks inherent in trying.

Understanding the Importance of Ideological Underpinnings

Fourth, it might be useful to understand what ideological positions underlie or motivate the creation of books about members of parallel-culture groups and how those differing motivations are reflected in the texts. One of the complicating factors in discussions of authenticity may be that different groups (insiders and outsiders) and different members of those groups at different times create children's literature to fulfill different functions. As has been pointed out, Black writers and activists historically have produced literature intended to, among other things, reinforce positive self-concepts in Black children, and counter and contradict prevailing negative images and representations. From Du Bois's expressed desire in 1920 to make African American children realize that they are "normal and beautiful," to Sandra Pinkney's and Myles Pinkney's *Shades of Black* (2000), that goal has been an implicit or explicit aspect of African American children's literature. At the risk of overgeneralizing, I would suggest that a substantial portion of African American children's literature over the past three decades has been shaped by or at least informed by a desire to affirm, empower, and inform Black children. At the same time, African American writers have also wanted to tell, for all readers, the story of African American life and history as seen from their perspective.

Historically, non–African American writers have shared some of those goals (e.g., providing information about African American history or historical figures), but also have been influenced by different ones. During the 1940s, for example, there was a widespread attempt to use children's books to foster better human relations. Florence Crannell Means (1940), a highly respected White author, wrote that she was attempting to "grow race friendship while trying in the compass of a shelf of books to make a mosaic of young America" (p. 40). Thus she created well-crafted and well-received books featuring protagonists from various parallel-culture groups (e.g., Mexican American, Native American, African American) in an attempt to help her readers better understand each other. She tried to enhance her fiction by making the effort to get to know something about the lived experiences of people in the groups about which she wrote, spending time in their communities. Clearly she intended to paint a "true picture" of the lives she wrote about. She also wrote that she wanted to help the White "Priscillas" of the nation understand why some girls like "Rabbit-Girl, Willie-Lou, and O Mitsu San" are "backward and slow of adjustment" (p. 35). Since Rabbit-Girl, Willie-Lou, and O Mitsu San are Native American, African American, and Japanese American, respectively, it would appear that her primary audience may have been the "Priscillas," and her primary goal to eliminate or at least mitigate *their* prejudices. Means's statement about backwardness is also a reminder that it is extremely difficult, if not impossible, for even the best-intentioned and most talented writer to escape the influence of her social and cultural environment.

More recently, Ann Cameron (1992) indicated that her central concern is the recognition of our common humanity, the ways in which we are all alike. She noted that her Julian character, who is portrayed as Black, was created as "an Everychild—a child living in an unspecified anywhere, who has adventures within the reach of every child" (p. 30). She further asserted that what entitles any writer to "draw the portrait of a culture or cultures" is "knowledge, imagination and sympathy" (p. 30). It is the nature and depth of the knowledge component that often comes into question.

Books about African Americans, created from such a perspective, can be well crafted and appealing. Children across various cultural groups can enjoy them, and in the case of the Julian books, African American children and their parents can find their physical selves reflected in the books. When he was younger, my great nephew enjoyed Cameron's books in part because he has an uncle named Julian, with whom he shared some of the humorous incidents in the story.

Cameron professes no interest in reflecting in those books any of the distinctiveness, or what Virginia Hamilton called the eccentricity, of African American life and culture. In fact, she notes that the Julian stories grew out of one told to her by a South African friend. The point is that, although one can certainly read Cameron's books in a way that Dan Hade (1997) refers to as reading multiculturally, asking how race and gender "mean" in her books, it is also useful to understand that she did not set out to create a culturally authentic work. One might ask how such texts reconcile the difference between "drawing the portrait of a culture," and casting a character as an Everychild based on the idea that "we are all the same."

Cameron's stated purpose serves as a contrast to Nikola-Lisa's (2002), who professed his intention to incorporate an African American perspective into his work. The final published text of his Christmas book tells the story of the Nativity using lyrical collective nouns (e.g., a warmth of doves) and a refrain, "And a black baby Jesus—Hallelujah!" Synthia Saint James's colorful, stylized paintings, which of course portray the Holy Family as Black, amplify the text and capture its celebratory spirit. Once the African American church context and the African American discourse pattern are eliminated, the result is a lovely book with a poetic text that plays up and celebrates what comes across as a novel idea—the infant Jesus cast as a Black baby. A critic might fairly ask whether the author successfully represents an African American perspective, since that is one of his expressed goals. How does this perspective manifest itself in the published book? In this case, is "appearance" and the phrase "a black baby Jesus" enough?

Not every author writes about his or her motivations, and it is not always possible to know what authors intended with specific books, although one can make inferences from the resulting text. Some would argue that this is not a valid line of inquiry or criticism. I would contend, however, that discussions of cultural authenticity can be informed by understandings about the ideological positions from which authors are creating and viewing their creations. Critics may still want to inquire into whether or not a work seems to be culturally authentic, or how race and culture function in the work, but they will also understand that examining some texts may reveal mainly the strategies some authors use to avoid having to deal with a particular cultural perspective.

Final Reflections

Finally, we need to recognize and acknowledge the importance of the sociopolitical and economic context in which the debate about cultural authenticity is situated. Only if we ignore history can we be surprised by the political underpinnings of the debate and the tensions or the emotional intensity that characterize discussions around the issue of cultural authenticity in children's books. There are a number of sticky questions embedded in the controversy over cultural authenticity. Whose perspectives are privileged in the publishing of so-called multicultural children's literature? What does it signify that just over half the books by African Americans published in 2001 were written by non–African Americans? What factors affect opportunities for people of color to be published, particularly at a time when bottom line considerations appear to drive publishing decisions more than any other factor? Whose needs are being served in the current emphasis on multiculturalism? These are political questions, but that does not make them irrelevant to the discussion. Eloise Greenfield (1979) once argued,

> There is a viewpoint . . . that holds art to be sacrosanct, subject to scrutiny only as to its aesthetic value. This viewpoint is in keeping with the popular myth that genuine art is not political. It is true that politics is not art, but art is political. Whether in its interpretation of the political realities, or in its attempts to ignore these realities, or in its advocacy of a different reality, or in its support of the *status quo*, all art is political and every book carries its author's message. (p. 3)

The controversy around cultural authenticity is related in part to the notion that the messages—the underlying values, images, and themes —in books by outsiders may not be those most valued by a given group. If a people view their story as anchor, compass, and sail—functioning to bind members to the group, to guide, and to empower—then passing that story on to children becomes an important responsibility for the group's literary artists. Given our society's strong traditional belief in the power of books to influence children's minds and transmit cultural values, it shouldn't be a surprise that people who identify as members of parallel cultural groups, who have felt themselves discriminated against and marginalized by the larger society, maintain a desire to tell their own stories.

That is why the debate sometimes encompasses questions about who has the right to tell which stories, with the result that White writers sometimes feel as if there is a concerted effort to keep them from writing about people of color. In reality, as Jacqueline Woodson (2003) points out in this volume, "This movement isn't about white people, it's about people of color. We want the chance to tell our own stories, to tell them honestly and openly" (p. 45). Reflected in those stories is likely to be what Ralph Ellison (1953/1964), writing about African Americans, called a "concord of sensibilities" (p. 131) that is shared by members of a group and that shapes their group identity. African American writers tend to reflect this particular concord of sensibilities in their texts, and in part this is what critics miss when they suggest that a text is lacking in cultural authenticity. The same is true of readers, critics, and writers of literature from other parallel cultural groups.

Asserting the need to "tell our own stories" is not the same as censoring or restricting the freedom of writers to choose their own topics. It does mean, however, that writers need to recognize that, when they try to cross cultural gaps to write about a cultural experience different from their own, they must find a way to deal effectively with the limitations of their experience and knowledge. Virginia Hamilton (1975) rightly championed the right of authors to write what they choose, but she also added a word of caution:

> I am free to write about the time of the world as I wish. I must be; and I am confined only by the measure of my knowledge. For all writers this must be so, and never should they be intimidated into believing otherwise. And yet there is nothing so jarringly real as reality. If we discover the knowledge that we think is true is not nearly so, we are apt to hear the thunder and to weather the storm of those who know more. (p. 120)

As long as the sociopolitical context remains as is, these storms over cultural authenticity will continue to arise. Perhaps if we take some time to reflect, rethink, and reconsider the issues, we will be more understanding of the conditions that give rise to the tempest, less startled by the thunderclaps, and more appreciative of the potential of storms to clear the air.

References

Cameron, A., Narahashi, K., Walter, M. P., & Wisniewski, D. (1992, January). The many faces in children's books. *School Library Journal, 38,* 28–33.

Clifton, L. (1987). In the inner city. *Good woman: Poems and a memoir, 1969–1980.* Brockport, NY: BOA Editions.

Du Bois, W. E. B. (1919). The true Brownies. *The Crisis,* 18, 285–86.

Ellison, R. (1953/1964). *Shadow and act.* New York: Vintage Books.

Gates, H. L. (1988). *The signifying monkey.* New York: Oxford University Press.

Greenfield, E. (1975, December). Something to shout about. *The Horn Book, 51*(6), 624–26.

Hade, D. D. (1997). Reading multiculturally. In V. J. Harris (Ed.), *Using multiethnic literature in the K–8 classroom.* Norwood, MA: Christopher-Gordon.

Hamilton, V. (1975, April). High John is risen again. *The Horn Book, 51*(2), 113–21.

Hamilton, V. (1995). Laura Ingalls Wilder Award Acceptance Speech. *The Horn Book, 71*(4), 436–41.

Horning, K. T., Kruse, G. M., & Schleisman, M., with Lindgren, M. V., & Elias, T. (2002). *CCBC choices 2002.* Madison: Cooperative Center for Children's Books, University of Wisconsin.

Hughes, Langston. (1932). Books and the Negro child. *Children's Library Yearbook, 4*, 108–10.

Larrick, N. (1965). The all-white world of children's books. *Saturday Review, 11*, 63–65, 84–85.

Means, F. C. (1940). Mosaic. *The Horn Book, 16*(1), 35–40.

Nikola-Lisa, W. (2002). Hallelujah: A black/white baby Jesus. *The New Advocate, 15*(2), 133–43.

Rollins, C. H. (Ed.). (1941). *We build together: A reader's guide to Negro life and literature for elementary and high school use.* Urbana, IL: National Council of Teachers of English.

Shepard, R. A. (1971). Adventures in blackland with Keats and Steptoe. *Interracial Books for Children, 3*(4), 3.

Sims, R. (1982). *Shadow and substance: Afro-American experience in contemporary children's fiction.* Urbana, IL: National Council of Teachers of English.

Soter, A. O. (1999). *Young adult literature and the new literary theories: Developing critical readers in middle school.* New York: Teachers College Press.

Woodson, J. (2003). Who can tell my story? In D. L. Fox & K. G. Short (Eds.), *Stories matter: The complexity of cultural authenticity in children's literature* (pp. 41–45). Urbana, IL: National Council of Teachers of English.

Children's Books Cited

Armstrong, W. H. (1969). *Sounder.* New York: HarperCollins.

Etter. L. (1969). *Fast break forward.* New York: Hastings House.

Hunt, B. S. (1951). *Stories of Little Brown Koko.* Chicago: American Colortype.

Keats, E. J. (1962). *The snowy day.* New York: Viking.

Nikola-Lisa, W. (2000). *Hallelujah! A Christmas Celebration.* New York: Atheneum.

Pinkney, S. (2000). *Shades of Black: A celebration of our children.* New York: Scholastic.

Steptoe, J. (1969). *Stevie.* New York: Harper & Row.

Yarbrough, C. (1989). *The shimmershine queens.* New York: Putnam.

II The Perspectives of Authors, Illustrators, and Editors on Cultural Authenticity

3 Who Can Tell My Story?

Jacqueline Woodson

We speak a different language in my grandmother's house. When the family is alone together or with close friends, our language flows into a southern dialect essenced with my younger brother's (and sometimes my own) hip-hop-of-the-moment idioms—what was once *good* became *fresh* and is now *the bomb*. What was once *great* was then *hype* and now *phat* and so on. My younger brother and I listen to music that plays with language, that pushes against grammatical and linguistic walls. We speak this language to those who understand and then we come home and this language gets blended into the language that is spoken in my grandmother's house. What is spoken in her house is the language of a long time ago, before we were shipped off to college, before my exposure to Chaucer and James and the Brontës. It is not the stereotypical "I be, you be" that has made its derogatory way into others' perception of "black dialect." And it is more complex and less frustrating than the whole Ebonics argument, although the seed of the argument is truly the essence of our language. It tells its own story, our language does, and woven through it are all the places we've been, all that we've seen, experiences held close, good and bad. You don't have to be a part of my family to understand what my grandmother means when she turns a phrase in a way that makes some friends knit their eyebrows and glance at me for help. You just need to have been a part of the experience.

A friend once asked if it was hard to speak "standard" English. I had never thought of Standard English as that. I had always thought of it as the language spoken on the outside, the language one used to procure scholarships, employment, promotions. Like putting on a nice suit—one that you feel good in in the outside world but wouldn't choose for a lazy Sunday afternoon. Having majored in English with a concentration in British Literature and Middle English, I have come to love all aspects of the English language—have come to love sitting down with the writings of James and Pound as much as I love sitting down to Sun-

This chapter is a revised version of an essay that originally appeared in *The Horn Book Magazine*, 1998, 74(1), 34–38. Reprinted with permission.

day dinner at my grandmother's house. Each event is buttered thick with experience and language. But at my grandmother's house, her experiences and the memories have filtered through her to us and by extension become our own. James's *Portrait of a Lady* doesn't do this. Nor does Pound's version of *The Seafarer*. But if I take the beauty of these works and filter my own experience through them, I can create something that is mine. And by this means, through the different, complicated elements of language and experience, through being and reading and listening and re-creating, I have come to understand the world around me—and myself as a writer.

At conferences, I am often asked to speak about my experiences as a writer. I talk about the early days, about what propelled me to write certain books. I talk about my friends, my goals as a writer, my home life, even my pets. Invariably, there is the question-and-answer period. Invariably, there is The Question. Although it is phrased differently, it always comes. At every conference, at every adult speaking engagement, at my breakfast table at the Coretta Scott King Awards, at my dinner table at the Newbery/Caldecott, even at book signings. *How do you feel about people writing outside of their own experiences? How do you feel about white people writing about people of color?*

More than the question, it is the political context in which it is asked that is annoying. As our country moves further to the right, as affirmative action gets called into question, as race-related biases against people of color soar, as the power structure in our society remains, in many ways, unchanged, why, then, would a person feel comfortable asking *me* this question?

When I asked my white writer friends how they answer this question, I was less than surprised to find that none of them had been asked. Why was it then that white people (because I have never been asked this by someone who was recognizably a person of color) felt a need to ask this of me? What was it, is it, people are seeking in the asking? What is it about the power structure our society was built and still rests upon that leads a white person to believe that this is a question that I, as a black woman, should, can, and must be willing to address?

In the early days, I couldn't see past the anger of constantly having this question hurled at me to the political ramifications of not only the question but the dynamic of the asking. And to the fact that what was happening in the moment of the question had always been happening. As my twenty-something activist mind wrapped around this idea, I began to speak. It was Audre Lorde who said, "Your silence will not protect you." As I came to understand what Lorde meant by this, I became grateful to those who weren't silent, who weren't afraid to take the chance and ask this question of me. And I became grateful for the chance to no longer be silent. Their asking afforded me the opportunity to have a dialogue, and through this dialogue to learn more about how people were thinking. True, I didn't like some of the thoughts, but I knew what they were and came to understand that it was safer to know what people were thinking than not. I realized that, like the backlash against affirmative action, there was a swelling wave against "multiculturalism." There were few who believed that the movement shouldn't exist (and these few were made known to me only through friends). But there were many who believed that while the movement to get a diversity of stories into classrooms and libraries was important, one didn't need to be a person of color to tell these stories. This did and continues to surprise me. When I bring stories like this to my grandmother's table, my family and friends look at me as though I've grown a third eye—or worse, never grew any. They remind me that the "art" of other people "telling our story" isn't new, that people have always attempted to do it in literature, radio, film. And I trace back my own childhood memories of the *Our Gang* series where white members of the cast appeared in blackface, to the novels of my childhood where people of color were often represented in subservient positions, to the present-day dilemma of others attempting to speak in "black English," to the films of my childhood where people of color were oftimes represented as maids, brutes, and temptresses.

As I grew older, as the negative misrepresentations of people of color showed up again and again, understanding replaced the anger. I realized that no one but me *can* tell my story. Still, I wondered why others would want to try. When I say this, that a person needs to tell his or her own story, people argue that this view is myopic, that if this were the case, there would only be autobiography in the world.

One of my novels, *If You Come Softly* (1998), is a story about the love affair between two fifteen-year-olds. In the novel, the boy is black and the girl is white and Jewish. As I sat down to write this novel, I asked myself over and over why I needed to write it. Why did I need to go inside the life of a Jewish girl? More than the need, what gave me the right? Whose story was this? And the answers, of course, were right in front of me. This, like every story I've written, from *Last Summer with Maizon* (1992) to *I Hadn't Meant to Tell You This* (1994) to *From the Notebooks of Melanin Sun* (1995), is my story. While I have never been Jewish, I have always been a girl. While I have never lived on the Upper West Side, I have lived for a long time in New York. While I have never been a black male, I've always been black. But most of all, like the characters in my story, I have felt a sense of powerlessness in my lifetime. And this is the room into which I can walk and join them. This sense of being on the outside of things, of feeling misunderstood and invisible, is the experience I bring to the story. I do not attempt to know what it is like to come from another country. Nor do I pretend to understand the enormity of the impact of the Holocaust.

What I know is this:

Tomorrow is Yom Kippur—a holy day of fasting and atonement. My partner and I will attend service at sundown, as we have done for the past few years. While I am not Jewish, my partner is, and we observe and respect each other's religious beliefs and plan to raise our children with our two sets of religious values. In this way I have stepped inside the house of my partner's experience. It is not my house, nor will it ever be, but there are elements of it we share. I know the struggle of Jewish people and experience the sting of anti-Semitism through the stories told over dinner, through what I hear from people who do not know the relationship I am in. I know what it is like to be hated because of the skin you were born in, because of gender or sexual preference. I know what it is like to be made to feel unworthy, disregarded, to have one's experiences devalued because they are not the experiences of a dominant culture. I cannot step directly into my character's experience as a Jewish girl, but I can weave my experiences of being black in this society, a woman in this society, and in an interracial relationship in this society, around the development of my character and thus bring to the creation of Ellie a hybrid experience that will, I hope, ring true. I don't want to tell the story of Ellie and Jeremiah because it is the "in" thing to do. I don't want to shortchange anyone that way. Nor do I want to exploit people through my writing. When I write of people who are of different races or religions than myself, I must bring myself to that experience, ask what is it that I, as a black woman, have to offer and/or say about it? Why did I, as a black woman, need to tell this story? I say this, because there is always, of course, one's position of power. I have read books where this position isn't named, where white authors write books "about" families of color with no white characters figuring into the story, and I wonder how this is different from the demeaning stories I read as a child, the television I watched, the movies I was taken to. I wonder why is that author standing in that room watching without adding or participating in the experience, without changing because of the experience? Why is that author simply telling someone else's story?

I realized in the middle of writing *If You Come Softly* that more than wanting to write about a boy and a girl falling in love, I wanted to write about the relationship between blacks and Jews. And here, at this point, where boy met girl, where different worlds and belief systems sometimes collided, was a story I knew well. A house I had been inside of.

Once at a conference I met a woman who had written a book about a family of color. "What people of color do you know?" I asked. "Well," she answered. "It's based on a family that used to work for mine."

This family had stepped inside this woman's kitchen, but she had not been inside theirs. And having not sat down to their table, how could she possibly know the language and the experiences and the feelings there? How could she know who they were when they took their out-side clothes off at the end of the day and moved from their outside language to the language they shared with family and close friends? How could she know what made them laugh from deep within themselves—a laughter that is not revealed in the boss's kitchen—and what made them cry—the stomach-wrenching wails one hides from the outside world? And most of all, why was it this woman needed to tell this story?

As publishers (finally!) scurry to be a part of the move to represent the myriad cultures once absent from mainstream literature, it is not without some skepticism that I peruse the masses of books written about people of color by white people. As a black person, it is easy to tell who has and who has not been inside "my house." Some say there is a move by people of color to keep whites from writing about us, but this isn't true. This movement isn't about white people; it's about people of color. We want the chance to tell our own stories, to tell them honestly and openly. We don't want publishers to say, "Well, we already published a book about that," and then find that it was a book that did not speak the truth about us but rather told someone-on-the-outside's idea of who we are.

My belief is that there is room in the world for all stories, and that everyone has one. My hope is that those who write about the tears and the laughter and the language in my grandmother's house have first sat down at the table with us and dipped the bread of their own experiences into our stew.

References

Woodson, J. (1992). *Last summer with Maizon*. New York: Dell.

Woodson, J. (1994). *I hadn't meant to tell you this*. New York: Delacorte.

Woodson, J. (1995). *From the notebooks of Melanin Sun*. New York: Scholastic.

Woodson, J. (1998). *If you come softly*. New York: Putnam.

4 "Around My Table" Is Not Always Enough

W. Nikola-Lisa

The poignancy of Jacqueline Woodson's (2003) question of "Who can tell my story?" really hit home. It made me think about why many of my picture books explore the world of multicultural relationships. Although I agree with the major premise—that one has to sit at another's table and experience another's world before writing about it—I find, at least in my own work, that that's not always enough.

First of all, a thought about those who sit around my table. Like a growing number of families in America, this past December we sat around the table to celebrate both the Christian and Jewish holidays. I am a white, middle-aged male of Christian upbringing who lives in Chicago. My wife is Jewish, raised in a secular Jewish environment. My children—by another marriage—are Catholic (though my oldest daughter, when asked, claims "Pedestrian"). My wife's sister, who regularly joins us for the holidays, is also Jewish, and a vegetarian as well, as is her adopted daughter of African American descent. My own persuasions, now encompassing more than my earlier Christian beliefs, take me a bit further east, as I've been a student of Chinese history and philosophy ever since my undergraduate days when I majored in comparative religion.

From this description, I could certainly point to those who sit around my table and say that I have sustained "authentic" experience with a variety of people, enough to justify my writing about different ethnic and racial groups. (And, if this did not satisfy the inquirer, I could always point to the fact that I live plunk in the middle of a multiethnic neighborhood.)

But that wouldn't really hit the nail on the head. In other words, the motivation I have for exploring multicultural issues is not lodged necessarily in the personal relationships I presently have, but rather in some uncomfortable scenes from my past.

This chapter is a revised version of an essay that originally appeared in *The Horn Book Magazine*, 1998, 74(3), 315–18. Reprinted with permission.

I grew up in the South—a "cracker"—living in Texas as a child, and Florida as an adolescent and young adult. My mother was hard-working and caring, but she was not particularly inclined toward people of different ethnic and racial backgrounds, and the word "nigger" and other such derogatory words were a part of my listening vocabulary from an early age. In fact, my mother, at various times a school or county nurse, usually did not have many positive things to say about the folks she "served" by day's end. So, during the most formative years of my life, I grew up with fairly negative stereotypes of nonwhites—and as such, my personal experience was somewhat skewed, contributing ultimately to some disquieting cultural experiences. Here's a couple that are seared into my mind.

When I was about nine, living in rural southern Texas, my friends and I (all of whom were white) used to have range wars with the Mexican-American children who lived on the other side of a line of trees that divided our property. My friends and I would gather at our fort, and with rifles in hand—typically BB-guns and pellet guns—we'd storm through the scrub brush to ambush the Mexican children playing on the other side of the trees. With guns a-blazing, we'd come running and hollering.

The Mexican children would scream and yell, the girls running into their houses, the boys galloping out to meet us. We did this on a regular basis—you know, boys just having a little bit of fun. The problem, however, was that the Mexican boys had no guns—they couldn't afford them. They'd pick up whatever was handy—rocks, sticks, bottles—and hurl them at us as we ran past firing our guns *Rifleman*-style from the hip. When we'd had enough, we'd retreat to our fort, smug in our "victory."

As a child, I never stopped to think once about the oddity—indeed cruelty—of my actions. It was all quite natural given my environment: Anglo and Mexican culture just did not mix in south Texas when I was growing up, not in a friendly way. In fact, I was doing no more than acting out my fantasies set in motion daily by all the Westerns I was watching on television (and probably acting out some latent anger set upon me by a not-so-nice stepfather as well).

Now, fast-forward ten or twelve years, to the late sixties. I'm visiting a girlfriend in Bloomfield Hills, a posh suburb of Detroit. It was my first year in college; she was one year behind me and attending an exclusive private school. At one point I found myself hitchhiking on the outskirts of Detroit with one of her friends, who was African American.

As we stood on the shoulder of the road, we fell into an interest-ing conversation that started this way: "How do you think we'll get a ride faster, if the white guy puts his thumb out, or if the black guy does?" Remember, this was Detroit, and there were certain considerations to be made. But being from the South and not knowing Detroit that well, and being somewhat impatient with the situation, I jumped in and said, "Hey, what's the big deal? Why don't we just do it this way: Eenie, meenie, miney, moe, catch a nigg . . . nigg . . . nigg . . ."

Well, as they say, I have seen the enemy, and it is myself. To this day, that experience haunts me. The friend I was hitchhiking with made me say the N word, say it loud and clear right to his face—salt rubbed into the wound—and then suggested that I put my thumb out after I lay down in the middle of the road.

In my reading of the "authenticity" debate, it seems to hinge pri-marily on personal relationships, i.e., sitting around the table and com-ing to understand firsthand another's perspective before writing about it. But there is a different type of experience that can also lend grist to the mill: those raw, sometimes awkward, sometimes painful cultural experiences that, once faced, bring long-held, unconscious negative at-titudes and behaviors sharply into relief.

When I look at what motivates me as a writer, especially when I write a text that has multicultural dimensions to it, it is not just the per-sonal relationships I currently sustain but those confrontations with my past that inform and propel my writing. The impression these experi-ences have left, moreover, can be distilled into one fundamental idea: that American life is riddled with unparalleled duality—between rich and poor, young and old, black and white. As I look at the books I have published that reflect a multicultural perspective, I see this theme again and again.

In *Bein' with You This Way* (1994), the cumulative verse plays off of differences: "Light skin. / Dark skin. / Long legs. / Short legs. / Thick arms. / Thin arms . . . Different— / Mm-mmm, / but the same, / Ah-ha!" I wanted children to know that although we are all physically dif-ferent—and certainly different in other ways as well—still we are all the same, or at least similar in that we share the same sense of human identity. *America: My Land, Your Land, Our Land* (1997), which also plays off of the notion of opposites, is more pointed—perhaps even a little too self-conscious—in its delivery and message. The initial pairings—"Wood Land Farm Land / Wet Land Dry Land"—are decidedly geo-graphic, but as the text moves forward I begin to entertain concepts that are more socioeconomic and psychological in nature: "Hard Land Soft

Land / Rich Land Poor Land / Fast Land Slow Land / My Land Your Land." The book ends, however, with the dialectical synthesis "Our Land / America, the Beautiful!"

This, in a nutshell, is what is at work in most of my writing that involves multicultural issues: it is the belief that we must first recognize our differences, and indeed celebrate them, but ultimately we must transcend them as well—though without sacrificing our own personal and cultural sense of identity. It is in the act of transcendence, of finding a new, even higher level of synthesis, that our future as a multiethnic, multiracial nation lies—but we have a long way to go.

As Woodson states so eloquently, personal relationships sustained over time are critically important, and certainly are the most important vehicle for enabling us to achieve that greater sense of unity. But let us also understand the important role that negative intercultural experiences can play in heightening our awareness of our own prejudices. Too often we have the tendency to bury them in our shame.

In the professional literature, we talk a lot about why children need multicultural literature; there are a hundred and one reasons why children should grow up in a world where every ethnic and racial group is authentically represented. The fact, though, is that we grownups often need it the most. We're the ones carrying around years of baggage. For myself, I recognize that my interest in multicultural literature comes first from my own self-interest, the need to face myself. You see, I'm afraid I still have a lifetime of unpacking to do!

References

Nikola-Lisa, W. (1994). *Bein' with you this way*. New York: Lee & Low Books.

Nikola-Lisa, W. (1997). *America: My land, your land, our land*. New York: Lee & Low Books.

Woodson, J. (2003). Who can tell my story? In D. L. Fox & K. G. Short (Eds.), *Stories matter: The complexity of cultural authenticity in children's literature* (pp. 41–45). Urbana, IL: National Council of Teachers of English.

5 Authentic Enough: Am I? Are You? Interpreting Culture for Children's Literature

Susan Guevara

When I first started illustrating children's literature, I was often called on to illustrate educational texts because of my Hispanic surname. This seemed ironic since my upbringing was mostly Anglo, in tradition and lifestyle: Anglo neighborhood, Anglo kids at my school, Anglo Evangelical church.

In the last ten or so years of my receiving these calls, publishers of children's literature have intensified their quest to create adequate backlists of multicultural literature. Being thorough began as simply as matching a Hispanic author with a Hispanic illustrator. Different criteria, however, were invoked for the literature and the art. I have been asked many times to "tone down" the depiction of non-Anglo cultures: tone down facial features, tone down color, remove iconography that might suggest a religious heritage or belief. I have been told in no uncertain terms to Anglicize the work, presumably for fear of creating stereotypes. Even so, the bylines read right. Backlists grew. Awards were created.

In this growing world of multicultural literature, educators are asking questions. The questions are complex, in part because of discrepancies in the depiction of certain cultures and in part because it is the nature of education to delineate. How *is* cultural authenticity in children's literature defined? Is a Hispanic surname qualification enough? Or do the requirements include a specific upbringing, a certain technical style, a Spanish mother tongue?

I have been asked to speak numerous times, as a biracial illustrator, about illustrating multicultural literature. This term "biracial" has piqued my curiosity. What information does it give you, the reader, about me, the artist? If an author/artist creates from her or his experience, intuition, and research, is that artist/author's creation truly authentic to a specific culture? I have only my own experience from which to find answers to these questions. The response to my work from educators and publishers alike may suggest a certain definition for cultural authenticity. But the only way to truly understand the complexity of the definition is to understand the complexity of the question. And to understand the complexity of the question we must understand something about those who create the work. There is no either/or definition for cultural authenticity. There is no simplistic scale upon which either you or I can weigh the artist or his or her work. The question, the work, and the artist must be set in context. Context gives breadth and enhances meaning—and frequently forces us to relinquish our convictions.

My Saturday y domingo weekends with first my maternal grandparents and then my paternal grandparents left me feeling curious more than anything. Such different sets of grandparents I had! Grandma and Grandpa Keller lived at the top of a hill in Antioch, California. They had a big rectangular pool in their backyard and an organ in their step-down living room. Grandpa Keller smoked cigarette after cigarette and squashed each butt in the overflowing ashtray on the family room table. He gave me a cold hotdog wiener wrapped in a paper napkin each time we visited his meat market. My Grandma Keller made Christmas gifts by hand for each of sixteen grandchildren. One year she meticulously sewed tiny sequins all over the dresses she'd made for my sister's Barbie doll. She made a coat and jacket for my baby doll from the leftover material of the coat my mother had made me. She told jokes I understood and she made funny faces to make us all laugh.

My Grandpa Joe, my father's father, had one glass eye and one arm missing from the elbow down, both from accidents at the steel mill. He and Grandma Mary lived in a tiny house in the old part of Antioch. Their house always smelled of fresh tortillas and carne asada. The dampness from the cellar crept up the tiny stairs to the kitchen along with the smell of laundry soap. Grandma Mary was not much taller than I. She had a full bosom under her blue and white apron and gold filigree earrings gracing the edges of her soft brown face. Grandma Mary clucked softly, constantly, "palabritas"—little cooing Spanish words I didn't understand. My Grandpa Joe would sigh and "Ay!" or "Ay! Chihuahua!" whenever there was a pause in the conversation. Then he would say something in Spanish, softly, almost under his breath, that would cause my father to laugh loudly. My Grandpa Joe's eyes would water up; a private chuckle would move his chest up and down as he sat in the armchair of their tiny living room. Sometimes my father would explain the joke my grandpa had made in Spanish. As a little girl I sometimes understood the humor. And sometimes I did not.

If I am biracial then so is my sister. But even as siblings our two experiences have been so different—the difference in what speaks to each of us from our distant heritage, the difference in how we were treated by others as children and as adults, the difference in how we view ourselves and the world. All of that experience is different for my sister, Louellen, than it was and is for me. And both of our individual experiences are still far from the stereotypes of what might be considered authentic Latino culture.

Several years ago I was invited to the Southwest to receive an award for the work in the picture book *Chato's Kitchen* by Gary Soto (1995). I was giving a couple of presentations and asked my sister to accompany me to help me schlep my loads of school appearance "stuff." We were greeted by our host who spoke first to my sister, thinking she was me. I quickly put out my hand and introduced myself and then my sister, Louellen. There was a short awkward moment at the confusion. When we reached the car transporting us to our hotel, another host opened the trunk and instructed my sister in Spanish where to place her bag. I was spoken to in English.

I realize that intermingling Spanish and English in one sentence, "Spanglish," is common in Hispanic communities, but I can't help wondering if the difference in who was spoken to in Spanish and who was spoken to in English was tied somehow to unconscious ideas of race and culture. You see, my sister's hair is jet black, her eyes are nearly black, and her skin is dark olive, like my father's. She has the right appearance. Never mind that the extent of her Spanish language comprehension is *¡Hola!* and *Gracias.* I do not have the right appearance for the supposedly culturally authentic stereotype. My features are more like those of my mother. No puedo hablar espanol muy bien pero estoy hacienda lo major possible!

Those simple actions of our hosts seem to me to be the epitome of the unpredictability of culture. In our search for ourselves, our own identities, my sister is drawn to our Anglo/French/German background. She's done extensive research on our heritage and traced my mother's side of the family back to Hugh Capet, King of France in the late 900s. Her house is English Tudor in style, filled with art from France, and includes an extensive collection of reproductions of the Eiffel Tower. The latest is a 16-inch version in chocolate.

In contrast, I've always been drawn to our Mexican American heritage. I've made many attempts at learning to speak Spanish (my efforts still mangle the language horribly); my house is filled with art and objects from Mexico and South America; and I create altars during particular holidays and during times of grief and challenge. As we were growing up, my sister was teased for having dark skin. Her in-laws disowned her husband because he married a "Mexican" whose father was only an electrician. I never faced these challenges. Does either one of us have an authentic Latino background?

If individual experience makes this definition of authenticity arbitrary, why is it even necessary to create the definition? Perhaps for educators (and publishers) to have a guideline for choosing books that adequately depict the experience of Latino children. But again, how can we define culturally authentic? By appearances? By experiences? Are early memories of creating an altar in one's home more authentic than an adult experience of living with a Mexican family and helping them to create their altar in celebration of Dia de los Muertos? Are there clear-cut authentic experiences of culture? Do those experiences have rigid boundaries? In creating art, does intuition have any culturally authentic value?

I do not believe there are clear-cut, rigid guidelines for the definition of cultural authenticity. And as a book illustrator, I absolutely do not begin with the question, "Is this an authentic story?" I begin with, "Does this story move me?" Do I feel a connection to this story? Can I experience viscerally and/or in memory the scent, the shape, the color, the light of the world of this story? If the script is really good, I can walk around in the world of the author's words. What I can't envision from my own experience, I research.

Chato's Kitchen is the kind of manuscript every illustrator hopes for. This story gave me wings. Wings to fly in and around and above Chato's barrio. I envisioned a sneaky cat, a cool cat, with a skinny *bigote* and a scrappy goatee. The memory of a Mexican waiter in the Yucatán, his cat eyes and gold tooth and short neck, merged with a photo of my sister's *gato*. The sketches sang. I copied color from the Mexican American muralist Gronk and learned, post art-school, how bright colors are even brighter when surrounded by muted colors and black.

Finding a calavera cat in a book of Jose Posada's broadsides set off fireworks. The balance of life and death in Mexican tradition married with the old tale of the nine lives of cats. The skeleton symbol became the climax for the Chato book when the low-riding, belly-scraping sausage dog, Chorizo, enters Chato's front door. If cats have nine lives, these vatos are about to move down to eight. The cats were initially all bones draped with clothes. But the strong black-and-white skeleton image frightened the publisher who feared reviewers would stop on that page. The concern was not whether the critic would say something positive or negative, only that the critic would stop. At conferences when I've shown a slide of the pre-corrected spread to educators, I've been told it was fortunate the change was made; otherwise, their school never would have purchased the book. When I show the same slide to school kids as I read the story aloud, they laugh every time. They laugh to see those two "cool cats" look so scared out of their fur.

And just as the opportunity to address the true Mexican tradition of Dia de los Muertos was stifled by putting fur back on those cats, the entire picture book itself was in danger of being banned in one Central California county. The baggy pants and baseball cap I gave Chato, the bandana and the plaid shirt buttoned once at the neck on Novio, set off alarms about gangs in the minds of certain folks. And the alarms didn't ring the same for everyone. Some felt I was condoning gang behavior. Others felt I was saying this is the only way you can be if you are Latino—a gang member. For all it was the issue of dress and identity. Both of these complaints express a fear of being boxed into a stereotype that none consider "right" or desirable.

But children, even middle graders, see these "barrio" cats and laugh! They adore them. They believe they *are* cool. Yet they know, because the story has told them so, that no matter how cool those cats appear to be, they are really just regular guys. Those cats are as frightened as a little kid would be when confronted with someone bigger, potentially tougher or meaner. Clothes don't make the cat. We have seen the loveable fool and he is us. He is me.

When I began the sketches for *Chato's Kitchen*, I feared I didn't have the "right" upbringing to illustrate this story. My Grandma Mary and Grandpa Joe were Jehovah's Witnesses and their house didn't have the Catholic iconography I wanted to put in Chato's house. I wanted to have a certain look to Chato's East Los Angeles home. Without using the exact words, my concern was for a culturally authentic representation. I wondered how I would get into the "right" house to take photographic reference. I was given the name of the head of the San Francisco State University Ethnic Studies Department, Dr. Jose Cuellar, who is also a member of Dr. Loco's Rockin' Jalapeno Band. I made an awkward request for help in illustrating this story truthfully. He suggested I check out the Hernandez Brothers, creators of the alternative comic *Love and Rockets*.

"And visit Galería de la Raza in the San Francisco Mission district," he said. "They sell true Mexican stuff. And you know what, Susan? You can even buy some doodads and put them in your own house."

The fool is me. His statement wasn't unkind or critical, it was just pointed and the arrow pierced my ignorance.

What is there about me that I can trust to be true to Chato's Mexican American world? Who is my father? My father loves his family. The sky can crumble, and as long as his family is safe and healthy my father is happy. My father loves food. He loves the pleasure of eating a meal slowly, carefully. Even if it is not the best-cooked meal, my father takes pleasure in the fact that he is enjoying a meal. If it is a meal with his family on the patio, a glass of wine, candles to keep the bugs at bay—that moment could not be better for my father. My father wakes up each morning and is pleased he is alive. He thanks God for this blessing and then prays for his family. He has his tea, his cereal, and his hot sauce. I have even seen my father put Tabasco sauce on cereal. My father has a passion for life and a corazon d'oro. This very afternoon we spoke about how to resolve a bad auto purchase I've made. I bought a used lemon from a dealer.

"I feel so helpless to know how to help you," he said.

"Ah, it's good for me to go through this," I answered. "It's a real pain and it makes me tired, but it's making me stronger and smarter."

"Tu tienes el corazon de tu padre," he answered. And I do. I have a passion for life. At times it may get buried in my propensity to think too much, but still it is there, underneath. Is this passion authentically Mexican American?

Once I had addressed the challenge of thinking about my own Mexican American heritage, I rented every movie I found set in Latino culture. The most useful was Cheech Marin's *Born In East L.A.* I paused the video and drew Cheech's "cool" walk from the still on the screen. I drew the interiors of his mother's living room right down to the altar on the fireplace mantle. The walk became Chato's as well as the altar.

My mother has a relentless curiosity driving her interests. She wants to *know* things, to understand about everything in the universe. She wants to know how things have changed since the beginning of time, how things grow now, so much so that she is a master gardener for the University of California Master Gardener program. She loves contemplating how the world functions, how to understand God. It's this kind of curiosity that took me to East Los Angeles and later, for the second Chato book, *Chato and the Party Animals* (Soto, 2000), back to the projects there. It's this curiosity that helped me record the detail of the neighborhoods, the slouch of a vendor, the bounce of a child, the duty of a mother, every bit I could suck up from a brief couple of visits. Is that curiosity authentic to a FrancoAngloDeutschephile? And did it help me produce a work noted as authentically Mexican American?

Asking questions is a natural part of my work and when they come from someone in my reading audience I trust that finding the answer, first for myself, then for my readers will help me grow. But was it the curiosity from my mother's side or the passion from my father's side or the tendency towards meticulous attention to detail from both of them, that impelled me to address the criticism of gang representation from the first Chato picture book in *Chato and the Party Animals?*

No matter the answer, my actual experience with gangs is nil. The most I could say after much reading and research and speaking with others with more experience came through a tiny sketch I made of the face of a half-black, half-white cat. Something about the drawing moved me. Later I realized that is how gangs are perceived and even how gangs perceive themselves. From educators and parents I've heard the phrase, "NOT in my house, and NOT in my classroom." Punto. There is no discussion of what gangs mean, what sense of family and belonging they might rigidly convey. The fear is palpable. For those within the gang it seems there is no room for error. You are in or you are out. You have protection or you do not. The only middle ground is that lost space where children lay dead.

These black-and-white cats that appear in *Chato and the Party Animals* are a symbol of this either/or attitude. Novio Boy has lost his sense of connection. He is about to slip away. He hangs out with the black-and-white vatos but can't find what he's really looking for. Then he heads to Chato's house and finds his true family is waiting for him. Gangs I don't know about but family I do. They are our roots, our arbol de vida, our way of connecting ourselves to the rest of humanity and this earth.

Family can have many definitions. There is no "right" way to be in a family. There is no one way to express being Mexican American. There is no one way for anything because nothing in life is clear-cut. All of life is relationship, the relationship of one shade of gray next to the other. I'd like to take a side step here and consider a concept of authenticity that has intrigued me since I began art school.

Years ago I discussed at length the concept of the Feeling of Life in works of art with a dear colleague, the sculptor, Thomas Marsh. We coined the term, "The Difference." When a work contained "The Difference" it contained some unexplainable aspect of humanity so as to give it the allusion of being alive. It is "The Difference" the soul makes when it is in the physical body. It is "The Difference" that distinguishes the living from the dead. The dead are generic. Tom was my first anatomy teacher in art school. At the end of our second semester, the class viewed cadavers at the University of California at San Francisco School of Medicine. I was alarmed and enthralled to discover there was very little difference between a frail woman who died at 90 years old and a tattooed overweight man who died at 28 years old. Their physical distinctions carried no definition, or more precisely, carried no "Life." No "Soul." No "Difference." The dead are generic.

If we relate this concept of "The Difference" or "aliveness" to cultural authenticity in a work of literature, we can say the authentic work is a work that feels alive. There is something true from the culture that exists there. I believe that the emotional intuitive connection I need to have to initiate the work, to be able to walk around in the world of that story, is the same type of connection readers will have when they see themselves and their worlds affirmed in the story and pictures. The artist has his or her experience and the reader has his or hers as well. When those experiences are similar, there is a connection from the artist/author to the reader. A gap is bridged by the work. The work then creates a relationship between its creator and its reader. I believe this is a real relationship. I believe this is an authentic connection.

In a recent school visit in Fresno County, I presented to a small group of middle graders. I passed around a lot of photographs of my studio and my illustrations. At that time I was in the middle of completing *My Daughter, My Son, The Eagle, The Dove* by Ana Castillo (2000). It is a collection of Aztec chants retold from the original sixteenth-century Spanish translations. I shared some photographs of several illustrations from that book, and afterwards a young girl came up to me.

"Do you sell these?" she asked. I didn't understand the question.

"Do you sell these pictures?" she asked again. I think it was unclear the photos were of paintings that would appear in a book at a later date. She wanted the picture of the girl giving her mother a gift with grandma in the background pouring tamarindo into a glass. There are papeles picados hanging in celebration.

"Why do you want this picture?" I asked her.

"Oh, because it just reminds me of my family and my grandma and when we celebrated my mom's birthday."

I modeled that girl and mother in the illustration after an experience I had as a child. One night I ran up to my father sitting at the dinner table. It was near Christmas. My sister had teased me, saying she told my father what my gift to him was.

"Did Loulie tell you I bought you a comb for Christmas?" I demanded. With a perfectly straight face my father answered, "No." Then we looked at each other—my sister, my father, and I. It took a minute for my six-year-old brain to register what I had just done. I had told my father what I was giving him for Christmas. I burst out crying. My sister apologized and my father took me in his arms and comforted me. He told me a comb is a wonderful gift and he was really looking forward to receiving it. My mother put her arms around me and told me it was OK. It would still be fun for my father to open his gift. Eventually we all laughed and, I'm not sure, but probably each had a bowl of ice cream.

The grandma in the background was modeled after the señora I stayed with while living in Oaxaca for six weeks attempting once again to learn Spanish. The editor of the book felt strongly that the pearls around the grandmother's neck would make her less accessible to readers, less universal. My Oaxaca señora wore pearls every day. That is why I put them on the señora in the book. That detail was from my real experience.

And that young girl in Fresno saw something in this illustration that spoke to her of her real experience. She saw a life experience of hers affirmed in this picture. We shared an affirmation of our existence. This is where the most powerful meaning in creating a book forms for me. When creating a work of art for children's literature, there is the process and the product. It is at times frustrating for me, the artist, to have so much emphasis placed on only the product. There is *no* divorcing the process from the product.

Miguel Lopez, a friend and professor at the University of San Francisco, was relating a current controversy over another Anglo author's recent picture book. Her story is about a young boy involved in a gang. She retold her memory of this event in which all the characters were white. However, no direct reference was made to their race in the script. When the African American illustrator read the script he saw the characters through his life experience and painted them as African Americans. The result is a powerful book that addresses a real problem in an age-appropriate way. Even so, the author has received harsh criticism for writing about a black experience when she is white.

As Miguel told me this story, my body separated from my understanding. I was not Susan and yet I was Susan. It began to be clear that the person who creates the work, and the eyes and hands the work comes from, are really not so very important in the scheme of things. What is important is the devotion to the process. This devotion is discipline, acceptance, patience, and above all willingness (by publisher, editor, art director, author, and artist alike) to allow the product to take life. The breath of a book is made possible by faithfulness to the creative process. When the book is allowed to breathe it will become something separate from the creator. It is enlivened by the life experiences of the author/artist and the reader. It is a unique manifestation of creativity but it is not creativity. It is the process that ultimately is honored when a book lives, and that is more important than the book itself or any of its creators. Creativity is free. It is not kept hidden by God or the Cosmos or only for those who are privileged or talented or of a specific culture. It is available to any human who will be faithful to the process. In a culturally authentic work, the process is made manifest through the specific and the work is formed.

What is cultural authenticity? I believe if we look to what rings true for each of us as individuals; if we look to what we see ringing true for our students and colleagues, this is a good guideline. And I would say again, there are many shades of gray in what is "true," what is real and authentic to each of us. Life is not either/or like the vato gang cats and others would have us believe. I am aware that there was some discussion in the Pura Belpré Award committee as to whether I was depicting my culture or my father's in *Chato's Kitchen*. Those earrings on Mami mouse are my Grandma Mary's earrings. That plate of enchiladas with the one olive in the center of each is just like the plate that my father brought home every Thursday night from my Grandma Mary. And the altar in Chato's living room is a direct rip-off of the one Cheech Marin showed in his character's living room in *Born in East L.A.* My Mexican American grandparents were Jehovah's Witnesses, not Catholic.

Krishnamurti (1953) says "to understand life is to understand ourselves, and that is both the beginning and the end of education" (p. 14). Understanding oneself, as well as understanding others, requires a certain comfortableness with the inability to sketch only one cultural portrait that delineates all of us within that culture. It requires us to see shades of gray where fear would have us see, and believe in, only either/or definitions.

It is this very complexity that makes literature, and life, rich and varied. For an artist, complexity is inspiration. There is no end to the learning. And learning, or to use Krishnamurti's word, education, is the place where complexities can be laid out on the feasting table. Each of us can bring to the table our very own pot of soup. With that much to choose from, no one goes hungry. No one lacks for understanding or being understood. The table is for all of us.

References

Castillo, A. (2000). *My daughter, my son, the eagle, the dove: An Aztec chant* (S. Guevara, Illus.). New York: Dutton.

Krishnamurti, J. (1953). *Education and the significance of life.* New York: Harper.

Soto, G. (1995). *Chato's kitchen* (S. Guevara, Illus.). New York: Putnam.

Soto, G. (2000). *Chato and the party animals* (S. Guevara, Illus.). New York: Putnam.

6 The Candle and the Mirror: One Author's Journey as an Outsider

Judi Moreillon

There are two ways of spreading light: to be the candle or the mirror that receives it.

Edith Wharton, "Vesalius in Zante"

Is multicultural children's literature both a candle and a mirror? Is it a candle that illuminates the beauty of cultures other than one's own? Is it a mirror that reflects each person's unique customs and contributions to the fabric of our pluralistic society?

I am a middle-aged, European American, female school librarian, theoretically from the dominant American culture, except that as a female, a liberal, an educator, and a first-time author, using the word "dominant" to describe myself sticks somewhere in my throat. Nonetheless, I wrote a poem about my Sonoran Desert home and the Tohono O'odham American Indians who have thrived in this harsh climate for hundreds of years. This chapter chronicles one author's journey as an outsider, a journey that has taught me more than I had planned and changed me more than I had imagined it could.

Several years ago, I sat down one warm spring weekend and wrote the first draft of *Sing Down the Rain*. The poem was written for Barbara Williams's fourth-grade class to perform as a choral reading at a multicultural parent evening. In my school library, I collaborate with classroom teachers for instruction. Students don't come to the library for lessons on a regularly scheduled basis but rather after the classroom teacher and I have planned how we will integrate the resources of the library into the classroom curriculum. In this instance, our goal was to have students present the information they had learned about the saguaro fruit harvest and rain-making ceremony of the Tohono

This chapter is a revised version of an essay that originally appeared in *The New Advocate*, 1999, 12(2), 127–39. Reprinted with permission.

O'odham Nation. At the time I wrote it, I had no conscious thought of publishing the poem.

Drenched in the desert sun, I sat in my backyard on fat pillows, yellow pad and favorite pen in hand. I looked up at the old saguaro cactus that grows just outside our back fence. I imagined its white blossoms that appear each June. I looked past the tall cactus arms at the Santa Catalina Mountains that rise up behind our home and remembered the huge rain clouds that form over those mountains each July. I wrote the poem in praise of this place. Then I reviewed what the students, classroom teacher, and I had studied about the Desert People (Tohono O'odham means the "Desert People") who have been surviving in this harsh climate for centuries—long before refrigeration.

Donald Murray (1991) says we write to share what we know, and we write to answer our questions. The poem is about the beauty of the desert and its ecology. I moved to the Sonoran Desert from a soggy green place, northern California. I never expected to like the moon-like landscape of the Sonoran Desert, the dry heat, the barely noticeable season changes. However, in a very short time, I fell head over heels in love with this parched place. This love is the "what I know" foundation for the poem.

I reviewed our classroom-library study about the Tohono O'odham's sacred traditions to bring the annual rainfall to this region. I consulted several texts on the saguaro fruit harvest and the wine feast. Two of these resources, *Tohono O'odham: Lives of the Desert People* (Papago Tribe, 1984) and *Tohono O'odham: History of the Desert People* (Papago Tribe, 1985), were published by the Papago Nation (the name imposed on the Tohono O'odham by Spanish explorers). I also looked at texts published in the 1930s and 1950s by anthropologists who studied Tohono O'odham culture. The first draft of the poem was written to the best of my ability working solely from previously published materials.

The poem begins: "A dusty land bakes. Its washes run dry. / The blazing hot sun hovers high in the sky" (Moreillon, 1997). The poem was written to be performed by Barbara Williams's thirty students. Two students read the narrator parts, the first four verses and two verses near the end of the poem. In between those narrator parts, four students read each of seven voices: clouds, saguaros, flowers, women, grandparents, medicine man, and headman. In the manner of a cumulative folktale, each time a new voice is added to the poem the previous voices repeat. The final two verses of the poem were written to be read in unison, all the voices reciting together: "Thanks to the women, the headman, the wine, / The fruits that are harvested each summertime. / The cactus, their flowers, sweet blessings abound. / They all work together to sing the rain down. / The life-giving clouds, enormous and white, / Flowed over the mountain, a beautiful sight! / The bountiful clouds let precious rain fall / To bring cooling water—for one and for all" (Moreillon, 1997).

On the evening of the first performance, I listened as a fourth-grade class of Mexican American, African American, Asian American, and European American students performed a first-draft version of *Sing Down the Rain*. Not one Tohono O'odham student was among them. As I listened, I realized the choral reading format clearly communicated three essential aspects of this indigenous culture—the Tohono O'odham's long-standing oral tradition, the circular discourse pattern of American Indian languages, and the interdependent community described in the poem and built by the children during the reading. I noticed how these students enjoyed the performance aspect of the poem and how it supported struggling readers with its rhythm and rhyme and shared voices. Weeks later, I heard students talk about their reading and the information embedded in the text.

And then I remembered the students with whom I had worked at Elvira Elementary School, my first school library position in Tucson. At that time, around seventy-five students, about 10 percent of our student population, were bused to our school from the nearby San Xavier District of the Tohono O'odham Nation. As their librarian, I was troubled by the lack of children's literature, both fiction and nonfiction, that accurately and authentically portrayed the cultural and spiritual traditions of the Desert People. Like Bishop (1992), I believe that "literature reflects human life and children need to see themselves reflected in that humanity" (p. 43). On my school library shelves, these Tohono O'odham children were nearly invisible.

I was at the time completing my master's degree in library science at the University of Arizona and taking a course on storytelling and oral tradition taught by a professor from the Yoeme Nation, another southeast Arizona American Indian tribe. Our class read *Through Indian Eyes* (Slapin & Seale, 1992). After examining Slapin and Seale's criteria for evaluating American Indian children's literature, I purged my school library shelves of many titles that included stereotypical portrayals of Native peoples. I certainly wasn't anxious to author a book about an indigenous North American culture and open myself to the criticism, justified or not, leveled at outsider authors who appropriate another's culture in their literary work.

However, there was nearly nothing on the library's shelves that reflected the lives of Tohono O'odham students. There were a few books that referred to the Papago, or Bean Eaters, the name wrongly and pejoratively given to the Desert People by a Spanish trader, and a few books written by anthropologists (from the dominant culture, of course). I ordered several copies of the two slight paperback volumes I later used in writing my poem.

At Elvira School, I observed that the Tohono O'odham students, for the most part, were not efficient readers and writers. They were not independent library users. They didn't achieve academic success in our school. Was the lack of literary reflection responsible for their lack of success in written literacy? I believed then, as I do today, that the absence of children's literature about their culture was part of the problem and part of the answer:

> The cumulative message inherent in years of schooling in which children seldom see anyone in a book who resembles themselves and who shares their cultural values, attitudes, and behaviors, or in which children see themselves portrayed as laughable stereotypes, is that these children do not count and are not valued by the society at large. We should not be surprised, therefore, when such schooling results in negative attitudes toward that society and its institutions, and toward literature itself. (Bishop, 1994, p, xiii–xiv)

In the spring of that school year, I consulted with a Tohono O'odham scholar who discouraged me from writing about her culture. She believed, and still does, that if Tohono O'odham children need books, they should be written only by members of their culture. I consulted with an O'odham storyteller about pursuing publication of a story I had heard him tell, a story written by a Tohono O'odham student. We talked about the issues of intercultural understanding—would non–Tohono O'odham students understand the boy's story—as well as issues of logistics, parent permission, and cooperation. He didn't encourage or discourage me regarding contacting the boy's family, but he left me to discern his meaning, as a Native storyteller will. In wanting to promote the publication of a book that would reflect the culture of Tohono O'odham students, I felt like I was becoming a stereotype myself—a would-be cultural thief.

Issues of Authorship

Taxel (2003) reminds us that controversies surrounding multicultural education must be understood in the context of the sociocultural and political developments in American society. The American Right has ascended to prominence in our social and political institutions. It focuses its energy on a cultural crisis that it claims has resulted from educational reform movements, such as multicultural education, reforms that have lost sight of "traditional" values. It is in this context that thinking educators must continue our discussions about multicultural education and, in particular, multicultural children's literature.

According to the *Statistical Abstract of the United States: 2000* (U.S. Bureau of the Census, 2000), 11,100,000 of the 37,941,000 K–8 students enrolled in U.S. public and private schools in 1998 were "Black" or "Hispanic" (other ethnic groups are not included). With children of color rapidly approaching one-third of K–8 enrollment, discussions about multicultural education are critical. From the available statistics, it is difficult to determine the number of children's books published in a given year. *The Bowker Annual: Library and Book Trade Almanac* (Bogart, 2002) reports that 9,195 books were published for juveniles in 1998. The percentage of multicultural titles is not available in that resource or any other I could find. It's likely that the number of multicultural titles published in 1998 wasn't much more than double the 2 percent that featured African Americans reported by Bishop in 1985. It most certainly didn't approach the 29 percent reported by the *Statistical Abstract* (2000) that represented the percentage of Black and Hispanic students in our schools in 1998.

Discussions of multicultural literature often center on issues of authenticity and accuracy. The controversy surrounding the ethnicity of the author has created chasms between some authors and some educators. Lasky (2003) calls restrictions placed on authors a "literary version of ethnic cleansing" (p. 88). Cai (1997) tells us that "mainstream reader-response theories are on the side of those who uphold the relevance of the author's cultural identity and perspective regarding the creation of multicultural literature" (p. 210).

At the time I wrote the poem, I was very aware of this controversy and was sympathetic toward book reviewers like Slapin and Seale (1992) who attempted to set standards for authenticity and accuracy. Still, I thought I could meet their standards and, despite the warnings I'd heard about outsiders writing about another's culture, I pursued publication of the piece. When I submitted *Sing Down the Rain* for the very first time, I felt the poem was perfect for that publisher's list. That first rejection came swiftly and painfully, and it took me five months before I submitted the poem again, the second time to several publishers simultaneously.

After two years of the submission-rejection cycle, I was frustrated. Refused by eight publishers, my manuscript wasn't even rejected for the "right" reasons. Not one publisher mentioned my cultural background. They criticized and rejected the poem for being too repetitive, too poetic, not right for their list. One asked why I couldn't write a "story" about waking up in the early morning and harvesting the saguaro fruit? Despite these obstacles, I persisted.

One fortunate day, Michael Lacapa, Apache/Hopi/Tewa author and illustrator and a guest author in my school library, connected me with Steven Hill of Kiva Publishing, who became the book's publisher. I subsequently met Michael Chiago, a Tohono O'odham artist, who became the poem's illustrator, and reconnected with Tohono O'odham storyteller, Danny Lopez, who served as the cultural advisor for the text and collaborated with me to write the introduction to the book.

I don't know if it's right or wrong for outsiders to use their writer's art to tell an insider's story. I don't know if authenticity and accuracy concerns apply only to European American authors who write about people of color but not to authors of color who write about European American culture, or to men writing from the point of view of a female protagonist, or to heterosexuals writing about homosexual experiences. I don't know if it's ever possible to be skilled enough or to research thoroughly enough to be able to completely understand "the other." What I do know is that during the year and a half between acceptance and the birth of the book, I had the opportunity to revisit all my fears about writing from the outsider position.

While *Sing Down the Rain* was in the publication process, I attended a children's literature conference and participated in a workshop about bias in children's literature written for and about American Indians. From the moment I introduced myself as the author of a children's book on an American Indian theme, I was suspect. Some questions and comments directed at me, and the tone in which they were delivered, clearly communicated that the presenter and some of the participants were sure that my unpublished book would be biased, inaccurate, and inauthentic. This prejudgment was based on my ethnicity alone.

After the publication of my book, I received a copy of a hate letter mailed to my publisher in which the writer accused me of lacking cultural sensitivity and using Tohono O'odham children to peddle my book. (The letter was written about a public performance of the choral reading by the Topawa O'odham Dance Group; books were not sold at the event.) Even in higher education, I have been criticized by indigenous and other people who, without reading my book, have demanded to know what gives me the right to write about Tohono O'odham culture.

I understand that some people will never accept my having authored this book from an outsider position. I also know that my intentions to provide a literary reflection for Tohono O'odham students were good intentions, that my initial research was thorough, and that I sought Tohono O'odham insiders to help ensure authenticity and accuracy.

In my mind, there have always been two groups of readers for my book, Tohono O'odham and non–Tohono O'odham. When I first wrote the poem, non–American Indian student performers were my primary concern. How would the poem sound with four students performing each voice? Did the meter and rhyme support oral presentation? Would students recognize that the information they had studied was embedded in the poetic imagery?

Murray (1991) says there are questions to be answered through the writing process. For me those questions and answers came during the revision stage when Tohono O'odham students were uppermost in my mind. I wanted this work to be an authentic, accurate, and positive reflection of their cultural experiences. Regular consultation with my Tohono O'odham advisor helped ensure cultural accuracy. I sent Danny Lopez numerous drafts of the poem, and after he reviewed each one, we met in person to discuss the changes he recommended. For instance, in an early draft of the poem, I had used "majestic" to describe the rain clouds. Danny helped me make the connection between "majestic" and its origin in the concept of "royalty," a concept foreign to O'odham culture. "Majestic" and other inaccurate or inauthentic words were deleted from the poem. In that same draft, I had also used the line: "Then catching the wind with the feathers he found, the medicine man makes circles around. . . ." Danny informed me that the eagle feathers used by a medicine man in a ceremony were not simply found but rather had been given to him as part of a ritual. Constrained by the rhyme, I changed "found" to "bound." Danny's insider perspective filled in the gaps in my textbook-centered research.

Steve Hill, publisher and editor at Kiva Publishing, was also an ally for authenticity and accuracy. All of Kiva's titles concern American Indian themes, and *Sing Down the Rain* was to be Kiva's second children's book. Since the illustrations in a children's picture book must convey and supplement the information found in the text, Steve and I both wanted a Tohono O'odham artist to ensure visual authenticity.

Ultimately, in order to secure Michael Chiago's artwork, I commissioned the twelve original paintings that became the book's illustrations. Steve and I paginated the text, and Michael and I sat down together to decide the visual content of each two-page spread. Michael's paintings clearly portray the singular beauty of our Sonoran Desert and the unique cultural practices of his tribe, painted with his insider's eye.

When at last the book was ready for distribution, I knew each group of readers, Tohono O'odham and non–Tohono O'odham, would bring their individual cultures, values, personalities, and life experiences to the reading event. The "dynamics of the relationship between the author, the text, the reader, and their cultural environments" would all play a part in the reading transaction (Rosenblatt, 1978, p. 174). "The candle" and "the mirror" are what I've observed, heard, and felt since the publication of my book.

The Candle: Sharing with European American Students

At the time this book was published, I worked at Gale Elementary School with middle-class students, most of whom come from the dominant culture. As a result, I had the opportunity to observe European American students interacting with *Sing Down the Rain*. For most of them, my book was their first meeting in print with Tohono O'odham culture.

> The cumulative message for the children, mainly white and middle class, who see their own reflections exclusively, is that they are inherently superior, that their culture and way of life is the norm, and that people and cultures different from them and theirs are quaint and exotic at best, and deviant and inferior at worst. . . . (Bishop, 1994, p. xiv)

A third-grade teacher, Reesa Phillips, and I assembled text sets for small groups around the theme of place; students were to read and respond to the literature. *Sing Down the Rain* was among the desert books. The connection to the social studies curriculum came in the form of biomes, ecological systems governed by climate, not cultures. Each group of four students was divided into partners who partner-read each book in the text set. Some groups read in the classroom, and others came to the library.

On the first day of the literature study, Nathan and Eric came to the library and were the first in their group to read my book. I observed that they chose to read the book silently, one of the legitimate options but not appropriate for poetry. However, because the literature studies

Figure 1. Nathan's sketch.

were designed for students to seek support among their group members rather than relying on the teachers, I chose not to intervene. After the reading, students wrote about the story's characters, setting, and plot, and what the book made them think about. Then they were to sketch the message of the story.

Nathan wrote that the story was about how the Tohono O'odham survive in the desert and how they bring down the rain. He wrote, "It made me think of how beautiful the desert really is. I felt relaxed when I read this book." Then he drew a picture of cowboys and American Indians (see Figure 1). Eric wrote a similar summary and said, "It made me think about different tribes." Then he drew a conversation between two people, one wearing a feather on his head, the other wearing dark glasses (see Figure 2).

It was at this point that I conferenced with Nathan and Eric. It was difficult for me not to show my surprise at Nathan's image of cowboys and Eric's feathered character. I asked Nathan to tell me about his sketch. "The message," he said, "is about cowboys and Indians." I asked him to show me the cowboys in the book. He opened to the cover illustration which shows the Tohono O'odham dancing the raindance (see Figure 3). "See," he said with some impatience in his voice, "they're wearing cowboy hats and boots and jeans."

Together we looked at all the images of the People in the book. Nathan noticed that all the men depicted were dressed like cowboys. We read the introduction to the book, which the boys had skipped, and

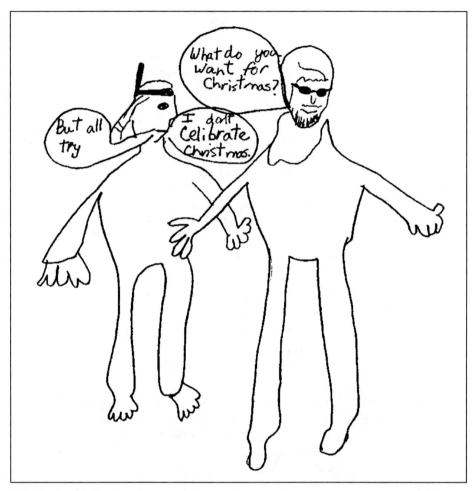

Figure 2. Eric's sketch.

talked about what life might be like on the reservation. Nathan agreed that these "cowboys" were also American Indians and that they dressed appropriately for their lifestyle.

Then I queried Eric about his sketch. His personal connection to the message was family traditions. From reading the book, he had learned that the Tohono O'odham had at least one different tradition from his own, the rain-making ceremony. He didn't believe that American Indians celebrated Christmas and thought they should "try" to celebrate Christmas. And although none of the illustrations in this book showed a Tohono O'odham wearing feathers, Eric's picture did. This symbol or stereotype of the feathered American Indian is one that many

Figure 3. Book cover.

students, and for that matter adults, use in sketches to contrast Native and non-Native characters.

I shared our conversation with Reesa, their classroom teacher. It was clear to us that these eight-year-old boys had brought their American Indian stereotypes to the reading. As clearly as I thought the "facts" were embedded in the text, these readers demonstrated that their initial understandings of the book were influenced by the previous knowledge they had brought to the reading. As Rosenblatt (1991) would argue, the meaning is what the readers constructed during their transaction with the text. Fortunately, their transaction didn't end with this initial reading. Reesa and I agreed that I should facilitate a discussion with all four members of this group.

The next time the literature study group met, I asked the students to reread the book aloud. For the other partners in the desert group,

Figure 4. Collaborative sketch.

Nicole and Anthony, this was a first reading. I invited Nathan and Eric to set the stage for the reading. They told their partners what they had learned about the Tohono O'odham peoples from reading the introduction. I read with the group to support Anthony, an emergent reader, who by the end of the poem, with the help of the rhyme, had memorized some of the lines.

After the reading, I asked the students to think of the voices as characters. How did the characters work together? Students talked about the life skill of "cooperation," a connection to a text set they had read earlier in the school year. The group went off to respond in their logs. I didn't see their collaborative sketch, recorded in Nicole's response log (see Figure 4), until the next day. For me, their collective sketch illustrated the interconnectedness of the environment and the People and indicated their understanding of the cyclical nature of this connection.

For me, this experience vividly demonstrated the transactional nature of the reading event. Even though the illustrator and I had been careful in our portrayal of Tohono O'odham culture, both in illustrations and in text, these students brought their prior knowledge to the reading and found "evidence" in the illustrations and the text for their preconceived notions of American Indian culture. Fortunately, with teacher intervention, their transaction developed beyond their initial reading. The context in which multicultural literature is shared and discussed is critical to increasing students' understanding of cultures other than their own.

At the same time, Janice Barnes's fourth-grade class at Gale School had been studying the Sonoran Desert and its plants, animals, and people with their student teacher Debbie Powell. They read *Sing Down the Rain* in the context of this study. Before my visit to their classroom, the students had an informational base about the customs and spiritual traditions of the Tohono O'odham. For them, the book stimulated their interest in the Desert People. I shared my experiences of working with students on the reservation and arranged for a cultural exchange between students from our school and fourth graders from Topawa Intermediate School on the main Tohono O'odham reservation. Gale students developed a long list of questions and a video to share the important features of our school and their classroom. Five students, a parent, and I drove eighty-five miles each way to deliver the videotape and ask our questions. Topawa students shared cultural artifacts with us, answered our questions, and invited us to lunch.

The thank-you notes by Gale students, written after our cultural exchange, showed what they valued: "Thank you for letting me hold the drum" (Paul to Kendall). "Your library was bigger (than ours) and had a cool kiva (performance pit)" (Paul to Christopher). "Thank you for singing to us" (Michelle to Trashina). "I like your lunch" (Chris to Nacho). "Thank you for eating with me" (Danielle to Naomi). In this second instance, the book acted as a bridge, an invitation to inquire about cultural differences and similarities, an invitation to reach out and make connections. During the following school year, we continued to build understanding between our culturally isolated students through a pen-pal program and field trips to each other's schools.

Classroom teachers, librarians, and parents won't always be there to guide students in their transactions with multicultural literature, but when we are, we must create an instructional context in which multicultural literature can make a significant impact on readers' responses. It is worth our time to study effective strategies for the best use of multicultural literature for all students.

The Mirror: Sharing the Book with O'odham Children

My first author visits were at Santa Clara Elementary School, where O'odham students are a minority among a Mexican American majority. I noticed how shyly but proudly the O'odham students shared their experiences and knowledge of their cultural traditions. It seemed that this was the first time they had been asked to do so. Jonathan recounted the experience of waking up before daylight and going with his aunt to harvest the saguaro fruit. His classmates listened.

Several weeks later, Jonathan was one of the narrators when we introduced *Sing Down the Rain* to the Tucson community. Michael Chiago and I held a public celebration at the Arizona Historical Society. In addition to a book signing and a display of the original paintings, multiethnic students from the fifth-grade classes at Santa Clara performed the choral reading, among them the younger siblings and cousins of my former Tohono O'odham students. Malinda and Jonathan, both O'odham, took the responsibility to learn and perform the narrator voice for the poem. All the students glowed in the applause following each of three performances that day. Parents were proud of their children's participation, and a local public television station covered the event. Many Tohono O'odham living in Tucson attended. Rosie Geronimo, a teacher from Topawa Intermediate School on the O'odham reservation, was in the audience and asked if her students could perform the reading sometime in the future. One month later they did.

At the same time I was working in Tucson with the Santa Clara students, Jennifer Roy, a colleague who teaches at Baboquivari High School in Sells, Arizona, on the Tohono O'odham reservation, shared my book with her eleventh-grade Honors English students. The letters they wrote to me after listening to the book are among my treasures. LaNell wrote, "It is good to see that a non–Tohono O'odham has taken an interest in our culture. It's always exciting when a book for children is published, but it is even more exciting when it is about their own culture." Daniel wrote, "The way you tell it is just like how it is. Anyone who is not Tohono O'odham and doesn't know (about) the wine feast can really see a clear picture of what it is all about." Eva wrote, "Your book *Sing Down the Rain* gave me a good feeling to know that someone else is reading about our people. . . ."

These students saw themselves—their culture—reflected in this book written by an outsider and were pleased that other readers will learn about their traditions. They were no longer invisible.

At an intergenerational evening of storytelling and song, elders and students sang traditional songs, a storyteller told a traditional story about the first saguaro cactus, and seventh-grade students from Baboquivari Middle School performed the choral reading of *Sing Down the Rain*. The audience offered responses such as, "It makes me proud to be O'odham. Thank you for an uplifting evening." "I remember my late grandmother would tell us stories while making baskets. I miss that." "It was good to see the young children entertaining the elders." "This was a very informative and nice presentation for the young parents and the community. I felt touched by it and that my daughter was part of the presentation." "As old as I am, I have never been into our O'odham culture. I hear about this and that but never to really listen. I am glad I came with my daughter who participated in the activities." "This evening's event was very good. More culture should be taught in school."

Tohono O'odham parents and grandparents have bought the book for their children and grandchildren. The book has acted as an invitation to encourage older members of the Nation to tell their stories. Beyond a doubt, the best thing this book could do on the reservation is to inspire Tohono O'odham to write down their stories. Said one elder to her grandchildren after sharing the book with them, "And that was written by a non–Tohono O'odham. Imagine what you could write!"

The Light

All children deserve literature that reflects the cultural diversity of our society and world. They deserve honesty from the writers of their books. They deserve books that are authentic and accurate. When an author who has written a book from outside his or her own culture shows up at a school for an author visit, students should be surprised to learn that he or she isn't a member of the culture depicted in the book. Authors, illustrators, publishers, parents, and teachers each play a critical role in developing children's knowledge and attitudes. All children deserve books that will inspire them and offer them expanded perspectives and worlds of possibility.

If the goal of multicultural education is "to transform society into one in which social justice and equity prevail" (Bishop, 1997, p. viii), then multicultural children's literature is instrumental in spreading the light. It is my hope that as educators and authors we will continue our discussions about the authorship of multicultural literature as it relates to authenticity and accuracy. I hope that educators will share observations about the impact of these texts on students' attitudes and understandings. I also hope that publishers, who are predominantly European

American, and children's book authors who don't work directly with students in classrooms will participate in these discussions and learn from teachers' observations. As a result, I trust that authors, publishers, teachers, and parents will exercise great care by choosing to author, publish, and/or share work that authentically and accurately reflects underrepresented people.

My journey of authoring from an outsider's perspective has taught me many things. Learning requires change; for me, some of those changes have been painful lessons. Unlike a politician who thrives on controversy, I'm a rather shy person who prefers to let a book or a story speak for me. I do regret the criticism I have brought upon myself as a result of the publication of this book because it hurts. But I don't regret the work. The book is a beautiful reflection of the Tohono O'odham and our Sonoran Desert home, and it has made a significant impact on many students.

Some of the children who have experienced *Sing Down the Rain* as a "candle" have developed understanding and compassion for people who are culturally different from themselves. For some Tohono O'odham students who have experienced this book as a "mirror," it is a testimony to a high value placed on their unique traditions. For other children the book has served as an invitation to join the literacy club (Smith, 1988).

"Literature educates not only the head, but the heart as well" (Bishop, 1994, p. xiii–xiv). The transformational power of multicultural literature has been summed up by mainstream fourth grader Danielle, from Gale Elementary School, and Tohono O'odham fourth grader Kendall, from Topawa Intermediate School. Said Danielle in her thank-you note to her new Tohono O'odham friend, Laurel, "That one game (toka) for girls was really neat and I would like to come again and stay all day." Said Kendall when asked what he thought of the book *Sing Down the Rain*, "My dad gave it to me, and I carry it in my backpack all the time. I can take it out and read it whenever I want." The candle and the mirror—may we never allow the light to go out.

References

Bishop, R. S. (1992). Multicultural literature for children: Making informed choices. In V. J. Harris (Ed.), *Teaching multicultural literature in grades K–8* (pp. 37–53). Norwood, MA: Christopher-Gordon.

Bishop, R. S. (1994). *Kaleidoscope: A multicultural booklist for grades K–8.* Urbana, IL: National Council of Teachers of English.

Bishop, R. S. (1997). Foreword. In T. Rogers & A. O. Soter (Eds.), *Reading across cultures: Teaching literature in a diverse society* (pp. vii–ix). New York: Teachers College Press.

Bogart, D. (2002). *The Bowker annual: Library and book trade almanac, 2002* (47th ed.). Medford, NJ: Information Today.

Cai, M. (1997). Reader-response theory and the politics of multicultural literature. In T. Rogers & A. O. Soter (Eds.), *Reading across cultures: Teaching literature in a diverse society* (pp. 199–212). New York: Teachers College Press.

Lasky, K. (2003). To Stingo with love: An author's perspective on writing outside one's culture. In D. L. Fox & K. G. Short (Eds.), *Stories matter: The complexity of cultural authenticity in children's literature* (pp. 84–92). Urbana, IL: National Council of Teachers of English.

Moreillon, J. (1997). *Sing down the rain.* Santa Fe, NM: Kiva.

Murray, D. (1991). Getting under the lightning. In B. M. Power & R. Hubbard (Eds.), *Literacy in process: The Heinemann reader* (pp. 5–13). Portsmouth, NH: Heinemann.

Papago Tribe (1984). *Tohono O'odham: Lives of the desert people.* Salt Lake City: University of Utah Printing Services.

Papago Tribe (1985). *Tohono O'odham: History of the desert people.* Salt Lake City: University of Utah Printing Services.

Rosenblatt, L. M. (1978). *The reader, the text, the poem: The transactional theory of the literary work.* Carbondale, IL: Southern Illinois University Press.

Rosenblatt, L. M. (1991). The reading transaction: What for? In B. M. Power & R. Hubbard (Eds.), *Literacy in process: The Heinemann reader* (pp. 114–27). Portsmouth, NH: Heinemann.

Slapin, B., & Seale, D. (1992). *Through Indian eyes: The native experience in books for children* (3rd ed.). Philadelphia: New Society Publishers.

Smith, F. (1988). *Joining the literacy club: Further essays into education.* Portsmouth, NH: Heinemann.

Taxel, J. (2003). Multicultural literature and the politics of reaction. In D. L. Fox & K. G. Short (Eds.), *Stories matter: The complexity of cultural authenticity in children's literature* (pp. 143–64). Urbana, IL: National Council of Teachers of English.

U.S. Bureau of the Census (2000). *Statistical abstract of the United States: 2000.* [Electronic version]. Washington, DC: U.S. Government Printing Office. Retrieved November 20, 2002, from http://www.census.gov/prod/www/statistical-abstract-us.html.

7 A Mess of Stories

Marc Aronson

One gray Sunday morning early in 1994, I popped a blues tape into the cassette player, opened up my *New York Times* magazine, and found a wonderful, personal article on blacks and Jews. Written by an African American author named Joe Wood, the piece got to the heart of multiculturalism. After describing his upbringing in a middle-class Jewish high school, his experiences at Yale, and his friendship with a Jewish classmate who seemed to know more about black culture than he did, Wood came to some conclusions:

> If Dan was "black" in any way, it was in precisely the same way that I was a "Jew." . . . I love Dan not because he's Jewish or, in some sense, black, and not because I am black or, in some sense, Jewish. While our tribes, and their memories, and their stories, did make us, they also have nothing to do with it. The heart, after all, is raised on a mess of stories, and then it writes its own.

Yes. That is exactly what multiculturalism means: the "mess of stories" we receive and those we write. As a footnote, I was listening to a tape, not a CD, because it had been sent to me by an African American friend I met playing basketball many years ago. We quickly discovered a mutual interest in Billie Holiday, and ever since then he has been sending me tapes and I have been sending him books on black history and culture to give to his children. I believe that kind of crossing and mixing, that sharing of cultures, stories, songs, dreams, and visions, has been, and is, the great secret, and also the great truth, of multiculturalism. Our culture is not given to us by our genes; it is not inevitable; it is not monolithic; and it does not stand still.

The multiculturalism that parades "authenticity" and pretends that *a* culture has *a* view that belongs to *a* people is now something of a shibboleth in children's books. Undoubtedly earnest in intention, it has contributed to the most exciting recent development in our industry—the publication of authors and illustrators from a wide variety of back-

This chapter is a revised version of an essay that originally appeared in *The Horn Book Magazine*, 1995, 71(2), 163–68. Reprinted with permission.

grounds and heritages. But that view of cultural diversity is also wrong. In editorial meetings throughout the land, proposals for books about a certain group are greeted with the ritual question: Is he black, is she Latina, are they Cherokee? Supposedly, this is an appeal for authenticity. In reality it is an amalgam of cynicism, marketing strategy, laziness, guilt, and some real interest in new artists and authors. The books this kind of blinkered thinking produces pose a real problem for reviewers. As a panel of leading children's book reviewers pointed out in *Evaluating Children's Books* (Hearne & Sutton, 1993), they are put into a political quandary: Should they judge all books by the same standards—thus seeming to denigrate the literature of underrepresented groups—or should they make exceptions for obviously weak books that are ethnically pure? Is the only thing that matters in judging a book the ancestry of the author?

No. The multiculturalism I propose is much harder to write. I say that if we look closely at any culture we will see all kinds of conflicting and mixed values, all sorts of opinions, and many different points of view. We may even find that the best representatives of a culture do not belong to it. Now be clear, be very clear, I am not calling for Disneylandesque, "We Are the World" flabbiness. I am not encouraging glib, tourist once-overs or deadly missionary depictions of "Little Brown Brothers." I am calling for more authenticity, not less. I am calling for the intellectual honesty that recognizes the complexity of culture. My argument for this kind of complexity relies on a discussion of music.

Let's begin with a song, and a singer, familiar to many of us. Try listening to Odetta singing that well-known song "Children Go Where I Send Thee" (from *The Tin Angel*). The song begins:

> Children go where I send thee
> How shall I send thee?
> I'm gonna send thee one by one
> One for the little bitty baby

After a count through ten numbers that stand for various apparently New Testament figures, we return to the baby, who was "Born, born, born in Bethlehem."

Obviously this is a Christian song, more precisely a gospel tune. A second version makes that last point especially well. In her 1961 recording at a jazz club (*Nina Simone at the Village Gate*), Nina Simone chides the audience, asking if anyone has ever been to a revival meeting. Her sideman mutters that they probably haven't even heard of one. As the song takes off, Simone tells the audience that they're in one now.

Clearly, at that time the song was so much a part of African American culture that Simone expected both the lyrics and the context to be entirely unfamiliar to a white audience.

I once had a boss who wanted to make "Children Go Where I Send Thee" into a picture book, a wonderful idea. I got interested, then, in where it had come from and what all the numbers meant. So I went to the library and looked through various histories of folk songs. As it turns out, John and Alan Lomax recorded the song in 1942 as performed by inmates of Arkansas's Gould Penitentiary. But that was not where it was composed. Ozark versions had been written down in the 1930s. One Arkansas family claimed it had belonged to them alone for a hundred years. Maybe, but others had it, too. Researchers have found old Cornish versions of the "Dilly Song," which had similar lyrics. An article in an 1891 issue of the *Journal of American Folklore* extended its history further than that. It turns out there is a 1625 version in the British Museum. There are Latin and German variants that are even earlier, as well as alternates in French, Provençal, and Spanish. But this long trail does finally have an end. Here is the source from which what we now think of as a paradigmatically African American song probably descended: "Had Gadya."

Yes, "Had Gadya," a song that is sung in the Jewish Passover service. In English the title is "An Only Kid," and it is a counting song that is also linked to "Green Grow the Rushes, O" and "The House That Jack Built." Over hundreds of years of borrowing and sharing, "Had Gadya" has taken on these new identities. With what kind of absolute hubris can we, today, pull up the ladder and say one song is African American and the other is Jewish and never the twain shall meet? What ahistoric right have we to deny hundreds of years of borrowing, stealing, fighting, loving, imitating, and oppressing?

Let's look at some more selections that show the problems with ethnic authenticity. First, try listening to Harry Belafonte doing his very careful version of "Hava Nageela" (*Harry Belafonte: A Legendary Performer*). Not only did he practice his Hebrew, he worked hard to capture the inflections and singing style appropriate to the song. On the same recording there is also a version of "Danny Boy" that begins with an invocation of the troubles in Ireland that sounds like it might be heard in a Dublin pub.

Even more "authentic" is my favorite recording of all time, Jesse Norman singing Richard Strauss's "Four Last Songs" (Norman, n.d.). To my taste this is a perfect recording of a demanding piece. Clearly she has taken the kind of care Belafonte employed and raised it to a higher power. European-style classical music is her medium, and she has approached it with the rigorous training, the devotion to craft, the passion for the music that can only be found in the very greatest artists. No one who is not a Nazi could possibly question her right to perform the music. Of course, since Strauss himself was rather too comfortable with the Nazis, that very qualification shows that art cannot, must not, be judged solely by the treasured traditions of its creators.

The next three pieces I have in mind raise more complicated problems. First, if you can find it, try listening to a CD called *Salsa No Tiene Frontera* by Orquestra de la Luz. The lyrics of the title song explain the problem this wonderful salsa recording creates for ethnic essentialists. The chorus is a declaration of faith—"salsa no tiene frontera" (salsa has no borders)—and a "rap" section, translated loosely as the following, explains why this declaration is necessary:

> The Orchestra of the Light plays hot salsa. It's rich, it's rich, it's rich, in this environment. Don't be surprised that we are Japanese. The whole listening audience should hear this. Dance! Enjoy! It's good, it's good, it is really good.

Yes, this "hot" salsa group is made up of Japanese musicians. Here again, musicians' talents, devotion to the music, and passion for their work have made a wonderful creation that would not exist if we guarded music with cranial calipers and birth certificates.

What, then, of this next piece, "Babalu (Orooney)" by Slim Gaillard *(Laughing in Rhythm: The Best of the Verve Years)*? Gaillard, an African American hipster who Jack Kerouac thought was God, sang in his own language, Vout. This track satirizes the very Latin music the Japanese musicians have worked so hard to master, yet it is authentic in its own way. Gaillard's music has the integrity, the honesty, the autonomy of parody. But that sort of borrowing and experimenting is exactly what folk performers have done for thousands of years.

"Paisach in Portugal" is a joke-filled klezmer piece originally composed by Mickey Katz. The version I have in mind is played by Don Byron *(Don Byron Plays the Music of Mickey Katz)*. Byron is a very serious, dreadlocked, African American jazz musician. When he first heard this music, he was studying at the New England Conservatory of Music. As he explained in the playbill for a concert in Brooklyn, "I immediately responded to the mischief in the music, where the clarinetist would play the most *out* thing he could think of. . . . As time went by, I developed my own voice in that language." Byron has found his spiritual/musical paternity in Katz, a klezmer genius who is now best known for being Joel Grey's father. He treats Katz's music with the kind of respect and seriousness Norman brings to Strauss. Authentic? Yes. Even though he is an African American playing a klezmer piece. But if a Passover song can turn into an African American spiritual, why can't African American jazz music turn into a Passover parody?

Again Byron puts it well: "I spent hundreds of hours transcribing Katz's records; I feel entitled to that knowledge, entitled to participate. . . . I'm not doing Jewish music or classical music instead of doing black music. I play what I like."

Why can we allow this cultural crossing in music and not in books for children? Why can't our authors, after sufficient preparation, do what they like? Time and again a minority artist who has gotten a start through the affirmative action of ethnic essentialism talks about being pigeonholed, trapped in a racially defined subject ghetto. Why can't we have the freedom to say that it would be fascinating to have a black writer contemplate the Holocaust, to have a Native American describe the Great Migration, to have a Jewish author think about the Trail of Tears? We need to have the courage of our elective affinities. Is that hard? Yes. Will authors be open to the criticism that they are "covering"—stealing a minority culture for profit? Yes. Will earnest authors make mistakes by not knowing cultures well enough? Yes. But that just means they have to work harder. I repeat, I am not suggesting a return to the days of white authors doing pallid books about "exotic" people. Instead I am challenging all authors to trust their passions, while still demanding the highest standards of artistry, honesty, and understanding. I want to create more options and opportunities for all talented and committed artists, no matter how they fill out their census forms.

If we take away the false certitudes of ethnic essentialism, if we are honest, rigorous, and thorough enough to look deeply at peoples and myths and ways of life around the world, we will find what Joe Wood discovered: We have a mess of stories, and then we write our own. We will recognize that our world is not made up of cultures forged separately one by one and guarded by skin color, religion, gender, class, or ethnicity. We came into this world two by two, and just as the wonderful mixture of our parents' genes made us, the incredible tapestry of world traditions lies beneath all of our songs and stories. Tracing those tangled lineages gives us our heritage. In that task we must be rigorous, attuned to the complexity of cultures, willing to recognize the limitations of our own points of view. But as we examine those threads, as we come to know them and cherish them, we can also weave our own new multicolored, and multicultural, robes; robes that will clothe our children with new beauty as we send them off to the future.

References

Belafonte, H. (1978). *Harry Belafonte, a legendary performer* [sound recording]. New York: RCA.

Byron, D. (1992). *Don Byron plays the music of Mickey Katz* [sound recording]. Beverly Hills: Elektra Nonesuch.

Gaillard, S. (1994). *Laughing in rhythm: The best of the Verve years* [sound recording]. New York: Verve. (Original work published 1946)

Hearne, B., and Sutton, R. (Eds.). (1993). *Evaluating children's books: A critical look: Aesthetic, social, and political aspects of analyzing and using children's books.* Urbana-Champaign, IL: University of Illinois, Graduate School of Library and Information Science.

Norman, J. (n.d.). *Richard Strauss Vier Letzte Lieder/Four last songs Jesse Norman Gewandhausorchester Leipzig* [sound recording]. K. Masur, conductor. Phillips 411 052-2.

Odetta, & Mohr, L. (1993). *The Tin Angel* [sound recording]. Berkeley: Fantasy. (Original work published 1953)

Orquesta de la Luz. (1991). *Salsa no tiene frontera* [sound recording]. New York: BMG Victor.

Simone, N. (1991). *Nina Simone at the Village Gate* [sound recording]. Hollywood: Roulette Jazz.

8 To Stingo with Love: An Author's Perspective on Writing outside One's Culture

Kathryn Lasky

Recently I attended my son's high school graduation at the Cambridge Rindge and Latin School in Cambridge, Massachusetts. The field house was crammed with at least three thousand people who were there to watch a graduating class of nearly five hundred receive their diplomas. Strung from the rafters of this field house were the flags of seventy different countries representing the seventy different nationalities of the student population of the high school. Of the half dozen commencement speakers, ranging from the valedictorian to the main speaker, there was not one who did not make a special point of mentioning, if not celebrating, the cultural diversity that was part and parcel of the Cambridge Rindge and Latin High School experience. It was amazing to be a part of this event.

Now, I come from the Midwest. Thirty years ago you could not even buy a bagel in Indianapolis, Indiana. I attended a private girls' school where I was one of three Jews; the rest were mostly Episcopalians, with a scattering of Presbyterians. I spent six years playing the role of a shepherd in the school Christmas pageant because of my swarthy looks, and it was assumed that if Jews weren't moneylenders or scribes perhaps they had been shepherds. The three angels were always shimmering blondes. This, of course, was before multiculturalism. This was before "multi" anything.

As a first-year high school student, I was taught Ancient History from a droll old book written by a fellow named Breasted. The book had a very ominous note in the front that referred to something he called

---

This chapter is a revised version of an essay that originally appeared in *The New Advocate*, 1996, 9(1), 1–7. Reprinted with permission.

"Orientalism." Mr. Breasted seemed to lump together everything east of Greece as Orientalism. And Orientalism was bad, very bad because the farther east you got the more people did not look like you—the noses might flatten, the eyes tilt, the skin turn tawny "unnatural shades." I can remember my high school history teacher's lecture on Xerxes and the battle of Salamis. Had that wily Oriental (who actually happened to be Persian) succeeded, Greece, the Parthenon, the Attic Theater, Sophocles, Phidias, the dialogues of Plato, and western civilization would all have been eliminated!

This indeed was a curriculum that was taught passionately in my school where blondes were angels and Jews were shepherds. Years later I wrote a novel about all this called *Pageant* (1986), which celebrated the agonies of being a young person in the context of this unmitigated, monolithic, unicultural background.

So we have certainly come a long way from those days. Now you can buy bagels everywhere, and no longer are we taught history from books that talk about creeping Orientalism. And you can bet that no school would ever get away with only blonde angels and Jewish shepherds. Multiculturalism has come into full bloom. We have inhaled deeply its fragrant scent and become nearly heady on the fumes. There is a pervasive euphoria about our evolution as a sensitive, caring people dedicated to teaching our children about the richness of all heritages and exposing them to the diversity within our American culture. There is almost an air of self-congratulation—dare I say smugness? For indeed we have formed a new elite, a politically correct elite that celebrates all creeds and colors and coaxes all voices to sing their separate strains loud and clear. We are the polar opposites of those nutty fanatics who preach against the perils of a New World Order and One Worldism.

Now, if one detects a hint of reservation in my tone about all this, a nuance of doubt, perhaps—well, you are right. For amidst the celebration, I, as an author, have been made privy to another aspect of this passionate embrace of the multicultural. And I now wonder if, in fact, I do not detect the seeds of another kind of fanaticism in which self-styled militias of cultural diversity are beginning to deliver dictates and guidelines about the creation and publishing of literature for a multicultural population of readers.

Recently I was attending an American Library Association meeting and ran into an old friend, who told me a story about a woman who had served in the Peace Corps for several years in West Africa and had just had her first children's book published. It was a picture book and told a West African folktale. My friend, her mentor, was outraged that the publisher had refused to put the author/illustrator's photograph on the book jacket because she was white. I had never heard of such a thing. Was there a precedent for this? Had people really complained?

Issues of Origin and Setting

I do not follow the politics of the world of children's literature that closely, but apparently I had missed out on one of the big brouhahas of recent years, waged over *The Fortune-Tellers* (1992), a picture book written by Lloyd Alexander and illustrated by Trina Schart Hyman. The critics questioned how two decidedly Anglo artists dared to set this folktale in Africa. Well, I did not want to make any judgment. I read the book. It seemed beautifully told, with exquisite illustrations, but some people seemed to think that this story was a misappropriated one—one that would never happen in Africa, in Cameroon, one that was of a distinctly European heritage. My question at the time was how someone could be so absolutely certain that this story could never have happened outside of Europe? Perhaps it had not evolved in Africa, but why should it be considered so entirely out of place? If indeed the story did a disservice to African people, undermined or offended their traditions, then perhaps too much license had been taken. But I am still not sure how anyone can be so categorically certain that a well-told story is out of place and has no value in a context that was not that of its provenance.

One never knows where old stories might pop up, stories we might like to think of as being part of a unique tradition. A year ago I was in Madagascar working on a book about lemurs. After we had finished our stay with the lemurs, we made a very arduous journey to the west coast of Madagascar to a section where the Veso people live. The Veso have a fishing culture. They fish only with spears and occasionally a jigger line, sailing out beyond the reef in Polynesian-style proas. Their boats are made without power tools. They have lived essentially in the same manner for centuries. Indeed, both my husband and I, who are great fans of Captain Cook, were astonished to walk into the village of Beheloka and find thatched huts identical to the ones in the engravings by artists on Cook's voyages. It was as if we had stepped into a seventeenth-century, maritime, subequatorial world and seen it with the same eyes as Cook and his crew. Nothing seemed to have changed.

One night we sat listening while one of the village elders told us the tale of Palasus, the most beautiful daughter of an ancient Veso queen. We listened in translation, for the Veso mostly speak a dialect of Malagasy and our guide translated it into French, but within minutes the story began to have a familiar ring. Imagine my surprise when I realized that I was listening to an Indian Ocean version of Snow White. In this version it is not seven dwarves but seven fishermen. "Quest-ce que c'est d'origin de cette histoire?" What was the origin of this story? I asked. The answer: "Us. It is our oldest story."

They merely smiled pleasantly when I told them I had heard another version. They asked me to tell it and I did. Now, I am not a linguist, nor a folklorist, nor an anthropologist. I am not in the least equipped to track down the origin of the Veso folktale. Did they cop a Grimm's tale, or did the Grimm brothers have a friend on one of Cook's voyages who brought the Veso tale back to them? The timing would have been slightly off, but not by much. Cook was sailing around there in 1770 and brothers Jacob and Wilhelm were cranking up in the early 1800s.

That, however, does not really seem to be the point. The point is that both tellings of the Snow White story or the *Ampelsoa,* as it is called by the Veso, were successful because they were stories well told. In the Veso story the wicked Queen is transformed into a large dolphin who must swim forever around the bay of her daughter's village to protect it from evil forces—maybe James Cook with the brothers Grimm on board!

The case of the Madagascar version of Snow White, and that of *The Fortune-Tellers* by Lloyd Alexander and Trina Schart Hyman, have introduced the issue of provenance and geographical misappropriation in relation to storytelling and literature. Critics raise issues in regard to context and setting, but in my opinion the questioning so far has been less than sophisticated. Too often these issues have not been explored within the conventions of responsible and enlightened literary criticism. There is a propensity to make special case scenarios for multicultural literature. At the heart of the provenance issue is the contention by some people that certain stories must unfold against specific backdrops that are consonant with their source.

This seems simplistic to me. Taken at its crudest, this approach would say that a Norse myth in the Florida Keys will not work, even if it is very well written. I disagree. First, it is my belief that it is virtually impossible to say with complete certainty that a particular story would not be told in a particular setting on our planet Earth. Second, I feel that such a response does not explore, on a serious level, the function of setting and context as part of the craft of writing. Hence, a double disservice is rendered that reflects on the true value of multiculturalism, for it suggests that issues of cultural diversity in education are a passing fancy, a trend that needs only to meet current guidelines to be politically correct and is not subject to the more rigorous standards by which we measure art. Playing fast and loose with aesthetic standards ultimately demeans the craft of writing and storytelling itself.

As an author I do not make artistic judgments based on notions of political correctness. Every single day in my life as a writer I make many decisions that have to do just with the setting in a novel or picture book. I work my way toward each decision by figuring out what is going to work in the convoluted matrix of plot, character, mood, and tone of a story. What will be believable and express the intent of the whole endeavor?

Issues of Authorship

A much thornier question than that of origin and setting is the one of authorship. It is, of course, an issue closely related to and indeed inextricably involved with that of provenance. As writers elect to write about a culture other than their own, the voices of the critics are becoming increasingly strident. We are told with greater frequency that certain stories may be told only by certain people. I strongly disagree. I feel that if this dictate were extrapolated, it would result in authors only being able to write their own story over and over. Furthermore, if authors can write only about their own culture, would not the corollary be that editors must follow suit and not edit material outside their own ethnic or cultural experience? We must seek African American editors for African American stories, Jewish ones for Jewish stories, Native American ones for Native American stories. Everything eventually must be perfectly aligned in terms of gender, sexual preference, race, creed, or ethnic origin. And then, only then, would we get the perfect book for our multicultural audience.

To me this is not only ridiculous but dangerous. It represents a kind of literary version of ethnic cleansing, with an underlying premise that posits that there is only one story and only one way to tell it.

I was upset recently when a publisher discouraged me from attempting a book on Sarah Breedlove Walker, or Madame Walker as she was known, who came from my hometown and was one of the first women millionaires. She was also African American. She made her money developing hair products for African American people. I was told that it was a losing battle for a white person to take on a subject like Madame Walker. The book would be panned by critics and wouldn't sell.

I was appalled. I was on the brink of begging to do this book because I am truly crazy about Madame Walker. But I realized it was a losing battle. These critics in essence have some publishers running scared. So I just said to this editor, "You realize that this is censorship?" And he said yes, he did. And wasn't it a shame? Eventually, my book, *Vision of Beauty: The Story of Sarah Breedlove Walker* (2000), was successfully published to unanimously excellent reviews, and no one ever brought up the fact that I wasn't African American.

Nearly every critic who writes or speaks on this subject of authorship starts by saying that he or she would never dream of prescribing what an author or illustrator should or should not write, but then they go right ahead and do just that, while making extravagant allusions to artistic freedom. The critics' first premise is that a distinction must be made between what they often call "universal stories," those stories that can be experienced by all children throughout the world through all times, and those stories which are "culturally specific." They state that culturally specific books can only be created well by those who come from within a culture.

This statement serves notice to anyone who might be considering writing outside his or her own culture. It is precisely within this kind of rhetorical climate that a writer's freedom is inhibited and prescriptions are made as to who should write which stories. The second premise of many who claim to carry the banner of multiculturalism concerns that of authentic voice. It has been said that great stories are told from the inside out and therefore a writer from another culture has no chance of capturing the true voice in which the story must be told. I would agree with the first part of that statement—great stories are told from the inside out, but great artists, even those not of a particular culture, can indeed find the real voice. They can go inside out, even if they have not been there before. That is the whole meaning of being a great artist. It rankles me that no one questions, for example, when an actor such as Meryl Streep takes on a role with a perfectly pitched accent of another culture, but the equivalent is considered less than genuine when done by an author.

It is true that many of us work out of the unique topographies of our hearts and minds, what we know the best through our own experience. And it is our own experience that is the natural starting point for many of us, especially in our first artistic efforts. But we must not be held to that point.

Any serious discussion of literature cannot present such strictures as the ones I have just discussed. The injunction against writing outside one's own culture is a frightening one because it is too easy to imagine it being extrapolated to bizarre conclusions. By the new rules of this multicultural game, I would be destined to keep writing about Midwestern Jewish girls of Russian extraction. I have done that twice already. What if I wanted to write a novel about a Sephardic Jew? Am I to be told that I can never capture the Sephardic voice? That this is a voice parched by the winds of North Africa, salted by the brine of the Mediterranean, forged in the pressure cooker of the Spanish Inquisition. My family are not Sephardim, nor are they Eshkenazy Jews. At this rate, I would never get west of Warsaw.

Writing Powerfully outside One's Own Culture

How paltry indeed would be the offering if artists had listened seriously to these specious arguments. I might as a reader have been deprived of my two favorite books of the last twenty years.

The most recent of the two is *The Remains of The Day* (1993). The author, Kazuo Ishiguro, is Japanese. He is much too young to have even been born in the period in which his story is set. How indeed does a not-yet-middle-aged Asian capture so perfectly the nuances, the speech, of an English butler of a manor house of the 1930s? How indeed? He is an artist—a consummate artist.

And then there is the second book. Here is how it begins:

> Call me Stingo, which was the nickname I was known by in those days, if I was called anything at all. The name derives from my prep school days down in my native Virginia.

Thus William Styron, a non-Jew, southern male, opens his masterpiece about the horrors of the Holocaust and the extraordinary Sophie. This was hardly the first book I read about the Holocaust. As a teenager, I had been profoundly moved by Anne Frank's *Diary of a Young Girl* (1993), and then a few years later seared by Elie Wiesel's harrowing novel *Night* (1982), but the Holocaust book that touched me to my very soul was Styron's *Sophie's Choice* (1999). I am not saying it is a better book. It was simply told in a way that stirred me more deeply. And I am a Jew. So why should I find this southern gentile voice more moving? I cannot answer the question. It is mysterious like art itself. I sometimes think when I reflect upon *Sophie's Choice* that it is a story as much about innocence as it is about horror. It is the very choice that Styron made to use the young, naïve, southern male as the narrative channel for this story of ultimate horror that gave it a kind of distance that, in the end, for me, made it infinitely the most powerful book about the Holocaust that I have ever read.

It seems to me that the new insistence on certain rules for authorship and provenance of a story (or who writes what and where) is indeed threatening the very fabric of literature and literary criticism. It is as if the critics are imposing a strange kind of double standard in which books are not allowed to stand or fall according to their own merits or deficiencies. The books are being prejudged when it is said that no author should write outside his or her own culture, for they cannot successfully capture the authentic voice in which the story was meant to be told.

This is detrimental for the following two reasons: Is there just one voice in which a story must be told? Is there only one version of a story to tell? I hope not, for obviously this is not just verging on censorship; it is censorship. Secondly, are we in fact weakening the conventional standards by which we judge, appreciate, and read literature? Is it okay if you are the right color or ethnic origin to write poorly? The first criterion for publication should always be that the book is good literature. While authenticity and accuracy are important, just because an author is from a particular ethnic group does not mean that the book is automatically good or that it is necessarily authentic.

It seems to me that the people who make these pronouncements about the creation of literature for a culturally diverse reading population are in the long run reductionists. They understand very little about the creative process. They indeed want to reduce the creation of fiction to a set of variables that rests on the shaky hypothesis that certain people have certain voices, and it is within these voices that certain stories are best told.

This kind of thinking undermines what is at the very heart of the creative process. Henry James said it best when he wrote of the creative act as one that involved "the mystic process of the crucible [in which] there was a transformation of material under [the] aesthetic heat" of the artist's craft. A writer can have all the right credentials in terms of ethnic background and culture but can still fail if he or she does not have the aesthetic heat. Such heat is not the product of ethnicity. It transcends ethnicity. It is within the realm of the artist.

In one of my books, a historical novel about the Underground Railroad entitled *True North* (1996), I elect to tell the story of the Underground Railroad from a dual perspective, that of a fourteen-year-old fugitive slave girl and that of a fourteen-year-old white New England heiress, a Boston Brahmin, descendant of one of the oldest of the original Puritan families. As I wrote the book, I fully expected to be criticized by various people for assuming the voice of a nineteenth-century African American. How dare she write out of an experience which is not her own? How dare she presume upon this part of history, to explicate, to explore, to present this human tragedy?

The irony, of course, is that I have no more authority to write as a Boston Brahmin than I do as a fugitive black slave. I have no more claim or kinship to that unique experience than I do to slavery. When I began contemplating this novel, both experiences were foreign to me—remember, I am the daughter of midwestern Jews by way of Russia. I grew up in shopping malls, dreaming about rock and roll and Jack Kennedy and his New Frontier. But as I said before, I have written about that already, and life is too short to tell the same story twice. I hope to tell all my stories well, and if I don't, it will not be because of my color, or ethnic origin. I shall fail simply because I am an inferior artist. In short, the heat won't be there—the aesthetic heat.

References

Alexander, L. (1992). *The fortune-tellers.* New York: Dutton.

Frank, A. (1993). *Anne Frank: The diary of a young girl.* New York: Bantam.

Ishiguro, K. (1993). *The remains of the day.* Vintage Books.

Lasky, K. (1986). *Pageant.* New York: Four Winds Press.

Lasky, K. (1996). *True north: A novel of the Underground Railroad.* Scholastic.

Lasky, K. (2000). *Vision of beauty: The story of Sarah Breedlove Walker.* Cambridge, MA: Candlewick Press.

Styron, W. (1999). *Sophie's choice.* New York: Modern Library.

Weisel, E. (1982). *Night.* New York: Bantam Books.

9 Multiculturalism Is Not Halloween

Thelma Seto

I have followed the debate regarding multicultural literature for children with interest for quite some time. As a Japanese American writer who was born and raised in the Middle East—Syria, Lebanon, and Iran—I have struggled with the issue of cultural identity and cultural borrowings all my life. I feel very strongly that it is morally wrong for Euro-American writers to "steal" from other cultures in order to jump on the multicultural bandwagon, unless they have direct, personal experience in the country where that culture originates—more than simply being a tourist or doing research in the library. Katherine Paterson is an example of a writer whose work is informed by more than a superficial understanding of another culture. Not only does she write about a culture with which she has personal experience, but, judging from the integrity of her books set in Japan, she does so very successfully.

It is a different matter to "steal" from another culture without understanding that culture with one's heart. In such writing, there is a very noticeable lack of integrity—something is missing at its core. Writing is, above all else, a moral issue. If writers are not honest at the deepest level, their work will be hollow, no matter how well they know their craft or how well-developed and interesting their characters and plots may be.

This issue of cultural theft and misrepresenting other people brings two recent incidents to mind. The first is a story my Euro-American cousin told me about trick-or-treating with her six-year-old daughter. A women educated in two of the best higher-education institutions in this country, my cousin spent several weeks sewing her daughter's costume and on Halloween night was especially careful in applying make-up to her daughter's face. Her little girl went as Little Black

---

This chapter is a revised version of an essay that originally appeared in *The Horn Book Magazine*, 1995, 71(2), 169–74. Reprinted with permission. Copyright retained by the author.

Sambo, in blackface. My cousin saw absolutely nothing wrong with this, saying Little Black Sambo is a well-known American literary character: "He is part of the public domain, and I'll do anything I want with him."

At the time my cousin told me this story, I hoped she was pulling my leg. After following the debate on multicultural literature in my own career, I have come to the conclusion that not only was she serious but that her disturbed thinking is commonplace among Euro-Americans.

Why is the image of a blue-eyed, blonde child in blackface so appalling to me? Why, for that matter, am I so offended every Halloween when I scoop out handfuls of candy and nuts to the countless ninjas and samurai, fundamentalist Muslim terrorists, and camel-less sheiks that parade past my door? Am I so very strange that I find it personally terrifying to live in a society where racist misrepresentations of non-Europeans are considered cute or funny or even poetic, either at the front door on Halloween or between book covers on our children's bookshelves?

What do Halloween and multicultural children's literature have in common? Is there not a metaphor here for Euro-American writers who produce "multicultural" literature and reach out their candy bags at their publishers' doors? Beyond the issue of personal gain, what better way to control the images of "otherness" than to define the cultural discourse by representing everyone yourself and silencing those who demand the right to represent themselves?

The second incident relating to this issue was a "multicultural" play I saw several years ago—a play that was lauded in the arts scene as "cutting edge." In fact, it was mishmash, written by a French Canadian theater group, describing the history of the Chinese in Canada. The Chinese characters were played by French Canadian actors with white nylon stockings pulled over their faces so that their features were flattened and indistinguishable. They were the only ethnic group in the play whose features were thus erased. And, of course, the characters of supposed Chinese ancestry ran a Chinese laundry, gambled, and sold their daughters into sexual slavery.

Multiculturalism is not Halloween. You cannot put on one mask and "become" Asian. It is not a matter of exchanging a Euro-American setting or face or national costume for an Asian American or African American or Latin American one. Euro-American writers cannot write from the point of view of an Asian American child because they have not lived that child's reality—they cannot have; they do not have that child's identity, culture, or family history. In the case of Asian Americans, our family histories on this continent are full of traumas Euro-American writers cannot imagine; nor can they understand how those traumas have been passed on generation after generation and what they mean. Euro-American writers cannot understand Asian American culture if they have not grown up in Asian American homes. As a mixed-race Asian American with both Asian American and Euro-American extended family, I think I speak with authority on this point. The differences are both enormous and intimate. My Euro-American cousins haven't a clue about the culture I share with my Japanese Canadian cousins. And, beyond that, neither side of the family has the foggiest idea what my invisible cultures, those of Syria, Lebanon, and Iran, are about.

Multiculturalism is a matter of bringing the broadest diversity of writers to the table. It is pluralism. It was with great consternation that I read Jane Yolen's (1994) "An Empress of Thieves." It was very telling to me that Jane Yolen grew up in a household that kept her cultural heritage a secret; I believe this is the reason Euro-Americans resist multiculturalism in its truest sense. It would be far more interesting to me, as both a writer and a reader, to see Yolen and other Euro-American writers rediscover their own heritages and write about those cultures, rather than about cultures they do not understand and have no connection to. Just as culture cannot be donned as a mask, it cannot be whitewashed through family secrets, either; it is a part of all of us, whether our parents have the wisdom to consciously pass it on or not. Furthermore, when Euro-Americans "take on" one of my cultures, I feel quite violated. It is a form of cultural imperialism—that euphemism for cultural rape. I do not wish to attack the work of individual artists—that is beside the point and we all need to support one another's work in a society that so devalues writers—but I can pick out specific examples if I must. Sadly, they are more plentiful than their culturally truthful and respectful counterparts.

If there is a dearth of multicultural children's literature on publishers' lists today, and non-Euro-American writers have not yet broken into the children's literature market—we *are* out there—it would be far more fruitful for publishers to seek out translators who might bring to American children the literature of other cultures and nations. There are certainly many deserving writers from other countries who would be delighted to find a broader audience for their work. And those of us in the United States whose families originally hail from those countries are starved to read those works.

Yolen says we are presently in a period of "Balkanization" in children's literature. So be it. Non-Euro-Americans need to tell our own stories, as only we can tell them. Non-Asian writers cannot tell my story. It is a story they cannot know specifically because it has not yet been told. And as an Asian American—whose people have been silenced and made invisible by Euro-Americans since our first ancestors came to this continent in the 1600s (ten years before the Pilgrims, I might point out)— I will not allow writers who do not have Asian ancestry to pretend to tell my story.

You cannot separate politics from literature, as most of us from the Third World are well aware. For centuries Euro-Americans have defined us, rewritten our histories, our cultures, our religions, even our languages—and profited handsomely from these efforts. For centuries in this country we have found caricatures of ourselves in Euro-American books. These caricatures have translated, in real life, into lynchings; race riots against our communities; gross anti-immigrant movements; military aggression in our homelands, such as the Gulf War against Iraq and the atomic bombings of Hiroshima and Nagasaki; and racially motivated individual beatings, rapes, cross burnings, and murders. Euro-American writers must be shockingly sure of themselves if they think they can get at the truth of my life in some library, and must also be in very deep denial if they think they do no one harm in wearing a Halloween mask in order to publish one more book. If any writer needs to wear a Halloween mask to portray me—or any other person of color—in order to be published, that book is one that doesn't deserve to be in print.

I urge Euro-American writers to look again at the issue of cultural thievery. There are very real consequences to it, especially in books for children. When a Euro-American writer pens a novel that is full of well-meaning but unconscious racial and cultural stereotypes, he or she hurts the children of that heritage who are inevitably given that book, hurts their self-image, and, down the road, this translates into internalized racism and racial violence. In addition, those books feed children who are not of that ethnicity all kinds of unwholesome and untruthful ideas about other racial or cultural groups. This hurts everyone, for racism affects Euro-Americans as well as people of color in this country.

Euro-American writers falsely portraying others contribute to horrors such as the Los Angeles riots of 1992. When I was a preteen, my father educated me about the world of his youth—that of the Yellow Peril Scare on the West Coast in the early 1900s—through a book written by Gene Stratton-Porter. I believe the images in that book, and in other books of that time, live today in the minds of those children—now adults—who read them, some of whom promulgate the same stereotypes in their own writing. I cannot possibly convey to you how much that particular book hurt me with its racist portrayal of the "Yellow Invasion." I thought of Gene Stratton-Porter as I watched the coverage of the L.A. riots on television, seeing African American, Latino, and Euro-American alike burning and looting an Asian American neighborhood with glee and impunity. Tell me, now, that it doesn't matter what our children read, as long as they do read. It matters very much.

As writers, we play a profound and important role in this society. We need to take ourselves a good deal more seriously than we have, to question our motives—in terms of personal gain—in relation to the greater good of the society, and to be clearer about the difference between right and wrong. Although as a writer I am affected by everything I read and experience, and use these things both consciously and unconsciously, I still believe it is wrong to steal. And I am not so egotistical, or ignorant, as to think I am qualified to write a book from a Native American or Latino or African American point of view.

I hope all writers—but especially Euro-American writers who subscribe to the belief that cultural theft is quite acceptable—will ponder the issues I have raised and spend time at the start of every writing day cultivating a smidgen of humility and grace. I would certainly welcome a book exploring the pain of a Euro-American child growing up without knowledge of his or her ancestral culture. That is a book I have not yet read and one I know needs to be written for the spiritual healing of countless Euro-American children, as well as this country as a whole. I promise to buy it.

Reference

Yolen, J. (1994). An empress of thieves. *Horn Book, 70*(6), 702–5.

III Political Correctness and Cultural Authenticity

10 Beyond Political Correctness

Hazel Rochman

*M*ulticulturalism is a trendy word, trumpeted by the politically correct with a stridency that has provoked a sneering backlash. There are PC watchdogs eager to strip from the library shelves anything that presents a group as less than perfect (Beard & Cerf, 1992). The ethnic "character" must always be strong, dignified, courageous, loving, sensitive, wise. Then there are those who watch for authenticity: how dare a white write about blacks? What's a Gentile doing writing about a Jewish old lady and her African American neighbors? The chilling effect of this is a kind of censorship and a reinforcement of apartheid.

It's easy to laugh at the lunatic fringe. According to PC labeling, I should change my name to Hazel Rochperson. They comfort me that I am vertically challenged (short), my husband is differently hirsute (bald), my mother is chronologically gifted (old), my brother differently abled (brain-injured), and some of my best friends are people of size (fat). Not at all comforting are the same kind of euphemisms from the corporate world: words like *downsizing* (firing workers). Then there's *ethically different* (corrupt) and *caloric insufficiency* (hunger), or a new one for hunger, *misnourishment*.

But the greatest danger from the politically correct bullies is that they create a backlash, and that backlash often consists of self-righteous support for the way things are. Whether we are weary or indignant, we wish the whiners would just go away. Or we focus on the absurd and on the names, and then we can ignore real issues of prejudice and hatred that keep people apart. Ethnic cleansing is the current euphemism: it's an attack on multiculturalism, and it isn't funny at all.

In promoting books with young people, we have to resist the extremes: the mindless conformity to the PC of multiculturalism but also the backlash. The pretentious jargon is only now catching up with what we've been doing all along—teaching and sharing great books from everywhere, stories that grab us and extend our view of ourselves.

Growing up in South Africa, I didn't think that anyone could write a good story about where I lived. I was an avid reader, but books were about English girls in boarding school or lovers running wild on the windy moors. My romantic dreams came from Hollywood. Gangsters were in Chicago, and poor people were noble heroes struggling far away in the Dust Bowl in Oklahoma. I certainly didn't think that there could be an interesting story about blacks where I lived. They were servants, not individuals like me with complex feelings and difficult moral choices, not like my family and friends, or people in books.

Apartheid didn't seem to have much to do with me. I grew up in a liberal home. I wasn't allowed to make racist remarks. I thought I was a good person. I didn't see what was going on around me. I took it all for granted. I never noticed that there were no black kids my age in my neighborhood, not one black student in my school. I just accepted that the woman who cooked and cleaned for us lived in a room in the backyard. We knew only her first name or referred to her as the "girl"; I never thought that her children lived far away or that she was forced to leave them in order to come and look after me. I remember vaguely that one of her children died. I never asked her about her life. Read a story about her? From her point of view? What point of view?

As editor of *Somehow Tenderness Survives: Stories of Southern Africa* (1988), I included Doris Lessing's "The Old Chief Mshlanga," a story very close to my experience of growing up white and privileged and apart. In the story, the teenage girl calls black people "natives," a derogatory term in Africa, with racist overtones of being primitive, uncivilized. The natives were "as remote as the trees and rocks." They were "an amorphous, black mass," and, of course, their language was "uncouth" and "ridiculous." It's as if the white girl is asleep or blind. Then she meets a black man, the old Chief Mshlanga; he once owned the whole district before the whites came and "opened it up." She sees him as a person, not just a native, and that starts waking her up to the world around her. First, it seems quite easy: Why can't they all live together, black and white, without elbowing each other out of the way? But she discovers that you can't just set things right with "an easy gush of feeling, saying: I could not help it. I am also a victim."

She comes of age—as I did under apartheid—with the shocking awareness that the universe you've always taken for granted is evil.

Another story in the collection is from Mark Mathabane's (1986) autobiography *Kaffir Boy: The True Story of a Black Youth's Coming of Age in Apartheid South Africa.* Mathabane grew up in the ghetto of Alexandra Township, barely ten miles from where I lived on a tree-lined Johannesburg city street. But it was another universe, unimaginable to me when I was growing up. Like the overwhelming majority of whites, I never set foot there, and I blocked out any awareness of its daily life.

Until two or three years ago, Mathabane's book was banned in South Africa. You can see why. Not only does he describe the cruel oppression, he makes us see that black child as an individual, like me. Mathabane's family are people. They aren't amorphous saintly victims, nor are they wild savages. They're definitely not the innocent, mysterious primitives in the popular safari-adventure stories of "dark Africa." Racism dehumanizes, but a good story defeats the stereotype. It makes us imagine that boy's life in all its complexity and connects it to ours.

It's not just South Africa. Just as I, a white child in Johannesburg, saw the blacks around me as undifferentiated "natives," so Maya Angelou (1971), growing up in segregated Stamps, Arkansas, couldn't see whites as individuals: "People were those who lived on my side of town. I didn't like them all, or, in fact, any of them very much, but they were people. These others, the strange pale creatures that lived in their alien unlife, weren't considered folks. They were whitefolks" (p. 21).

They all look alike. *We* are individuals.

A good book can help to break down those barriers. Books can make a difference in dispelling prejudice and building community: not with role models and literal recipes, not with noble messages about the human family, but with enthralling stories that make us imagine the lives of others. A good story lets you know people as individuals in all their particularity and conflict; and once you see someone as a person—flawed, complex, striving—then you've reached beyond stereotype. Stories, writing them, telling them, sharing them, transforming them, all enrich us and connect us and help us know each other.

But it's insulting to say that a book is good *because* it's multicultural. Betsy Hearne, editor of the *Bulletin of the Center for Children's Books*, was appalled at a recent conference to hear people recommend a book only because it was multicultural, as if no further evaluation were needed.

And Yet . . . Beyond Recipes and Role Models

How do you evaluate books across cultures? Are there special criteria? What are the pitfalls? And in a time of declining book budgets in libraries and school media centers, when librarians do have to select very carefully, how do you balance all the demands of literary quality and popular appeal and intellectual freedom and curriculum support and multiculturalism? And how do you make kids want to read?

Of course, these issues aren't new, and there are no simple answers. As the arguments about political correctness reach a crescendo, I find myself agreeing and disagreeing with everybody. If there's one thing I've learned in this whole multicultural debate, it's not to trust absolutes. I say something and then immediately qualify it with "And yet. . . ." And it's usually because I find a book that upsets all my neat categories. That's what good books do: they unsettle us, make us ask questions about what we thought was certain. They don't just reaffirm everything we already know.

Underlying much of the PC debate is the demand that each book must do it all. Let's face it, a lot of kids don't read much for fun, especially as they get older. They don't have time. They get their stories, their dreams, their escape entertainment, without effort from TV and video and commercials. For many students, reading isn't a need and a pleasure. It's a drag. Something you do for a grade, if you have to.

The poet Katha Pollitt (1991) says that it's because young people read so little that there's such furious debate about the canon. If they read all kinds of books all the time, particular books wouldn't matter so much. If you think that the book you're promoting is the only one kids are ever going to read on a subject—about the pioneers or about Columbus or about the Holocaust or about apartheid—then there's intense pressure to choose the "right" book with the "right" message. If we don't watch out, reading becomes only therapy, only medicine. We start to recommend books because they give us the *right* role models, depending on what's considered "right" in the current political climate.

Censors think that readers treat a story like a recipe or a self-help manual with directions to follow, so that you go out and do literally what you're reading about. I'm not sure what happens when we read. It's mysterious. A story grabs us; a phrase sings and won't let us be; a street or a room gives us a view; the conflict in a character startles us into seeing ourselves in a new way.

The paradox is that if we give young people didactic tracts, or stories so bland that they offend nobody, we're going to make them read even less. For books to give pleasure there has to be tension and personality, laughter and passionate conflict. That's what will grab kids and touch them deeply—and make them want to read.

A good story is rich with ambiguity. You sympathize with people of all kinds. Read Anne Fine's funny young adult novels, like *My War with Goggle-Eyes* (1989), and you get swept up into furious family quarrels about relationships and about ideas, where neither side wins. The best books glory in conflict. This is especially so with political themes, where everything can degenerate into propaganda if the characters become mouthpieces for worthy ideas. Susan Sontag (1992) uses a wonderful expression: "Literature is a party," she says. "Even as disseminators of indignation, writers are givers of pleasure" (p. xviii).

The novelist E. L. Doctorow says that one of the things he most admires about George Bernard Shaw is that "he gave the best speeches to the people he disagreed with. . . . You have to allow the ambiguity. You have to allow for something to be itself and its opposite at the same time" (quoted in Moyers, 1989, p. 90).

Censors on the left and the right can't allow for ambiguity. One of their constant mistakes is to take what the narrator says, or what one character says, as the voice of the author. The Canadian novelist Margaret Atwood complains, "It's amazing the extent to which readers will think that everything anybody in any of your books says is an expression of your own opinion. Literature just doesn't work like that" (quoted in Sumrall, 1992, p. 76). If you judge every character to be the author, then you can never allow debate in a book, never have a protagonist who has an ugly or erroneous thought, never have a narrator who's less than perfect—perfect, that is, according to the current fashion.

A library collection does have to satisfy all kinds of requirements. But each book can't do it all. When Walter Dean Myers spoke at the Columbia Children's Literature Institute in 1990, someone in the audience asked him why he wrote a book about black kids playing basketball—it's such a stereotype, why was he feeding it? "Every book I write," he replied, "can't take on the whole African American experience." He said he had written other books in which kids did other things. But, he said, he likes basketball; lots of African American kids like basketball; and this one book is about that world.

One book doesn't carry the whole ethnic group experience. In Sook Nyul Choi's *Year of Impossible Goodbyes* (1991), chosen as an ALA Best Book for Young Adults, the Japanese occupiers of North Korea during World War II, as seen through the eyes of a young Korean girl, are cruel and oppressive enemies. Japan-bashing is a problem in the U.S. now, but that doesn't affect the truth of this story. You could read that book with Yoko Kawashima Watkins's *So Far from the Bamboo Grove* (1986), about a Japanese girl on the run from cruel Koreans after World War II. Or with Yoshiko Uchida's fiction and autobiography about how Japanese Americans were treated here during World War II.

What's more, one writer is not the representative of a whole ethnic group. Maxine Hong Kingston, who wrote the classic memoir *The Woman Warrior* (1976), complains about "the expectation among readers and critics that I should represent the race. Each artist has a unique voice. Many readers don't understand that. What I look forward to is the time when many of us are published and then we will be able to see the range of viewpoints, of visions, of what it is to be Chinese American" (quoted in Sumrall, 1992, p. 77). Nor does one reviewer speak for a whole ethnic group. Phoebe Yeh, a children's book editor at Scholastic, says that she is a reader before she is Chinese. I'm a Jew, but I can't speak for all Jews. Nor for all South Africans, not even for all South Africans who are anti-apartheid.

And every time an artist or writer does something, it doesn't have to be about her or his race. Sheila Hamanaka's book *The Journey* (1990) is based on her five-panel mural painting. It shows the World War II experience of Japanese Americans, including her own family, who were herded up and sent to concentration camps. It's a story of prejudice and injustice, personal and official, and Hamanaka is passionate about what happened to her people. But some of Hamanaka's books aren't focused on the Japanese American experience at all. *A Visit to Amy-Claire* (Mills, 1992) is a picture book about a family, about sibling rivalry, and the family happens to be Asian American. Recently, Hamanaka illustrated a delightful picture book, *Sofie's Role* by Amy Heath (1992), about a family bakery, and there are no Asian characters at all.

Accuracy and Authenticity

Now, there are people who say that Hamanaka should stick to stories about Asians. Or that Lloyd Alexander's (1991) *The Remarkable Journey of Prince Jen (Booklist's* Top of the List winner for fiction in 1991) can't be any good because Alexander can't really know the Chinese tradition. Or that Chinese American Ed Young can't illustrate African American folklore because he can't really know the culture. One of the most violent debates swirling around the issue of multicultural literature relates to accuracy and authenticity.

Of course accuracy matters. You can get a lot of things wrong as a writer, an artist, or a reviewer when you don't know a place or a culture. Junko Yokota (1992), who's from Japan, has pointed out some important errors in Japanese costume and custom in picture books published in the United States. For example, she shows that one illustration has characters wearing their kimonos in a style that only dead people are dressed in; another shows characters with chopsticks in their hair;

a third depicts food in a manner appropriate only when served to deceased ancestors. I'm from South Africa, so I know that culture better than the average American does, and in reviewing a book about apartheid I might find things that others might miss.

And yet . . . that isn't the whole story. Sometimes I worry that I know too much, that I can't see the forest for the trees, that steeped as I am in the South African culture, I can't always know what an American teenager doesn't know. Would an American reader be confused by something that I take for granted? One of the things that does help me is that I no longer live in South Africa, so to some extent I can see things from outside as well as in—from both sides of the border.

So what about those who say that an American can never write about Japan, that men can't write about women? In fact, some take it further. Only American Indians can really judge books about American Indians, or books about Jews must be reviewed only by Jews. And further still, you get the ultimate extreme, blacks should read only about blacks, or Latinos about Latinos, locking us into smaller and tighter boxes.

What I hear echoing in that sort of talk is the mad drumbeat of apartheidspeak. Apartheid made laws on the basis of so-called immutable differences. Not only should whites and blacks be kept absolutely apart and educated separately, but among blacks, each "tribe" should be separate, so that Zulus should live only with Zulus and be taught in Zulu about Zulus to do things that only Zulus do. The apartheid planners said that the only work blacks could do was simple manual labor, that science and abstract thinking weren't part of their culture, and that their training should prepare them to be good servants. It's so absurd that it's hard to believe how much of it was carried out, and with untold suffering to millions.

When I went back to South Africa in 1990, I interviewed Nadine Gordimer for *Booklist* at her home in Johannesburg. I asked her if she felt that as a white she could write about black experience, and how she answered those who said she was using black suffering. She got angry. "How does a writer write from the point of view of a child?" she said. "Or from the point of view of an old person when you are seventeen years old? How does a writer change sex? How could the famous soliloquy of Molly Bloom have been written by James Joyce? Has any woman ever written anything as incredibly intimate? I mean, how did Joyce know how a woman feels before she's going to get her period?"

Then, in 1992, I interviewed Virginia Hamilton. She spoke about her frustration in not being allowed to write *outside* the black experience. "People won't allow it; critics won't allow it," she said. "If I would do a book that didn't have blacks, people would say, 'Oh, what is Virginia Hamilton doing?' I feel the limitation," she explained. "I'm always running up against it and knocking it down in different ways, whichever way I can. But I know that it's there and will always be there. I mean, there were people who said in the middle of my career, 'Now Virginia Hamilton has finally faced who she is.' Well, how dare they?"

In a wonderful article called "What Mean We, White Man?" Roger Sutton (1992) sums it up this way: "Literature, language, is a way to jump out of our own skins. If we cannot reach beyond the bounds of race, ethnicity, sex, sexual orientation, and class, literature is useless, leaving writers few options beyond Joni Mitchell–style confessional lyrics."

And yet . . . only gifted writers can do it, write beyond their own cultures. Fiction and nonfiction are full of people who don't get beyond stereotypes because the writer cannot imagine them as individuals. Traveling to foreign places—or reading about them—isn't necessarily broadening. Many tourists return from their experience with the same smug stereotypes about "us" and "them." Too many books *about* other countries, written without knowledge or passion, take the "tourist" approach, stressing the exotic, or presenting a static society with simple categories. Some writers who try to tackle a country's complex political and social issues seem to think that in a book for young people it's fine to do a bit of background reading and then drop into a country for a few weeks, take some glossy pictures, and go home and write a book about it.

There's nothing wrong with writing a book about travel, about how it feels to be in a foreign place, even about finding a foreign place exotic. But don't pretend you're writing about the place or the people there. If the book takes a tourist approach, just touching down from the cruise ship for some local shopping, then you get the kind of nonfiction photo-essay so common in children's literature, where the pictures are arranged so that the child—usually attired in national dress—goes on a "journey," a journey that allows the book to include some colorful scenery and local customs.

Yes, authenticity matters, but there is no formula for how you acquire it. Anybody can write about anything—if they're good enough. There will always be inauthentic or inaccurate books, and defining authenticity on some exclusionary basis or other won't change a thing. The only way to combat inaccuracy is with accuracy—not with pedigrees.

Saints, Role Models, and Stereotypes

The savage savage is a stereotype, but the noble savage is, too. Both are designed to set up borders, to keep "them" far away from "us."

Michael Dorris, who acted as consultant for the Native American list in *Against Borders* (Rochman, 1993), said in a *New York Times* article about the depiction of American Indians in the movie *Dances with Wolves:* "Readers and viewers of such sagas are left with a predominant emotion of regret for a golden age now but a faint memory. In the imaginary mass media world of neat beginnings, middles and ends, American Indian society, whatever its virtues and fascinations as an arena for Euro-American consciousness raising, is definitely past tense" (n.p.). Beverly Slapin and Doris Seale, in *Through Indian Eyes: The Native Experience in Children's Books* (1992), show how often American Indians are presented as whooping savages in paint or feathers, or as cute, make-believe figures for kids to playact in costume, or as noble savages, generic and distant, as in dusty museum panoramas.

Lionel Trilling said that James Agee's text for *Let Us Now Praise Famous Men*, published in the early 1940s, about poor tenant families in the South, was the most realistic and the most important moral effort of his generation. Even so, Trilling pointed out "a failure of moral realism" in the book. "It lies in Agee's inability to see these people as anything but good. He writes of these people as if there were no human unregenerateness in them, no flicker of malice or meanness, no darkness or wildness of feeling, only a sure and simple virtue, the growth, we must suppose, of their hard, unlovely poverty. He shuts out, that is, what is part of the moral job to take in. What creates this falsification is guilt—the observer's guilt at his own relative freedom" (quoted in Hersey, 1988).

When I was compiling the stories about apartheid for *Somehow Tenderness Survives*, I struggled at first with that kind of reverential, patronizing guilt. I looked for stories that had the right line—brave, good, strong, beautiful people succeeding in the fight for freedom—and I felt a great deal of pressure to include role-model stories.

But several things stopped me from choosing that kind of propaganda. First, reviewing the books on South Africa for *Booklist,* I had seen too many politically correct anthologies with the right balance and the reverential attitudes that just weren't being read. You can't harangue people into reading, however worthy the cause. There has to be the pleasure of story, character, passionate conflict, and language if you're going to grab readers and make them want to read on.

Second, I listened to Nadine Gordimer when she came to speak in Chicago. She is politically militant, unequivocally committed to Nelson Mandela and the struggle against racism. But she is just as adamant that the correct attitude doesn't make a good story. She writes about betrayal, as well as courage. About people.

Ethnicity, Universals, and a Sense of Place

Of course it's great to read about your own culture and recognize yourself in a book, especially if you have felt marginalized and demonized. The writer Jamaica Kincaid, who grew up in Antigua, talks about the joy she felt when she first read the books of fellow Caribbean Derek Walcott (the 1992 winner of the Nobel Prize for Literature): "I thought we were just the riffraff of the British Empire until I read this man and thought: 'Oh yes, that is me. That is us'" (Kincaid, 1992, n.p.). Katha Pollitt says that, however much she hates the "self-esteem argument," she has to admit that it meant something to her when she was growing up to find a female poet in an anthology.

But it isn't always as direct as that. Mark Mathabane remembers reading a battered copy of *Treasure Island* and realizing that there were other possibilities beyond his ghetto township. Similarly, Richard Wright, in *Black Boy* (1945), describes how books gave him "new ways of looking and seeing," offering him hope that there was a world beyond the one in which he was trapped. "It was not a matter of believing or disbelieving what I read, but of feeling something new, of being affected by something that made the look of the world different" (pp. 272–273). I love the Yiddish idiom and the shtetl setting in the stories of Isaac Bashevis Singer: he makes me laugh; he makes me remember my mother's stories and her love of Singer; and he gives me a sense of my family and who I am. But I also get immense pleasure and the shock of recognition when I read Sandra Cisneros's stories in *The House on Mango Street* (1989), about a young Chicana girl, Esperanza, coming of age in Chicago. Esperanza says her great-grandmother "looked out of the window her whole life, the way so many women sit their sadness on an elbow" (pp. 10–11). That image makes me catch my breath. It makes me think of so many women trapped at home. I remember my mother-in-law, an immigrant from Lithuania, well educated, spirited, but a stranger, who got stuck in the rigid role prescribed for her in Cape Town's Jewish community. She used to sit like that, chin in her hands, elbows on the table, angrily watching us eat the food she'd cooked. And just as I love Cisneros, so non-Jews can find themselves in the humor and humanity of Singer's shtetl stories.

Amy Tan's *The Joy Luck Club* (1989) does give you an idea of what it's like to grow up Chinese American, and that is a good reason to read it. It's important for Asian Americans to read about themselves in books, and it's important for everybody else to read good books about them. It does show women struggling for independence, and that does give me pleasure. But it isn't reverential; the people aren't always wise and admirable. The extraordinary success of *The Joy Luck Club* has little to do with our need to know about "other" cultures. This book is a best-seller because, rooted as it is in the Chinese American experience, it explores the complexity and conflict, the love and anger, between mothers and daughters everywhere.

I was on the committee that selected Virginia Hamilton as the 1992 U.S. nominee for the international Hans Christian Andersen Award. When the nomination was announced, some people said that she didn't have a chance of world recognition because foreigners wouldn't understand her, wouldn't read her, wouldn't translate her. She was too idiomatic, too difficult, too local, they said. They were wrong. She won. And, in fact, her books have been widely read in countries like Japan for years.

We're too quick to say, "Kids won't read this." We each live in a small world and talk to people like ourselves and reinforce each other, and we think everyone agrees with us. If you choose good stories and if you promote them, it's not true that books in translation or about foreign cultures are only for the "gifted," that young people won't read books with a strong sense of a foreign place. Singer (1977) says that the opposite is true, that the more a story is connected with a group, the more specific it is, the better. In an opening note to *When Shlemiel Went to Warsaw* (1968), he says: "In our time, literature is losing its address" (n.p.). That's such a wonderful pun—losing its sense of place, its identity, and because of that, losing its ability to speak, to address an audience. (It's interesting that for him place isn't so much a landscape or a physical environment—"in a village somewhere in the Ukraine"—it's really that idiom, that individual voice, rooted in a particular group and its way of life.) Singer says that in writing for children, he's not concerned with using only words that the child will understand. "Unknown words don't stop the child," he says. "But a boring story will" (pp. 13–14). E. B. White said the same about *Charlotte's Web*: "Children are game for anything. I throw them hard words and they backhand them over the net. They love words that give them a hard time" (quoted in Gherman, 1992, p. 93).

It's obvious that for mainstream young people, books about "other" cultures are not as easy to pick up as *YM* magazine, or as easy to watch as *Beverly Hills 90210*. And, in fact, they shouldn't be. We don't want a homogenized culture. If you're a kid in New York, then reading about a refugee in North Korea, or a teenager in the bush in Africa, or a Mormon in Utah involves some effort, some imagination, some opening up of who you are. In talking about books with kids, I always start with a story set where they are, here and now. Then once they're listening, I move to other cultures, in this country and across the world and back again.

Stories about foreign places risk two extremes: either they can overwhelm the reader with reverential details of idiom, background, and custom, or they can homogenize the culture and turn all the characters into mall babies. There's always that tension between the particular and the universal, between making the character and experience and culture too special, and making them too much the same. On the one hand, we don't want to be bogged down in reverential details about the way of life and the deep mystical meaning of everything the protagonist sees; we don't want to wade through thickets of idiom, background, and culture before we can get to the story. And yet . . . the pleasures of a good story emerge most forcibly from a vividly evoked, particularized setting. Details make a world. Take *Shabanu: Daughter of the Wind*, by Suzanne Fisher Staples (1989), about a young Muslim girl living with her nomadic family in the desert of Pakistan. Shabanu has spirit and intelligence and that's dangerous in a girl, especially when at the age of twelve she's promised in marriage to an old man. As we get to care for Shabanu and what happens to her, we imagine what it must be like to be her. At the same time, the story is rooted in the particulars of her culture, and the sense of her place is deeply felt. The important thing is that there's no sense of the exotic; the desert is very much there but not as scenery or travelogue. This book is remarkable in showing a sense of individual personality within a tight structure.

Glossaries and Names

When I was compiling *Somehow Tenderness Survives*, my editor, Charlotte Zolotow, and I were reluctant to have a glossary. We felt that readers would get the meaning of strange words from context. If you know there's a glossary, it makes you stiff and wary, instead of allowing you to give yourself over to the world of the story. What persuaded us that we did need a glossary was the fact that the racist categories and racist insults needed clarification. Most Americans didn't know that *kaffir* was the worst insult, the equivalent of *nigger* here; they didn't know that *native* is derogatory. In fact, it's a sign of the shame of apartheid that it has spawned such an exact list of racist names.

This chapter started with a joke about names. And yet . . . what you call people does matter, especially in a society where groups are angry and divided. When Malcolm Little dropped the last name that had been given to his family by slave owners and took on X to stand for the "true African family name that he never could know," he was making a powerful statement about his identity (Malcolm X & Haley, 1965, p. 199). His renaming was like a rebirth: he was freeing himself from the self-hatred that kept him enslaved. To call a man a "boy," as many whites do in South Africa, is a vicious racist insult. If servants are nameless, they aren't people.

Sensationalism and Sentimentality

Books about apartheid, about slavery, about the Holocaust can be grim. Do you give young people books about racial oppression and mass suffering? How do you evaluate such books?

Young people want to know about these things, and it is important that they know. But, whether it's fiction or nonfiction, the account shouldn't exploit the violence; it shouldn't grab attention by dwelling on sensational detail. Nor should it offer slick comfort; the Holocaust did not have a happy ending. Nor should it fall back on exhortation and rhetoric; after a while, words like *horror, atrocity,* and *terrible* cease to mean anything.

The best stories tell it from the point of view of ordinary people like Anne Frank, like us. Holocaust accounts like Ida Vos's *Hide and Seek* (1991) or Isabella Leitner's *The Big Lie* (1992) succeed through understatement, allowing the facts to speak for themselves, true to the Jewish child's bewildered point of view. (Why must she wear a star? What does it mean, going into hiding?) There are no gimmicks like time travel or easy escape; no rhetoric, no tears, no hand-wringing about *atrocity* and *horror.* Stories like these defeat stereotype. They overcome the evil institution, not by making the character a heroic role model or a proud representative of the race, not by haranguing us with a worthy cause, but by making the individual a person.

Against Borders

When I wrote my book *Against Borders,* I felt overwhelmed at first by the demands of political correctness. How was I going to choose the "right" books for the essays and resource lists? The watchdogs from right, left, and center would pounce: How could you put that in? How could you leave that out? Even with my great editors and wise advisors and consultants, there were going to be so many *problems.*

My husband is a long-time apartheid fighter. "Not *problems*," he said. "*Riches.*"

And that's really the point about the whole multicultural debate. When I lived under apartheid, I thought I was privileged—and compared with the physical suffering of black people, I was immeasurably well off—but my life was impoverished. I was blind, and I was frightened. I was shut in. And I was denied access to the stories and music of the world. Groups like Ladysmith Black Mambazo were making music right there, and I couldn't hear them. I didn't know that in the streets of Soweto there were people like Nelson Mandela with a vision of nonracial democracy that would change my life. I was ignorant, and I didn't know I was ignorant. I thought I was better than someone like Mark Mathabane's mother because she spoke English with an accent; I didn't know that she and others like her were fluent in multiple languages. I didn't know anything about most of the people around me. And because of that I didn't know what *I* could be.

Borders shut us in, in Johannesburg, in Los Angeles and Chicago, in Eastern Europe, in our own imaginations.

References

Alexander, L. (1991). *The remarkable journey of Prince Jen.* New York: Dutton.

Angelou, M. (1971). *I know why the caged bird sings.* New York: Bantam.

Beard, H., & Cerf, C. (1992). *The officially politically correct dictionary and handbook.* New York: Villard.

Choi, S. N. (1991). *Year of impossible goodbyes.* Boston: Houghton-Mifflin.

Cisneros, S. (1989). *The house on mango street.* Houston: Arte Publico Press.

Dorris, M. (1991, 24 February). Indians in aspic. *New York Times,* p. 417.

Fine, A. (1989). *My war with Goggle-Eyes.* New York: Bantam.

Gherman, B. (1992). *E. B. White: Some writer!* New York: Atheneum.

Hamanaka, S. (1990). *The journey: Japanese Americans, racism, and renewal.* New York: Orchard.

Heath, A. (1992). *Sofie's role.* New York: Four Winds.

Hersey, J. (1988). Introduction. J. Agee & W. Evans, *Let us now praise famous men.* Boston: Houghton Mifflin.

Kincaid, J. (1992, October 9). I thought we. . . . *New York Times,* p. x.

Kingston, M. H. (1976). *The woman warrior: Memoirs of a girlhood among ghosts.* New York: Knopf.

Leitner, I., with Leitner, I. A. (1992). *The big lie: A true story.* New York: Scholastic.

Malcolm X, & Haley, A. (1965). *The autobiography of Malcolm X.* New York: Ballantine.

Mathabane, M. (1986). *Kaffir boy: The true story of a Black youth's coming of age in apartheid South Africa.* New York: NAL/Dutton.

Mills, C. (1992). *A visit to Amy-Claire.* New York: Macmillan.

Moyers, B. D. (1989). A world of ideas: Conversations with thoughtful men and women about American life today and the ideas shaping our future. New York: Doubleday.

Pollitt, K. (1991, September 23). Why do we read? *The Nation,* p. x.

Rochman, H. (Ed.). (1988). *Somehow tenderness survives: Stories of Southern Africa.* New York: Harper & Row.

Rochman, H. (1990, September 15). The *Booklist* interview: Nadine Gordimer. *Booklist, 86,* 100–101.

Rochman, H. (1992, February 1). The *Booklist* interview: Virginia Hamilton. *Booklist, 88,* 1020–21.

Rochman, H. (1993). *Against borders: Promoting books for a multicultural world.* Chicago: American Library Association.

Singer, I. B. (1968). *When Shlemiel went to Warsaw & other stories.* New York: Farrar, Straus & Giroux.

Singer, I. B. (1977). Untitled. *Children's Literature, 6.*

Slapin, B., & Seale, D. (1992). *Through Indian eyes: The native experience in books for children.* Philadelphia: New Society.

Sontag, S. (1992). Introduction. In S. Sontag (Ed.), *Best American essays, 1992* (p. xviii). New York: Ticknor & Fields.

Staples, S. F. (1989). *Shabanu, daughter of the wind.* New York: Knopf.

Sumrall, A. C. (1992). *Write to the heart: Wit and wisdom of women writers.* Freedom, CA: Crossing Press.

Sutton, R. (1992, August). What mean we, white man? *VOYA: Voice of Youth Advocates.*

Tan, A. (1989). *The joy luck club.* New York: Putnam.

Vos, I. (1991). *Hide and seek* (T. Edelstein & I. Smidt, Trans). Boston: Houghton Mifflin.

Watkins, Y. K. (1986). *So far from the bamboo grove.* New York: Lothrop.

Wright, R. (1945). *Black boy: A record of childhood and youth.* New York: Harper & Row.

Yokota, J. (1992, September 12). Looking beyond the literary and visual images to raise the level of cultural consciousness. Paper presented at the meeting of the Chicago Children's Reading Round Table Conference, Chicago, IL.

11 The Complexity of Debates about Multicultural Literature and Cultural Authenticity

Violet J. Harris

Imagine yourself as a child reading *More Stories Julian Tells* (Cameron, 1986). You enjoy the book because Julian's antics are like your own or because he physically resembles you. Now, think about the sense of triumph you feel when your third-grade class takes a required, standardized reading test and one of the selections is an excerpt from this book. You are familiar with the story and believe that you can answer the questions. Now, visualize yourself looking at the illustration that accompanies the text and seeing that Julian is no longer a Black child but is now White.

This scenario actually occurred when third graders in Illinois completed a reading test (Cameron, Durham, Long, & Noffke, 2001). A teacher described her reaction to the deracination of *More Stories Julian Tells*:

> I almost couldn't believe that the creators of the test had finally included a story about a delightful African-American family. The librarian and I have both read the "Julian" stories to my students. Just a moment later, I saw the illustrations. I cannot begin to tell you how shocked and furious I was when I saw these. The African-American family was White! I could not believe they'd made these characters White! What nerve! And neither could my students. Even worse were the looks I kept getting from the students. As each of the fifteen students with this test form reached the story with the incorrect illustrations they looked up at me, looked at their test booklet, looked up at me, looked at the illustrations in the test booklet. I tried to quietly tell them to finish their tests. (p. 190)

This chapter is based on an article originally published in 1996 in *The New Advocate*, 9(2), 107–22, entitled "Continuing Dilemmas, Debates, and Delights in Multicultural Literature."

When the teacher engaged students in a discussion about the changes in the illustrations, one girl wondered if "perhaps the test makers didn't think Black people were good enough to be in the test" (p. 190).

This incident highlights some of the concerns that arise in discussions and debates about cultural authenticity and children's literature. First, the question of who can write about what culture is seemingly answered for those critics who suggest that Whites cannot write about a racial or ethnic group that differs from them without being subjected to political correctness (Lasky, 2003; Galbraith, 2001). Ann Cameron is White, and she has had a career relatively free of criticism about her creation of Black characters. In fact, one might argue that her books reflect the type of universalism deemed so necessary by some. By that, I mean that Blackness or what some perceive as culturally authentic Blackness is not a necessary ingredient for her stories. Julian's experiences are the same for those of any child in comparable circumstances in the United States. Second, the institutionalization of her books in reading series and standardized tests is an aim for many writers who are typically labeled "diverse," "culturally diverse," or "multicultural." This goal has been achieved with some success for a few major writers such as Virginia Hamilton and newer writers such as Linda S. Park. Third, the example highlights the unintentional effects and emotional harm that result from well-meaning but unenlightened gestures.

Such experiences are likely to occur as long as stratification, whether based on race, ethnicity, or gender, exists. These experiences are all the more poignant as we struggle with conflicting ideas about national identity, religious freedom, tolerance, and our place in a world community made seemingly smaller by technology in the wake of the tragedy of September 11, 2001. Recurring talk about cultural authenticity makes the debates both exhilarating and frustrating. For me these debates highlight conceptions of identity, authorial strictures, cultural authenticity, and "willful critical blindness" (Morrison, 1992).

What's in a Name? Conceptions about Identity

Confusion exists about how to refer to members of a group: Black or African American, Chicano/Chicana or Mexican American, gals or women, GLBT (gay, lesbian, bisexual, or transgender) or queer, and deaf or hearing impaired. That the groups are not monolithic should be obvious, but the reality is that individuals who do not possess these identities often resort to stereotypes or sweeping generalities about those who embody them. Not so long ago, "nigra," "Jap," "Injun," "gimp," and, less frequently, "sand nigger" for individuals of Middle Eastern descent, were common terms in print and electronic media. Some individuals still slip occasionally and feign ignorance about the negative reactions generated by their use of these epithets. Adding to the confusion is the popularity of musical forms, for instance, rap and hip-hop, that use terms considered derogatory by Blacks, women, and those who are GLBT. These artists and others who adopt the terms in various forms of communication suggest that they are subverting traditional connotations and, consequently, diffusing the ability of these words to wound the psyches of those to whom they are directed. An example of this intention is *Nigger: The Strange Career of a Troublesome Word* by Harvard law professor Randall Kennedy (2002). The reactions to the book have been mixed, with some questioning the necessity for its publication (Williams, 2002) or the use of the N-word as a pejorative or term of endearment (Tyehimba, 2001). Clearly, the subversion of stereotypes and demeaning names works for a few but not for all.

The increasing numbers of biracial and multiracial individuals have engendered new discussions about how a group with certain characteristics should be named or identified. Some write about "hybridity," shifting and interrelated identities, and the social construction of race (Tatum, 2000), arguing that traditional conceptions of race, for example, are not valid given our knowledge about biology and various social and cultural factors that affect an individual's identity. Radical feminist Gloria Anzaldúa (1987) popularized terms such as "mestizo" and "borderland cultures" to signify what occurs when cultures merge, forcefully or voluntarily. Then, there are the individuals who simply want to assume the identity of "American" without any other marker of identity appended or hyphenated.

Naming is clearly political and indicative of the power (or lack of it) wielded by a group. Perhaps it is best to allow individuals or groups to self-identify in the manner they wish. Author Julius Lester self-identifies as a Jewish American although his physical attributes suggest a Black person and his early writings suggested some ideological association with Blackness (Moore, 2001). Rudolfo Anaya, author of the classic *Bless Me, Ultima* (1972) and children's books such as *The Farolitos of Christmas* (1995) and *Roadrunner's Dance* (2000), described himself in these terms in an interview: "I am what I write. I belong to only one race, the human race. My Hispanic, New Mexican culture has shaped my identity, but so have people, books, travel, dreams, life in general. I feel very close to the people of New Mexico and the landscape, so this community appears in my stories" (Battle, 2001, p. 105).

The terms "minority" and "non-White" engender similar considerations. I tend not to use these terms for several reasons. *Minority* always seems to imply inferiority. *Non-White* acquires an absurdity that could become comical if the same method were used to make other distinctions, non-males, for example. Virginia Hamilton offered the term "parallel cultures" as a replacement for "minority cultures." This term seemed less hierarchical and more accurate, so I adopted it.

Other terms—for example, "race" and "ethnicity"—evoke similar linguistic conundrums. *Race* and *ethnicity* are not synonymous. However, the historic development of academic studies that focused on racial issues resulted in their being tagged with the label "ethnic." The conflating of race and ethnicity is evident in the terms "multiethnic" and "multicultural." Here, *multiethnic* refers to groups such as those of African, Asian/Pacific Islander, Latino/Latina, or Native American ancestry. In some instances it would refer to those of European descent, but conceptions about "Whiteness" seem to have supplanted ideas associated with White ethnics (Babb, 1998). In contrast, *multicultural* can include race, ethnicity, gender, class, and other elements that denote difference.

"Culture," too, embodies a multitude of meanings. *Culture* as used in this chapter refers to beliefs, attitudes, values, worldviews, institutions, artifacts, processes, interactions, and ways of behaving. It is not static but occasionally fluid and flexible; at other times, it seems unyielding and stifling. Over the past two decades, some exciting discourse emerged about culture and/or literature ignited by individuals such as Edward Said, Stuart Hall, Stanley Fish, Toni Morrison, Catherine Stimpson, and Henry Louis Gates Jr. Their ideas and those of others who followed in their wake offered a new way to talk about literature and the influence of identity, culture, and politics on its creation and interpretation.

Consensus does not exist about definitions and conceptions of multiculturalism. Should the focus remain on race, gender, and class? Is a more expansive conception required that includes disability, linguistic variation, sexual orientation, religion, and other categories of difference? What counts as multicultural literature, and who are the multiculturalists who advocate its use?

Moving toward Tolerance

I was not born a multiculturalist. My support for the ideology emerged gradually and remains in a state of flux. I came to support some of the tenets of multiculturalism because I strongly value and argue for the inclusion of African American literature and history in curricula. When individuals from other groups tacitly or overtly inquired about or argued for their group's inclusion, I was pushed toward multiculturalism. My struggles with conceptions of multiculturalism are evident in my past and emerging attitudes about literature featuring gays and lesbians.

Some years ago, a colleague inquired if I included books about gays and lesbians in my multicultural literature course. Mainly, my students read multiethnic literature with some attention to Appalachian Whites and Jewish people. I wanted to focus more on ethnic literature because racism, in all its manifestations, remains one of the most significant and vexing issues facing the country. If multiethnic literature incorporated characters or themes unique to gays and lesbians, then it was included, for example, Jacqueline Woodson's *The Dear One* (1993). However, the presence of gay and lesbian characters was not a main consideration.

Other reasons, such as discomfort and my perception that many gays and lesbians have not agitated for the equality of other groups in a public manner, shaped my decision. Even now I continue to struggle, and some of my current discomfort stems from religious beliefs. I was also somewhat angered by gays and lesbians who adopted the symbols and rhetoric of the modern civil rights movement with less of a public willingness to incorporate issues of race and ethnicity in public discourse. I had parallel concerns for other groups listed under the multicultural umbrella. Was I being homophobic and bigoted? Self-reflection and self-criticism suggested that I was. Still, the battle for including literature featuring gays and lesbians was one I did not wish to shoulder. I wanted to see and read about more gay and lesbian authors, poets, and illustrators "coming out of the closet" and enduring the opposition that those agitating for ethnic literature have borne. I wanted these individuals to display the bravery of one of my favorite writers, James Baldwin, who lived the paradox of being an artistic, gay, Black man in America.

I reasoned that sociocultural conditions existed that allowed gays and lesbians, particularly those who were White, to highlight other identities they possessed without having to reveal their sexual orientation. They could assume identities based in gender, occupation, region of birth, and any combination of these. Basically, they could "pass" as straights. Many people of color cannot shed their racial identities and exist solely as writer, poet, artist, editor, or reviewer. The inability to shed a racial marker seemed fundamentally unfair. In time, my dogmatism about the issue lessened as self-criticism suggested that if I wanted others to share multiethnic literature, then I should also practice what I advocated. Over the years, I read essays written by bell hooks, Cornell West, Marlon Riggs, and Audre Lorde in which they argued for inclusiveness in human rights struggles, including those who were GLBT. Their writings urged analysis of the ways in which an individual embodies many identities that are fluid and which exert influence in ever-changing ways. Lectures by dancer Bill T. Jones were also powerful. Now, I include pioneering novels about people who are GLBT, as well as current novels such as the series The Pride Pack. The decision to include the books is also eased as more authors who are GLBT and White have exited the closet and made public their identities, such as M. E. Kerr and Marion Dane Bauer.

Authorial Strictures

Another, related dilemma is the demand by some that authors of literature we label "multicultural" create characters who are "role models." The stories must either uplift or inspire or correct and usurp stereotypic works. Positive images are preferred and deemed crucial. Novels that include lessons that inform readers of the group's history and ongoing struggles are a preferred type of didacticism. Illustrator George Littlechild shares his interpretation of this ascribed function of the literature:

> I think being from the "other," not belonging to the majority, had everything and nothing to do with what I've become. Unbeknownst to me, I have become a voice for the people through my art and through my writing. I would be the last person to understand, as a child, that [becoming a voice] could possibly be my future. Being a catalyst for change has been the most phenomenal experience, as a person, but also as a person of Native American ancestry. In my mother's culture, it's all about the gift, and the gift is giving. In doing so there's this universal feeling that everything I have is yours. So that's what my art is all about. Knowing that with my books and my art, that I touch people's lives, that it helps people, it changes people's lives, to me that's the gift. (qtd. in Mendoza, 2001, p. 323)

Occasionally, literature written by people of color who identify as GLBT is considered to have a political agenda or is criticized as too sociological (Gates, 1992). Author Jacqueline Woodson (2001) dissected the intentional political nature of her works in a panel of authors on the politics of writing. One author indicated that he did not believe his writing was political or that it should be. Woodson suggested that his maleness and Whiteness allowed him the freedom to write in an apolitical manner. She argued that she lacked the luxury of separating the political from the creative. Her works were intended to provide a cultural space for readers relegated to the margins of culture. In numerous books, she demonstrates the value of the "Other" and their creative processes and products. As a consequence, the reader, especially the "Other," is transformed.

Many factors account for the emphasis that many readers, critics, parents, and others place on sociopolitical concerns. Books with stereotypes, inaccuracies, and hurtful sections remain in publication. A case in point is the response to Anne Rinaldi's (1999) novel *My Heart Is on the Ground* by members of Oyate, an organization devoted to First Peoples/Native American issues (Atleo et al., 2002). *My Heart Is on the Ground* is the fictionalized account of one character's experience in a boarding school for Native children. The book's cover jacket appears on the Oyate Web site with a red line drawn through it, an intense, succinct, visual reminder of members' evaluation of the book. Members of Oyate provide a documented listing of what they consider to be historical inaccuracies, lack of cultural authenticity, and literary appropriation. Oyate members compare examples from Rinaldi's work with examples written by Native authors and conclude that this book "reflects what can go wrong when a non-Native author writes about Native cultures" (Atleo et al., p. 7). Oyate members acknowledge the successful marketing of the series Dear America, of which the book is a part, but they lament that *My Heart Is on the Ground* will be many children's only introduction to this aspect of Native American history.

We cannot compel an author to assume the mantle of defender of race, gender, or class. Most want an outlet for their creativity. A few accept the mantle willingly without compromising standards of excellence. Virginia Hamilton (1993) created the category "liberation literature" in her attempts to imbue the reader with a literary experience that entertained and transformed:

> Books of mine such as *Many Thousand Gone*, *Anthony Burns*, and *The People Could Fly* I term Liberation Literature. In this literature, the reader travels with the character in the imagined world of the book and bears witness to the characters' trials and suffering and triumphs. To the extent that the protagonist finds liberty, so too does the witness, the reader, recognize the struggle as a personal one and perceive a spiritual sense of freedom. (p. 375)

Woodson, Hamilton, and many others create works that appeal to children while maintaining fidelity to their personal philosophies and refusing to compromise on literary quality.

Bemusement and a measure of anger characterize the response of a few authors placed in the multicultural category. Allen Say (1991), for instance, has written about his discomfort with "identity" issues. He discussed further how he reconciled his heritage with his artistic sensibilities and the expectations of others. Say's primary concerns are artistic and literary excellence, not his or his readers' race or ethnicity.

Authenticity and Authorial Freedom

One of the more divisive questions relates to authenticity and authorial freedom. Can a person write about another culture? Or, do some members of a group possess a "prior epistemological claim to the territory" by virtue of their membership (Galbraith, 2001)? And how authentic are the resulting portrayals? A sampling of opinions from the first section of this book captures conflicting perspectives. Writer Thelma Seto (2003) declares that writing outside one's culture is a moral offense akin to the most egregious theft. She critiques "racist misrepresentations" and states forcefully that hegemonic control of "cultural discourse" allows European Americans to idealize "Whiteness" and relegate everything else to a representation of the "Other." In contrast, Marc Aronson (2003) urges the existence of "intellectual honesty" that recognizes the complexity of culture along with an elimination of what he terms "ethnic essentialism." He ponders, "Why can we allow this cultural crossing in music and not in books for children? Why can't our authors, after sufficient preparation, do what they like?" (p. 82). Aronson argues that extensive preparation, immersion in the culture, and practice worked for musicians and that a comparable strategy would benefit writers.

Aronson (2001) ignited a firestorm of criticism and support for his advocacy of eliminating "race-based" literary awards such as the Coretta Scott King and Pura Belpré Awards. He argued that these and other awards were no longer needed because people of color had recently been the recipients of several major literary awards such as the Newbery Medal and the Printz Award. Author Virginia Hamilton (2001), scholars Rudine Sims Bishop (2001) and Henrietta Smith (2001), and editor Andrea Davis Pinkney (2001) took Aronson to task for his inaccuracies about the criteria for the Coretta Scott King Awards, his undue enthusiasm about racism being eliminated from the publishing industry, and his criticism of groups that target their awards to members of particular racial or ethnic groups.

We share certain experiences because we are humans or share a particular nationality. Other experiences stem from differences that offer innumerable privileges for some and oppressive strictures for others. Historical truths require artistic excellence and not artistic dilettantism if propaganda, stereotypes, and mediocrity are to be avoided. It is the exceptional writer or illustrator who successfully depicts this anguish, hurt, and hope. For instance, Tom Feelings needed twenty years and lengthy sojourns in Caribbean and African countries in order to create paintings conveying the unspeakable horror and degradation of the Middle Passage, or what some call the African Holocaust. His book *The Middle Passage: White Ships/Black Cargo* (1995) should give pause to any writer or artist who blithely takes on another's culture. These realities are not pleasant and they can engender complicated responses among students (Willis & Johnson, 2000). Historical truths, however, cannot be sugarcoated. Nor should willful, collective amnesia about history prevent children from knowing the truth.

Very few individuals argue for their right to depict people with disabilities, those with bilingual proficiencies, the elderly, or religious minorities, because it is taken for granted that any author can write about these cultural groups, with or without having these experiences in their own lives. Debates about race create primordial responses that indicate a racial chasm that appears permanent. A more important question is not the authorial freedom of European American authors to write about any group or culture they wish. Rather, it is the authorial arrogance of some European American authors who demand freedom to write about any group or culture they wish without subjecting their work to critical scrutiny. They seem guilty of what Toni Morrison (1992) labels as "willful critical blindness." Morrison argued that Blacks were crucial to the creation of many artistic, cultural, and political moments in history but their impact has been ignored, omitted, and unacknowledged. Further, these European American authors ignore or refuse to acknowledge literary and critical history, including the fact that for years members of parallel cultures were denied access to publishing. Fondre (2001) documented the manner in which "Whiteness" is privileged in literature discussion groups in a children's literature course for preservice teachers. Many of the students enrolled in the course epitomized the ideas put forth by Morrison.

For hundreds of years, European Americans have written about African Americans; with few exceptions, the works have been one-note variations of the same refrain. Notably, the authors produced comic Negroes such as Sambo, Epaminondas, and Little Brown Koko, contented slaves such as Amos Fortune, unnamed sharecroppers as in *Sounder* (Armstrong, 1969) and fathers who willingly sacrifice their lives so that a "White" character can recognize the error of his racism. It is the rare "White author"—for example, Mary White Ovington, Milton Meltzer, Arnold Adoff, Robert D. San Souci, Juanita Havill, or Katherine Paterson—who creates an artistic, multifaceted, and plausible depiction of African Americans.

Author Kathryn Lasky (2003) in her chapter in this book illustrates the complexities and contradictions of these issues. She warns against "a kind of literary version of ethnic cleansing, with an underlying premise that posits that there is only one story and only one way to tell it" (p. 88). She recounts a discussion with an editor about her desire to write a biography of Sarah Breedlove Walker or Madame C. J. Walker. The editor informed Lasky that the "book would be panned by critics and wouldn't sell" (p. 88). Why? According to the editor, her "Whiteness" was the central factor. Lasky labeled this as censorship.

Any author who creates a biography of Walker should be held to standards of biographical and literary excellence that include accuracy, authenticity, and style. The author must recreate the social, political, and cultural milieu in which Madame C. J. Walker lived. The complex status, roles and feelings of and about African American hair and Madame Walker's almost mythical role in the creation of African American beauty rituals must be understood. This culture is explored in *Saturday at the New You* (Barber, 1994), a picture book about the social interactions in a beauty shop, and in the revolutionary subtext of Alexis De Veaux's *An Enchanted Hair Tale* (1987) with its emphasis on braids and "locks." The intimate camaraderie among males in barbershops is lovingly portrayed in *Haircuts at Sleepy Sam's* (Strickland, 1998) and *A Handbook for Boys* (Myers, 2002). Unquestionably, hair is a serious and sometimes comic topic among Blacks. The process and terminology of "straightening" hair—the "hot comb," oiling the scalp, "nappy edges," sectioning of the hair, and the problem of "reversion" when the "pressed" hair is wet—must be described in a convincing manner.

Further, the author must convey Walker's role in and importance to several sociopolitical and cultural movements before her death in 1919. Walker's home served as a cultural salon for prominent individuals. Walker's daughter continued her legacy of cultural activism. Her business acumen enabled hundreds of African American women to become economically liberated from the kitchens of White women who typically did not pay them a fair wage. These women felt exhilaration when they did not have to answer to "gal" or "auntie" or leave their families and work for subsistence wages. Unless a White author immerses herself in research, discussions with others, and contact with artifacts, the rhythm of her text is likely to be Revlon not Ultra Sheen, *Life* magazine rather than *Ebony* magazine, the bland sounds of Pat Boone rather than the whoops and hollers of Little Richard. It might be far more interesting, artistic, and insightful if Lasky created a picture book or novel depicting a White girl's appreciation of an African American woman as a hero.

Several picture books about Black children's hair have been written, including Nikki Grimes's *Wild, Wild Hair* (1997). One of the most famous books about Black hair is Carolivia Herron's *Nappy Hair* (1997), the catalyst for a major school-district and media problem. Herron (2000) indicated in a personal communication that she had selected an illustrator who spent months studying and drawing various examples of Black hair; but that illustrator was not selected for her picture book.

Lasky (2000) did write a picture book biography of Madame C. J. Walker, *Vision of Beauty*. She attempts to add authority in an author's note in which she states that she spent time with A'Lelia Perry Bundles, Walker's great-great-granddaughter. Lasky also notes that Bundles shared information with her about Walker and that they both resided in the suburbs of Indianapolis. The book received generally favorable reviews, but there were questions about research and historic accuracy. For example, Lasky refers to the material worn to cover the hair of Black women during slavery and thereafter as a "do rag." The "do rag" actually emerged among Black men who "processed" their hair, a style and use of the material epitomized by "doo-wop" groups in the 1950s and 1960s.

Other biographies about Madame Walker, for example, *Madam C. J. Walker* (Bundles, 1991), *Madam C. J. Walker: Building a Business Empire* (Colman, 1994), *Madam C. J. Walker: Self-Made Millionaire* (McKissack & McKissack, 1992), and *Madam C. J. Walker: Self-Made Businesswoman* (Yannuzzi, 2000), offer information about Walker and the political, cultural, and social milieus that are not found in the Lasky biography. The differences in tone and content may be attributed to the fact that these books were not written in picture book format and a sense that there is less authorial distance between these authors and the subject matter.

Lasky (2003) also argues that this "new insistence on certain rules for authorship and provenance of a story (or who writes what and where) is indeed threatening the very fabric of literature and literary criticism" (p. 91). This statement is without foundation. The major journals devoted to literary criticism of children's literature—*Horn Book Magazine, The Lion and the Unicorn, Children's Literature Association Quarterly,* or *Children's Literature in Education*—do not have editors who are people of color. The majority of the articles published in these journals do not relate to multiculturalism or any of its attendant controversies, even though the number of articles about multiculturalism has increased significantly. Further, book publishing in its various aspects—editorial, marketing, and sales—remains overwhelmingly the province of Whites. How have proponents of multiculturalism managed to "take control" of the production, dissemination, and evaluation of this cultural product without even knowing it? While there have been some changes recently, in that Rosalinda B. Barrera, Sarah McCarthey, and I assumed editorship of *The New Advocate* from 2000–2003, and Andrea Davis Pinkney assumed responsibility for the children's division of Houghton Mifflin in 2002, the overall world of children's publishing and literary criticism remains White.

I view the near impossibility of authors of color being able to write about "nonracial" issues as far more important than the competition and critical heat that European American authors feel. Moreover, the authors who protest the most are not in the vanguard arguing for the same freedom for writers of color. One could argue that a slightly different situation exists for those who are GLBT. For example, Lesalea Newman, the author of *Heather Has Two Mommies* (1989), writes a wonderful picture book, *Remember That* (1996), in which readers need not reference the fact that she is GLBT. W. D. Myers attributes this situation to the inability of editors to envision the possibility of writers assuming multiple perspectives:

> The publishing world touts itself as very liberal, but I keep challenging people to name books written over the last 20 years by Blacks that are on non-black subjects. So when you have a black writer who says, "I've got this great idea about space monkeys that talk," he or she is turned down. And what they are allowed to write about very often reflects the editor's opinion. (qtd. in Sutton, 1994, p. 26)

One notable exception is Julius Lester's (2001) *When Dad Killed Mom* that does feature Whites as the protagonists. The novel received good to excellent reviews.

Virginia Hamilton, despite being one of the most honored writers in the world, faced some barriers. When Rochman (1992) asked Hamilton, "Do you consider yourself a black writer?" she responded: "And an American writer. And a woman. I'm all of those things. . . . My themes are universal" (p. 1021).

How many times has a European American author been asked, "Do you consider yourself a White writer?" Not often enough. We ignore the construction and historical development of Whiteness as equivalent to "American." Everyone else is the exotic, the different, the "Other" stripped of any symbolic designation of "American."

Some editors ignore Hamilton's assertions that she is an American writer and capable of creating stories outside a predetermined Black experience:

> But it's very difficult when you're a black writer to write outside of the black experience. People don't allow it; critics won't allow it. If I would do a book that didn't have blacks, people would say, "Oh, what is Virginia Hamilton doing?" Yet a white writer can write about anything. . . . I feel the limitation. I'm always running up against it and knocking it down in different ways, whichever way I can. But I know that it's there and will always be there. I mean there were people who said in the middle of my career, "Now Virginia Hamilton has finally faced who she is." Well, how dare they? (Rochman, 1992, p. 1021)

Hamilton's artistic abilities and literary philosophy suggest that any stories she would have created about European Americans would have multifaceted characters, intriguing plots, and creative narrative forms. No shortcuts in the form of stereotypes or formulaic plots were likely to litter her work, as they do with some authors who write cross-racially or, in the jargon of the day, across borders.

I do not want to suggest that a European American author, one without disabilities, or a man, for example, cannot create artistic, culturally authentic literary works. Many works exist in which the author has stepped outside of a primary or secondary identity to write about others who are unlike him or her. Michael Dorris wrote novels with exquisite female characters, for example Rayona in *A Yellow Raft in Blue Water* (1987) and *The Window* (1997). Other characters in these novels represent a multitude of identities, yet Dorris captured the essence of their humanity without resorting to bad characterization or stereotypes. What continues to befuddle me is that some authors who write about people of color do not acknowledge their privilege or the sense of entitlement they possess that affords them chances to write about any topic imaginable even when they acknowledge that their works are stereotypic. M. E. Kerr (1998) indicates that gender identity, not her Whiteness or sexual orientation, is the factor that she has had to confront in different ways in her career as writer. Kerr assessed the arguments about who can write about whom in a chapter with a witty title, "Must You Be a Cake to Write a Cookbook?" She relates the response of W. D. Myers to her novel about an interracial romance among young adults: "'Well,' he said, in a noncommittal tone, with a shrug, 'they were different.' I wasn't sure then what he meant, but a while later, older and wiser, I understood" (p. 203). What Kerr understood was that the Black female protagonist sounded as if she had stepped off a plantation in the 1800s: "Oh, honey, honey, I'd like to die imagining you without your allowance, child. . . . Lord take pity on you, without your 'lowance, you gonna be reduced to poverty level" (p. 203). Kerr has indicated that the character would be written differently now but maintains the right for a writer to create characters "who are unlike him in color, religion, ethnic background, or sexual orientation" (p. 205). Still, she has the unacknowledged freedom to revise or create a new novel with an interracial affair.

In contrast, Jean Marzollo underwent a different level of introspection as she thought about writing a biography of scientist George Washington Carver (Spodek, Barrera, & Harris, 2002). She attributed the reluctance of editors to accept a biography written by her not to her Whiteness but to the editor's belief that Carver was not considered someone who fought for civil rights. Marzollo also praised the bravery and broadminded attitude of Andrea Davis Pinkney, then editorial director of Jump at the Sun Books, in asking her to write a series of picture books, *Shanna's Princess Show* (2001) and *Shanna's Doctor Show* (2001), featuring a Black girl as the main character Shanna. "Andrea asked me to write a series about a little black girl. Andrea felt that it was not a criterion to pick a black author to write about a black child, that it would be better to pick somebody who knew something about young children. That was important to her. But I think that she deliberately paired me with Shane Evans. . . . She is a big thinker and I might add, an excellent children's book author, as well as an editor" (Spodek, Barrera, & Harris, pp. 97–98).

Author Jacqueline Woodson (2001) has spoken of her frustration with being pegged as a Black, lesbian author. However, she adamantly supports the idea that an individual must have experienced some things in order to write about them:

> Like many people of color, I am constantly being told that my work, my self, my truths are lesser than someone who is not of color. I am constantly being asked to believe that what I have achieved is a result of a publisher's or an employer's or an awards committee's need to fill a long empty hole with a lesser-than product of color. I have watched the burden of this buckle African Americans. (p. 49)

When an author writes that she only wants to write a story about people who "happen to be" African American, Asian/Pacific Islander,

Latino/Latina, or Native American (Cameron, 1992), I question the need to eliminate the essence of feelings, experiences, and aspects of culture that shape who a people are. How many others are likely to develop the understanding of the "Other" as detailed by Woodson? Still, questions about authenticity, insider/outsider views, and authorial freedom remain unresolved.

Political Correctness

Individuals engaged in the efforts to make multicultural literature available to children must pursue candid and honest discourse on the topic. Some feelings will be hurt and a few acquaintances may part company. However, those who continue to raise the issues must not be silenced with accusations of "political correctness." Few who use the phrase choose to make explicit their conceptions of the term. One of the assignments in my undergraduate children's literature course is the reading and analysis of trends in Caldecott books published from 1960 through the current year. Each semester, several students label the appearance of literature from parallel cultures as award winners in the 1970s–1990s as political correctness. They question whether members of the committee bowed to outside political pressure. Although I explain how Caldecott winners and honor books are selected, some persist in this belief. They cling to the explanation of political correctness even though I critique the exclusionary policies of many publishing companies and booksellers in earlier historic periods. Rarely will a student who adopts this stance characterize the periods of exclusion as indicative of White supremacist ideology. Nor apparently, do some authors, teachers, librarians, and parents. Conversations are necessary if progress, no matter how incremental, is desired.

Conclusions

Undeniably, progress is evident in the attempts to institutionalize the creation, publication, and dissemination of multicultural literature. It would have been unthinkable five years ago to expect that Andrea Davis Pinkney would be selected to head the children's division of a major publishing company. While laudable, such appointments may suggest incorrectly that similar inclusiveness is evident in all aspects of publishing. Novelist Walter Mosely's stalwart efforts to create a publishing program in the City Colleges of New York City are a testament to the ongoing efforts that are needed. The program has been established and some individuals have received their endorsement as potential editors.

The children's books now being published are more expansive in terms of genre, themes, narrative structure, and illustrations. For example, Laurence Yep writes a series, The Goblin Pearls, that is notable for its humor, adoption of tropes from movies filmed in the 1930s and 1940s, and multifaceted nature of the Asian American characters. Walter D. Myers (1999) introduced a different kind of narrative structure in *Monster* that was instrumental in his selection as the recipient of the first Printz Award. Nonfiction has included a greater number of controversial topics and attempts to correct histories in books about slavery, World War II, the labor movement, and women's movements. GLBT has achieved a more noticeable status, as evidenced by an increase in the number of GLBT novels published and by series such as The Pride Pack. Poetry exhibits a resurgence and robustness in quality that is quite remarkable, for example Naomi Shihab Nye's (1998) *The Space between Our Footsteps*. The publication of the sons and daughters of some of the pioneering authors, Chris Myers, Javaka Steptoe, a plethora of Pinkneys, and Jaime Adoff, suggests that multicultural literature has achieved a measure of permanency.

Permanency cannot be maintained, however, if teachers, parents, librarians, and children are not encouraged to read and share the literature. They need guidance to understand that multicultural literature can speak to their sense of humanity, that they can find themselves in the literature. After all, groups usually listed as a part of multicultural literature have had to find themselves in the pages of literature featuring Whites. That type of border crossing needs to become typical rather than atypical.

Supporting multiculturalism forces an individual to engage in a great deal of critical self-reflection. What constitutes multicultural literature? What does it mean to be an "American"? Why are some groups classified as "them" or the "Other"? Who has access to publication and what are the effects of differential access to publishing? How do popular culture, books, and textbooks create images that are reinforced by societal institutions? What accounts for the appeal of stereotypic texts? Will children enjoy reading the texts we label multicultural? Yet, the ultimate purpose of literature is to engage the reader in an aesthetic experience. While the issues discussed in this chapter are crucial, our debates and efforts are worthless if children do not have an opportunity to read the literature.

References

Anzaldúa, G. (1987). *Borderlands/La Frontera = The new Mestiza*. San Francisco: Aunt Lute.

Aronson, M. (2001). Slippery slopes and proliferating prizes. *Horn Book, 77,* 271–78.

Aronson, M. (2003). A mess of stories. In D. L. Fox & K. G. Short (Eds.), *Stories matter: The complexity of cultural authenticity in children's literature* (pp. 78–83). Urbana, IL: National Council of Teachers of English.

Atleo, M., Caldwell, N., Landis, B., Mendoza, J., Miranda, D., Reese, D., Rose, L., Slapin, B., & Smith, C. (2002, September 12). Avoid *My heart is on the ground* [Review of the book *My heart is on the ground*]. *Oyate.* Available at http://www.Oyate.org/books-to-avoid/my Heart.html.

Babb, V. M. (1998). *Whiteness visible*. New York: New York University Press.

Battle, J. (2001). A conversation with Rudolfo Anaya. *The New Advocate, 14*(2), 103–09.

Bishop, R. S. (2001). Letter to the editor. *Horn Book, 77*(5), 501–2.

Cameron, A. (1992, January). Untitled article. *School Library Journal, 38,* 29–30.

Cameron, A., Durham, N., Long, Y., & Noffke, S. E. (2001). Multiple choices: A tale of testing in four voices. *The New Advocate, 14*(3), 189–96.

Fondre, S. (2001). "Gentle doses of racism": Whiteness and children's literature. *The Journal of Children's Literature, 27*(2), 9–13.

Galbraith, M. (2001). Hear my cry: A manifesto for an emancipatory childhood studies approach to children's literature. *The Lion and the Unicorn, 25*(2), 187–205.

Gates, H. L. Jr. (1992). *Loose canons: Notes on the culture wars*. New York: Oxford University Press.

Hamilton, V., (1993). Everything of value: Moral realism in the literature for children. *Journal of Youth Services in Libraries, 6,* 363–77.

Hamilton, V. (2001). Letter to the editor. *Horn Book, 77*(5), 504.

Kennedy, R. (2002). *Nigger: The strange career of a troublesome word*. New York: Pantheon.

Kerr, M. E. (1998). *Blood on the forehead: What I know about writing*. New York: HarperCollins.

Lasky, K. (2003). To Stingo with love: An author's perspective on writing outside one's culture. In D. L. Fox & K. G. Short (Eds.), *Stories matter: The complexity of cultural authenticity in children's literature* (pp. 84–92). Urbana, IL: National Council of Teachers of English.

Mendoza, J. (2001). Becoming a voice: A conversation with George Littlechild, illustrator. *The New Advocate, 14*(4), 321–28.

Moore, O. (2001). Othello, Othello, Where art thou? *The Lion and the Unicorn, 25,* 375–90.

Morrison, T. (1992). *Playing in the dark: Whiteness and the literary imagination.* Cambridge, MA: Harvard University Press.

Pinkney, A. D. (2001). Awards that stand solid ground. *Horn Book, 77,* 535–39.

Rochman, H. (1992, February 1). The *Booklist* interview: Virginia Hamilton. *Booklist, 88,* 1020–21.

Say, A. (1991, December). Musings of a walking stereotype. *School Library Journal, 37,* 45–46.

Seto, T. (2003). Multiculturalism is not Halloween. In D. L. Fox & K. G. Short (Eds.), *Stories matter: The complexity of cultural authenticity in children's literature* (pp. 93–97). Urbana, IL: National Council of Teachers of English.

Smith, H. (2001). Letter to the editor. *Horn Book, 77*(5), 505.

Spodek, B., Barrera, R. B., & Harris, V. J. (2002). In touch with kids: A conversation with Jean Marzollo. *The New Advocate, 15*(2), 91–100.

Sutton, R. (1994). Threads in our cultural fabric: A conversation with Walter Dean Myers. *School Library Journal, 40*(6), 24–28.

Tatum, B. D. (2001). The complexity of identity: Who am I? In M. Adams, W. J. Blumenfeld, R. Castañeda, H. W. Hackman, M. L. Peters, & X. Zúñiga (Eds.), *Readings for diversity and social justice* (pp. 9–14). London: Routledge.

Tyehimba, C. (2001, November). Society: Nigger? Please. *Savoy, 1*(9), 68–71.

Williams, K. (2002, January/February). [Review of the book *Nigger: The strange career of a troublesome word* by R. Kennedy.] *Quarterly Review of Black Books, 24,* 33.

Willis, A., & Johnson, J. (2000, September). A horizon of possibilities: A critical framework for transforming multiethnic literature instruction. *Reading Online* [Online]. Available: http://readingonline.org/articles/willis/index.html.

Woodson, J. (2001, Spring/Summer). Fictions. *Obsidian, 3*(1), 48–50.

Children's Books Cited

Anaya, R. A. (1972). *Bless me, Ultima.* Berkeley, CA: Tonatiuh-Quinto Sol International.

Anaya, R. (1995). *The farolitos of Christmas.* New York: Hyperion.

Anaya, R. (2000). *Roadrunner's dance.* New York: Hyperion.

Armstrong, W. H. (1969). *Sounder.* New York: Harper & Row.

Barber, B. E. (1994). *Saturday at the New You.* New York: Lee & Low.

Bundles, A. P. (1991). *Madam C. J. Walker.* New York: Chelsea House.

Cameron, A. (1986). *More stories Julian tells.* New York: Knopf.

Colman, P. (1994). *Madam C. J. Walker: Building a business empire.* Brookfield, CT: Millbrook.

De Veaux, A. (1987). *An enchanted hair tale.* New York: Harper & Row.

Dorris, M. (1987). *A yellow raft in blue water.* New York: Holt.

Dorris, M. (1997). *The window.* New York: Hyperion.

Feelings, T. (1995). *The middle passage: White ships/black cargo.* New York: Dial.

Grimes, N. (1997). *Wild, wild hair.* New York: Scholastic.

Herron, C. (1997). *Nappy hair.* New York: Knopf.

Lasky, K. (2000). *Vision of beauty: The story of Sarah Breedlove Walker.* Cambridge, MA: Candlewick Press.

Lester, J. (2001). *When dad killed mom.* San Diego: Silver Whistle.

Marzollo, J. (2001). *Shanna's doctor show.* New York: Jump at the Sun/ Hyperion.

Marzollo, J. (2001). *Shanna's princess show.* New York: Jump at the Sun/ Hyperion.

McKissack, P., & McKissack, F. (1992). *Madam C. J. Walker: Self-made millionaire.* Hillside, NJ: Enslow.

Myers, W. D. (1999). *Monster.* New York: HarperCollins.

Myers, W. D. (2002). *Handbook for boys.* New York: HarperCollins.

Newman, L. (1989). *Heather has two mommies.* Boston: Alyson.

Newman, L. (1996). *Remember that.* New York: Clarion.

Nye, N. S. (1998). *The space between our footsteps: Poems and paintings from the Middle East.* New York: Simon & Schuster.

Rinaldi, A. (1999). *My heart is on the ground: The diary of Nannie Little Rose, a Sioux girl.* New York: Scholastic.

Strickland, M. R. (1998). *Haircuts at Sleepy Sam's.* Honesdale, PA: Boyds Mills.

Woodson, J. (1993). *The dear one.* New York: Dell.

Yannuzzi, D. A. (2000). *Madam C. J. Walker: Self-made businesswoman.* Berkeley Heights, NJ: Enslow.

12 "Authenticity," or the Lesson of Little Tree

Henry Louis Gates Jr.

It's a perennial question: Can you really tell? The great black jazz trumpeter Roy Eldridge once made a wager with the critic Leonard Feather that he could distinguish white musicians from black ones—blindfolded. Mr. Feather duly dropped the needle onto a variety of record albums whose titles and soloists were concealed from the trumpeter. More than half the time, Eldridge guessed wrong.

Mr. Feather's blindfold test is one that literary critics would do well to ponder, for the belief that we can "read" a person's racial or ethnic identity from his or her writing runs surprisingly deep. There is an assumption that we could fill a room with the world's great literature, train a Martian to analyze these books, and then expect that Martian to categorize each by the citizenship or ethnicity or gender of its author. "Passing" and "impersonation" may sound like quaint terms of a bygone era, but they continue to inform the way we read. Our literary judgments, in short, remain hostage to the ideology of authenticity.

And while black Americans have long boasted of their ability to spot "one of our own," no matter how fair the skin, straight the hair, or aquiline the nose—and while the nineteenth-century legal system in this country went to absurd lengths to demarcate even octoroons and demi-octoroons from their white sisters and brothers—authentic racial and ethnic differences have always been difficult to define. It's not just a black thing, either.

The very idea of a literary tradition is itself bound up in suppositions—dating back at least to an eighteenth-century theorist of nationalism, Johann Gottfried Herder—that ethnic or national identity finds unique expression in literary forms. Such assumptions hold sway even after we think we have discarded them. After the much ballyhooed "death of the author" pronounced by two decades of literary theory, the author is very much back in the saddle. As the literary historian John

---

Guillory observes, today's "battle of the books" is really not so much about books as it is about authors, authors who can be categorized according to race, gender, ethnicity, and so on, standing in as delegates of a social constituency.

And the assumption that the works they create transparently convey the authentic, unmediated experience of their social identities—though officially renounced—has crept quietly in through the back door. Like any dispensation, it raises some works and buries others. Thus Zora Neale Hurston's *Their Eyes Were Watching God* has prospered, while her *Seraph on the Suwanee*, a novel whose main characters are white, remains in limbo. *Our Nig*, recently identified as the work of a black woman, almost immediately went from obscurity to required reading in black and women's literature courses.

The case of Forrest Carter, the author of the best-selling *The Education of Little Tree*, provided yet another occasion to reflect on the troublesome role of authenticity. Billed as a true story, Carter's book was written as the autobiography of Little Tree, orphaned at the age of ten, who learns the ways of Indians from his Cherokee grandparents in Tennessee. *The Education of Little Tree*, which has sold more than 600,000 copies, received an award from the American Booksellers Association as the title booksellers most enjoyed selling. It was sold on the gift tables of Indian reservations and assigned as supplementary reading for courses on Native American literature. Major studios vied for movie rights.

And the critics loved it. *Booklist* praised its "natural approach to life." A reviewer for the *Chattanooga Times* pronounced it "deeply felt." One poet and storyteller of Abenaki descent hailed it as a masterpiece—"one of the finest American autobiographies ever written"—that captured the unique vision of Native American culture. It was, he wrote blissfully, "like a Cherokee basket, woven out of the materials given by nature, simple and strong in its design, capable of carrying a great deal." A critic in *The (Santa Fe) New Mexican* told his readers: "I have come on something that is good, so good I want to shout 'Read this! It's beautiful. It's real.'"

Or was it?

To the embarrassment of the book's admirers, Dan T. Carter, a history professor at Emory University, unmasked "Forrest Carter" as a pseudonym for the late Asa Earl Carter, whom he described as "a Ku Klux Klan terrorist, right wing radio announcer, home grown American fascist and anti-Semite, rabble-rousing demagogue and secret author of the famous 1963 speech by Gov. George Wallace of Alabama: 'Segregation now . . . Segregation tomorrow . . . Segregation forever.'" Forget Pee-wee Herman—try explaining this one to the kids.

This is only the latest embarrassment to beset the literary ideologues of authenticity, and its political stakes are relatively trivial. It was not always such. The authorship of slave narratives published between 1760 and 1865 was also fraught with controversy. To give credence to their claims about the horrors of slavery, American abolitionists urgently needed a cadre of ex-slaves who could compellingly indict their masters with first-person accounts of their bondage. For this tactic to succeed, the ex-slaves had to be authentic, their narratives full of convincing, painstaking verisimilitude.

So popular did these become, however, that two forms of imitators soon arose: white writers, adopting a first-person black narrative persona, gave birth to the pseudoslave narrative; and black authors, some of whom had never even seen the South, a plantation or a whipping post, became literary lions virtually overnight.

Generic confusion was rife in those days. The 1836 slave narrative of Archy Moore turned out to have been a novel written by a white historian, Richard Hildreth; and the gripping *Autobiography of a Female Slave* (1857) was also a novel, written by a white woman, Mattie Griffith. Perhaps the most embarrassing of these publishing events, however, involved one James Williams, an American slave—the subtitle of his narrative asserts—"who was for several years a driver on a cotton plantation in Alabama." Having escaped to the North (or so he claimed), Williams sought out members of the Anti-Slavery Society, and told a remarkably well-structured story about the brutal treatment of the slaves in the South and of his own miraculous escape, using the literacy he had secretly acquired to forge the necessary documents.

So compelling, so gripping, so *useful* was his tale that the abolitionists decided to publish it immediately. Williams arrived in New York on New Year's Day, 1838. By January 24, he had dictated his complete narrative to John Greenleaf Whittier. By February 15, it was in print, and was also being serialized in the abolitionist newspaper *The Anti-Slavery Examiner*. Even before Williams's book was published, rumors spread in New York that slave catchers were on his heels, and so his new friends shipped him off to Liverpool—where, it seems, he was never heard from again. Once the book was published, the abolitionists distributed it widely, sending copies to every state and to every Congressman.

Alas, Williams's stirring narrative was not authentic at all, as outraged Southern slaveholders were quick to charge and as his abolitionist friends reluctantly had to concede. It was a work of fiction, the

production, one commentator put it, "purely of the Negro imagination"—as, no doubt, were the slave catchers who were in hot pursuit,
and whose purported existence earned Williams a free trip to England
and a new life.

Ersatz slave narratives had an even rougher time of it a century
later, and one has to wonder how William Styron's *The Confessions of
Nat Turner*—a novel that aroused the strenuous ire of much of the black
intelligentsia when it was published in 1976—might have been received
had it been published by James Baldwin. "Hands off our history," we
roared at Mr. Styron, the white Southern interloper, as we shopped
around our list of literary demands. It was the real thing we wanted,
and we wouldn't be taken in by imitators.

The real black writer, accordingly, could claim the full authority
of experience denied Mr. Styron. Indeed, the late 1960s and early '70s
were a time in which the notion of ethnic literature began to be consoli-
dated and, in some measure, institutionalized. That meant policing the
boundaries, telling true from false. But it was hard to play this game
without a cheat sheet. When Dan McCall published *The Man Says Yes*
in 1969, a novel about a young black teacher who comes up against the
eccentric president of a black college, many critics assumed the author
was black, too. The reviewer for *The Amsterdam News*, for example, referred to him throughout as "Brother McCall." Similar assumptions
were occasionally made about Shane Stevens when he published the
gritty bildungsroman *Way Uptown in Another World* in 1971, which detailed the brutal misadventures of its hero from Harlem, Marcus Garvey
Black. In this case, the new voice from the ghetto belonged to a white
graduate student at Columbia.

But the ethnic claim to its own experience cut two ways. For if
many of their readers imagined a black face behind the prose, many avid
readers of Frank Yerby's historical romances or Samuel R. Delany's science fiction novels are taken aback when they learn that these authors
are black. And James Baldwin's *Giovanni's Room*, arguably his most ac-
complished novel, is seldom taught in black literature courses because
its characters are white *and* gay.

Cultural commentators have talked about the "cult of ethnicity"
in postwar America. You could dismiss it as a version of what Freud
called "the narcissism of small differences." But you also see it as a salu-
tary reaction to a regional Anglo-American culture that has declared
itself as universal. For too long, "race" was something that blacks had,
"ethnicity" was what "ethnics" had. In mid-century America, Norman
Podhoretz reflected in *Making It*, his literary memoirs, "to write fiction

out of the experience of big-city immigrant Jewish life was to feel one-self, and to be felt by others, to be writing exotica at best; nor did there exist a respectably certified narrative style in English which was any-thing but facsimile-WASP. Writing was hard enough but to have to write with *only* that part of one's being which had been formed by the accul-turation-minded public schools and by the blindly ethnicizing English departments of the colleges was like being asked to compete in a race with a leg cut off at the thigh."

All this changed with the novelistic triumphs of Saul Bellow and Philip Roth—and yet a correlative disability was entered in the ledger, too. In the same year that Mr. Styron published *The Confessions of Nat Turner*, Philip Roth published *When She Was Good*, a novel set in the ru-ral heartland of gentile middle America and infused with the chilly humorlessness of its small-town inhabitants. This was, to say the least, a departure. Would critics who admired Mr. Roth as the author of *Goodbye, Columbus* accept him as a chronicler of the Protestant Corn Belt?

Richard Gilman, in *The New Republic*, compared Mr. Roth to a "naturalist on safari to a region unfamiliar to him" and declared him-self unable to "account for the novel's existence, so lacking is it in any true literary interest." Maureen Howard in *Partisan Review* said she felt "the presence of a persona rather than a personal voice." To Jonathan Baumbach, writing in *Commonweal*, the book suggested "Zero Mostel doing an extended imitation of Jimmy Stewart." "He captures the rhythms of his characters' speech," Mr. Baumbach says of Mr. Roth, "but not, I feel, what makes them human." If the book was written partly in defiance of the strictures of ethnic literature, those very strictures were undoubtedly what made the book anathema to so many reviewers.

And what if *When She Was Good* had been published under the name Philip McGrath? Would the same reviewers still have denounced it as an artistic imposture? Does anyone imagine that Zero Mostel would have come to mind? Yet there is a twist in the tale. Even a counterfeit can be praised for its craft. For some, the novel's worth was enhanced precisely because of its "inauthenticity"—because it was seen as an act of imagination unassisted by memory.

Under any name, Kazuo Ishiguro's *Remains of the Day*—a novel narrated by an aging and veddy English butler—would be a tour de force; but wasn't the acclaim that greeted it heightened by a kind of criti-cal double take at the youthful Japanese face on the dust jacket? To take another example, no one is surprised that admirers of Norman Rush's novel *Mating* would commend the author on the voice of its female narrator. Subtract from the reality column, add to the art column. Thus

Doris Grumbach, who commended Mr. Roth's novel for its careful observation, concludes her own review with an assessment of technique: "To bring off this verisimilitude is, to my mind, an enormous accomplishment." Would she have been so impressed with the virtuosity of a Philip McGrath?

Sometimes, however, a writer's identity is in fact integral to a work's artifice. Such is the case with John Updike's *Bech: A Book*, the first of two collections of short stories featuring Mr. Updike's Jewish novelist, Henry Bech. The 1970 book opens with a letter from the protagonist, Henry, to his creator, John, fussing about the literary components from which he was apparently jury-rigged. At first blush (Bech muses), he sounds like "some gentlemanly Norman Mailer; then that London glimpse of *silver* hair glints more of gallant, glamorous Bellow. . . . My childhood seems out of Alex Portnoy and my ancestral past out of I. B. Singer. I get a whiff of Malamud in your city breezes, and am I paranoid to feel my 'block' an ignoble version of the more or less noble renunciations of H. Roth, D. Fuchs and J. Salinger? Withal, something Waspish, theological, scared and insultingly ironical that derives, my wild surmise is, from you."

What is clear is that part of the point of John Updike's Bech is that he is *John Updike's* Bech: an act Cynthia Ozick has described as "cultural impersonation." The contrast between Bech and Updike, then, far from being irrelevant, is itself staged within the fictional edifice. You could publish *Bech* under a pseudonym, but, I maintain, it would be a different book.

Conversely—but for similar reasons—one might argue that exposing the true author of *Famous All Over Town*, a colorful picaresque novel set in a Los Angeles barrio, was a form of violence against the book itself. Published in 1983 under the nom de plume Danny Santiago, the book was hailed by Latino critics for its vibrancy and authenticity, and received the Richard and Hinda Rosenthal Foundation Award from the American Academy of Arts and Letters for an outstanding work of fiction. But Santiago, assumed to be a young Chicano talent, turned out to be Daniel L. James, a septuagenarian WASP educated at Andover and Yale, a playwright, screenwriter and, in his later years, a social worker. And yet Danny Santiago was much more than a literary conceit to his creator, who had for twenty years lost faith in his own ability to write; Danny was the only voice available to him. Judging from the testimony of his confidant, John Gregory Dunne, Mr. James may well have felt that the attribution was the only just one; that *Famous All Over Town* belonged to Danny Santiago before it quite belonged to Daniel James.

Death-of-the-author types cannot come to grips with the fact that a book is a cultural event; authorial identity, mystified or not, can be part of that event. What the ideologues of authenticity cannot quite come to grips with is that fact and fiction have always exerted a reciprocal effect on each other. However truthful you set out to be, your autobiography is never unmediated by literary structures of expression. Many authentic slave narratives were influenced by Harriet Beecher Stowe; on the other hand, authentic slave narratives were among Stowe's primary sources for her own imaginative work, *Uncle Tom's Cabin*. By the same token, to recognize the slave narrative as a genre is to recognize that, for example, Frederick Douglass's mode of expression was informed by the conventions of antecedent narratives, some of which were (like James Williams's) whole-cloth inventions.

So it is not just a matter of the outsider boning up while the genuine article just writes what he or she knows. If Shane Stevens was deeply influenced by Richard Wright, so too were black protest novelists like John O. Kilens and John A. Williams. And if John Updike can manipulate the tonalities of writers like Saul Bellow, Bernard Malamud, and Philip Roth, must we assume that a Bruce Jay Friedman, say, is wholly unaffected by such models?

The distasteful truth is that like it or not, all writers are "cultural impersonators."

Even real people, moreover, are never quite real. My own favorite (fictional) commentary on the incursion of fiction upon a so-called real life is provided by Nabokov's Humbert Humbert as he reflects upon the bothersome task of swapping life stories with a new and unwanted wife. Her confessions were marked by "sincerity and artlessness," his were "glib compositions"; and yet, he muses, "technically the two sets were congeneric since both were affected by the same stuff (soap operas, psychoanalysis, and cheap novelettes) upon which I drew for my characters and she for her mode of expression."

Start interrogating the notion of cultural authenticity and our most trusted critical categories come into question. Maybe Danny Santiago's *Famous All Over Town* can usefully be considered a work of Chicano literature; maybe Shane Stevens's *Way Uptown in Another World* can usefully be considered within the genre of black protest novels. In his own version of the blindfold test, the mathematician Alan Turing famously proposed that we credit a computer with intelligence if we can conduct a dialogue with it and not know whether a person or machine has been composing the responses. Should we allow ethnic literatures a similar procedure for claiming this title?

At this point, it is important to go slow. Consider the interviewer's chestnut: are you a woman writer or a writer who happens to be a woman? A black writer or a writer who happens to be a black? Alas, these are deadly disjunctions. After struggling to gain the recognition that a woman or a black (or, exemplarily, a black woman) writer is, in the first instance, a writer, many authors yet find themselves uneasy with the supposedly universalizing description. How can ethnic or sexual identity be reduced to a mere contingency when it is so profoundly a part of who a writer is?

And yet if, for example, black critics claim special authority as interpreters of black literature, and black writers claim special authority as interpreters of black reality, are we not obliged to cede an equivalent dollop of authority to our white counterparts?

We easily become entrapped by what the feminist critic Nancy K. Miller has called "as a" criticism: where we always speak "as a" white middle-class woman, a person of color, a gay man, and so on. And that, too, is a confinement—in the republic of letters as in the larger policy. "Segregation today . . . Segregation tomorrow . . . Segregation forever": that line, which Asa Earl Carter wrote for George Wallace's inauguration speech as Governor, may still prove his true passport to immortality. And yet segregation—as Carter himself would demonstrate—is as difficult to maintain in the literary realm as it is in the civic one.

The lesson of the literary blindfold test is not that our social identities don't matter. They do matter. And our histories, individual and collective, do affect what we wish to write and what we are able to write. But that relation is never one of fixed determinism. No human culture is inaccessible to someone who makes the effort to understand, to learn, to inhabit another world.

Yes, Virginia, there is a Danny Santiago. And—if you like that sort of thing— there is a Little Tree, too, just as treacly now as he ever was. And as long as there are writers who combine some measure of imagination and curiosity, there will continue to be such interlopers of the literary imagination. What, then, of the vexed concept of authenticity? To borrow from Samuel Goldwyn's theory of sincerity, authenticity remains essential: once you can fake that, you've got it made.

13 Multicultural Literature and the Politics of Reaction

Joel Taxel

Few issues in today's contentious social and cultural environment evoke as much heated debate as do the subjects of political correctness and multiculturalism. This chapter explores the complex issue of political correctness and the challenges it poses to those concerned with the creation, production, distribution, and consumption of children's literature. The discussion addresses questions that speak to the very nature and function of children's literature and to its status as art and entertainment and as a source of role models and ideology for children's "impressionable" minds. I will also explore the relationship between the politically charged question of cultural authenticity and whether books about African Americans are to be written only by African Americans, books about Native Americans by Native Americans, and so forth, and the freedom of writers to write without restriction.

Multiculturalism and Multicultural Literature for Young People

Multiculturalism refers to education that addresses the interests, concerns, and experiences of individuals and groups considered outside of the sociopolitical and cultural mainstream of American society. In the United States, multicultural education is often interpreted as a reference to groups such as African Americans, Native Americans, Asian Americans, and Hispanic Americans. Smith (1993) describes a broader interpretation of multiculturalism, one that is inclusive of handicapped persons, gay and lesbian individuals, indeed "any persons whose lifestyle, enforced or otherwise, distinguishes them as identifiable members of a group other than the 'mainstream'" (p. 341). Nieto (1996) suggests that

This chapter is a revised version of an essay that originally appeared in *Teachers College Record*, 1997, *98*(3), 417–48. Reprinted with permission.

multicultural education "challenges and rejects racism and other forms of discrimination in schools and society and accepts and affirms the pluralism (ethnic, racial, linguistic, religious, economic, gender, among others) that students, their communities, and teachers represent" (p. 307).

The term "multicultural literature" is used in a variety of ways. Cai and Bishop (1994) argue that the critical factor is the relation between the literature and the larger pedagogical intentions of multicultural education. They believe that despite general agreement that multicultural literature "is about some identifiable 'other'" who is different "from the dominant white American cultural group" (pp. 57–58), problems exist because the definition of multicultural literature has more to do with its ultimate purpose than its literary characteristics. Multicultural literature thus is best considered a pedagogical construct with the goal of "challenging the existing canon by expanding the curriculum to include literature from a variety of cultural groups" (p. 59).

Cai and Bishop (1994) suggest that multicultural literature actually consists of at least three distinct kinds of literature. The broadest of the categories is "world literature," said to include all literature. In the United States, world literature is meant to include the literature of underrepresented peoples. "Cross-cultural literature" refers to works about the interrelations of peoples from different cultures, as well as books about people from specific cultural groups that are written by individuals not of that group. This group of books has been the focus of the most vociferous and bitter controversies. "Parallel culture literature" refers to books written by individuals from parallel cultural groups such as African Americans, Native Americans, and Hispanic Americans. Their works represent the "experiences, consciousness, and self-image developed as a result of being acculturated and socialized within these groups" (pp. 65–67).

The Need for Multicultural Literature

Demands for multicultural literature, and for multicultural education, were an outgrowth of the civil rights and women's movements of the sixties and seventies (Cai & Bishop, 1994; Johnson-Feelings, 1990; Smith, 1993) when educators began scrutinizing the representations found in curriculum materials and literature for young people. Harris (1993a) points out that while African Americans have been depicted in general literature since the seventeenth century, these portrayals have been stereotyped and unauthentic. Derisive and disparaging treatments of women, African Americans, and other racial and ethnic minorities also filled the pages of the textbooks that dominated American schools in the nineteenth century (Elson, 1964), as well as much of the first half of the twentieth century. Especially significant was the relationship between the distorted representations of historically oppressed groups in textbooks and children's literature and the overall distribution of power and resources in society (Apple, 1979; Taxel, 1981).

Criticism and protest during the past several decades did contribute to an overdue opening up of American literature and culture in general to the voices of long-silenced groups. Shacochis (1995) contends that the past fifteen years "have constituted a golden age in American literature because those who have been cast to the periphery by the centrifuge of Western history and the power dynamics of American power are telling their stories in greater number than ever before" (p. 14). Harris (1993b), citing the "unprecedented artistic and literary excellence" of the literature created in the 1980s and 1990s, suggests the dawning of a "golden age in African-American children's literature" (p. 59). Bishop (1991) is a bit more cautious in her assessment, noting that of five thousand children's books published in 1990, African Americans wrote only 1 percent. Even when one considers nonblack authors writing about African Americans, the number does not increase appreciably. However, unlike the books of previous decades, most current books about African Americans are parallel-culture literature; they are written and illustrated by African Americans themselves. There are exceptions, and many of the criticisms and controversies related to African American children's literature focus on these cross-cultural literary exceptions.

Most critics agree that representations of girls and women in literature are richer and more varied today than twenty years ago. However, progress often is contradictory, and some question the nature and the extent of the "progress" actually made. Ernst (1995), for example, notes, "while the number of females in books has increased, research indicated that the stereotypical behaviors with which they have been portrayed have not been changed" (p. 68). In addition, an overwhelming number of children's books feature males who are central characters who continue to have a disproportionate number of positive characteristics attributed to them. Progress in gender representations also has been undercut by the remarkable popularity of formulaic romance series and by the phenomenally popular series books targeted at various age groups (Christian-Smith, 1990). The latest of these mass-market phenomena, The American Girls series, is self-consciously constructing an image of the American girl and is being marketed via direct mail along with high-priced dolls and an unending list of clothes, accessories, and curriculum materials for use in schools. Analysis of this series not only provides a fascinating glimpse of the mass-market construction of a very particular notion of gender, but important insight into critical, insufficiently discussed and understood developments in the political economy of publishing (Story, 2002).

The Political Economy of Publishing

Children's books are products of our culture "whose existence straddles various realms, including education, entertainment, illustration, and literature" and which serve as agents of "socialization, [of] politicization, and of formal education" (Johnson-Feelings, 1990, p. 1). Apple (1986), Christian-Smith (1990), and Luke (1988) argue that changes in trade-book and textbook content and form are best understood when examined in the context of the systems of production, distribution, and consumption that shape the publishing industry. Johnson-Feelings (1990) referred to the publishing industry as "part of an entire structure of interrelated institutions in this country which respond to ever-changing political sentiment and to the economic imperatives of making a profit from the sale of a product—in this case books" (p. 9). Christian-Smith (1990) sees the adolescent romance novels that dominate the shelves of shopping center and mall bookstores less as traditional literary creations than as products of marketing research that are written to carefully prescribed formulas and marketed much like any other commodity. Another revealing illustration of how political sentiment and economic considerations contribute to important changes in the kinds of books made available to young people is found in the 1965 Elementary and Secondary Education Act's provision of money for school and public libraries. This act of Congress effectively created the market for books about black children (Sims, 1982), a development that was instrumental in paving the way for the growth of multicultural children's literature.

Contemporary children's book publishing in the United States is undergoing the same process of integration, consolidation, and downsizing evident in other sectors of the economy. In recent years, publishing companies that once were independently owned enterprises have been purchased by large multinational corporations such as Viacom/Paramount/Simon & Schuster and Rupert Murdock's publishing and media empire (Harris, 1994; Nodelman, 1996). The increasing importance of the bottom line in these conglomerates undermines publishers' willingness to publish new, novel, or experimental books, or books having a limited market. Nodelman (1996) notes that while old independent publishers were businesspeople, they "tended to view their work not only as a way of making money, but as a humane contribution to the quality of life and literature." In contrast, editors today are under enormous pressure "to produce little beyond the kinds of books that are most likely to achieve wide sales" (p. 95). Some observers fear that these changes in the ownership of publishing houses will result in fewer multicultural books being published (Harris, 1996).

Other factors are affecting the business of producing and selling books for young people. Changes in tax laws, for example, now make it unprofitable for publishers to warehouse books, and publishers increasingly are finding it necessary to reduce their backlists. Titles that had been in print for decades are no longer available. Once again, the bottom line is that only titles that sell widely remain in print (Nodelman, 1996). Further exacerbating these trends is the replacement of the independent bookstores that once dominated the industry by bookstore chains like Waldenbooks and B. Dalton. This concentration of economic power "threatens the diversity of what gets published" and results in the same "mainstream" books appearing in virtually all stores (Nodelman, 1996, pp. 95–96).

The market for children's books itself is being divided into ever finer segments to be exploited through the proliferation of mass-market books (e.g., series books, television and movie tie-ins). On the positive side, we have seen the growth of a small group of powerful editors and writers who have considerable freedom and latitude to publish pretty much what they please. These editors and writers produce that segment of the thousands of books published each year that is consistent with the highest standards of literary and artistic excellence. Some of what they publish is new, novel, and experimental. The books of Francesca Lia Block (1989, 1993) come to mind. It also is important to note that an increasing number of these high-quality books are the creations of African American artists and illustrators who have become major powers in the field (e.g., Pat Cummings, Virginia Hamilton, James Ransom, Patricia McKissack, Walter Dean Myers, Jerry and Brian Pinkney, Mildred Taylor). While Harris (1996) is confident that major writers like Hamilton and Myers "will not have to worry about finding publishers receptive to their work," she is concerned that "unknown talents may remain unpublished" (p. 117). Clearly, there is a gap between the kinds of books critics celebrate and the books that sell. There is little doubt that the ability of writers and editors to maintain their independence in the face of the relentless bottom-line imperative will go a long way in determining the future not only of multicultural children's literature but also of high-quality children's literature itself.

These important developments in the publishing industry, along with changes in the political landscape, provide critical context for understanding the controversies that surround multicultural children's literature which are the central concern of this chapter.

Challenges to the Multicultural Movement in Children's Literature

Many in our increasingly conservative political culture regard multiculturalism as "a catchall term for a panoply of evils, all bent on undermining Western Culture" (Cope & Kalantzis, 1993, p. 87). McCarthy (1993) argues that conservatives have responded to multiculturalism with a "virulent reaffirmation of Eurocentrism and Western culture in debates over school curriculum and educational reform" (p. 290). Attacks on multiculturalism and multicultural literature are usefully considered in relation to "political correctness (PC)," which is defined in an article in *Time* as a movement that seeks "to suppress thought or statements deemed offensive to women, blacks or other groups" (Allis, Bonfante, & Booth, 1991, p. 13). Advocates of political correctness are said to favor banishing unfavorable speech, opinions, and attitudes about women and minority groups from college campuses and from the pages of children's literature. PC also has been labeled "the enforcement arm of multiculturalism" (Ozersky, 1991, p. 35).

Proponents of political correctness are viewed as exerting an undue influence on children's literature. A 1993 review of children's books in *Newsweek* began with the observation that "kids' books" have fallen "into the clutches of the politically correct, the multiculturalists and every other do-gooder with an eat your spinach attitude." While noting that the emphasis on "being good—respecting others, respecting yourself, allowing for cultural differences" is difficult to criticize, Jones (1993) wonders "whatever happened to old fashioned fun like gluing your sister's hair to the bedpost" (p. 54).

Other, more serious charges are raised in this book by Kathryn Lasky (2003) and Hazel Rochman (2003), both of whom applaud many aspects of the movement to make children's literature truly multicultural but fear that things may have gone too far. Lasky (2003) approvingly cites the positive benefits of multicultural education in teaching children about rich cultural heritages within North American culture. She nevertheless is deeply concerned about the "politically correct elite" who manifest a "fanaticism" that leads them to act as "self-styled militias of cultural diversity" (p. 85). She sees these individuals as delivering dictates and guidelines about who can create books for children from diverse cultural backgrounds.

Lasky (2003) also discusses the complex relationship between multicultural children's literature and important issues such as context and setting. Ignoring these matters, she argues, suggests that "issues of cultural diversity in education are a passing fancy" or a politically correct trend that is not subject to rigorous artistic standards. Lasky insists that as an author, she does "not make artistic judgments based on notions of political correctness" (p. 88).

Another important issue raised by Lasky (2003) is that of authorship. When authors choose to write outside of their own cultures, Lasky says, critics maintain that in order to write effectively about a culture, one must be "of" or "inside" that culture and that "certain stories may be told only by certain people" (p. 88). Extrapolating from the (supposed) stricture suggesting, for example, that one must be African American to write about African Americans, Native American to write about Native Americans, and so forth, Lasky wonders if this requires us to seek only African Americans to edit African American stories and Jewish Americans to edit Jewish stories until everything is "perfectly aligned in terms of gender, sexual preference, race, creed, or ethnic origin." Lasky sees these strictures as "dangerous" (p. 88).

Similar themes are echoed in Rochman's (1993) *Against Borders: Promoting Books for a Multicultural World*, a passionate, compassionate, and wonderfully literate plea for "great books from all cultures" to "break down apartheid" (p. 12). In a chapter in this volume based on her earlier work, Rochman (2003) maintains that

> *multiculturalism* is a trendy word, trumpeted by the politically correct with a stridency that has provoked a sneering backlash. There are PC watchdogs eager to strip from the library shelves anything that presents a group as less than perfect (Beard & Cerf, 1992). The ethnic "character" must always be strong, dignified, courageous, loving, sensitive, wise. Then there are those who watch for authenticity: how dare a white write about blacks? . . .
>
> But the greatest danger from the politically correct bullies is that they create a backlash, and that backlash often consists of self-righteous support for the way things are. (p. 101)

Does Children's Literature Really Have a PC Problem?

Because Lasky and Rochman in many respects are advocates of multicultural literature, their criticisms are especially troubling and demand response. I am convinced that they seriously exaggerate the power of those who raise questions about the cultural content of children's literature and that they (perhaps unwittingly) provide aid, comfort, and ammunition to those who pose the real threat to the future of children's literature. Their references to "literary ethnic cleansing," to "politically correct bullies," and to "self-styled militias of cultural diversity" include few specifics, let alone the names of these people and how they manage to exercise such intimidating power. Harris (2003) notes that Lasky's claim that individuals are mandating who can write about whom is without foundation. She also points out that the major journals of criticism and discussion of children's literature do not have editors who are people of color, that the book-publishing industry remains "overwhelmingly the province of Whites," and the majority of articles they publish do not focus on multicultural issues.

Just as disturbing is the virtual absence of discussion about the sociohistorical and political context that has shaped current debates about multicultural children's literature. There is no recognition, let alone appreciation, of the relation between the vulgar, racist representations of African Americans, Native Americans, and other groups historically found in literature, films, and other cultural artifacts and "the legitimation of authority and inequality in society" (McCarthy, 1993, p. 290). A related point is that neither Lasky nor Rochman acknowledges that members of parallel cultures were denied consistent access to publishing until the 1960s and that African American writers and illustrators of children's books still do not enjoy equal access to the publishing industry. "This is often the case even after they have already published books which are successful financially and critically" (Johnson-Feelings, 1990, pp. 4–5, 12). Bishop (1996) gets to the heart of the matter when she suggests that

> to ignore the historical role of race and racism in American children's literature is naive at best, and allows one to take the issue out of its rightful context and to redefine it in terms of "political correctness," an easy put-down for anyone who questions the authority of people used to unquestioned privilege. (p. viii)

Despite these criticisms, Lasky and Rochman do raise important issues that require our attention—for example, whether an ethnic character must "always be strong, dignified, courageous, loving, sensitive, wise" (Rochman, 2003, p. 101). Harris (2003) speaks of "the demand by some that authors of literature we label 'multicultural' create characters who are 'role models'" and of the need for stories that "either uplift or inspire or correct and usurp stereotypic works. Positive images are preferred and deemed crucial" (p. 121). Bishop suggests that among the primary criteria for selecting multicultural texts is that a book "should contribute in a positive way to an understanding and appreciation of persons of color and their cultures" (qtd. in Nodelman, 1996, pp. 132–133).

These questions touch on the very nature and function of children's literature: its status as art, as entertainment, as a source of role models and ideology for young, impressionable minds, and whether it is proper to deem it "political." We might also ask whether authors of books for young people have a unique social responsibility and, if so, what the relation is between that responsibility and the freedom of authors to write without guidelines and restrictions. While it is presumptuous for anyone to claim to have definitive answers to these complicated and vexing questions, it is apparent that this frequently emotional debate is often reduced to a case of good guys versus bad guys, of racists and sexists versus those committed to justice and equity.

These points are dramatically illustrated by the way these matters have been debated recently. Yolen (1994) makes an earnest plea for the right of storytellers to be free to tell whatever story they choose and warns of an increasing movement toward "the Balkanization of children's literature. We are drawing rigid borders across the world of story, demanding that people tell only their stories" (p. 705). In a later post on the "childlit list" of the "Children's Literature: Criticism and Theory" bulletin board, Yolen reiterates her stance and concludes by saying that

> we are going through an interesting time of re-examination. But in our eagerness to right historical wrongs, let us not forget that the stories (and storytellers) will report all this years from now. And if any of us are still around to hear or read these stories, we are going to be awfully surprised at what they think we said! (Yolen, personal communication, March 19, 1995)

Seto (2003) is neither moved nor swayed by Yolen's concerns about the possible "Balkanization" in children's literature. She warns that it is wrong for Euro-American authors to "'steal' from other cultures," and that these authors must not write outside their own culture unless they have direct personal experience with the culture they are writing about. "When Euro-Americans 'take on' one of my cultures," Seto writes, "I feel quite violated. It is a form of cultural imperialism—that euphemism for cultural rape" (p. 95).

Seto's strong language reflects the anger that Harris (2003) suggests is understandable. Seto's comments contain an implicit and emphatic rejection of the long-cherished notion that literature and other art forms exist "for their own sake," the idea that literature or literary quality "transcends the contingencies of race and gender and the like" (Cope & Kalantzis, 1993, p. 104).

Carus publisher and author Marc Aronson (2003) points out that when these issues actually get played out in the boardrooms of publishing houses, they often do so in complex and contradictory ways that frequently belie good intentions. While Aronson applauds the recent increase in the publication of authors and illustrators from diverse backgrounds, he feels that "the multiculturalism that parades 'authenticity' and pretends that *a* culture has *a* view that belongs to *a* people is now something of a shibboleth in children's books" (p. 78). He concludes with a plea for "cultural crossing," for black writers to contemplate the Holocaust, for Native Americans to describe the Great Migration, for Jewish authors to think about the Trail of Tears (p. 82). Back on the Internet, Kwame Dawes (personal communication, March 16, 1995) focuses on the critical issue of cultural appropriation:

> What is at stake here is not simply a writer's freedom to write about whatever he or she chooses, but the silencing of voices that need to be heard if we are to truly create harmony and mutual respect in a culturally diverse society. . . . That recently white writers have been forced to cope with questions of "What gives you the right to write about another culture?" is not a bad thing. It is good because it now forces writers to be more careful, more aware of the implications of what they write. Does it stop us from writing outside our cultures? No. Should it? No. But it does make us more careful, and that is not a bad thing.

Critic Peter Neumeyer (personal communication, June 2, 1995) chimes in with a reverential plea for us to honor literature's special status as art:

> In the Internet conversations, I sense that often the discussion begins with moral-political screening. And ends there too. If so, that's too bad for the children. Yes, Literature is an Example. But it's not a simple one, even for children; it's not facile and platitudinous. It's merely the most true (Keats) rendering available to us of the Life we humans have on this planet, in its wonder and awfulness and indefinableness. Literature aspires to Understanding. Not to preaching.

Kathleen Horning (personal communication, March 16, 1995) raises an issue that must be faced if we are ever to get beyond the name-calling and good-guy versus bad-guy dichotomizing that so often characterizes discussion of these issues:

> The real question seems to be: can we honestly criticize the cultural content of their work without being labeled "politically correct," "oversensitive," "bitter," or told that we "have a chip on our shoulder?" Can we discuss the storyline, characters, language and style of the book itself, instead of hearing endlessly about the noble intentions, careful research, childhood friends and personal life philosophy of the author?

We read a final posting from Perry Nodelman (personal communication, March 16, 1995):

> I'm not suggesting that men shouldn't write about women, or Christians about Jews. I'm only suggesting that readers need to be conscious of the degree to which ALL fiction holds a distorting mirror up to reality, and to be willing to always distrust writers as well as enjoy them. . . . A key example of voice appropriation, incidentally, is the one we specialists in children's literature like to absolutely ignore: Just about ALL children's literature describes childhood as represented by adults. It's ALL voice appropriation, and presents childhood as we adults want children to imagine it. It would be very manipulative of us if we didn't do our best to make children conscious of that fact.

Children's Literature, Political Correctness, and the Selective Tradition

Even though the advocates of multiculturalism do not have nearly the power ascribed to them by cultural conservatives, this does not mean that they are powerless. Indeed it is in the territory between public perception and actual conditions in the editorial rooms of publishing houses, in the review media, in bookstores, in classrooms in our nation's schools, and on college campuses that the struggle for a curriculum and a literary canon that includes all Americans is being waged.

Our response to assertions that multicultural characters must be role models, or to the claim that authorship of multicultural books should be the exclusive province of members of parallel cultural groups themselves, is to a significant degree a function of how we view literature's place in and relation to society. That is, do we see literature existing for its own sake, as an object to be contemplated and revered and therefore considered to be outside of politics, ideology, and even history? Or is literature an artifact of the culture that must be situated in its sociohistorical and political context in order to be understood? Despite considerable discussion over the years (Taxel, 1986, 1991), and an understanding that not even the "most apparently simple book for children can be innocent of ideological freight" (Hunt, 1992, p. 18), resistance persists to the idea that literature and other forms of creative expression have political and ideological dimensions. The viewpoint that art is inherently and unavoidably political is clearly articulated by noted author Eloise Greenfield (1985):

> There is a viewpoint . . . that holds art to be sacrosanct, subject to scrutiny only as to its esthetic value. This viewpoint is in keeping with the popular myth that genuine art is not political. It is true that politics is not art, but art is political. Whether in its interpretation of the political realities, or in its attempt to ignore these realities, or in its distortions, or in its advocacy of a different reality, or in its support of the status quo, all art is political and every book carries its author's message. (p. 20)

I find it difficult to conceive an argument suggesting that authors of children's books operate in a political and ideological vacuum and pursue their artistic vision without constraint. Like other cultural artifacts, children's literature is a product of convention that is rooted in, if not determined by, the dominant belief systems and ideologies of the times in which it is created. While the total elimination of boundaries and conventions in writing for young people would contradict the very idea of children's literature (i.e., if there are no boundaries, why have children's literature?), one hopes there always will be writers and editors who challenge convention and extend the boundaries with sense and aesthetic sensitivity. In any event, it undoubtedly is the case that while boundaries and conventions change, they never are eliminated altogether.

The point here is that it is impossible to understand the evolution of children's literature without situating the books of a given era in the sociocultural and political milieu of that period. Pressures and forces, direct and indirect, subtle and not so subtle, influence the writing, publication, and review of books and are part of the social landscape that includes the culture and economics of publishing. Present-day concerns about the way historic victims of oppression are represented in literature simply are the latest manifestations of this phenomenon.

Thankfully, the most abhorrent and loathsome of the caricatures and stereotypes of the racist and sexist history of American children's literature (Harris, 1993a) are absent from most contemporary books. However, newer, more subtle stereotypes and representations are still to be found in books for young people, as well as in films, on television, and throughout popular culture. Many of these objectionable representations are found in cross-cultural books, books about a specific cultural group written by individuals not of that group. Cai and Bishop (1994) point to research suggesting that many works of cross-cultural literature reinforce rather than dispel ignorance. It is for this reason that some of the most impassioned controversies instigated by proponents of a multicultural children's literature relate to books about the experiences of African Americans written by European American authors. *Ben's Trumpet* (Isadora, 1979), *Jake and Honeybunch Go to Heaven* (Zemach, 1982), *Sounder* (Armstrong, 1969), *The Cay* (Taylor, 1969), *The Slave Dancer* (Fox, 1973), and *Words by Heart* (Sebestyen, 1979) all were reproved for subtle and not-so-subtle stereotyping, racism, and questionable authenticity (e.g., Banfield & Wilson, 1985; Moore, 1985; Sims, 1980; Taxel, 1986; Trousdale, 1990). Trousdale (1990), for example, suggests that African American characters in books like *Sounder* (Armstrong, 1969) and *Words by Heart* (Sebestyen, 1979) manifest a "submission theology" in which African American characters are "docile [and] submissive towards whites, and accepting of injustice and oppression" (p. 137).

It is significant to note that while Cai and Bishop (1994) emphasize the difficulty of acquiring the perspective of a group other than one's own, they do not deny the rights of outsiders to portray cultural groups to which they do not belong. Instead, they underscore "the need for outsiders to fill in the cultural gap themselves before they can close it for others" (p. 67). Cai and Bishop insist that "literature from parallel cultural groups has a unique role to play in multicultural literature programs, because writers from these groups best represent their own cultures" (pp. 66–67). Vandergrift (1993) provides an important note of caution to those who assume rigid and dogmatic positions on this critical question:

> The belief that only one of a culture can write authentically about that culture . . . would deny the very nature of aesthetic composition and perhaps eliminate children's literature, which is, of course, almost always written by adults. It is true that adults were once children, but, nonetheless, the insider argument, if carried to its logical conclusion, would result in a literary canon composed solely of autobiographies. (p. 356)

We live in a time of heightened sensitivity and mounting pressure to move beyond stereotypes and clichés in writing about historically oppressed cultures. Clearly, there is growing, and warranted, impatience with the "willed scholarly indifference" (Morrison, 1993) of many toward taking this criticism seriously and recognizing both the obvious and the less readily apparent manifestations of racism, sexism, and other forms of prejudice.

One consequence of this impatience is that some academics, critics, and writers express anger and occasionally appear didactic and dogmatic in their views of what literature for young people should be like. A recent post of the "Children's Literature: Theory and Criticism" bulletin board, for example, contained an objection to the racism voiced by the title character in *The Great Gilly Hopkins* (Paterson, 1978). What this reader failed to recognize is the dramatic change in Gilly's character over the course of the novel, that there is a "healing difference" between Gilly's initial racism and "the loving acceptance" she later shows (Gouch, personal communication, October 9, 1995). Even Johnson-Feelings (1990), whose volume is an unqualified celebration of the "promise of African American literature for youth," observes that some efforts to combat stereotyping can easily manifest "a tendency to go too far in the other direction and present characterizations which are too ideal, too one-dimensional, too stereotypical toward the other extreme" (p. 52).

Recognition of the existence of occasional excess, however, is a far cry from the alarmist rhetoric of Lasky and Rochman, or the claim of author/illustrator Diane Stanley (1993) that American children's literature is in the grips of the "doctrine of political correctness." Stanley's suggestion is that the current climate limits the ability of authors to tell the stories they choose to tell in the way they see fit. This contention is supported by Lasky's (2003) report that because she is white, she was "discouraged" by a publisher from writing a book about Sarah Breedlove "Madame" Walker, one of the first American female millionaires, who was African American. Lasky also reports, however, that among her books is *True North* (Scholastic, 1996), a historical novel about the underground railroad that is written from the dual perspectives of a fugitive slave girl and a white New England heiress. And Lasky did eventually publish her book about Sarah Breedlove Walker.

Author Walter Dean Myers (1993) offers an assessment of our current situation that is quite different from the one offered by Stanley and Lasky. Myers contends that the present moment is not one where the freedom of authors and illustrators is being restricted, but rather that writers now (finally) are being asked to show more care and respect when writing about the experiences of minorities and women. Bishop (1996) makes a similar point:

> I wish Ms. Lasky well in the publication and reception of her book on the Underground Railroad. I doubt seriously that anyone will criticize her for daring to take on the perspective of a 14-year-old nineteenth-century fugitive slave. Someone may, however, criticize the way in which she portrays that fugitive slave and that is something I think any critic has the right to do. (p. viii)

Henry Louis Gates Jr. (1992) suggests that no past exists without cultural mediation and that, however worthy, the past "does not survive by its own intrinsic power." A crucial function of literary history, Gates concludes, is to disguise that mediation and "to conceal all connections between institutionalized interests and the literature we remember" (p. 34). Given the historic role of culture, including literature for young people, in providing legitimacy for racial and gender-related injustice and oppression, why are we surprised that there are those who are sensitive, angry, and occasionally dogmatic? How could it be otherwise? Does anyone truly believe that the progress made in the past several decades in opening children's literature to long-silenced voices would have been possible without the loud protests of those determined to unmask the connections between institutional interest and literature? Does change in any deeply rooted institutional pattern or cultural practice occur without the efforts and energies of those willing to offend? A central thesis of this chapter is that attacks on multiculturalism are a backlash against those who have demanded long-overdue changes in children's literature, on college campuses, and throughout society. It is disturbing that otherwise thoughtful critics choose to focus on occasional excess and lose sight of the enormous contributions of those who simply are asking that their cultures and experiences be treated with sensitivity and accorded the respect they deserve.

If there is a real threat to the future health and vitality of children's literature, I doubt very seriously that it comes from those concerned with the accuracy and authenticity of representations of women and minorities. Rather, the threat lies in the crass commercialism and the bottom-line mentality that is ubiquitous in our mass culture and is rooted in the profound changes in the publishing industry that could lead to more homogenization and uniformity in books (Harris, 1994).

While thankful for the growing number of talented authors and illustrators who are encouraged by bold and innovative editors willing to take chances, I am troubled by the remarkable amount of junk published that reflects the desire to play it safe, to appeal to the lowest common denominator, to capitalize on the latest fads, and to publish sequels or copies of somebody else's bestseller. These practices have become generic to television and film, and throughout our culture industry. The skyrocketing price of books also threatens to make purchase of the best of children's literature impossible for an increasingly large portion of the public. If unchecked, this trend will virtually assure the proliferation of the worst of the series and other mass-market books that take up all but a fraction of the space in mall bookstores and supermarkets.

Again, the threat to children's literature today lies in these largely ignored developments, not from those who express consternation or outrage over the persistence of stereotypes or hackneyed clichés in writing about minority cultures.

What Does All of This Mean?

Despite what the liberal media would have us believe, there is no conspiracy to prescribe an orthodoxy on children's literature replete with guidelines and a new censorship. This is not to say that changing long-standing conventions in relation to how we write about the cultures and histories of long-oppressed groups is easy. I take very seriously the concerns voiced by Jane Yolen and Marc Aronson, as well as by Kathryn Lasky and Hazel Rochman. Nevertheless, the insistence of peoples from the diverse cultures that make up the United States that their history and culture be treated with respect, dignity, and sensitivity is hardly unreasonable, and the dividends derived from taking their demands seriously already have begun to accrue. Does anyone seriously dispute that protest, sometimes loud and strident, played an important role in the demise of the virtually all-white world of children's books and helped pave the way for the likes of Mildred Taylor, Gary Soto, Virginia Hamilton, Walter Dean Myers, Sheila Hamanaka, Jerry and Brian Pinkney, and others?

Debates about multiculturalism and political correctness in children's literature, to a significant degree, are debates about social responsibility (Little, 1990; Meltzer, 1989; Taxel, 1990). While we must continue to insist that books for young people be literature and not propaganda, I find it impossible to imagine anyone arguing that those who write for young people do not have a special responsibility. Author Michael Rosen grappled with the issues faced by writers who take seriously both their artistic and social responsibilities. He also addressed the widespread denigration of social awareness that goes along with labeling something "PC." Noting that *Publishers Weekly* had described his marvelous *Elijah's Angel: A Story for Chanukah and Christmas* (Rosen, 1992) as "the politically correct holiday book of the season," Rosen (1995) suggests that the term has come to connote something "obviously arch and artificial." I share his outrage and sadness "that a persuasive magazine would cavalierly perpetuate an idea that politically correct is passé, as if it were high time we all got back to political incorrectness" (p. 24).

Raising issues of this sort implies an understanding that what children read plays an important role in shaping their perceptions of the diverse peoples of our world. Clearly, authors need to be cautious in creating characters, developing plots, and articulating themes that deal with subjects about which certain groups have every right to be sensitive. A precariously thin line exists between this position and the need for authors to have the freedom to create (Paterson, 1994). Kathryn Lasky (2003) understandably shares this concern and argues that despite the claims of critics that they "would never dream of prescribing what an author or illustrator should or should not write," they proceed to "go right ahead and do just that, while making extravagant allusions to artistic freedom" (p. 89). For Violet Harris (2003), however, the critical question is not about authorial freedom but the "authorial arrogance" of some authors who wish to write about any subject "without subjecting their work to critical scrutiny" (p. 124). It is apparent that straddling the line between freedom and responsibility is not now, and never will be, easy. My reading of current criticism is that despite the claims of Lasky and Rochman, most, if not all, critics would prefer to err on the side of giving authors more freedom, rather than less. These critics are equally insistent, however, that writers be willing to accept criticism when warranted.

It also seems clear that all parties in this dispute need to have greater confidence in the ability of young people to deal with the many difficult issues raised by this controversy. My confidence comes from my experiences, and those of teachers around the country, of sharing books with young people. West, Weaver, and Rowland (1992), for example, conclude their account of sharing several controversial books about Columbus with children with a plea that reading should "be regarded as exploration, a voyage of discovery, as invitation, rather than as a tool of didacticism or moralizing," and that we need to discuss stories that "challenge our expectations, that force us to confront new ideas and to grapple with long held beliefs" (p. 262). Having students wrestle with the debates raised by controversial books is an effective way to address some of the difficult issues raised in this chapter. Comparative reading of Sebestyen's (1979) *Words by Heart* and Taylor's (1976) *Roll of Thunder, Hear My Cry*, for example, leads to discussion of the many striking similarities and differences between these books as well as a host of important literary and political issues. Experiences of this sort illustrate that response to literature is never easy to predict. Young children are strong and resilient and, with the guidance of caring and skillful teachers, are capable of handling complex and controversial issues when they are presented in a developmentally appropriate fashion.

In view of the alarming increase in the power of the fundamentalist Right that is seeking to eliminate even seemingly innocuous materials from schools, this may not be the best time to raise these issues. However, I am convinced that we must endeavor to open and even widen the dialogue on these important concerns. Above all, we need to understand better how debates about multiculturalism have been turned into attacks on the important progress made by the women's and civil rights movements through gross overstatements of fact and outright distortion. We must urge publishers to build on the encouraging progress made in recent years in creating a literature that accurately and honestly reflects a rich cultural mosaic, as well as the very highest literary and artistic standards. As teachers, we need to create conditions in our classrooms that encourage students to read freely, discuss, and write about these books. Finally, we must be steadfast in our resistance to those seeking to roll back the progress made in the long and painful struggle for justice and equality.

Author's Note

My sincere thanks to JoBeth Allen, Andrew Gitlin, and Claudia Taxel for their helpful comments and suggestions on early drafts of this chapter.

References

Allis, S., Bonfante, J., & Booth, C. (1991, July 8). Whose America? *Time, 138*(1), 12–17.

Apple, M. W. (1979). *Ideology and curriculum.* New York: Routledge & Kegan Paul.

Apple, M. W. (1986). *Teachers and texts: A political economy of class and gender relations in education.* New York: Routledge & Kegan Paul.

Aronson, M. (2003). A mess of stories. In D. L. Fox & K. G. Short (Eds.), *Stories matter: The complexity of cultural authenticity in children's literature* (pp. 78–83). Urbana, IL: National Council of Teachers of English.

Banfield, B., & Wilson, G. (1985). The black experience through white eyes—The same old story once again. In D. MacCann & G. Woodard (Eds.), *The black American in books for children: Readings in racism* (2nd ed., pp. 192–207). Metuchen, NJ: Scarecrow Press.

Bishop, R. S. (1991). Evaluating books by and about African-Americans. In M. Lindgren (Ed.), *The multicolored mirror: Cultural substance in literature for children and young adults* (pp. 31–40). Fort Atkinson, WI: Highsmith Press.

Bishop, R. S. (1996). Letter to the editors. *The New Advocate, 9*(2), vii–viii.

Cai, M., & Bishop, R. S. (1994). Multicultural literature for children: Towards a clarification of a concept. In A. H. Dyson & C. Genishi (Eds.), *The need for story: Cultural diversity in classroom and community* (pp. 57–71). Urbana. IL: National Council of Teachers of English.

Christian-Smith, L. K. (1990). *Becoming a woman through romance.* New York: Routledge.

Cope, B., & Kalantzis, M. (1993). Contradictions in the canon: Nationalism and the cultural literacy debate. In A. Luke & P. Gilbert (Eds.), *Literacy in contexts: Australian perspectives and issues* (pp. 85–177). St. Leonards, Australia: Allen and Unwin.

Elson, R. M. (1964). *Guardians of tradition: American schoolbooks of the nineteenth century.* Lincoln: University of Nebraska Press.

Ernst, S. (1995). Gender issues in books for children and young adults. In S. S. Lehr (Ed.), *Battling dragons: Issues and controversy in children's literature* (pp. 6–78). Portsmouth, NH: Heinemann.

Gates, H. L. (1992). *Loose canons: Notes on the culture wars.* New York: Oxford University Press.

Greenfield, E. (1985). Writing for children—A joy and responsibility. In D. MacCann & G. Woodard (Eds.), *The black American in books for children: Readings in racism* (2nd ed., pp. 19–22). Metuchen, NJ: Scarecrow.

Harris, V. (1993a). African American children's literature. The first one hundred years. In T. Perry & J. W. Fraser (Eds.), *Freedom's plow: Teaching in a multicultural classroom* (pp. 167–81). New York: Routledge.

Harris, V. (1993b). Contemporary griots: African-American writers of children's literature. In V. Harris (Ed.), *Teaching multicultural literature in grades K–8* (pp. 55–108). Norwood, MA: Christopher-Gordon.

Harris, V. (1994). Multiculturalism and children's literature: An evaluation of ideology, publishing, curricula, and research. In C. K. Kinzer & D. J. Leu (Eds.), *Multidimensional aspects of literacy research, theory, and practice: Forty-third yearbook of the national reading conference* (pp. 15–27). Chicago: National Reading Conference.

Harris, V. (1996). Continuing dilemmas, debates, and delights in multicultural literature. *The New Advocate, 9*(2), 107–22.

Harris, V. (2003). The complexity of debates about multicultural literature and cultural authenticity. In D. L. Fox & K. G. Short (Eds.), *Stories matter: The complexity of cultural authenticity in children's literature* (pp. 116–34). Urbana, IL: National Council of Teachers of English.

Hunt, P. (1992). *Literature for children: Contemporary criticism.* New York: Routledge.

Johnson-Feelings, D. (1990). *Telling tales: The pedagogy and promise of African American literature for youth.* New York: Greenwood.

Jones, M. (1993). Kid lit's growing pain. *Newsweek, 122,* 54–57.

Lasky, K. (2003). To Stingo with love: An author's perspective on writing outside one's culture. In D. L. Fox & K. G. Short (Eds.), *Stories matter: The complexity of cultural authenticity in children's literature* (pp. 84–92). Urbana, IL: National Council of Teachers of English.

Little, J. (1990). A writer's social responsibility. *The New Advocate, 3*(2), 79–88.

Luke, A. (1988). *Literacy, textbooks, and ideology: Postwar literacy instruction and the mythology of Dick and Jane.* New York: Falmer Press.

McCarthy, C. (1993). After the canon: Knowledge and ideological representation in multicultural discourse on curriculum reform. In C. McCarthy & W. Crichlow (Eds.), *Race, identity, and representation in education* (pp. 289–305). New York: Routledge.

Meltzer, M. (1989). The social responsibility of the writer. *The New Advocate, 2*(3), 155–57.

Moore, O. (1985). Picture books: The un-text. In D. MacCann & G. Woodard (Eds.), *The black American in books for children: Readings in racism* (2nd ed., pp. 183–91). Metuchen, NJ: Scarecrow Press.

Morrison, T. (1993). *Playing in the dark: Whiteness and the literary imagination.* New York: Vintage.

Myers, W. D. (1993, June). Is this book politically correct? Truth and trends in historical fiction for young people. Symposium conducted at the meeting of the American Library Association Annual Convention.

Nieto, S. (1996). *Affirming diversity: The sociopolitical context of multicultural education.* White Plains, NY: Longman.

Nodelman, P. (1996). *The pleasures of children's literature* (2nd ed.). White Plains, NY: Longman.

Ozersky, J. (1991). The enlightenment theology of political correctness. *Tikkun, 6*(4) 35–39.

Paterson, K. (1994). Cultural politics for a writer's point of view. *The New Advocate, 7*(2), 85–91.

Rochman, H. (1993). *Against borders: Promoting books for a multicultural world.* Chicago: American Library Association.

Rochman, H. (2003). Beyond political correctness. In D. L. Fox & K. G. Short (Eds.), *Stories matter: The complexity of cultural authenticity in children's literature* (pp. 101–15). Urbana, IL: National Council of Teachers of English.

Rosen, M. J. (1995). Seed crystals. *The New Advocate, 8*(1), 17–28.

Seto, T. (2003). Multiculturalism is not Halloween. In D. L. Fox & K. G. Short (Eds.), *Stories matter: The complexity of cultural authenticity in children's literature* (pp. 93–97). Urbana, IL: National Council of Teachers of English.

Shacochis, B. (1995). The enemies of imagination. *Harpers, 291,* 13–15.

Sims, R. (1980). Words by heart: A black perspective. *Interracial Books for Children Bulletin, 11*(7), 12–15,17.

Sims, R. (1982). *Shadow and substance: Afro-American experience in contemporary children's fiction.* Champaign, IL: National Council of Teachers of English.

Smith, K. P. (1993). The multicultural ethic and connections to literature for children and young adults. *Library Trends, 41*(3), 340–53.

Stanley, D. (1993, June). Is this book politically correct? Truth and trends in historical fiction for young people. Symposium conducted at the meeting of the American Library Association Annual Convention.

Story, N. (2002). *Pleasant Company's American Girls collection: The corporate construction of American girlhood.* Unpublished doctoral dissertation, University of Georgia, Athens.

Taxel, J. (1981). The outsiders of the American revolution: The selective tradition in children's fiction. *Interchange on Educational Policy, 12*(2–3), 206–28.

Taxel, J. (1986). The black experience in children's fiction: Controversies surrounding award winning books. *Curriculum Inquiry, 16*(3), 245–81.

Taxel, J. (1990). Notes from the editor. *The New Advocate, 3*(2), vii-xii.

Taxel, J. (1991). Roll of thunder, hear my cry: Reflections on the aesthetics and politics of children's literature. In W. H. Schubert & G. Willis (Eds.), *Reflections from the heart of educational inquiry: Understanding curriculum and teaching through the arts* (pp. 301–11). Albany: SUNY Press.

Trousdale, A. M. (1990). A submission theology for black Americans: Religion and social action in prize-winning books about the black experience in America. *Research in the Teaching of English, 24*(2), 117–40.

Vandergrift, K. E. (1993). A feminist perspective on multicultural children's literature in the middle years of the twentieth century. *Library Trends, 41*(3), 354–77.

West, J., Weaver, D., & Rowland, R. (1992). Expectations and evocations: Encountering Columbus through literature. *The New Advocate, 5*(4), 247–63.

Yolen, J. (1994). An empress of thieves. *The Horn Book Magazine, 70*(6), 702–05.

Children's Books Cited

Armstrong, W. (1969). *Sounder.* New York: Harper & Row.

Block, F. L. (1989). *Weetzie bat.* New York: HarperCollins.

Block, F. L. (1993). *Missing angel Juan.* New York: HarperCollins.

Fox, P. (1973). *The slave dancer.* New York: Dell.

Isadora, R. (1979). *Ben's trumpet.* New York: Greenwillow.

Lasky, K. (1996). *True north: A novel of the Underground railroad*. New York: Scholastic.

Paterson, K. (1978). *The great Gilly Hopkins*. New York: HarperCollins.

Rosen, M. (1992). *Elijah's angel: A story for Chanuka and Christmas*. San Diego: Harcourt Brace Jovanovich.

Sebestyen, O. (1979). *Words by heart*. New York: Bantam.

Taylor, M. (1976). *Roll of thunder, hear my cry*. New York: Penguin.

Taylor, T. (1969). *The cay*. New York: Doubleday.

Zemach, M. (1982). *Jake and Honeybunch go to heaven*. New York: Farrar, Straus & Giroux.

IV The Perspectives of Educators on Cultural Authenticity

14 Can We Fly across Cultural Gaps on the Wings of Imagination? Ethnicity, Experience, and Cultural Authenticity

Mingshui Cai

The debate over who can create valid books about a particular culture has been raised intermittently since the late 1960s. For a time, the debate centered on widely circulated books about African Americans written by White authors, such as *Sounder* (Armstrong, 1969), *Words by Heart* (Sebestyen, 1979), *A Girl Called Boy* (Hurmence, 1982), *Ben's Trumpet* (Isadora, 1979), and *Jake and Honeybunch Go to Heaven* (Zemach, 1982). These books have been criticized for containing negative images and even racist overtones. The debate often centers on whether only an insider can write culturally authentic literature about ethnic experiences, or whether outsiders can use imagination to successfully capture ethnic experiences (Bishop, 1992).

This insider versus outsider debate is not just a verbal battle over the question of who can portray cultural authenticity in literary creation but also involves a power struggle over whose books get published. Some books by outsiders have been published and defended on the basis of their literary merits and quality of imagination, no matter how much they distort reality or stereotype people of the culture they attempt to represent (Bishop, 1984). In the name of literary excellence, cultural imposition has been perpetuated by the publication of these pseudo "multicultural" books. It is ironic that literary excellence is posed against

This chapter is a revised version of an essay entitled "Imagination, Ethnicity, and Cultural Authenticity" that appeared in *Multicultural Literature for Children and Young Adults: Reflections on Critical Issues* by Mingshui Cai. Copyright © 2002 by Greenwood Publishing Group, Inc., Westport, CT. Reprinted with permission by Greenwood Publishing Group, Inc. The essay appeared originally in *The New Advocate*, 1995, *8*(1), 1–16.

cultural authenticity as if falsifying reality and stereotyping characters do not violate the basic principles of literary creation.

This kind of literary evaluation emanates from a mentality that regards marginalized cultures as nonentities to be toyed with or trampled underfoot. The evaluation typically seems to be done in a nonpolitical form, but actually "furthers certain political uses of literature all the more effectively" (Eagleton, 1983, p. 209). Implicitly or explicitly, the literary and social-political aspects of the insider versus outsider issue are interrelated.

In this chapter, I address the literary question: Can we cross cultural gaps on the wings of imagination? The power of imagination has been used as a protective umbrella even for blatantly biased or poorly researched multicultural works. It also has been drawn upon as a source of inspiration for outsider authors to venture into unfamiliar cultures. Thus, the function of imagination in the creation of multicultural literature is an issue central to the insider versus outsider debate. If we clarify this issue, we not only shed some light on a literary question but also on the sociopolitical side of the debate.

The Crux of the Issue

In terms of literary creation the crux of the insider versus outsider issue is not the relationship between authors' ethnic background and literary creation but rather the relationship between imagination and experience. The realities reflected in multicultural literature are the culturally specific realities that ethnic groups experience. Ethnic literature is usually defined on the basis of its focus on the unique experiences of an ethnic group. For example, Asian American literature is literature that reflects the experiences of Asian Americans (Yokota, 1993). Ethnic literature is therefore culturally specific (Bishop, 1992).

Cultural authenticity is the basic criterion for evaluating multicultural literature. "The purpose of authentic multicultural literature," as Howard (1991) puts it, "is to help liberate us from all the preconceived stereotypical hang-ups that imprison us within narrow boundaries" (p. 92). If we agree with Howard, we accept cultural authenticity as a major criterion for evaluating a book. When imagination departs from the reality of ethnic culture, it leads to misrepresentation or distortion of reality. Lack of imagination may result in uninspired, insipid writings, but misrepresentation of reality is even worse; it perpetuates ignorance and bias and defeats the purpose of multicultural literature. Cultural authenticity is a basic criterion in the sense that no matter how imaginative and how well written a story is, it should be rejected if it *seriously* violates the integrity of a culture.

Cultural authenticity is a basic criterion for evaluating realistic literature, not a demand for "literature-as-propaganda." Putting the criterion of authenticity first does not mean neglecting other criteria for literary excellence, to which we subject all kinds of literature. We should collapse the dichotomy between a good and an authentic story. As Taxel (1986) points out, "demands for realistic, nonstereotyped characters, and for historical and cultural accuracy and authenticity in writing . . . need not conflict with the demand for literary excellence" (p. 249).

Those who believe only insiders can write valid literature about ethnic experiences hold a determinist view of the relationship between the author's ethnicity and the creation of authentic multicultural literature. According to this view, the reality of ethnic culture is inaccessible to any outsiders even if they have plenty of direct and indirect experience with that culture and a powerful imagination. Gates (2003) repudiates this determinist view in his comments on *The Education of Little Tree* (Carter, 1976): "No human culture is inaccessible to someone who makes the effort to understand, to learn, to inhabit another world" (p. 142). *The Education of Little Tree* is an example of a book written by an outsider and accepted as culturally authentic by insiders. The irony is that the author was not only an outsider but also a racist. Although this is an atypical example, it makes it impossible to insist that only insiders are able to write culturally authentic literature about ethnic experiences.

On the other hand, those who argue that outsiders can also write culturally authentic books through imagination overestimate the power of imagination to cross cultural gaps. In her debate with the author of *A Girl Called Boy*, Bishop (1984) cogently argued that White authors often fail to authentically reflect Black experience in their books because they have not been socialized into the ways of living, believing, and valuing that are unique to Black Americans. She emphasized the difficulty of an outsider acquiring the perspective of an ethnic culture. Those who believe in the all-powerful imagination do not seem to recognize the difficulties involved in crossing cultural gaps and tend to be carried away by their imagination. This imagination-omnipotent view is abetting the publication of books that distort ethnic realities and stereotype ethnic people, and it should command the serious attention of anyone who supports multiculturalism.

To further address the relationship between imagination and experience in the creation and critique of multicultural literature, I consider how cultural boundaries can pose challenges to outsiders who try to write about cultures other than their own, why it is important for an author to acquire the perspective of a culture before attempting to write about it, and how "brute facts" of cultures can impose constraints on an author's imagination. I illustrate my points with a comparative study of two novels.

Cultural Boundaries

People who believe in the outsider's power of imagination to cross cultural gaps raise questions about the uniqueness of ethnic realities, cultural identities, and the cultural specificity of ethnic literature. For example, Aronson (1993) states,

> No modern culture arose alone and "belongs" solely to a particular people. In modern America, it is very difficult to say where one ethnic group ends and another begins. Since we live in a shared society, and since we all grew up in worlds that are inflected with the accents of other cultures . . . we can all claim an "authentic" connection with many different cultures. (pp. 390–91)

It is true that every ethnic group in modern American society has a mixed cultural heritage, part of which is their traditional root culture and part of which is the American mainstream culture. But the duality of this cultural heritage, the influence of the mainstream culture or other cultures, has not obscured the distinction between the cultures of different ethnic groups. Since there are no autonomous regions for ethnic groups in the United States, geographically it is hard to say where one ethnic group ends and another begins. But in terms of tradition, customs, attitudes, beliefs, values, and experiences, each ethnic group has defining features that are culturally specific. If we map the cultural characteristics rather than the locations of people of different ethnic backgrounds, we see the distinct parameters of each culture that do belong solely to that ethnic group. As Wilson points out:

> We share certain mythologies. A history. We share political and economic systems and a rapidly developing, if suspect, ethos. Within these commonalities are specifics—specific ideas and attitudes that are not shared on the common ground. These remain the property and possession of the people who develop them. (qtd. in Bishop, 1992, p. 41)

Banks (1979) states that in the United States there exist "ethnic subsocieties which contain cultural elements, institutions, and groups which have not become universalized"(p. 247). If we deny this, then we deny the existence of ethnic cultures and ethnic literature.

Multiple acculturation, or mutual influence among cultures, enables all of us to claim some connection with many different cultures. But the key issue is the strength and authenticity of that connection. Banks (1979) proposes a four-level hierarchy of cross-cultural competency to provide a yardstick for testing "authentic connection" with another culture:

Level I: The individual experiences superficial and brief cross-cultural interactions.

Level II: The individual begins to assimilate some of the symbols and characteristics of the "outside" ethnic group.

Level III: The individual is thoroughly bicultural.

Level IV: The individual is completely assimilated into the new ethnic culture. (p. 251)

If an author's cross-cultural competence is at the first level, for instance, having visited a Chinatown, eaten some Chinese food, and read a couple of books about Chinese culture, can that author claim "authentic connections" with the Chinese culture and therefore be considered qualified to write a book about Chinese Americans? If most of us had achieved a high level of cross-cultural competence and could claim "authentic connections" with different cultures, then there would be true mutual understanding between different ethnic groups. Cultural rapport would result and racial tension would be greatly reduced. To overestimate people's cross-cultural competence is to lower the goal for multicultural education and to lose sight of the difficulties involved in the creation of multicultural literature.

Ethnic Perspective

A difficult task confronting writers who try to authentically reflect the reality of an ethnic culture, whether or not they are from that culture, is to grasp the perspective of that culture. An ethnic perspective is "a world view shaped by an 'ideological difference with the American majority'" (Bishop, 1984, p. 148). This perspective is reflected in culturally specific ways of living, believing, and behaving. The key is to take on the group's perspective "like actors who take on a role so thoroughly that they come to be identified with it (and occasionally act it out in real life)" (Miller-Lachmann, 1992, p. 17).

Authors of multicultural literature act as cultural messengers, but they may unconsciously impose their perspectives on the culture they are trying to re-create, exhibiting what Nodelman (1988) calls "cultural arrogance." As an example of unconscious cultural arrogance, he cited the translation of an Oriental tale in a collection called *Best-Loved Folk Tales of the World* (Cole, 1982). The story is about a woman who believes she is fated to marry one specific man. But the man proposes too late and dies of remorse. On the day of her wedding to another man, she stops by the grave of her true lover and says, "If we are intended to be man and wife, open your grave three feet wide" (p. 351). The grave opens instantly, and she jumps into it. Finally, the couple turn into rainbows. This story reflects a cultural belief that relationships among people, be it lovers or friends, are determined by fate. But the title of the story is mistranslated as "Faithful Even in Death," which, Nodelman believes, distorts the story to accommodate non-Oriental cultural assumptions:

> It implies that the woman's faithfulness is a matter of choice on her part, and therefore, a virtue that is being rewarded, whereas the story itself makes it clear that the woman had no choice but to love the man she was meant to love, and that the situation has nothing to do with virtue or reward. Only someone whose conception of story derived from European fairy tale could have distorted this tale making the moral health of the characters the driving force behind the events of the plot. (p. 232)

The subtleties and nuances of cultural beliefs and behaviors can be elusive to an outsider. In order to give authentic representation of an ethnic culture, an author must make the effort to enter the world of that culture, which can not be entered just on the wings of imagination, no matter how imaginative the author.

Insiders who want to write about their own ethnic cultures have great advantages over outsiders, but they also need to observe and learn. An ethnic group's perspective is not inherited through genes but acquired through direct and indirect experiences. "Just as authors from outside a group can write convincingly about that group, being a member of the group is no guarantee that an author's perspective will be with the group" (Miller-Lachmann, 1992, p. 18).

Lawrence Yep engaged in six years of research in libraries and universities to find the information needed to reconstruct a picture of what life was like in the Chinatown of the 1900s for his book *Dragonwings* (1975). Yep (1987) tried to understand the background that shaped him and "to develop a special sense of reality, a Chinese sense rather than an American sense" (p. 488). This "special sense of reality" is an equivalent of an ethnic perspective. It is this "special sense of reality" plus his powerful imagination that distinguishes his works from those that stereotype the Chinese. Some multicultural books fail not because the authors are unimaginative but because they have not acquired a culturally specific perspective.

Brute Facts

There is no denying that imagination is a great creative power, but imagination is limited by reality. As Rabinowitz (1987) points out, "brute facts" impose great constraints and limitations on the author's imagination, especially in historical fiction. This is also true of multicultural literature. Cultural differences are brute facts that limit the author's imagination and put constraints on literary choices to be made.

When an author writes about the Chinese dragon dance, for example, he or she has to work within the restraints of cultural conventions and represent the facts of the dance authentically. The picture book *Chin Chiang and the Dragon Dance* (Wallace, 1984) features the dragon dance, but the dance is confused with the lion dance. In the dragon dance, the head and tail of the dragon are held up with poles rather than directly by the hands as in the lion dance.

Another example is the picture book *The River Dragon* (Pattison, 1991), which contains ludicrous misrepresentations of cultural facts. It shows ancient Chinese people eating fortune cookies and swallow meat, and a dragon chasing the reflection of a moon to its death. Many know that the fortune cookie is an American invention, although not many people know that Chinese people eat the nest that a special species of swallow makes with secretion from its mouth. They do *not* eat swallow meat. The notion of the dragon chasing the moon is alien to Chinese culture and the god of the river would not die in the river.

Sometimes insider authors may also present inaccurate cultural information if they have not done sufficient research. The well-known Chinese American author Amy Tan (1991), for example, misrepresents some cultural details in her novel *Kitchen God's Wife*. For the most part, the story takes place in China during World War II, and, on the whole, the book truthfully recaptures that period in Chinese history from an insider's perspective. Nevertheless, it does contain minor inaccuracies. For example, a fortune-teller brags that "she had the luckiest fortune stick" for her customers (p. 121). This would immediately betray the fortune-teller as an impostor. A fortune-teller may boast accurate prophecy with fortune sticks but will never promise good fortune for a customer.

A more serious instance of inaccuracy occurs in the plot line when the protagonist/narrator is jailed, falsely accused by her husband. Her aunt comes to her rescue by telling the Kuomintang officials that they have imprisoned a relative of a high-ranking Communist leader, and since the Communists are soon coming to take over, they had better release her. This is historically untrue. Communists and Kuomintang were sworn enemies. Although they formed a united front twice against common enemies—once against the imperial rulers and another time against the Japanese invaders—they are fundamentally antagonistic toward each other. In the civil war period that followed the Second World War, they were again engaged in cutthroat battles. Before Kuomintang fled to Taiwan, they killed many communists held in prison. What the aunt says could only endanger her niece's life. Two chapters earlier, several characters talk about the enmity between the two parties: "All this talk about unity among all the parties—nonsense. If the Kuomintang find out we have a daughter who is a Communist—ssst!—all our heads could be rolling down the street" (p. 338). The inaccuracies in the novel show that the American–born and raised Chinese writer has not completely grasped the realities in the land of her ancestors. Nevertheless, these minor inaccuracies are outweighed by the authentic portrayal of the characters and historical spirit.

Brute facts are not just visible facts in the external reality but also invisible facts in the internal reality. Philips (1983) distinguishes visible and invisible culture. The former refers to the physical aspects of culture, while the latter refers to the mental and behavioral aspects. The brute facts of the invisible culture are especially difficult to grasp. True, authors can write about lives never directly experienced, but they need at least indirect experience as a basis for their imagination.

Imagination, as Coleridge defines it, has two functions. In terms of human perception, the function of imagination enables us to "grasp the forms first and then to visit and revisit them in our mind's eye thereafter" (Warnock, 1976, p. 204). In terms of literary creation, imagination enables the author to recreate "something out of the materials which we have acquired from perception" (p. 92). Imagination "dissolves, diffuses, dissipates, in order to re-create" (Coleridge, quoted in Leask, 1988, p. 136). Poetic imagination is a faculty to re-create rather than to create experience.

Ethnic experiences can never be accessed by imagination without any direct or indirect perception. For example, in *Children of the River* (Crew, 1989), the Cambodians believe that if you ruffle a child's hair you may scare away the child's intelligence or soul and that if you step over a person lying on the ground it is bad luck for that person. If the author has not read about or heard Cambodians talk about these culturally specific facts, can she get to know these facts by sheer imagination? One may imagine the fears of losing one's intelligence or soul, because they are common to human sensibility, but one cannot imagine the culturally specific situations in which the fears occur.

One of Hemingway's aesthetic principles provides a balanced view of the relationship between imagination and reality. According to Meyers (1985), Hemingway believed that "fiction must be founded on real emotional and intellectual experience and be faithful to actuality, but also be transformed and heightened by imagination until it becomes truer than mere facts" (p. 138). Faithfulness to truth is the essence of this principle. When engaged in writing, Hemingway "liked to know how it really was; not how it was supposed to be" (cited in Meyers, 1985, p. 138). To create an imaginary world of another culture, authors should never start with "how it was supposed to be."

Reality is distorted when the power of imagination is elevated to unlimited heights. In our postmodern era, the romantic dream that imagination is able to transcend reality to create a realm "in the full liberty of aesthetic play" (Schiller, quoted in Kearney, 1988, p. 186) has collapsed before the onslaught of realities. We can no longer make extravagant claims for imagination.

A Comparative Study of Two Novels

Historical fiction is often used as an example of imagination's power to harness experience (Bishop, 1984; Aronson, 1993). We can never experience the lives of those who lived before us but we can write historical fiction by relying on research and imagination. None of the people living now met Columbus personally, but many write about him. Imagination can synthesize the bits and pieces of information into an artistic representation, and, where information is not available, imagination will be relied on to restore the damaged tapestry of history (Fleishman, 1971). If it were imperative to write from direct experience, then there would be no historical fiction.

The question is: Who presents the real historical figure, the real Columbus? Whose work is true both to the facts and to the spirit of that historical period? Examination of biographies about Christopher Columbus reveals that we get as many images of Columbus as the perspectives from which he has been portrayed. If a historical novel distorts the facts and spirit of the past, does it succeed or fail? Of course, it fails, no matter how imaginative the author. Authenticity is the first criterion for historical fiction and for multicultural literature as well.

The author's ability to take on the perspective of other people living in the past or in other cultures is crucial to authenticity. Comparing books on the same subject may shed some light on this point. The Chinese involvement in the construction of the Transcontinental Railroad is the focus for many novels. Lawrence Yep (1993) has published a novel, *Dragon's Gate*, which I compare to *The Footprints of the Dragon* by Vanya Oakes (1949).

Both books imaginatively represent the trials and tribulations the Chinese experienced, and the courage and tenacity they demonstrated in overcoming the obstacles in their way. But there are some major differences between the two books. In Oakes's book, the White railroad bosses all treat the Chinese workers nicely. The only villains in the book are a Chinese foreman named Lee and his friend Mosquito. While the White bosses are kindly and benevolent, Lee acts like a slave driver, a falsification of history which covers up brutal exploitation of Chinese workers by White bosses. Can one truly believe that in that historical period there was no racial discrimination against and oppression of the Chinese?

The Chinese workers, especially the main character Hip Wo, are presented as workaholics, accepting the inhuman working conditions with very little complaint; to the contrary, they exhilarate in meeting the challenges of their work, no matter how dangerous. For example, when a group of Chinese workers is buried beneath an avalanche while battling against a severe snowstorm, their fellow workers are stunned with horror, but no one complains or protests. Hip Wo rationalizes that, "In such a great task as this there are always some who must perish" and urges others to continue working: "Come, there is work to be done. . . . There is nothing to be done for them" (p. 176). Neither he nor any other Chinese worker says anything about a decent burial for the dead. These images of Chinese workers are stereotypes.

In striking contrast, Yep's *Dragon's Gate* presents historical facts and realistic portraits of Chinese workers. It shows that Chinese workers were not only subjected to harsh living conditions and a dangerous working environment, but also victimized by White bosses. The arch villain in Yep's book is a White foreman called Kilroy. Another villain, the Chinese interpreter Shrimp, is only a hatchetman working for Kilroy. This foreman treats the Chinese as subhumans, relentlessly driving them to work under dangerous circumstances. He whips anyone who dares to defy him. He never calls a Chinese by his name; he addresses every

Chinese as John—someone without any identity. He prohibits his son Sean from befriending the Chinese boy, Otter, who is the narrator of the story. When he finds Sean having a meal together with Otter, Kilroy yells at Otter, "I said go, you filthy little heathen. You eat with your own kind" (p. 154). In *The Footprints of the Dragon*, you do not find this kind of racist slur, let alone mention of racist oppression.

Unlike the submissive and workaholic stereotypes in Oakes's book, the Chinese workers in Yep's book voice their grievances and fight for their rights when they can no longer put up with the inhuman treatment. After some workers are buried by an avalanche, the others refuse to go on working and insist that they look for the bodies in the snow. "We not send bodies home, their ghosts not happy" (p. 223), one of them argues. Yep's treatment of this incident is not only realistic but also culturally authentic. The Chinese believe that if the dead are not buried in their hometown, their ghosts will wander the world, howling all the time. In the end of the story, the Chinese workers stage a strike demanding basic human rights. As Yep points out in the afterword, the strike has a basis in history; however, it was ignored by the media during that period of time and later by authors like Oakes who wrote about the Chinese builders from a narrowly White perspective.

An author's perspective determines what he or she selects to include in a book. As Taxel (1992) points out, "narratives are value-laden selections from a universe of possibilities and . . . different selections tell different stories" (p. 22). Omission can be a form of distortion just as fabrication is.

Yep not only selected historical facts that are ignored or covered up by authors who hold an outsider's perspective, but also included details that capture the way Chinese workers looked at events, ideas, and people around them. In the new world, the Chinese workers experienced culture shocks and the novelty of a different culture. They perceived this unfamiliar world from a Chinese perspective, as in this discussion by Chinese workers trying to understand the Western concept of time: "Westerner will waste most anything—food, money, land—but not time. One T'ang hour makes two of theirs. They sliced up the hours into finer and finer portions . . . into minutes and minutes into seconds" (p. 92).

Yep shows various ways in which the Chinese view the world differently from the Westerners. When Otter first sees Sean eat with a fork, his first reaction is, "How do you keep from hurting yourself with that thing?" which looks like a "miniature metal rake" to him (p. 149). When two White men are fighting, Otter and other Chinese workers are puzzled as to why they do not use their feet. "Don't they know they have feet," Otter asks (p. 159). Obviously, the author is able to see through the Chinese workers' eyes and write about them from inside out. In Oakes's book, there is little description of the reactions of the Chinese workers to cultural differences because the author does not get inside the characters' minds or feelings. As a result, the characters appear to be two-dimensional.

Both Oakes and Yep demonstrate considerable power of imagination to evoke scenes of the past which neither of them has directly experienced. However, Yep's insider's vision coupled with careful research leads him to include historical facts that undo the stereotypes of Chinese laborers. If, without imagination, authors "would have been manipulating stick figures across a historical landscape" (Aronson, 1993, p. 391), then without drawing on historical facts, authors might have been creating phantoms in a realm of fantasy. The same holds true for multicultural literature.

There is a span of forty-five years between the two novels. Time has changed people's perspectives. An author of today would view the Chinese experiences during that period from a perspective very different from that commonly held in the past. Few would view Chinese laborers as subhumans or would make fun of their demand for an eight-hour working day, as one correspondent did in 1867 (Yep, 1993). Even people from parallel cultures have changed their self-perceptions, liberating themselves from the influence of the dominant culture that once degraded and demeaned them.

As people's perspectives change, their presentations of reality change, too. Perspective rather than imagination is the commanding factor in the creation of historical novels or multicultural literature. If *The Footprints of the Dragon* were written today, it might not be published, not because it is not imaginative but because it does not fit with the widely accepted version of that historical and cultural reality from the present-day perspective.

Concluding Thoughts

Before authors try to write about another culture, they should ask themselves whether they have acquired the specific perspective of that culture, in other words, whether they have developed a culturally specific sense of its reality. To bridge cultural gaps for their readers, authors should first cross these gaps themselves. If an author makes persistent efforts to understand a culture, he or she may finally be able to look at the world from the perspective of that culture and write about that culture as authentically as authors from that culture.

A good example of an author who makes earnest efforts to get inside a culture is Suzanne F. Staples, the author of *Shabanu* (1989), a powerful book about desert people in Pakistan. She studied their language, did research on their culture, mingled with them as much as she could, and was able to identify with them to the point of "laughing at the same things very spontaneously as they did." She had lived in Asia for about twelve years and was familiar with much of the culture before writing her novel. As she puts it, to write about another culture, a writer should not only be a better observer and listener but also be more empathetic, wanting to "be under somebody else's skin" (Sawyer & Sawyer, 1993, p. 166).

One can only hope that outsiders make similar painstaking efforts to take on perspectives of cultures other than their own before they write about them. If outsiders believe that they can fly across cultural gaps only on the wings of imagination, then, at best, they will create mediocre literature. Silvey (1993) points out that, in the past, great pieces of literature have come from an insider perspective because outsiders have not engaged in in-depth research. She predicts that "the great writers and illustrators for children of parallel cultures will, on the whole, continue to come from members of those cultures" (p. 133), unless changes are made to bring imagination and research together. Her prediction is based on her belief that "writers create best the landscape that they know—in their minds or in their hearts" (p. 133).

The goal of the multicultural literature movement is to give voice to those who have been historically silenced and to give authentic faces back to those whose images have been distorted. To achieve this goal, authors and illustrators from mainstream culture should work at taking on the perspective of other cultures. If they indulge in imagination without doing serious, in-depth research, there is a danger of imposing their perspective on the experiences of the people they portray and so perpetuating stereotypes and misrepresenting cultures other than their own.

References

Aronson, M. (1993). Letter to the editor. *The Horn Book, 69*(4), 390–91.

Banks, J. A. (1979). Shaping the future of multicultural education. *Journal of Negro Education, 48,* 237–52.

Bishop, R. S. (1984). A question of perspective. *The Advocate, 3,* 145–56.

Bishop, R. S. (1992). Multicultural literature for children: Making informed choices. In V. J. Harris (Ed.), *Teaching multicultural literature in grades K–8* (pp. 37–54). Norwood, MA: Christopher-Gordon.

Eagleton, T. (1983). *Literary theory: An introduction.* Minneapolis: University of Minnesota Press.

Fleishman, A. (1971). *The English historical novel.* Baltimore, MD: The Johns Hopkins Press.

Gates, H. L. Jr. (2003). "Authenticity," or the lesson of Little Tree. In D. L. Fox & K. G. Short (Eds.), *Stories matter: The complexity of cultural authenticity in children's literature* (pp. 135–42). Urbana, IL: National Council of Teachers of English.

Howard, E. F. (1991). Authentic multicultural literature for children: An author's perspective. In M. V. Lindgren (Ed.), *The multicolored mirror: Cultural substance in literature for children and young adults* (pp. 91–100). Fort Atkinson, WI: Highsmith Press.

Kearney, R. (1988). *The wake of imagination: Toward a postmodern culture.* Minneapolis: University of Minnesota Press.

Leask, N. (1988). *The politics of imagination in Coleridge's critical thought.* New York: St. Martin's Press.

Meyers, J. (1985). *Hemingway: A biography.* New York: Harper & Row.

Miller-Lachmann, L. (1992). *Our family, our friends, our world: An annotated guide to significant multicultural books for children and teenagers.* New Providence, NJ: Bowker.

Nodelman, P. (1988). Cultural arrogance and realism in Judy Blume's *Superfudge. Children's Literature in Education, 19*(4), 230–41.

Philips, S. U. (1983). *The invisible culture: Communication in classroom and community on the Warm Springs Indian Reservation.* New York: Longman.

Rabinowitz, P. J. (1987). *Before reading: Narrative conventions and the politics of interpretation.* Ithaca, NY: Cornell University Press.

Sawyer, W. E., and Sawyer, J. C. (1993). A discussion with Suzanne Fisher Staples: The author as writer and cultural observer. *The New Advocate, 6*(3), 159–69.

Silvey, A. (1993). Varied carols. *The Horn Book Magazine, 69*(2), 132–33.

Taxel, J. (1986). The black experience in children's fiction: Controversies surrounding award winning books. *Curriculum Inquiry, 16*(3), 245–81.

Taxel, J. (1992). The politics of children's literature: Reflections on multiculturalism, political correctness, and Christopher Columbus. In V. J. Harris (Ed.), *Teaching multicultural literature in grades K–8* (pp. 1–36). Norwood, MA: Christopher-Gordon.

Warnock, M. (1976). *Imagination.* Berkeley: University of California Press.

Yep, L. (1987). A Chinese sense of reality. In B. Harrison and G. Maguire (Eds.), *Innocence and experience: Essays and conversations on children's literature* (pp. 485–89). New York: Lothrop, Lee and Shepard

Yokota, J. (1993). Literature about Asians and Asian Americans: Implications for elementary classrooms. In S. M. Miller & B. McCaskill (Eds.), *Multicultural literature and literacies: Making space for difference.* Albany: State University of New York Press.

Children's Books Cited

Armstrong, W. H. (1969). *Sounder.* New York: Harper & Row.

Carter, F. (1976). *The education of Little Tree.* New York: Delacorte.

Cole, J. (1982). *Best-loved folktales of the world.* Garden City, NY: Doubleday.

Crew , L. (1989). *Children of the river.* New York: Delacorte.

Hurmence, B. (1982). *A girl called boy.* New York: Ticknor & Fields.

Isadora, R. (1979). *Ben's trumpet.* New York: Greenwillow.

Oakes, V. A. (1949). *Footprints of the dragon: A story of the Chinese and the Pacific railways.* Philadelphia: Winston.

Pattison, D. (1991). *The river dragon* (J. and M. S. Tseng, Illus). New York: Lothrop, Lee & Shepard Books.

Sebestyen, O. (1979). *Words by heart.* New York: Bantam.

Staples, S. F. (1989). *Shabanu: Daughter of the wind.* New York: Knopf.

Tan, A. (1991). *The kitchen god's wife.* New York: Putnam.

Wallace, I. (1984). *Chin Chiang and the dragon's dance.* New York: Atheneum.

Yep, L. (1975). *Dragonwings.* New York: HarperCollins.

Yep, L. (1993). *Dragon's Gate.* New York: HarperCollins.

Zemach, M. (1982). *Jake and Honeybunch go to heaven.* New York: Farrar, Straus & Giroux.

15 Accuracy and Authenticity in American Indian Children's Literature: The Social Responsibility of Authors and Illustrators

Elizabeth Noll

Native stories deal with the experiences of our humanity, experiences we laugh and cry and sweat for, experiences we learn from. Stories are not just for entertainment. We know that. The storyteller and writer has a responsibility—a responsibility to the people, a responsibility for the story and a responsibility to the art.

Lenore Keeshig-Tobias, "Not Just Entertainment"

O ne of the ways children learn about the world is through the books they read and the books that are read to them. Literature has the power to help children construct knowledge, to provide new perspectives on problems and issues they face, and to shape attitudes. Books that present accurate and authentic depictions of children's cultural backgrounds validate those cultures and communicate to all children a strong, positive message about our diverse society. When literature excludes certain cultures or contains misinformation and warped images, however, children's identities, attitudes, and understandings are negatively influenced. Bishop (1992) notes:

> If literature is a mirror that reflects human life, then all children who read or are read to need to see themselves reflected as part of humanity. If they are not, or if their reflections are distorted and ridiculous, there is the danger that they will absorb negative messages about themselves and people like them. Those who see only themselves or who [are] exposed to errors and misrepresentations are miseducated into a false sense of superiority, and the harm is doubly done. (p. 43)

This chapter is a revised version of an essay that originally appeared in *The New Advocate*, 1995, *8*(1), 29–43. Reprinted with permission.

Historically, children's literature has reflected the ideology of the dominant culture in society. This ideology, indicative of a primarily white authorship, reinforces a selective tradition in which "certain meanings . . . are selected for emphasis and certain other meanings . . . are neglected or excluded" (Williams, 1977, p. 115). The exclusion and distortions of oppressed groups in children's literature not only reflect but also perpetuate societal racism and inequitable social relations (Slapin & Seale, 1998; Taxel, 1981). Thus, children's literature becomes a means by which society transmits selective cultural understanding (Bishop, 1992; Kelly, 1974).

As people of color have spoken out against prejudice and racism, especially since the Civil Rights movement, there has been a slow trickle-down effect to children's literature. Long-overdue publication of books by members of nondominant cultures and increasing cultural consciousness on the part of white authors and illustrators have resulted in the emergence of culturally authentic literature. These books provide a powerful vehicle for confronting racism. The accurate information and rich images they convey have the capacity to break down negative stereotypes and encourage understanding and appreciation of different cultures.

Yet the fact that some children's literature presenting distorted views of cultures continues to be written and published strongly suggests that many authors, illustrators, and publishers are either ignorant of or unconcerned about the social and political impact of their books. Children's literature does not exist as an entity unto itself, "subject to scrutiny only as to its aesthetic value" (Greenfield, 1985, p. 20), but is inextricably linked to cultural assumptions that are communicated in the literature. These assumptions, along with children's prior experiences, influence the personal understandings children construct as they engage with text and illustrations.

Because authors and illustrators play a part in children's developing knowledge and attitudes, it is critical that they be responsible to their young audiences for portraying cultures accurately and authentically. In this chapter, I explore the challenges of creating culturally accurate and authentic literature through an examination of the portrayal of American Indian cultures in children's literature.

Determining Accuracy and Authenticity

Accuracy and authenticity of cultures are concerns in children's literature due to the prevalence of books created by "outsiders" to the cultures being portrayed. These outsiders often have limited knowledge of or personal experience with the culture they have chosen to depict. Their representations in text and illustrations grow out of their own cultural and literary experiences and understandings of underrepresented cultures. Thus, it is not surprising that literature created by outsiders frequently contains misinformation and disparaging stereotypes.

Defining who is an "insider" and who is an "outsider" is not necessarily as uncomplicated as it may appear. Being an American Indian author or illustrator does not make one an insider to all indigenous cultures, only to the individual's own culture. Furthermore, simply being of Navajo ancestry, for example, does not guarantee that an individual who has been raised outside of the culture can accurately portray what it means to be Navajo.

It is also true that the cultural understandings of "insiders" may differ greatly depending on their upbringing. Such would be the case for Navajos raised on a reservation versus those raised in an inner city. All authors and illustrators draw from their individual cultural experiences. Although their depictions of Navajo culture will not be identical, each will be authentic within its own context. Still, there are disagreements within cultures about the validity of depictions in literature. For example, the illustrations in *Monster Slayer* (Browne, 1991), though done by Navajo artist Baje Whitethorne, are not regarded as accurate by some Navajos (Kathy Short, personal communication, April 27, 1994).

For readers unfamiliar with the culture portrayed in a particular piece of literature, determining accuracy and merit is not always easy. There are, however, a number of resources available to help educators, parents, and others evaluate and select multicultural literature. The Council on Interracial Books for Children has published material on stereotyping, racism, and sexism, including *Guidelines for Selecting Bias-Free Textbooks and Storybooks* (1980) and, more specifically, *Unlearning "Indian" Stereotypes: A Teaching Unit for Teachers and Children's Librarians* (Racism and Sexism Resource Center for Educators, 1981). Though dated, these resources are still widely accepted. Slapin and Seale's *Through Indian Eyes: The Native Experience in Books for Children* (1998) is an excellent collection of critical reviews and essays on American Indian children's literature. In addition, their volume provides a list of specific criteria for evaluating literature. More recent reviews of children's literature by Slapin and Seale and others may be found at www.oyate.org, a Web site that is committed to portraying Native lives and histories honestly through a variety of means. Oyate is especially interested in the writing and illustrations of Native people.

Finally, Kuipers's *American Indian Reference Books for Children and Young Adults* (1995) offers evaluative criteria to guide selection of non-fiction American Indian books that can be adapted easily for fiction and for literature about other ethnic groups. Among her suggestions, Kuipers (1995) recommends examining the qualifications of authors and asking questions such as:

- Is the American Indian culture evaluated from the perspective of Indian values and attitudes rather than from those of another culture?

- Does the author recognize the diversity among tribes, cultures, and lifestyles?

- Does the literature recognize the American Indian people as an enduring race, not vanishing or assimilated?

- Are Indian languages and dialects respectfully portrayed?

- Does the literature portray realistic roles for American Indian women? (pp. 21–27)

It is important for those of us who share literature with children to raise these and other questions with them, to explore issues of stereotyping and prejudice, and to help them develop an appreciative yet critical stance toward literature. In acknowledging the existence of literature that is problematic, Lass-Kayser (1978) also emphasizes the importance of "hav[ing] books of diverse opinions, against whose ideas we could compare our own, to include or exclude whatever we choose to make ourselves better people, thinkers and readers" (p. 16). Furthermore, she looks to "young people's literature on Indians . . . to help us adults help children do this very thing" (p. 16).

Recognizing Culturally Offensive Images

For both writers and readers of children's literature who are outsiders to a particular culture, recognizing offensive images and language may be especially difficult when the distortions are consistent with their own cultural and literary experiences. To complicate matters further, these distortions may appear in otherwise sensitively written books.

Amazing Grace (1991), written by Mary Hoffman and illustrated by Caroline Binch, is the story of a young, imaginative Afro-Caribbean girl who faces racial discrimination. On one page, Grace imagines herself to be "Hiawatha, sitting by the shining Big-Sea-Water. . . ." The accompanying illustration depicts her in a common stereotypic Indian pose: wearing a full headdress, with long braids and a painted face, her arms folded across a bare chest, and sitting "Indian style." It is both ironic and unfortunate that this book, while intending to expose discrimination in one culture, perpetuates a distorted view of another.

In *Ten Little Rabbits* (Grossman & Long, 1991), the author and illustrator use rabbits instead of humans to present various American Indian cultural traditions. Illustrator Sylvia Long's depiction of "cute" animals dressed up like Indians is dehumanizing and condescending to the cultures she intends to represent. Furthermore, as McCarty (1995) points out, *Ten Little Rabbits* "perpetuates the monocultural stereotype that all Indian people are alike. In this case, they just wear different blankets" (p. 98).

In some children's literature the presence of any particular American Indian culture is so vague that accuracy is nearly impossible to determine. This monocultural portrayal of American Indians is a reflection of the authors' lack of recognition of the uniqueness of individual tribal cultures. Bishop (1992) describes this type of multicultural literature as universal, or generic. Typically, as in *The Yesterday Stone* (Eyvindson, 1992) and *My Grandmother's Cookie Jar* (Miller, 1987), neither the text nor the illustrations provide sufficient clues to define a particular tribe. Perhaps in these cases doing so is not the authors' and illustrators' intent, but even so, the cultural images conveyed in both books are questionable.

In *The Yesterday Stone*, the text is inexplicit and is potentially misleading. Young Anna's grandmother has a special stone which, when polished, produces images of the past. In the story she helps Anna find her own stone. As Anna drags a magnet across the ground, searching for the right stone, her grandmother says, "Be gentle. Ever so gentle. Your stone needs time to speak." The cultural origins of this practice are unclear. Perhaps the author was trying to convey oneness with nature, but the message communicated to young readers instead may be that American Indians have superhuman powers that allow them to communicate with inanimate objects.

My Grandmother's Cookie Jar, another generic picture book, centers on themes of family, love, and death. As in *The Yesterday Stone*, a girl whose features suggest an American Indian ancestry listens to her grandmother tell stories about the past. A cookie jar resembling an Indian's head contains the stories, and with each cookie a different adventure is told. When Grandma suddenly dies, the child's grandfather presents her with the cookie jar, "The jar is full of Grandma's love and Indian spirit. If you tell one of Grandma's stories with each of the cookies . . . then her spirit, and the spirit of those who went before her, will live on." Though no particular American Indian culture is portrayed, the notion that the spirit of anyone might live on in a cookie jar is puzzling at best.

Providing readers with factual information should be a basic responsibility of all authors and illustrators. Yet all too often, the written and artistic depictions of indigenous people and their cultures created by those outside of a culture suggest a disregard for accuracy. Virginia Driving Hawk Sneve, Lakota author of numerous books for children, comments, "There are non-Indian writers who have never even met an Indian but who do most of their writing from . . . what has been written in the past, and that's damaging" (V. Driving Hawk Sneve, personal communication, November 1993).

In *Knots on a Counting Rope* (1987), written by Bill Martin Jr. and John Archambault and illustrated by Ted Rand, it seems evident that neither the authors nor the illustrator did adequate background research. The "counting rope" around which the story is based has no significance in any American Indian culture, nor do the customs and dress represent a specific culture. Furthermore, as Slapin and Seale (1998) point out, the language and conversation are unauthentic. The romantic imagery in expressions such as "I hear it in the wounded wind" projects a stereotypical view of American Indian speech, and the depiction of the boy constantly interrupting his grandfather shows an ignorance of culturally appropriate behavior.

The Magic Weaver of Rugs: A Tale of the Navajo (Oughton & Desimini, 1994) contains a number of cultural inaccuracies, particularly in the illustrations, according to Navajo educators from Rough Rock, Arizona (T. L. McCarty, personal communication, May 18,1994). Neither the women's dress and hairstyles nor the rug designs are representative of Navajo culture, and the landscapes, which show saguaro cacti, do not accurately depict the terrain on the Navajo Reservation. In addition, the forbidding character of Spider Woman is portrayed far differently in appearance, disposition, and actions than the same figure in the well-known Navajo narrative.

Developing Cultural Consciousness

Though challenging, being an outsider to a culture does not necessarily preclude one from authentically depicting that culture. Gates (2003) notes that our personal histories do affect our abilities to write authentically about another culture, but that any culture is accessible to those who make a concerted effort to learn about and understand another world.

Non–American Indians whose work shows an understanding of the nuances of the culture they represent often have lived or worked on a reservation, thereby following Metis author Maria Campbell's advice: "If you want to write our stories then be prepared to live with us" (qtd. in Keeshig-Tobias, 1992, p. l00). Similarly, Joseph Bruchac, an Abenaki author of numerous books for children, suggests that "one way for a non-Native to gain this knowledge is by listening with care and respect to those who are within [the culture] rather than those who view it from the outside" (Dresang, 1999, n.p.). A number of non-Native writers and artists have done just that, basing their work on long-term, first-hand experiences with the cultures they portray. For example, white author Margaret Kahn Garaway draws on years of living and teaching young children on the Navajo Reservation in her portrayal of Native customs in *The Old Hogan* (1989a). Her depiction is well supported by the illustrations of Navajo artist Andrew Emerson Bia. Garaway's second book, *Ashkii and his Grandfather* (1989b), though rather didactic in style, also shows an understanding of Navajo relationships and lifestyle.

Similarly, author Paul Pitts, who also has lived and worked on the Navajo Reservation, presents the disparity between Navajo perspectives and mainstream cultural values in *Racing the Sun* (1988). Through the eyes and experiences of twelve-year-old Brandon, a Navajo boy being raised in a white, middle-class environment, Pitts skillfully exposes and counteracts a number of negative stereotypes. The author explains to his readers that he is committed to learning about the Navajo culture and that, to ensure the authenticity of his book, he has relied on the advice of a number of Navajo friends and colleagues.

Culturally specific humor is not easy for non-Native authors to grasp, but in *Who-Paddled-Backward-with-Trout*, Howard Norman (1987) effectively uses humor to tell about a young Cree boy who wants to earn a new name. Not only has Norman lived with the Swampy Crees, he speaks Cree and translates Cree stories (Slapin & Seale, 1998). His intimate understanding of both Cree culture and language makes it possible for him to write a humorous story that does not ridicule the culture.

Finally, Paul Goble, a non–American Indian reteller and illustrator of numerous picture books, including *Iktomi Loses His Eyes: A Plains Indian Story* (1999) and *Storm Maker's Tipi* (2001), is known for the distinctive style and authenticity of his artwork. He is described as "offer[ing] readers a seamless interpretation of Plains Indian art and lore, with paintings as sparkling as quillwork and as brilliant as the night sky and with an exciting narrative that evokes the storytellers of old"

(Goble, 1988, n.p.). He writes of a long-term relationship with Native cultures:

> I have collected many books, and examined museum collections, and have lived for thirteen years in the Black Hills of South Dakota, close to the Crow and Cheyenne reservations to the west in Montana, and several Sioux reservations to the north and east of our home. I feel that I have seen and learned many wonderful things from Indian people. (Goble, *Dream Wolf*, 1990, n.p.)

Indeed, as Goble explains in *Iktomi and the Ducks* (1990), his Iktomi books are based on the stories he has been told by Edgar Red Cloud, the great-grandson of the famous Chief Red Cloud. Goble is an adopted member of the Oglala Sioux and Yakima tribes and has received many awards for his books.

Unlike some books by non–American Indians, the work of these authors represents *culturally* conscious literature (Sims, 1982). Such books accurately depict cultural traditions, behaviors, and language and present an authentic perspective while also drawing on human universals. Authors and illustrators who, like those described above, have had personal associations with an Indian culture are more apt to create books that, even if not presenting an insider's view, benefit from a deep personal understanding of the culture.

Writing and illustrating a book that is culturally authentic is difficult, perhaps impossible, when the author or illustrator has no experience with the culture. According to Kruse:

> The farther one is removed from the experience of heritage about which one is writing, the more barriers there are to success, the harder writers have to work to attain cultural authenticity, and the more sensitive they need to be in order not to use hurtful images and erroneous cultural information. (qtd. in Madigan, 1993, p. 172)

Authors and illustrators who have limited experience with a culture but are concerned about providing accurate information must seek out reliable sources. Previously published books or other accounts to which authors might refer often contain misinformation and negative stereotypes. By basing their information on such portrayals, authors run the risk of perpetuating distorted views. Consulting with members of the culture and eliciting feedback on book drafts might be helpful in cases where personal relationships have been established. Factual material can also often be obtained from American Indian museums and cultural centers. Jamie Oliviero, author of *The Fish Skin* (1993), a retelling of a Cree legend, consulted with elders of the Norway House and

Cross Lake communities. In addition, Oliviero spoke with many other authorities of the Cree culture to develop the correct setting for the story.

Perhaps some of the most authentic stories are those in which the author solicits the actual words of a member of the culture to tell a traditional narrative or describe contemporary life. Slapin and Seale (1998) contend that "'good' stories—the ones we like best—get on the pages the same way they are told; they have the same style, rhythm and cadence as they would if an Elder were telling them" (p. 280).

Two Little Girls Lost in the Bush: A Cree Story for Children (Bear, 1991) is such a story. Told by Glecia Bear, a well-known Cree storyteller, to her niece Freda Ahenakew, the story is presented in both Cree and English. Through careful translation of the text, Ahenakew retains Glecia Bear's style of speech and voice. The accompanying illustrations are the work of talented Cree artist Jerry Whitehead.

A Boy Becomes a Man at Wounded Knee (Wood, 1992) is a narrative in which the voice of a young Lakota storyteller, Wanbli Numpa Afraid of Hawk, is reflected in the written text. Nine-year-old Wanbli describes his participation in the Si Tanka Wokiksuye, or Big Foot Memorial Ride, which commemorated the one-hundred-year anniversary of the Wounded Knee Massacre. His narrative is rich in detail about the ride as well as about the Lakota culture. In similar format, Diane Hoyt-Goldsmith uses American Indian children to narrate *Apache Rodeo* (1995) and *Potlach: A Tsimshian Celebration* (1997). Books such as these offer readers rich portrayals and authentic perspectives of Native customs, lifestyles, and relationships.

Historical Multicultural Literature

For authors and illustrators of historical children's literature, the task of presenting accurate cultural information is even greater than it is for creators of contemporary literature. Firsthand accounts may be difficult or impossible to come by, requiring authors to rely on second- or thirdhand accounts of history for their body of knowledge. To complicate matters further, these accounts may contradict one another. Yet, even when the accounts agree, there is no assurance that they are accurate, only that they represent commonly accepted interpretations of history.

Authors of historical fiction tell a story based on a time or event in the past. Their challenge is to balance the telling of a good story with maintaining an accurate historical view. Taxel (1986) contends that their responsibilities differ from those of their nonfiction counterparts. He suggests two conditions for authors of historical fiction. The first is to determine whether the liberties taken are for the purpose of improving the overall literary quality of the piece. The second condition concerns whether or not the liberties taken result in a distorted or demeaning view of the culture or an attitude of superiority by others toward the culture.

In the perennially popular *Little House* books (Laura Ingalls Wilder) and the more recent *The Indian in the Cupboard* series (Lynne Reid Banks), there are a number of instances in which a demeaning view of American Indians is presented. In *Little House on the Prairie* (1971), Wilder writes: "The naked wild men . . . were tall, thin, fierce-looking. . . . Their eyes were black and still and glittering, like snakes' eyes" (p. 134) and "Their faces were bold and fierce and terrible" (p. 139). Elsewhere, the Indians are described as "dirty and scowling and mean" (p. 233). Later, the Ingalls' neighbor, Mr. Scott, comments, "The only good Indian is a dead Indian" (p. 284), a statement reflective of Mrs. Ingalls's sentiments expressed throughout the book.

This statement also is reflective of attitudes in the time period in which the *Little House* books take place. Fear of American Indians and racism were common among white settlers, and Wilder's description is an accurate representation of her own childhood experiences. Such is not the case in *Return of the Indian* (1986), which is perhaps as much fantasy as it is historical fiction. The distorted and demeaning cultural images in this book have no historical justification, and they in no way improve the overall literary quality. Banks writes: "Omri saw . . . the mindless destructive face of a skinhead just before he lashed out. . . . The Algonquin licked his lips, snarling like a dog" (p. 159). Slapin and Seale (1992) ask, "How could [a Native child] reading this fail to be damaged? How could a white child fail to believe that he is far superior to the bloodthirsty, sub-human monsters portrayed here?" (p. 122).

In both Wilder's and Banks's books, the Indians are also depicted as being inarticulate. Michael Dorris (1992), author of *Guests* (1999) and *The Window* (1997), among other books, notes, "It's hard to take seriously, to empathize with a group of people portrayed as speaking ungrammatical language. . . . Frozen in a kind of pejorative past tense, these make-believe Indians are not allowed to . . . be like real people" (p. 27).

It should be pointed out that both Wilder and Banks do include perspectives that differ from these distorted views. For example, in *Little House on the Prairie*, Laura wonders aloud why the Indians should have to move from Indian Territory to make room for the white settlers. And in *The Indian in the Cupboard*, Omri and his friend Patrick question whether it is right for them to control Little Bear and the other minia-ture human beings. These examples and the contrasting negative per-spectives quoted above offer ideal opportunities for initiating discus-sion with children about stereotyping and prejudice.

Joann Mazzio, author of adolescent contemporary and historical fiction, discusses the moral challenges she faces in providing accurate perspectives without perpetuating negative images. About researching and writing her historical novels, Mazzio says:

> First of all, before everything, if you're writing a novel for any-body, you have to tell a good story. But when you're writing his-torical fiction . . . you have to remember that sometimes this fic-tion might be their first exposure to a particular historical episode or a particular historical attitude. So you have a moral obligation to be as accurate as possible. In writing *Leaving Eldorado*, for ex-ample, I was always walking a tightrope in trying to present his-tory accurately and at the same time, making sure that I wasn't perpetuating negative stereotypes of the cultures my characters represent.
>   My next historical novel is on the expeditions of John Freemont and Kit Carson, and it will be more difficult than *Leaving Eldorado*. My protagonist will be a French American boy who will have to hold Freemont and Carson in awe because they were heroes of the time. He is going to admire them for the very things that we deplore these days, but that was part of his culture. Kit Carson will come into camp with the scalps of Indians he's killed and this is something the boy can't disapprove of because he is a prod-uct of his age. So here again I walk that tightrope. (J. Mazzio, personal communication, October 14, 1993)

Mazzio effectively copes with this challenge by creating predica-ments for her characters that force them to question commonly held beliefs of the time. In this way she is able to accurately portray the pre-vailing views of the era while also presenting an alternative view. Mazzio also strives for accuracy in her novels by carefully researching her topics. For *Leaving Eldorado* (1993), she consulted books, diaries, oral histories, periodicals, and catalogs published in the time period of her novel. She also visited museums to get a sense of the clothing of the era and became familiar with the geographic region in which her novel is set. The rich, detailed information she gathered is interwoven through-out her novel, providing factual accuracy and a sense of authenticity.

In contrast to Mazzio's novel are the young adult novels *The Place at the Edge of the Earth* (Rice, 2002) and *My Heart Is on the Ground: The Diary of Nannie Little Rose, A Sioux Girl* (Rinaldi, 1999) and the picture book *Brother Eagle, Sister Sky: A Message from Chief Seattle* (Seattle, 1991).

With the two young adult novels, both of which take place on the site of the Carlisle Indian Industrial School, it appears that neither Rice nor Rinaldi carefully researched Lakota culture of the late 1800s. Rice makes a number of factual errors, such as having the children refer to themselves as Indians (or, in Rinaldi's novel, Sioux) and having a child sing a death chant. Furthermore, as Slapin and Seale (n.d.) assert, there is no record of a student killing a principal at the school or of a student dying as a result of a lynching. Rinaldi's *My Heart Is on the Ground*, which is part of Scholastic's popular Dear America series, also contains numerous historical and cultural inaccuracies as well as stereotypical language. Her protagonist, Nannie, refers to her diary as "the white man's talking leaves" (p. 3) and writes of words not being "empty gourds, with nothing inside to quench our need, but full of meaning, from which I drink hope" (p. 29).

Brother Eagle, Sister Sky: A Message from Chief Seattle is based on misinformation about the speech given by Chief Seattle in 1854. As the creator and illustrator Susan Jeffers notes in the afterword: "The origins of Chief Seattle's words are partly obscured by the mists of time." Euphemisms aside, Chief Seattle's words have been obscured and distorted by the interpretations of many individuals, including Jeffers herself. In fact, according to some historians, these "interpretations" are not even based on Chief Seattle's speech. Rather, they are the interpretations of a screenwriter's 1971 fictitious version of the original speech, written for a film documentary on pollution.

Chief Seattle's speech, itself translated into English by Henry Smith many years after the fact, focused on the differences between American Indian and Christian spirituality. Selections from the speech appear in *Chief Seattle* (Buerge, 1992), which the author notes is the only written text based on a firsthand account. Unlike this book, fictionalized versions of Chief Seattle's speech do not reflect his original message. In *Brother Eagle, Sister Sky*, Chief Seattle is quoted as saying: "What will happen when the buffalo are all slaughtered?" and "When the view of the ripe hills is blotted by talking wires?" Had Jeffers done her research, she would have discovered that there were no buffalo within hundreds of miles of the chief's home and that the telephone was not even invented until after he died.

When questioned about her portrayal of Chief Seattle's message, Jeffers commented, "Basically, I don't know what he said—but I do know that the Native American people lived this philosophy, and that's what is important" (qtd. in Egan, 1992, p. 13). Apparently, Jeffers believes that her lack of accuracy is justified by her positive depiction of

American Indian values, and it appears that there are many who would agree with her. Even after a front-page exposé in the *New York Times*, sales of *Brother Eagle, Sister Sky* continued to soar (Murray, 1993). By 1999 almost half a million copies of the book had been sold (Slapin & Seale, n.d.).

At least as troubling as Jeffers's inaccurate portrayal of Chief Seattle's speech is her assertion of her right to speak for all American Indians. Although some might argue that this is an example of artistic freedom, such a "right" does not excuse Jeffers, or other children's authors and illustrators, from an examination of their responsibility to their young audiences and to the cultures they depict.

Conclusion

Writers and artists who choose to portray cultures to children through literature do have a responsibility to ensure that they are providing accurate information and authentic cultural images. Their work offers young readers a powerful means for developing personal understandings of the diversity and uniqueness of all people. It is crucial that those understandings be built upon a foundation of facts, not misinformation, distortions, and stereotypes.

The examples of children's literature depicting American Indian cultures discussed in this chapter are characteristic of literature about other cultures. Similar examples can be found in books that describe African Americans, Asian Americans, Latinos, and people of other ethnicities and cultures. There is a wide range in the quality of multicultural literature in terms of both its aesthetic value and its cultural accuracy. Some of the finest books are those that possess high quality on both counts, thereby offering children wonderfully rich opportunities to construct knowledge about their own and other cultures.

Authors and illustrators bear a responsibility to their young audiences, but they are not the only ones who influence children through literature. All of us—authors, illustrators, editors, publishers, librarians, teachers, and parents—share a role in supporting children's positive experiences with books. Together and individually, we must insist upon literature that is culturally accurate and authentic and that includes a strong representation by authors and illustrators of the cultures portrayed. As author Milton Meltzer (1989) tells us: "All of us . . . are joined in the collective effort to shape a world where every child may grow in the spirit of a community that fulfills the best in us" (p. 157).

References

Bishop, R. S. (1992). Multicultural literature for children: Making informed choices. In V. J. Harris (Ed.), *Teaching multicultural literature in grades K–8* (pp. 37–53). Norwood, MA: Christopher-Gordon.

Council on Interracial Books for Children (1980). *Guidelines for selecting bias-free textbooks and storybooks.* New York: Author.

Dorris, M. (1992). "I" is not for Indian. In B. Slapin & D. Seale (Eds.), *Through Indian eyes: The native experience in books for children* (3rd ed., pp. 27–28). Philadelphia: New Society.

Dresang, E. T. (1999). An interview with Joseph Bruchac. Retrieved August 4, 2002, from http://www.education.wisc.edu/ccbc/bruchac.htm.

Egan, T. (1992, April 21). Chief's 1854 warning tied to 1971 ecological script. *The New York Times*, pp. 1, 13.

Gates, H. L. Jr. (2003). "Authenticity," or the lesson of Little Tree. In D. L. Fox & K. G. Short (Eds.), *Stories matter: The complexity of cultural authenticity in children's literature* (pp. 135–42). Urbana, IL: National Council of Teachers of English.

Greenfield, E. (1985). Writing for children—A joy and a responsibility. In D. MacCann & G. Woodard (Eds.), *The black American in books for children: Readings in racism* (2nd ed., pp. 19–22). Metuchen, NJ: Scarecrow.

Keeshig-Tobias, L. (1992). Not just entertainment. In B. Slapin & D. Seale (Eds.), *Through Indian eyes: The native experience in books for children* (pp. 97–100). Philadelphia: New Society.

Kelly, R. G. (1974). Literature and the historian. *American Quarterly, 26,* 141–59.

Kuipers, B. J. (1995). *American Indian reference and resource books for children and young adults* (2nd ed.). Englewood, CO: Libraries Unlimited.

Lass-Kayser, M. J. (Ed.). (1978). *Books on American Indians and Eskimos: A selection guide for children and young adults.* Chicago: American Library Association.

Madigan, D. (1993). The politics of multicultural literature for children and adolescents: Combining perspectives and conversations. *Language Arts, 70,* 168–76.

McCarty, T. L. (1995). What's wrong with *Ten Little Rabbits? The New Advocate, 8*(2), 97–98.

Meltzer, M. (1989). The social responsibility of the writer. *The New Advocate, 2,* 155–57.

Murray, M. (1993). The little green lie. *Reader's Digest, 143*(855), pp. 100–104.

Racism and Sexism Resource Center for Educators (1981). *Unlearning "Indian" stereotypes: A teaching unit for elementary teachers and children's librarians.* New York: Author.

Sims, R. (1982). *Shadow and substance: Afro-American experience in contemporary children's fiction.* Urbana, IL: National Council of Teachers of English.

Slapin, B., & Seale, D. (Eds.). (1992). *Through Indian eyes: The native experience in books for children.* Philadelphia: New Society.

Slapin, B., & Seale, D. (Eds.). (1998). *Through Indian eyes: The native experience in books for children.* Los Angeles, CA: American Indian Studies Center, University of California.

Slapin, B., & Seale, D. (n.d.). Books to avoid. *Oyate* [Review of the book *The place at the edge of the earth*]. Retrieved August 4, 2002, from http://www.oyate.org/books-to-avoid/edgeEarth.html.

Taxel, J. (1981). The outsiders of the American revolution: The selective tradition in children's fiction. *Interchange on Educational Policy, 12,* 206–28.

Taxel, J. (1986). The black experience in children's fiction: Controversies surrounding award winning books. *Curriculum Inquiry, 16,* 245–81.

Williams, R. (1977). *Marxism and literature.* Oxford, England: Oxford University Press.

Children's Books Cited

Banks, L. R. (1980). *The Indian in the cupboard.* New York: Avon.

Banks, L. R. (1986). *The return of the Indian.* New York: Doubleday.

Bear, G. (1991). *Two little girls lost in the bush: A Cree story for children* (F. Ahenakew & H. C. Wolfart, Eds. and Trans.). Saskatoon: Fifth House.

Browne, V. (1991). *Monster slayer: A Navajo folktale.* Flagstaff, AZ: Northland.

Buerge, D. M. (1992). *Chief Seattle.* Seattle, WA: Sasquatch Books.

Dorris, M. (1997). *The window.* New York: Hyperion.

Dorris, M. (1999). *Guests.* New York: Hyperion.

Eyvindson, P. (1992). *The yesterday stone.* Winnipeg, Canada: Pemmican.

Garaway, M. K. (1989a). *The old hogan.* Cortez, CO: June Eck.

Garaway, M. K. (1989b). *Ashkii and his grandfather.* Tucson, AZ: Treasure Chest.

Goble, P. (1988). *Her seven brothers.* New York: Bradbury.

Goble, P. (1990). *Dream wolf.* New York: Bradbury.

Goble, P. (1990). *Iktomi and the ducks.* New York: Orchard.

Goble, P. (1999). *Iktomi loses his eyes: A Plains Indian story.* New York: Orchard.

Goble, P. (2001). *Storm Maker's tipi.* New York: Atheneum.

Grossman, V., & Long, S. (1991). *Ten little rabbits.* San Francisco: Chronicle.

Hoffman, M. (1991). *Amazing Grace.* New York: Dial.

Hoyt-Goldsmith, D. (1995). *Apache Rodeo.* New York: Holiday House.

Hoyt-Goldsmith, D. (1997). *Potlatch: A Tsimshian Celebration.* New York: Holiday House.

Jeffers, S. (1991). *Brother eagle, sister sky: A message from Chief Seattle* (S. Jeffers, Illus.). New York: Dial.

Martin, B. Jr., & Archambault, J. (1987). *Knots on a counting rope.* New York: Henry Holt.

Mazzio, J. (1993). *Leaving Eldorado.* Boston: Houghton Mifflin.

Miller, M. (1987). *My grandmother's cookie jar.* Los Angeles: Price Stern Sloan.

Norman, H. (1987). *Who-paddled-backward-with-trout.* Boston: Little, Brown.

Oliviero, J. (1993). *The fish skin* (B. Morrisseau, Illus.). New York: Hyperion.

Oughton, J., & Desimini, L. (1994). *The magic weaver of rugs: A tale of the Navajo.* Boston: Houghton Mifflin.

Pitts, P. (1988). *Racing the sun.* New York: Avon.

Rice, B. F. (2002). *The place at the edge of the earth.* New York: Clarion.

Rinaldi, A. (1999). *My heart is on the ground: The diary of Nannie Little Rose, A Sioux Girl.* New York: Scholastic.

Wilder, L. I. (1971). *Little house on the prairie.* New York: Harper & Row.

Wood, T., with Afraid of Hawk, W. N. (1992). *A boy becomes a man at Wounded Knee.* New York: Walker.

16 Accuracy Is Not Enough: The Role of Cultural Values in the Authenticity of Picture Books

Weimin Mo and Wenju Shen

Culture is largely a seamless and shared significant experience that pragmatically consists of organized events of patterned interactions (Bhugra et al., 1999). It influences the way we view ourselves, society, and human relations and interactions. It determines our assumptions about social behaviors or customs and reflects what we value and believe to be true. Our cultural perceptions crystallize early in our lives. In a way, culture is a psychological built-in software in each of us, providing us with a kind of sensitivity for cultural appropriateness.

Our cultural responses are, most of the time, spontaneous. Because of the spontaneity of cultural perception, it is not easy for us to view reality from a cultural perspective that differs from our own. According to Nostrand (1989), it takes years of careful study to make up for the native experience that begins in childhood. Therefore, mistakes of inauthentic cultural depiction are inevitable when only a few cluttered concepts are used as cues to create picture books.

For instance, both the literary and artistic work of *Tikki Tikki Tembo* (Mosel, 1968) have serious problems of cultural authenticity. The author does not reveal the source of the folktale. Culturally, Chinese full names will not go beyond four syllables. Therefore, to Chinese, the name of the protagonist, Tikki Tikki Tembo-No Sa Rembo-Chari Bari Ruchi-Pip Peri Pembo, sounds more like the name of a foreign aristocrat. The culture depicted in the illustrations seems to be more Japanese than Chinese. Even *The Horn Book*'s comments miss the point by saying that "the artist has extended the story with wonderful droll ink-and-wash drawings that combine imaginative beauty with a true Chinese spirit"(qtd. in Mosel, 1968, back cover).

Progress in Cultural Authenticity: Achievement over a Half Century

The mainstream culture in the United States has been strongly influenced by Eurocentrism. Historically, minorities were unfairly treated and their cultures depreciated. There have been all kinds of slurs, stereotypes, and assumptions that are racially coded for every minority group. Unfortunately, some of these have been passed on from generation to generation. Authors and illustrators are not immune to this influence, and it has been reflected in their picture books. These books, in turn, influence readers of the new generation, and so the issue of cultural authenticity remains an ongoing concern. In this chapter we examine cultural authenticity as related to picture books about Asians and Asian Americans.

Asian cultures and Asian Americans were once the least represented in picture books, but much progress has been made in the quantity and quality of books over the last half century. In 1976 the Council on Interracial Books for Children (CIBC) found that out of twenty-four books published from 1945 through 1976, twenty-two were considered to be racist, sexist, and elitist, and Asians were depicted as looking alike and living together in quaint neighborhoods of large cities and clinging to their outmoded traditions. Harada (1995) studied issues of ethnicity, authenticity, and quality in Asian American picture books from 1983–1993. The results indicated great improvement in the authenticity of picture books:

1. characters in more than 90 percent of the works are positive, non-stereotyped portrayals;

2. Asian-American characters assume a proactive role in resolving their own problems and forging cross-cultural bonds in almost 80 percent of the stories;

3. derogatory language and parodied speech are absent from all of the work;

4. historical information, when present, is accurately presented in all of the titles;

5. cultural details, when included, are authentically described in almost 70 percent of the work;

6. Asian-Americans are realistically depicted through illustrations and photographs in almost 80 percent of the books. (pp. 140–141)

When the results of the two studies are compared, it is encouraging to see the progress achieved over a half-century in the authenticity of picture books. However, when we further studied the findings and the focus on stereotypes, the question of what is authenticity came to our minds.

Accuracy versus Authenticity

We questioned whether authenticity equals nonstereotyped portrayals, positive images, lack of derogatory language, accurate historical information, and accurate cultural details. Surprisingly, Harada did not define authenticity in her study beyond stating that the first issue was "authenticity versus stereotyping" (p. 137). She also mentioned Yokota's elements of "cultural accuracy," which include "richness of details, authentic handling of dialogue and relationships, and sensitive treatment of issues" (p. 137).

In our opinion, authenticity is not just accuracy or the avoidance of stereotyping but involves cultural values and issues/practices that are accepted as norms of the social group. Although there is conceptual overlap, the various aspects of cultural accuracy do not constitute an appropriate definition for cultural authenticity. Strictly speaking, accuracy basically focuses on cultural facts instead of values. Yokota (1993) explained the elements of accuracy, stating that, first, "rich cultural details" give insight into the nuances of daily life." Second, "authentic dialogue and relationships" show how characters depicted in the story "really speak" instead of being "generic non-Caucasians." Third, "inclusion of members of a 'minority' group for a purpose" helps story characters "to be regarded as distinct individuals whose lives are rooted in their culture, no matter how minor the role in the story"(p. 160).

These elements only answer the question of whether the facts posited in the story believably exist in that culture. They do not tell whether these facts represent the values that most people of the social group do or do not believe.

The only element that Yokota directly relates to cultural values is the treatment of important cultural issues. Yokota briefly mentions, "There are many issues that are central to each culture. It is important to give these issues a realistic portrayal and explore them in depth so that readers may be able to formulate informed thoughts on them" (p. 160). But what does it mean to portray those issues and explore them in depth? That is what the issue of *authenticity* is all about! Obviously, that theme was not in the scope of Yokota's article, and she did not further elaborate on it.

The term "cultural accuracy" does not provide substantial conceptual content. The use of stereotyping as an antonym for accuracy is not as simple as flipping over a pancake to enable us to see the opposite side. It is difficult to examine the authenticity of multicultural children's literature without further clarifying such vague general terms as "richness of details," "authentic handling," and "sensitive treatment" in the sense of cultural values, especially those related to the "issues that are central to each culture." And we do believe there is a fundamental difference between the concept of authenticity and the concept of nonstereotyping.

The first two explanations of the word *authentic* listed in *Webster's New Collegiate Dictionary* (1989) are: "(1) authoritative, (2) worthy of acceptance or belief as conforming to fact or reality: trustworthy" (p. 117). These explanations shed some light on the nature of authenticity. Hearne (1993b) urged writers and illustrators to establish their cultural authority as authors of a particular narrative. That means they need to train themselves to distinguish the values, facts, and attitudes that members of the culture as a whole would consider worthy of acceptance or belief.

Some cultural facts and practices may be realistically reflected in the story but may not be considered authentic because members of the culture do not agree with each other on interpretation of their values. Moreover, within a culture, different values are constantly in conflict. New values, beliefs, and attitudes are fighting to take hold, while old ones, though dying, are still valid for a minority. For instance, people usually think of ancient China as a male-dominated society. However, before the Confucian ethical code sank its roots into Chinese culture, the original Chinese society was a matriarchal system. There was no seclusion of women at that time; divorce and remarriage were once popular (Lin, 1936).

Cultures also affect each other. They constantly absorb each other's values, attitudes, and beliefs; sometimes, they actively clash. Therefore, cultural values are not stagnant. When an author's version of a culture can be accommodated inside the range of values acceptable within that social group, a measure of authenticity has been achieved. That is why cameras may provide realistic pictures but not always authentic ones.

In this chapter, we examine several aspects of the connection between cultural authenticity and issues of cultural values. We particularly focus on the representation of values that some may say are accurate because they are or have been part of a culture, but that are not culturally authentic within a particular book. While cultural accuracy relies on a culture's social practices, cultural authenticity is based on whether or not the cultural practice represents its central code. In addition, even when the practice is part of a culture's central code, we believe that cultural authenticity should never be a license to introduce values that violate basic human rights.

Authenticity and Cultural Acceptance

A good case in point is the 1939 Caldecott winner *Mei Li*, written and illustrated by Thomas Handforth. Even by today's strict multicultural literature standards, *Mei Li* is a commendable book in terms of its authentic literary quality. A girl named Mei Li refuses to accept the inferior position the Confucian ethical code designated for women and has exciting adventures at the New Year Fair. The story reflects the essence of cultural values at that time. By the time the Ching Dynasty was overthrown in 1911, the oppressive and discriminative attitude about women, which was an important part of Confucian ideology, was severely renounced by the Chinese.

However, Handforth's judgment of aesthetic authenticity is not as accurate as his judgment of value authenticity. Problems in his artwork hurt its endurance as a magnificent book. For instance, the stone lions look like dogs and the characters unrealistically use fans in Peking's winter. A more significant error is his depiction of the bound feet of Mei Li's mother. It is not that the pictures are not realistic. There were many women in China in 1939 with bound feet. Nevertheless, this cruel practice of binding girls' feet had been hated since the day it started and was officially banned when the Ching Dynasty was overthrown in 1911. It was no longer a cultural value acceptable to most Chinese at the time this book was written. The practice of binding feet was viewed as a sexual fetish that had lost appeal long before being officially banned and was severely criticized as a symbol of seclusion and suppression of women (Lin, 1936).

Since the 1911 revolution, people in China have viewed bound feet as a symbol of women's humiliated past and an emotional scar. Since the deformation of feet could not be reversed, people held a cultural attitude of either paying no attention or avoiding mention of them. At that time many women with bound feet wore shoes for natural feet by stuffing cotton balls inside the shoe tips instead of wearing their own small shoes to cover their deformed feet.

A small sign of curiosity about bound feet from an "outsider" could stir up as much resentment as pulling a wig off a bald-headed person in public today. Only outsiders would go to China and enjoy the exotic flavor of bound feet. If a Chinese artist had created the illustrations for this picture book, the mother's feet would have undoubtedly looked natural without any deformation.

Throughout more than four thousand years of recorded history of China, foot binding was practiced only for about five hundred years. Depiction of bound feet twenty-seven years after it was banned should be justifiably rejected, especially considering the feelings about bound feet by the majority of Chinese people at that time. Based on these problems we could call *Mei Li*'s artwork nonstereotyped because the scenes were depicted realistically, but we would argue that the book is not authentic because it does not reflect the cultural values of that time period.

Authenticity and Cultural Values

Several studies indicate that folktales represent an extremely high percentage of multicultural picture books. They have "become, to many folklorists' horror, one of the primary tradition-bearers of the Twentieth Century" (Hearne, 1993a, p. 24). Cultural experience and research are the only ways to gain insights into the heart of a culture. No one holds an inborn patent on it. As Harada's study shows, cultural insiders "may not always identify with their own culture" (p. 138).

Ed Young has ingeniously re-created and/or adapted a number of Chinese folktales. His illustrations for Ai-Ling Louie's (1982) *Yeh-Shen: A Cinderella Story from China* and his illustrated adaptation *Lon Po Po: A Red Riding Hood Story from China* (1989) received critical acclaim, and the latter won the Caldecott Medal. However, two other books, one featuring his illustrations for Lafcadio Hearn's *The Voice of the Great Bell* (1989), and the other for *Red Thread* (1993), authored by Young himself, fail to meet our criteria for authentic understanding of cultural values.

In *The Voice of the Great Bell* a girl sacrifices her life by leaping into the lava of molten metal to become part of the great bell to save her father from the death penalty. Hearne (1993b) raises a question pertinent to evaluating this book: "How do contemporary adaptation and art reflect a folktale's culture of origin?" (p. 33). Although the theme of *The Voice of the Great Bell* rings with a strong Confucian ethical notion of filial piety, the retold story is problematic because of its didactic nature and the difference between the ideal and the actual practice of this value.

The original story is a literary illustration of the rules of filial piety laid out in Confucian classics like *Book of Rites* (Chai, 1967) that require children to make inhuman sacrifices, humiliating submission, and outrageous subservience. These rules also instill destructive guilt feelings. In ancient times, the rules of filial piety even enabled parents to let their children replace them in jail when they were convicted. This story bears a strong resemblance to one of the traditional didactic stories of *The Twenty-Four Examples of Filial Piety* (1995) in which a couple bury their son alive in order to save money for the man's ailing mother.

The didactic nature of this book violates the literary and aesthetic principles for authenticity because it does not reflect the "culture of origin." Didacticism reduces writing for children to a tool for "prolonging and preserving . . . values which are constantly on the verge of collapse" (Rose, 1984, p. 44). In spite of the fact that the ruling scholar-officials tried hard to impose these inhuman values, Chinese history has never lacked antiheroes who resisted their unreasonable implementation. In determining the authentic values of Chinese culture, distinguished scholar Lin (1936) cautions that "it would be dangerous to lend too much weight to academic theory, for the Chinese are always a realistic people and have a way of withering theories with a laugh" (p. 140).

In this sense, the author of the story wrongly judged the cultural authenticity of this value. While Chinese people still use the term "filial piety" to mean love for parents, the concept implied in the story goes far beyond the ways in which Chinese people actually thought about filial piety. Historically, children disliked the stories based in the Confucian ideal and adults laughed at them as extreme examples. Today, no Chinese believe that their children should die for them or accept using children as life insurance. Therefore, the story reflects an exaggerated example of a value within Chinese culture. The value is accurate but the book does not reflect the beliefs, attitudes, or actual practices of this value by Chinese people past or present.

Another question raised by Hearne (1993b) is, "What are the implications when these origins are—and are not—reflected accurately?" (p. 33). In other words, what sense do authors/illustrators expect young readers to make of a story when the culture's practices are or are not accurately reflected? Where do authors/illustrators stand when conflicting interpretations of a cultural code of conduct occur within a culture? *Red Thread* is another story that carries an overtone of Confucian teachings: arranged marriage. It is a traditional belief that the marriage god, so-called "The Old Man Under the Moon," ties each couple's ankles with a piece of invisible red thread in their previous lives to predetermine their fiancé/fiancée.

It is true that arranged marriage was once a popular practice in Chinese culture. The story does accurately reflect the fact that marriage was basically an alliance established between two families to build influential social connections. According to Confucian ideology, the matrimonial alliance between a man and a woman was nothing compared to the alliance established between two families. Marriage was a family affair, not an individual one. Usually most arranged marriages considered money or influential connections—everything but love.

Like *The Voice of the Great Bell*, the problem with *Red Thread* is its didactic nature. The story strongly advocates the irresistible divine power of predestined arranged marriage. The protagonist tries desperately, including hiring a killer, to change the marriage arranged by the "Old Man Under the Moon" but in the end he fails and it turns out that his wife is the girl he was predestined to marry. The resolution of the story suggests that the fate of arranged marriage is insurmountable.

In contrast to the Confucian teachings, stories about young people who rebelled and ran away from arranged marriages have always permeated Chinese history and history of Chinese literature. *Butterfly Lovers* (Tai, 2000) is one of the innumerable stories in which a young couple would rather die dreaming of becoming butterflies in their next lives and loving freely than to accept the arranged marriage. The popularity of these stories with readers tells the true story about this particular cultural value and the difference between its ideal and people's actual attitudes toward that value.

In both *Red Thread* and *The Voice of the Great Bell*, the value at the heart of the book is part of Chinese culture, but its authenticity is still problematic. The authenticity is questionable because the book does not reflect how that value actually played out in people's lives and thinking. As we noted earlier, cultural authenticity involves examining the connections between a social practice and the central code of a culture.

Authenticity and Cultural Commensurability

While we recognize the great diversity of values rooted in different cultures, we believe that all cultures have an overlapping area of values, especially in terms of the nature of humanity. These values are commensurate in the sense that they are compatible or appropriate to all cultures. This compatibility is based on the understanding that, in any culture, those who endorse values that are inhuman either have trouble forcing people to follow or fail to control the situation after a period of time. Therefore, there is legitimate moral ground for rejecting claims of authenticity for these inhuman values. Li (1998) argues:

> When a girl fights to escape female genital circumcision, or foot binding or arranged marriage . . . the relativist is obliged to "respect" the cultural or traditional customs from which the individuals are trying to escape. In so doing, the relativist is not merely disrespecting the individual but effectively endorsing the moral grounds for torture, rape, and murder. In moral issues, ethical relativists cannot possibly remain neutral—they are committed either to the individual or to the dominant force within the culture. (p. 30)

Authors and illustrators need to consider the implications of the cultural values they introduce in their stories. *Red Thread* seems to warn young people not to defy the divine decision in their arranged marriages. The author appears to be saying that any struggle to pursue freedom in love will end up in vain. For that reason, the story is committed to the inhuman values of the Confucian ethic code and violates the principle of literary authenticity. In fact, the once seemingly powerful practice of arranged marriages is no longer part of Chinese culture. The story may accurately reflect reality in history but this cultural value violated basic human rights and had enormous negative consequences, particularly for women. We have to question a story that promotes a cultural value that violates a basic human right, without raising any questions about its practice.

Some may hesitate before claims of the universality of values for fear of being accused of cultural hegemony. But the insistence of ethical relativists on the incompatibility of cultural values is a denial that values of different cultures in human history have overlapped and converged. Maybe it is advisable to bear in mind when introducing cultural values that certain articles in the United Nations Universal Declaration of Human Rights (1948) are particularly relevant to children's literature as rights that should be observed for all cultures:

> Article 1. All human beings are born free and equal in dignity and rights. . . .
>
> Article 3. Everyone has the right to life, liberty, and the security of person. . . .
>
> Article 5. No one shall be subjected to torture, or to cruel, inhuman or degrading treatment or punishment (qtd. in Ching, 1998, p. 69).

Authenticity and Cultural Conventions

The relationship between authenticity and intercultural conflict also needs to be considered. When a folktale is adapted from one culture to another, the author or illustrator has to consider the possible value conflict between the two cultures and the recipient culture's ability to accept the introduced value. Another reason *The Voice of the Great Bell* and *Red Thread* have elicited criticism is that these values run counter to those which are deeply held in the mainstream culture of the United States, the country in which they were published. Hearne (1993b) notes that "selection dictates how much a story will need to be adapted to translate from one culture to another and how readily it will be absorbed" (p. 34).

Like it or not, adaptation is, in a way, a process of cultural filtering. In fact, it started at the beginning of traditional literature. When literature was still shared orally, storytellers often tailored stories to fit their audience's taste. The variety of different versions of *Cinderella* and other stories verifies the early adaptations that humans made when different cultures learned and received values from others.

What values readers are able to accept is a complicated issue and is associated with the historic, social, economic, and material development of that cultural group. Other cultures do not always appreciate Americans' enthusiasm for introducing American values. Similarly, Americans are unable to accept such values as inequality and the neglect of individuality implied in the human relationships of Confucian ideology: a family, or even a nation, is run under communal principles and children/subjects are viewed as assets of their parents or emperor and are obliged to make sacrifices even against their own will—their human rights would, of course, be considered as internal affairs.

Whoever adapts a story from another culture has to consider how his or her own readers will receive that story. The author/illustrator has to answer Hearne's (1993b) question of whether the author selected the right story in the first place. An author decides which one story to retell out of all of the stories available within a particular culture, and that selection can be critiqued for intercultural authenticity.

Moreover, questions about cultural and artistic logicality may arise when adaptation occurs. Adaptation covers a wide range of changes, going from trivial cultural facts to story, characters, plot, and/ or settings. A couple of years ago, in an attempt to have proportional representation of different cultures, some publishers transplanted stories into a totally different culture in basal reading series by simply altering the character names and the setting of the story. Changes like those often cause problems of cultural and artistic logicality because language and human behaviors are, to a certain extent, culturally governed. That is what Yokota (1993) meant by "authentic dialogue and relationships"(p. 160). Without appropriate cultural changes, the awkwardness and inconsistence are clearly evident to an insider.

We recently adapted a Chinese folktale and ran into a cultural dilemma. In the story, there are several scenes that include descriptions of drinking. Exposing children to drinking is very sensitive in the United States. Many parents and educators are strongly opposed to this kind of exposure, whereas, in Chinese culture, drinking is a culturally controlled behavior. It is culturally disgraceful and humiliating to lose self-control and behave foolishly, and being drunk is not accepted as an excuse for follies. There is no drinking age in China, and so very young children are allowed by their parents to drink a little on festival occasions. Compared with North America, alcoholism is not a serious problem in China. In spite of the fact that the description is authentic, after balancing the two traditions, we reluctantly made an adaptation by changing the wine to green tea. The adaptation is compatible with the recipient culture and is still acceptable to the original culture.

As Hearne (1993b) points out, "Folktales are not born and nourished in isolation; they grow from social experience and cultural tradition"(p. 33). Folktales introduced from another culture often need to be modified in order to fit with the social conventions and values of the recipient culture. These modifications are appropriate as long as the adaptations are still culturally logical, although these changes can mean that readers from other cultures are not challenged to go outside their own cultural boundaries.

Authenticity in Artwork

What, then, is the relationship between authenticity and the artistic quality of multicultural picture books? Actually it is difficult to separate one from the other. A great number of picture books make a few mistakes in cultural depiction. It is unfair to accuse them of being stereotyped because, in most cases, the illustrators do not have a fixed pattern in their mind. Nevertheless, their errors in artwork can lead to inauthenticity. Some have dubious depictions of dresses, hairstyles, and architecture, making a tossed salad of Asian cultures. *Paper Crane* (Bang, 1985) is such a mixture of Chinese and Japanese cultures. Others mix Asian with Western cultures. The dragon in *Everyone Knows What a Dragon Looks Like* (Williams, 1976) appears to be more or less like the one in Trina Schart Hyman's *Saint George and the Dragon* (Hodges, 1984), thus making the title sound ironical. In *Ming Lo Moves the Mountain* (Lobel, 1982) the characters wear pointed slippers from the *Arabian Nights*. Lack of knowledge causes humorous errors in the illustrations that result in clothes and hairdos from different historical periods thirteen hundred years apart being thrown into the same story. Too often, illustrators borrow tasteless folk art like fan- or vase-shaped frames and brick-carving decorations or imitate awkward restaurant-style calligraphy and supposedly traditional paintings, only to expose their lack of experience and research. A high percentage of illustrators who make this type of mistake do not appear to be Asian, possibly indicating a lack of in-depth research.

Cultural authenticity includes the power of imagination and creative perception (Hearne, 1993b). In *Yeh-Shen*, Ed Young did not use much of the traditional graphic mode. Even the panel frames are not exactly the traditional ones. However, his authentic artistic expressions are embodied in the original use of the simple page design and blank space, which are very traditional. Even though pastel and watercolor are not traditional Chinese media, the shimmering effect of the merged watercolors and the lack of attention to lighting are very typical of Chinese paintings.

There are other subtle cultural influences implied in Young's artistic devices. For instance, he develops visual illusions for the motif of fish. The fish is not only an important character that represents the literary motif of magic power, but also a cultural symbol of good luck and prosperity.

The way Young transposes objects and characters is very poetic but not at all out of sync with the story. The bareness in composition could be compared to old-fashioned Peking opera that had very little sitting on the stage. As in the Shakespearean era, the audience has to fill in the scene with their imagined details. Ingenious artistic recreation is a distillation of an innovative interpretation of the reality, not of mechanical imitation.

These arguments do not imply that multicultural picture books can be written and illustrated only by authors and artists who are insiders to the cultures they portray in books. In fact, there are plenty of excellent picture books whose authors and illustrators are from different cultural backgrounds from the culture they depict. *Mama, Do You Love Me?* (Joosse, 1991) is a good example. The artist is not an Arctic Native Inuit, but her artwork is authentic. In addition to the accurate depiction of cultural details, its authenticity is also reflected through the logicality of its art form.

Based on our own backgrounds in art and illustration, we believe that an authentic art form can be interpreted from two aspects. First of all, the art form should serve its purpose, that is, the content of the story—helping readers visually perceive the accurate images of the characters and enriching the story with a detailed depiction of cultural reality. Secondly, an authentic art form should not be rigidly interpreted as the typical traditional style. On the contrary, powerful art forms often result from the daring exploration of different approaches to artistic expression and the innovative integration of styles from different cultures. The artist is involved in a creative process of recasting, transfiguring, transposing, exaggerating, creating illusions/subplots, and so on. In the history of art, there are many examples of such cross-cultural approaches. An authentic art form should lead readers to feel that its freshness and novelty come so naturally that they become part of the story as an organic whole.

Although the illustrations of *Mama, Do You Love Me?* are not made in the exact Inuit folk art style, the artist's audacious exaggeration and artistic transfiguration present a sense of simplicity found in authentic artifacts made by Inuit folk artists. Those illustrations are the result of the artist's careful research on the artistic expression of the culture and painstaking cultural experiences. The specific culture is clearly evident in the art but is so naturally blended into the book as a whole that it is difficult to exactly identify those elements.

Reflections on Authenticity

The authenticity of picture books, for both literary and artistic quality, is not simply a matter of nonstereotyping or accurate depiction. Cultural authenticity is a multidimensional issue. We take it for granted that the authentic values of any culture represent its genuine human side. However, cultural diversity can present its aesthetic richness only on the common ground of the converging values of humanity. While the field has made obvious quantitative progress in multicultural picture books, it is time to complicate the definition of authenticity and face the new qualitative challenges. Authors of picture books need to carefully select and adapt stories that authentically reflect the culture of origin and, at the same time, ensure that their value implications are compatible with both universal human rights and the values of the recipient culture. Illustrators need to establish their cultural credibility by engaging in active research on all aspects of the culture they are trying to depict instead of being satisfied with expressing only the exotic and superficial aspects of culture. They also need to focus on sharpening their artistic perception and imagination to enhance their artistic expressive capacity.

As authors and illustrators attend to these issues, various aspects of a culture, including cultural values, customs, and objects, will be accurately *and* authentically depicted in picture books. Picture books that are accurate *and* authentic constitute a rich cultural resource to support us in understanding, respecting, and appreciating ourselves and others. At the same time, they challenge us to reflect on cultural differences from the perspectives of humanity.

References

Bhugra, D., et al. (1999). Cultural identity and its measurement: A questionnaire for Asians. *International Review of Psychiatry, 11*(2/3), 244–49.

Ching, J. (1998). Human rights: A valid Chinese concept? In W. T. de Bary & W. Tu (Eds.) *Confucianism and human rights* (pp. 67–83). New York: Columbia University Press.

Council on Interracial Books for Children. (1976). How children's books distort the Asian American image. *Interracial Books for Children Bulletin, 7*, 3–23.

Harada, V. H. (1995). Issues of ethnicity, authenticity, and quality in Asian American picture books, 1983–93. *Journal of Youth Services in Libraries, 8*(2), 135–49.

Hearne, B. (1993a). Citing the source: Reducing cultural chaos in picture books, part one. *School Library Journal, 39*(7), 22–27.

Hearne, B. (1993b). Respect the source: Reducing cultural chaos in picture books, part two. *School Library Journal, 39*(8), 33–37.

Li, X. (1998). Postmodernism and universal human rights. *Free Inquiry, 18*(4), 28–31.

Lin, Y. (1936). *My country and my people.* New York: Reynal & Hitchcock.

Nostrand, H. L. (1989). Authentic texts and cultural authenticity: An editorial. *Modern Language Journal, 73*(1), 49–52.

Rose, J. (1984). *The case of Peter Pan: Or, the impossibility of children's fiction.* London: Macmillan.

Webster's Ninth New Collegiate Dictionary (1989). Springfield, MA: Merriam-Webster.

Yokota, J. (1993). Issues in selecting multicultural children's literature. *Language Arts, 70*(3), 156–76.

Children's Books Cited

Bang, M. (1985). *The paper crane.* New York: Greenwillow.

Chai, C., & Chai, W. (1967). *Li Chi: Book of rites: An encyclopedia of ancient ceremonial usages, religious creeds, and social institutions.* New Hyde Park, NY: University Books.

Handforth, T. (1938). *Mei Li.* Garden City, NY: Doubleday.

Hearn, L. (1989). *The voice of the great bell* (E. Young, Illus.). Boston: Little, Brown.

Hodges, M. (1984). *Saint George and the dragon: A golden legend* (T. S. Hyman, Illus.). Boston: Little, Brown.

Joosse, B. M. (1991). *Mama, do you love me?* (B. Lavallee, Illus.). San Francisco: Chronicle.

Lobel, A. (1982). *Ming Lo moves the mountain.* New York: Greenwillow.

Louie, A.-L. (1982). *Yeh-Shen: A Cinderella story from China* (E. Young, Illus.). New York: Philomel.

Mosel, A. (1968). *Tikki Tikki Tembo* (B. Lent, Illus.). New York: Henry Holt.

Tai, F. (2000). *Butterfly lovers: A tale of the Chinese Romeo and Juliet.* Dumont, NJ: Homa & Sekey.

The twenty-four examples of filial piety. (1995). Tainan, Taiwan: Shi Yi Cultural Affairs.

Williams, J. (1976). *Everyone knows what a dragon looks like* (M. Mayer, Illus.). New York: Four Winds Press.

Young, E. (1989). *Lon Po Po: A Red-Riding Hood story from China.* New York: Philomel.

Young, E. (1993). *Red thread.* New York: Philomel.

17 Artistic Triumph or Multicultural Failure? Multiple Perspectives on a "Multicultural" Award-Winning Book

Laura B. Smolkin and Joseph H. Suina

Perhaps the most carefully worked out use of color to suggest the meaning of a picture-book story is McDermott's Arrow to the Sun. *The book does not so much make use of conventional connotations of colors as it creates and sustains its own internal system of color significations.*

Perry Nodelman, *Words about Pictures:*
The Narrative Art of Children's Picture Books

I feel awful, not right. Like "poor things" [referring to the Kachina-like figures]. Like they shouldn't be there. It's just like they're making them just to make money. And when I saw that [Arrow to the Sun (McDermott, 1974)], already I felt funny. . . . When I asked you who or where it came from, I thought to myself it was probably a white man, or maybe a Hopi. And to white people all it means is making money. I don't know, it seems to me it's just not right.

Male artist, Rio Grande Pueblo member

This chapter explores the responses of a range of adults to one children's book, *Arrow to the Sun* (McDermott, 1974). We interviewed five adult Pueblo Indians; three were women, all classroom teachers, and two were men, one a teacher, the other an artist. We employed Benton's (1984) suggested questions as a protocol to explore personal responses to text and illustration, and to access personal connections to and emotional responses toward the book.

In attempting to assess a "multicultural" book, we have examined multiple traditions and multiple histories and determined that

This chapter is a revised version of an essay that originally appeared in *The New Advocate,* 1997, 10(4), 307–22. Reprinted with permission.

evaluating multicultural literature is not a simple matter of locating inaccuracies. In the pages that follow we share our explorations, confusions, and conclusions.

Multicultural Literature for Children: Accuracy, Authenticity, and Sensitivity

Horning and Kruse (1991) outline the history of critical reviews of multicultural literature, noting that prior to the 1950s, both the New York and Chicago Public Libraries had begun evaluating books for their portrayal of the African American experience. Interest in affecting the "All-White World of Children's Books," as Larrick (1965) would entitle her landmark article, intensified in the late 1960s with the founding of the Council on Interracial Books for Children (CIBC). With its twin functions of promoting authors and illustrators of color and providing "socially conscious criticism of children's books . . ., the CIBC had a tremendous impact upon the formerly all-white world of children's books" (Horning & Kruse, 1991, p. 3).

Multicultural literature for children has been defined in various ways in the more than fifty years it has been examined by children's literature critics. Cai and Bishop (1994) reflect upon the cause:

> As it is generally conceived, the definition of multicultural literature is contingent not on its literary characteristics, but on the purposes it is supposed to serve. . . . We are less concerned with the nature of the literature itself than with the way it can function in school settings. In this sense, *multicultural literature* is a pedagogical term, rather than a literary one. Rather than suggesting unifying literary characteristics, the term implies a goal: challenging the existing canon by expanding the curriculum to include literature from a wide variety of cultural groups. (pp. 58–59)

For Cai and Bishop, multicultural literature is "an umbrella term that includes at least three kinds of literature: world literature, cross-cultural literature, and 'minority' literature or literature from parallel cultures" (p. 62). The subject of our study, *Arrow to the Sun*, a Caldecott award-winning picture storybook created by a writer of one cultural group about a second cultural group, falls within the cross-cultural category. Cai and Bishop selected this term as it implies "that there may be gaps between the author's cultural perspective embodied in the literary work and the cultural perspective of the people his or her work portrays" (p. 63).

Gaps such as these lead to a continuing concern in the evaluation of multicultural literature: Does the literature accurately and authentically portray members of parallel (nondominant) cultures? Two other issues should be added to this question. The first is a point that Bishop, in her early writings, termed "cultural sensitivity" (Sims, 1982). Does the literature display a sensitivity to the concerns of the culture portrayed? The second, implied in the comments of the Rio Grande Pueblo artist whose words appear at the beginning of this chapter, has been explicitly stated by Stott (1992): "Are these activities just examples of cultural exploitation, the taking of property and possessions for their own (usually financial) benefit?" (p. 374). As Bishop (1992) indicates, such critiques generally are applied to individual books, and, "in cases where books have been denounced, the assumption has been that as an outsider, the author was unaware of the nuances of day to day living in the culture portrayed in the book" (p. 41).

Various criteria are suggested for evaluating the cultural accuracy and authenticity of multicultural literature, with picture books receiving special attention. Bishop (1992) urges selectors to examine pictures for "accurate, authentic, nonstereotypical presentations of people of color. Do they show variety in physical features among the people of any one group, or do they all look alike?" (p. 50). Hearne (1993) sets forth her own concerns in assessing picture book folklore. How much will a story "need to be adapted to translate from one culture to another, and how readily will it be absorbed?" (p. 34). "What happens when we apply new art to old stories?" (p. 35). Are "folk art motifs misappropriated from a culture or misapplied from one culture to another"? (p. 36). Finally, Stott (1984) is concerned that children see historic cultures honestly and fully depicted.

In this volume, Rochman (2003) thoughtfully contributes to conversations about accuracy and authenticity, thrusting at the borders bounding current evaluations of multicultural literature, questioning criteria such as those described above:

> If there's one thing I've learned in this whole multicultural debate, it's not to trust absolutes. I say something and then immediately qualify it with "And yet. . . ." And it's usually because I find a book that upsets all my neat categories. (p. 104)

Because our experiences with *Arrow to the Sun* upset some of our own absolutes, we found Rochman's phrase "and yet . . ." to have particular resonance. With this phrase in mind we explore the creation and various evaluations of *Arrow to the Sun.*

McDermott and the Creation of *Arrow to the Sun*

Illustrator Gerald McDermott (1975a), three times honored by the Caldecott award committee, explained his interest in an "ancient, pre-Conquest Pueblo Indian tale" (p. 127). Following his original decision to use folklore as his source for his cinematic efforts, McDermott chanced to meet Joseph Campbell, who noted that McDermott's selected tales generally represented a common theme—the hero quest. In such myths, the hero ventures into the world of the supernatural, overcomes obstacles, and returns with the ability to confer gifts on fellow human beings. Whereas protagonists in his other works (e.g., *Stonecutter*, 1975b; *Anansi the Spider*, 1972) had each failed at some point in their quests, the Boy of the Pueblo tale completes his undertaking. For McDermott (1975a), this tale was "a perfect example of the classic motif of the hero quest" (p. 127).

McDermott spent considerable time studying the motifs of Southwest Indian art. Nodelman (1988) comments on McDermott's evocation of "the paintings found on the walls of ancient Anasazi kivas" (p. 91). McDermott (1975a) makes mention of the rainbow motif "that appears in the sand paintings, pottery designs, and weaving of the Southwest" (p. 128). He demonstrates understanding of the harmony of Pueblo life, commenting that his Pueblo protagonist will not destroy the creatures he encounters in his trials as would be the case in the Greek and Hebrew tradition, but will "assume their positive qualities and put them at our service . . . [manifesting] . . . a kinship and reverence for the natural world" (p. 129). Still, McDermott (1988) makes clear that his role as artist allows him to transform traditional stories of other cultures:

> The goal of my quest as author and illustrator is to give contemporary voice and form to traditional tales; to release the spirit of the story through my own words and pictures. . . . It becomes a form of literature, not archaeology or anthropology. At its core is tradition, but the finished form is unmistakably that of the individual artist. (pp. 1–2)

In his critique of children's literature on Plains Indians, Stott (1984) commented on what he perceived to be McDermott's successfully sensitive portrayal of Pueblo life:

> Certainly if we are to come closer to such fine picture books as Gerald McDermott's *Arrow to the Sun* . . . we must increase our awareness of the traditional cultural backgrounds which these writer-artists have assimilated and integrated into their stories. (p. 118)

According to our Pueblo informants, McDermott and his book were welcomed in his visits to schools in several New Mexico pueblos. At one school, scenes from *Arrow to the Sun* were used as designs for T-shirts; at another, his text was translated into Keres (the language of several New Mexico pueblos). Stott's praise would seem to have been well merited.

The Pueblo Worlds

Despite McDermott's invitations to schools, despite reviews lauding the book as a work of art and as a culturally sensitive depiction, our interviews with informants revealed that *Arrow to the Sun* is neither welcomed nor celebrated by some members of the Pueblo world.

In considering reactions to McDermott's work among Pueblo people, it is appropriate to distinguish between Eastern Rio Grande Pueblos and Western Pueblos. As we have discussed elsewhere (Suina & Smolkin, 1995), repressive policies by the conquering Spaniards toward native religious practices had their greatest impact in the Eastern Rio Grande Pueblos. Along the river, with its fertile fields and its constant water supply, the Spaniards felt their greatest comfort and imposed their heaviest hand. Pueblos found further from these comforts experienced Spanish oppression, but never to the extent nor for the duration that their fellow Pueblo peoples along the river did. Dozier (1983) describes the reactions of the Spanish priests to native observances:

> Soldiers were called to enter Pueblo ceremonial rooms and punish the performers and their leaders. The missionaries employed drastic disciplinary measures in their attempt to wipe out the native religion. They whipped native religious leaders and executed repeat offenders. Periodically, Pueblo homes were raided for Katcina [sic] masks, prayer sticks, prayer feathers, and other objects considered sacred by the Indians. (p. 50)

Refusing to abandon their native religion, Eastern Rio Grande Pueblo peoples moved particular observances and ceremonies into concealment and secrecy, particularly those that entailed the masked Kachina figures. Today, among the Pueblo peoples there flares a tension between conservative Eastern Rio Grande Pueblo peoples and Western Pueblo peoples regarding the proper place of the Kachina.

To the traditional Pueblo Indians of the Southwest, a Kachina figure is as sacred as the Blessed Sacrament would be to a devout Catholic. Revered with the utmost respect and adoration, the Kachina is the spirit come to life, assuming a near-human form, as it brings blessings and retribution to humans. For believers, Kachinas come only when all requisite conditions have been "made proper," not before, not after, unless they should choose to appear out of their normal contexts. For humans to illustrate, make models, or choose to imitate Kachinas is to tamper with the forbidden realm of the supernatural, and is deemed sacrilegious.

Despite these injunctions, certain pueblos are renowned for their Kachina carvings. These dolls are not only found in homes, but along the roadsides and in shops, as Pueblo artists promote their sale as an economic endeavor. Particularly well known for their Kachina dolls are the most westerly pueblos of Zuni and the Hopi Mesas.

In the building of the Pueblo Cultural Center in Albuquerque, artists of various pueblos painted representations of Pueblo life on the walls surrounding a central plaza. A Zuni artist painted a Kachina figure from the winter Shalako ceremony. Eastern Rio Grande Pueblo tribes insisted that this work be removed; a Kachina figure in a public place was simply unacceptable. This dispute led to a political fracture; Zuni Pueblo withdrew from the council for almost two years. The figure was painted over; another took its place. Our artist informant from an Eastern pueblo shed light on this stance:

> Me, you'll never see me with a Kachina doll in my house. No, not me. I don't know, those Hopis and those Zunis, they just do it. But you'll never see me with a Kachina in my house. It is our way, our own way, that they [Kachinas] come only one time. And I tell my children that they are spirits. And they come so that they can be seen only just a certain time. You'll never see any drawings of them here [his house]. Only at that time when they're allowed to come, and only there and then.

Members of the Rio Grande Pueblos, including children, make definite distinctions about the conditions under which it is appropriate to see Kachina figures.

Another informant, also a member of an Eastern Rio Grande Pueblo, teaches in the elementary school of another of New Mexico's more conservative pueblos. Thumbing through our copy of *Arrow to the Sun*, she described the responses of the children in her school:

> Going back to where I teach, it's . . . known to be more conservative. I would think with drawings like this one on the front cover and some of the ones that are in the back [depicting Kachina-like figures], I don't know. I think we have the book [at the school library], but I know that some of the kids start saying, "Ka-tsi-nah" [her tone is reverent as she speaks the Keres word] and "That's not supposed to even be here" or that type of thing. If I

used this book, I think the only thing I would do is just read it. And their reaction is going to be, you know, the way they're brought up in the Pueblo, "We're not supposed to be looking at things like that" or "We're not supposed to be hearing things like that, or seeing things like that. . . ." It's more like some of the books over there are censored. . . . I think, I'm not sure, they go through a committee, but they know what kind of books can be on the library shelf. And one of the kids saw one of these and she was showing me. I guess she knew where it was because she brought it to me, and she said, "Look. This shouldn't be here in the library." Coming from a fourth grader to say that. And then she said, "Somebody at the Pueblo is going to get mad at this."

Still another of our Eastern Rio Grande Pueblo informants described a visit he had taken with his wife to a Hopi mesa:

It was on top of the mesa but a little ways down when you first get to it. There were some Santo Domingo (a conservative, very traditional Eastern Rio Grande Pueblo) ladies sitting there. They were selling bread and other things. I went over there. I recognized one of the ladies; we used to go to school together. I said to her, "But how come you're not up there watching?" She said, "We're not allowed to do that, only the men went up there." There was a couple of boys; they were down there. The Santo Domingo lady said, "Or like them too, they're not allowed to go." They [would] get whipped the next time their own Kachinas come.

Simply put, women, girls, and uninitiated young boys of this conservative pueblo are not allowed to see Kachinas out of the context of their own community's ceremonies.

As might be anticipated, given the historical perspective, our interviews with Western Pueblo members regarding *Arrow to the Sun* were quite different from responses in Eastern Pueblos. Two female teachers from a Western Pueblo maintained that each felt comfortable having the book in their homes and sharing the book with the children in their classrooms.

Our interviews indicate, then, that there is no monolithic "Pueblo" world from which *Arrow to the Sun,* "a Pueblo Tale," to use McDermott's words, originates. Depending on the particular pueblo, each of the nineteen varying from its closest neighbor, the book is welcome or unwelcome, its artwork stimulating interest and excitement or creating a concern with content.

Pueblo People's Concerns with Accuracy and Authenticity

In examining *Arrow to the Sun,* our Pueblo respondents noted many points addressed by Bishop, Hearne, and Stott regarding McDermott's

portrayal of their culture. They expressed concerns with misappropriation of cultural motifs, with the features of the characters, with issues
of cultural sensitivity, and finally with cultural exploitation.

Michael Lacapa (1995), Hopi-Tewa/Apache author and illustrator of children's books, asserted that American Indian children reading
Arrow to the Sun would not be looking for variations on patterns that
McDermott creates. Instead, sensitive to signs and meanings of their
own world, they would be looking for particular patterns that carry
specific denotations. Their response, suggested Lacapa, might be,
"'Wow! Look at those designs. Maybe it means something.' If you are
traditional, designs have meaning." Traditional symbols and tales, taken
"out of their original community and context" (McDermott, 1988, p. 1),
serving as the basic material for the artist's transformation, become
problematic when reintroduced into those communities.

Compositional elements of McDermott's illustrations were questioned by one of our Rio Grande Pueblo informants:

> I was looking for the pumpkin in these colors. These orange col-
> ors and the black colors [reminiscent of Halloween] . . . are not
> very significant in the Pueblo world. It's very strange to have
> those two colors together in the Pueblo world.

Colors, especially red, yellow, blue, white, and black, carry particular
meanings and significance in the Pueblo world. Clearly, this Pueblo re-
spondent does not share Nodelman's (1988) enthusiastic stance toward
McDermott's "internal system of color significations" (p. 144).

As for Bishop's concern with the features of the characters, one
of the Western Pueblo informants noted that Arrow Maker, with his
beard, appears Asian. This inaccuracy was noted by Lacy (1986) in her
analyses of Caldecott-winning illustrations: "Arrow Maker is portrayed
with a long beard, which is unheard of for an Indian elder" (p. 173). One
of the Rio Grande Pueblo informants specifically addressed the facial
features of the characters:

> You know, as a young child getting my first impressions of an-
> other culture, I think I would be a little bit frightened by some of
> the characters as they're illustrated. Even the Boy looks kind of
> scary, the sharp angles and so forth. Except every now and then,
> like the female character has a roundness about her, but the men
> are all very sharp, rough and angry faces or frightened faces.

What will non-Pueblo children think about this unknown culture of
angular-faced men?

This same question arises in terms of cultural sensitivity. One of
our Rio Grande Pueblo informants pondered the non-Puebloan's inter-

pretation of the kivas in which the Boy encounters his various trials with the serpent, the bees, the lightning, and the lions:

> The kiva in the book—the kiva is a holy place, and you're not going to find kivas filled with trials and tribulations such as . . . bees, and lightning, and lions, and serpents. You're not going to find them inside a kiva; a kiva is a place of worship, of peace.

One of the Western Pueblo women, however, saw the kivas differently. Unlike her Rio Grande Pueblo female counterparts, she was only rarely permitted in a kiva; she knew, however, that young men "go through certain ritual rites on their way to manhood" and speculated that the kiva scenes might reflect these rites of passage.

Another Pueblo informant expressed concern with the book's message that the members of his pueblo would shun a child:

> There's this beginning where he's not accepted by other boys in the pueblo, but that's usually not the case because Pueblo children are not usually shunned by their peers because they only have their mother.

This troubled response appeared in four of the five interviews with New Mexico Pueblo informants; it seemed as much a concern to the members of the Western Pueblo as to those of the Eastern Rio Grande Pueblos.

The major dilemma, however, for all three Eastern Rio Grande Pueblo respondents was the presence of the Kachina-like figures. The concern was not with misimpressions that non-Pueblos might receive of Pueblo culture, nor with a misappropriation of cultural motifs, but with violations of their own taboos:

> Not that the book says anything about Kachinas, but the figures themselves, like on the front page and in the places where, especially where the dance is occurring, the characters all look like Kachinas, and that's taboo to share in any way with Pueblo children outside of the context of the ceremony in the Pueblo.

McDermott's figures are interpreted by the Rio Grande Pueblo members as Kachina-like and, therefore, of a forbidden nature. For Rio Grande Pueblo children, then, *Arrow to the Sun* does not meet one of Bishop's (1992) essential criteria: "Consider the possible effect on a child's self-esteem. . . . Is there anything in the book that would embarrass or offend you if it were written about you or the group you identify with?" (p. 51).

Finally, there is Stott's (1992) consideration of exploitation of a culture for financial purposes. This is particularly evident in the words of the Rio Grande Pueblo artist in the opening of this chapter. For him, the sacred has been plucked from its proper place, causing it to be seen at inappropriate times, jeopardizing the harmony of the Pueblo world. In his eyes, it has been profaned, perhaps simply, he hypothesizes, "to make money." Nowhere has this concern with exploitation of parallel cultures been more strongly voiced than in Thelma Seto's (2003) "Multiculturalism Is Not Halloween." When nonmembers use cultural members' materials, distance, rather than increased closeness, may occur between members of parallel cultures and members of dominant cultures, thus enforcing existing stereotypes such as those expressed by the Pueblo artist or leading to intense anger such as Seto's.

From the comments of our informants, it would seem that *Arrow to the Sun* does not measure up to Stott's (1984) praise as a fine book that successfully assimilates and integrates traditional cultural background. It would seem, instead, to fail as a multicultural work. However, Rochman's phrase "and yet . . ." pushes us to consider further.

Reconsidering Accuracy and Authenticity

At least three key problems arise as authors address accuracy and authenticity in children's books; a fourth may be inherent in the process. First, evaluations of cultural authenticity may be based either solely on the author's insider perspective or on a single cultural member's response. Second, multicultural reviews themselves may contain inaccuracies. Third, perspectives on the book as a literary work may be absent. Finally, the very act of analysis may be culturally and traditionally inauthentic.

The first problem has been alluded to by Bishop (1992) and Noll (2003). No culture is monolithic (Aronson, 2003; Rochman, 2003); therefore, no single member of that culture can be seen as able to issue a final assessment of the cultural authenticity of a text. Despite Aronson's (2003) call "for the intellectual honesty that recognizes the complexity of culture" (p. 79), few, if any, critiques of a piece of multicultural literature have gone to the trouble of collecting viewpoints from multiple members of a culture. Authors of multicultural evaluations, if not "insiders" of the addressed culture, at best ask *an* individual they know who is from, or who is familiar with, a culture. Views of "insiders" may differ, even when considering subjects sacred to a culture. For example, during a visit to the Pueblo Cultural Center in Albuquerque, Laura was skimming through the children's book collection. A young clerk, who later identified himself as a member of a Western Pueblo, recommended *Arrow to the Sun:* "This was the most important book to me, growing up. It was about us, about our culture. It was my favorite book." The conclusion that *Arrow to the Sun* is a failure as a multicultural piece of literature wobbles against this additional perspective.

A second problem with multicultural evaluations is that they, too, may contain inaccuracies. For example, McCarty (1995) writes an excoriating analysis in "What's Wrong with *Ten Little Rabbits?*" She raises some important points. Critiquing Grossman's (1991) *Ten Little Rabbits,* McCarty queries, "What are we to make of rabbits dressed as Kachinas performing rain ceremonies . . . ?" (p. 97). As we shared the book and the article with our Pueblo students, they responded with surprise: "The Corn Dance, the Harvest Dance, is not a Kachina dance; it's a social dance."

A third problem with multicultural evaluations of children's literature is that emphasis in such evaluations is not on the literary work but on its appropriate use in school settings (Cai & Bishop, 1994). Multicultural evaluations generally exhort writers and illustrators to consider their social responsibilities when they are creating their art, but speak little to issues of appreciation of a work's artistic qualities. Children's author Jean Little (1990) addresses the predicament this creates:

> I do not believe that writers have a responsibility to society. I believe our only responsibility is to be faithful to the vision each of us is given, however fragmentary and imperfect, of the book which has claimed us as its author. Not to sell it short. Not to skimp on the work it demands. Not to manipulate it to show strong female protagonists . . . or to accomplish any number of other laudable aims that are, in fact, outside what the book itself is asking us to say. (p. 79)

Comments about social responsibility, accuracy, and authenticity are not necessarily welcomed by writers and illustrators who, in the Western tradition, are concerned with their personal freedom in the creative process.

Finally, evaluations that focus on a single aspect of a book, such as its cultural accuracy, may be seen as reproductive of the part-as-opposed-to-the-whole emphasis of much of Western society, which contrasts strongly with the holistic traditions of many parallel cultures. Swentzell (1982) illuminates this distinction:

> Separation and distinction are not primary qualities in Pueblo thinking. It is a system that does not have distinct, well-defined parts. The emphasis is not to break down into simpler constituents but rather to move to the larger whole. (p. 17)

Swentzell's statement accords well with the types of responses we received from our Pueblo informants. Despite the questions we posed, those most steeped in traditional life scarcely addressed specific aspects in pictures; instead, they either focused on a personal reaction or were concerned about how others might react.

Art in Tribal Traditions and Western Traditions: The Development of the Picture Book

Issues of assessment are not the only areas in which members of parallel cultures may differ from dominant society; perceptions of the place and role of art may be distinct as well. Examining the picture book in its historical perspective illuminates distinctions between Pueblo views of art and those of Western Europeans.

Kiefer (1995) sets forth a fascinating history of the picture book. She identifies its roots as the art-related component of communal religious ceremonies, citing first appearances in the Australian aboriginal "dreamings" of forty thousand years ago and in the better-known cave paintings of Europe some fifteen thousand years ago. Though the medium changed, the Egyptian papyri, speculates Kiefer, served a purpose similar to the dreamings and the cave paintings: "the book's audience probably remained a wide one, for even those who were not literate may have had access to the books in communal celebrations" (p. 72).

Poet Gloria Anzaldúa (1988) elucidates the role of such art in tribal, communal cultures. Art, she explains, is critical in enactments, an integral part of daily life, like the intricately decorated clay pot that holds seeds for spring planting or the carefully carved Kachina mask worn in a religious ceremony. Art is situated in its appropriate context; it expresses appropriate content—this is the view of art within the traditional Pueblo world. When artists violate these norms, they can be censored, to the point of being driven from their community (Smolkin & Suina, 1996a).

In contrast, Anzaldúa asserts, Western [European] cultures separate art from those who "witness" it:

> The aesthetic of virtuosity, art typical of Western European cultures, attempts to manage the energies of its own internal system such as conflicts, harmonies, resolution, and balances. . . . Its task is to move humans by means of achieving mastery in content, technique, feeling. (p. 32)

For the developing picture book, the dividing point between communal as opposed to virtuoso art is detectable in the illuminated manuscripts of the Middle Ages. According to Kiefer (1995), these works "show a move toward art for art's sake and also a move toward the expression of more individualistic painting styles" (p. 76). During the fourteenth and fifteenth centuries, Kiefer believes, "books also came to be valued, not for their magical or religious qualities, but as objects of art in themselves" (p. 80), becoming readily purchasable, collectible commodities. We believe that it is with this period that purchasers' concerns with selection for enhancing a collection first came to be associated with pictures in books.

The tradition of artistic experimentation continues today, attests Kiefer. The art form "intrigue[s] artists who have discovered the picture book as a challenging medium for their talents" (p. 87). Within the developed tradition of the picture book, Kiefer explains, artists are free to make stylistic selections from a range of choices, from a range of cultures, in order to express their meaning. The picture book as today's art object (Marantz, 1977) is securely located in the Western tradition.

Examining a Book within Its Own Tradition

Turner (cited in Bishop, 1992) declares that teachers "must acquire sufficient cultural breadth to be able to judge whether the black [African American] has created beauty according to a non-European model. . . . Literary work cannot be evaluated outside its own tradition" (p. 49). If Turner's statement is logically extended, then McDermott's *Arrow to the Sun* cannot be evaluated by those who lack sufficient breadth in their knowledge of picture book art to determine what is beautiful, nor can it be evaluated outside the developed Western tradition of the picture book. Resonating with the aesthetics of the Western world, representing the tradition from which the picture book derives, Kiefer (1995) presents a criterion quite different from those posed by Bishop, Hearne, and Stott. She asserts that "we must judge the book, therefore, not as to whether the illustrations match the definition of a particular period or culture, but as to whether the artist has chosen elements that enhance and extend the meaning of the book for today's reader" (p. 138).

Gerald McDermott works within the long-established tradition of graphic experimentation in the picture book. In *Arrow to the Sun*, he creates tension through his strong use of angularity, resolving it through the final two-page spread of a circle dance. This virtuoso performance, this resolution of conflict, was clearly discerned by one of our Western Pueblo informants:

> As Pueblo people, our designs on pottery are geometric, but they still have some of that curve. . . . The lines of the book are linear . . . 'til you get to the very end where the rainbow comes in at the last page. It opens it up a little bit more.

From the response of our Pueblo informant, McDermott has clearly chosen artistic elements that enhance the meaning of the book for that reader.

Gerald McDermott, then, follows the tradition of picture book artists who "are less interested in imitating styles than in evoking them—*less interested in accuracy than expression* [emphasis added]" (Nodelman, 1988, p. 96). Within this tradition, McDermott's work merits the Randolph J. Caldecott Medal, designed to honor the artwork of the most distinguished American picture book for children from a previous year's published works. Clearly, then, judging the book from its own traditions, *Arrow to the Sun* is an immense artistic success.

Beyond Dichotomies: Considering Pedagogies, Censorship, and Solutions

The book is an artistic triumph; the book is a multicultural failure. Libraries should purchase the book for its literary merit; teachers should avoid its use because it is culturally inaccurate and insensitive. Dichotomies such as these recur throughout the history of children's literature criticism (Ewer, 1995). They, too, can be seen as arising from a set of traditions—the traditions of children's literature.

The first books for children, explain Huck et al. (1997), served didactic, pedagogical purposes, imparting scholastic and moral principles. As evident from the remarks of Cai and Bishop (1994), pedagogical purposes continue as an important factor in children's literature. In fact, any use of any book with any child may be seen as pedagogical. Developing children's sensitivity toward cultural groups different from their own makes up a portion of the pedagogy of multicultural education, and this pedagogy makes certain demands of the picture books it employs. Developing children's appreciation of "virtuoso" art, be it literature, music, or painting, also is an educational process, emanating from another pedagogical stance, with its own set of requirements for picture books. Assisting children in critical readings of texts is yet another educational process, again requiring a particular pedagogy. When a book like *Ten Little Rabbits* or *Arrow to the Sun* is reviewed as being culturally inappropriate or inaccurate, and reviewers declare that such a book is not needed by any "teacher, librarian, or reading audience" (McCarty, 1995, p. 98), opportunities to move toward, and engage in, multiple pedagogies decrease, and apprehensions of censorship surface.

As Shannon (1989) has so aptly stated in his discussion of censorship, "A life around books is complex indeed" (p. 101). Ours is a society in which individuals, engaging in the collector's traditional dilemma of selection, must contend not only with an evaluation of the artwork itself, but with the concerns about selecting the "right" book (Rochman, 2003). Each book selection or deletion that a teacher or a librarian or a community makes is, at the same time, both an affirmation and a negation of what each believes "is appropriate knowledge for children" (Shannon, 1989, p. 103).

Our work with *Arrow to the Sun* has forced us to take another look at our own "absolutes." In general, we find ourselves in support of the American Library Association's position that readers should have the right to choose, and also in support of the Council on Interracial Books for Children's position that we must guard against covert censorship in which we unconsciously present only one side of an issue. However, our interviews in this study have compelled us to consider censorship (and selection) in new ways, beginning with the perspective of the Rio Grande Pueblo members.

Their schools, located on their reservations, federally funded in ways that recognize the sovereignty of Indian nations, present a unique case. Sometimes, as one of our informants explained, a book must be removed to "maintain the norms, keep the traditions, keep the truth as it is known here." If particular Pueblo communities do not want *Arrow to the Sun* in their school libraries, if the book contains motifs or images that Pueblo religion forbids to be seen out of a particular context, then the choice to exclude this book, made by a people who are witnessing the loss of their language and customs (Smolkin & Suina, 1996b), must be seen as a reasonable defense of Pueblo values and way of life.

We have been asked whether, in a logical extension of this position, we take as seriously the concerns of Christian fundamentalist groups regarding books that deal with topics such as witches or the supernatural. Though it is beyond the purview of this chapter to address this question in depth, we will say that our current work has caused us to be less readily dismissive of such concerns, less quick to apply the emotionally-laden label "censor." Still, we, like Taxel (1994), feel compelled to give greater weight to "the interests, concerns, and experiences of individuals and groups considered *outside* [emphasis added] of the sociopolitical and cultural mainstream of American society" (p. 94). The people of America's parallel cultures, often lacking the political power to make their voices heard, must, like the voices of our Pueblo respondents, be carefully heeded, especially regarding the arrogation of their cultural heritage.

With that stance, then, as we ponder the place of *Arrow to the Sun* in the multicultural classrooms of today's public schools, we choose to close with the thoughts of one of our Rio Grande Pueblo informants:

> For a teacher to use this in any beneficial way in the classroom, they would have to offset what's here with what's real in the Pueblo world today. . . . This kind of a book really is of use. . . . You can compare two sets of information, one that is more current to the Pueblo setting, and one that is based on *Arrow to the Sun*. The other, I think, would be if the teacher was fairly sensitive and knowledgeable about Kachinas, Pueblo traditions, and so forth, they could provide this book as a base of studying the real life, views, traditions, culture versus the liberties that the author took in the book. I think it would help to share with non-Pueblo children who can use this book without any fear, meaning that there's no restrictions or any fear of using the book like this, as to what and why Pueblo kids may be offended by this. I think there's a lot to be learned about beliefs and values of a group of people just from [this one] book.

Authors' Note

The data for this study were collected when we co-directed the Rural/Urban American Indian Teacher Education Program at the University of New Mexico. We particularly wish to express our gratitude to our Pueblo respondents for their willingness to assist in this study.

References

Anzaldúa, G. (1988). The path of the red and black ink. In R. Simonson & S. Walker (Eds.), *Multi-cultural literacy* (pp. 29–40). Saint Paul, MN: Graywolf Press.

Aronson, M. (2003). A mess of stories. In D. L. Fox & K. G. Short (Eds.), *Stories matter: The complexity of cultural authenticity in children's literature* (pp. 78–83). Urbana, IL: National Council of Teachers of English.

Benton, M. (1984). The methodology vacuum in teaching literature. *Language Arts, 61,* 265–75.

Bishop, R. S. (1992). Multicultural literature for children: Making informed choices. In V. J. Harris (Ed.), *Teaching multicultural literature in grades K–8* (pp. 37–54). Norwood, MA: Christopher-Gordon.

Cai, M., & Bishop, R. S. (1994). Multicultural literature for children: Towards a clarification of the concept. In A. H. Dyson & C. Genishi (Eds.), *The need for story: Cultural diversity in classroom and community* (pp. 57–71). Urbana, IL: National Council of Teachers of English.

Dozier, E. P. (1983). *The Pueblo Indians of North America.* Prospect Heights, IL: Waveland Press.

Ewer, H. (1995). The limits of literary criticism of children's and young adult literature. *The Lion and the Unicorn, 19*(1), 77–94.

Grossman, V. (1991). *Ten little rabbits.* San Francisco: Chronicle Books.

Hearne, B. (1993). Respect the source: Reducing cultural chaos in picture books, part two. *School Library Journal, 39*(8), 33–37.

Horning, K. T., & Kruse, G. M. (1991). Looking into the mirror: Considerations behind the reflections. In Lindgren, M. (Ed.), *The multicolored mirror: Cultural substance in literature for children and young adults* (pp. 1–13). Ft. Atkinson, WI: Highsmith Press.

Huck, C. S., Hepler, S., Hickman, J., & Kiefer, B. Z. (1997). *Children's literature in the elementary school* (6th ed.). Madison, WI: Brown & Benchmark.

Kiefer, B. Z. (1995). *The potential of picturebooks: From visual literacy to aesthetic understanding.* Engelwood Cliffs, NJ: Merrill.

Lacapa, M. (1995, June). Changing trends in American Indian children's literature. Speech delivered at the Second Annual American Indian Education Institute, Albuquerque, NM.

Lacy, L. E. (1986). *Art and design in children's picture books: An analysis of Caldecott Award–winning illustrations.* Chicago: American Library Association.

Larrick, N. (1965, September 11). The all-white world of children's books. *Saturday Review,* 63–65, 84–85.

Little, J. (1990). A writer's social responsibility. *The New Advocate, 2,* 79–88.

Marantz, K. (1977). The picturebook as art object: A call for balanced reviewing. *The Wilson Library Bulletin,* 148–51.

McCarty, T. (1995). What's wrong with *Ten Little Rabbits? The New Advocate, 8,* 97–98.

McDermott, C. (1972). *Anansi the Spider: A tale from the Ashanti.* New York: Holt.

McDermott, C. (1974). *Arrow to the Sun: A Pueblo Indian tale.* New York: Viking.

McDermott, C. (1975a). On the rainbow trail. *The Horn Book Magazine, 57*(2), 122–31.

McDermott, C. (1975b). *The stonecutter: A Japanese folk tale.* New York: Viking.

McDermott, C. (1988). Sky father, earth mother: An artist interprets myth. *The New Advocate, 1,* 1–7.

Nodelman, P. (1988). *Words about pictures: The narrative art of children's picture books.* Athens: University of Georgia Press.

Noll, E. (2003). Accuracy and authenticity in American Indian children's literature: The social responsibility of authors and illustrators. In D. L. Fox & K. G. Short (Eds.), *Stories matter: The complexity of cultural authenticity in children's literature* (pp. 182–97). Urbana, IL: National Council of Teachers of English.

Rochman, H. (2003). Beyond political correctness. In D. L. Fox & K. G. Short (Eds.), *Stories matter: The complexity of cultural authenticity in children's literature* (pp. 101–15). Urbana, IL: National Council of Teachers of English.

Seto, T. (2003). Multiculturalism is not Halloween. In D. L. Fox & K. G. Short (Eds.), *Stories matter: The complexity of cultural authenticity in children's literature* (pp. 93–97). Urbana, IL: National Council of Teachers of English.

Shannon, P. (1989). Overt and covert censorship of children's books. *The New Advocate, 2,* 97–104.

Sims, R. (1982). *Shadow and substance: Afro-American experience in contemporary children's fiction.* Urbana, IL: National Council of Teachers of English.

Smolkin, L. B., & Suina, J. H. (1996a, December). The influence of cultural change on Pueblo Indian grandparents' versus parents' presentation of *In my mother's house.* Paper presented at the annual meeting of the National Reading Conference, Charleston, SC.

Smolkin, L. B., & Suina, J. H. (1996b). Lost in language and language lost: Considering native language in classrooms. *Language Arts, 73,* 166–72.

Stott, J. C. (1984). Horses of different colors: The Plains Indians in stories for children. *American Indian Quarterly, 8,* 117–25.

Stott, J. C. (1992). Native tales and traditions in books for children. *American Indian Quarterly, 16,* 373–80.

Suina, J. H., & Smolkin, L. B. (1995). The multicultural worlds of Pueblo Indian children's celebrations. *Journal of American Indian Education, 34*(3), 18–27.

Swentzell, R. N. (1982). A comparison of basic incompatibilities between European/American educational philosophies and traditional Pueblo world-view and value system. Unpublished doctoral dissertation, University of New Mexico, Albuquerque.

Taxel, J. (1994). Political correctness, cultural politics, and writing for young people. *The New Advocate, 7,* 93–108.

18 Images of West Africa in Children's Books: Replacing Old Stereotypes with New Ones?

Vivian Yenika-Agbaw

Indeed, Africa, for some Americans, is one vast exotic place, perhaps a single gigantic country, where wild animals roam and where people cannot resist killing and perhaps eating each other.

Ungar, *Africa: The People and Politics of an Emerging Continent*

Western interest in non-Western cultures increased as European colonialism declined in Africa and other parts of the world. For many Westerners, movies, television, and stories are the most popular means of obtaining information about these cultures. These different art forms, particularly stories written for children and young adults, enable Western readers to develop certain visions of life in other parts of the world.

Film as a popular medium transmits cultural images that shape viewers' perceptions of a group of people. These images, whether good or bad, come to define a cultural group and become stereotypes through which outsiders recognize and talk about people from that particular culture. While movies such as *King Solomon's Mines* (1937) and *Congo* (1995) represent a stereotypical image of Africa as violent and primitive, *Out of Africa* (1986) celebrates Africa as a natural and romantic place, thus perpetuating another stereotype. Television news reports often depict Africa as a continent ridden with killer diseases that might someday wipe out every human soul on this earth or as a continent plagued by famine.

These art forms invent realities for how Africans are defined in our global community. In this chapter, I discuss the cultural authentic-

---

This chapter is a revised version of an essay that originally appeared in *The New Advocate*, 1998, *11*(3), 203–18. Reprinted with permission.

ity of the portrayal of West Africa in fiction for children and young adults. Because there is little research on African representation in children's literature, the precise images that dominate this genre are not known despite the popular belief that these images are largely negative (Khorana, 1994). I decided to focus on images because people tend to believe the images of themselves and others as portrayed in print and mass media (hooks, 1996; 1994). Children can be manipulated by these images to accept their positions in society as communicated by symbolic forms.

My discussion of images and cultural authenticity is framed within a postcolonial theoretical perspective. Postcolonial theory deconstructs colonial ideologies of power that privilege Western cultural practices (Giroux, 1992), challenges the historical representations of colonized groups (Adam & Tiffin, 1990), and gives voice to those at that margin (Spivak, 1990). Postcolonial theory thus provides a framework through which scholars can identify and resist subtle and blatant social injustices. By examining the cultural authenticity of children's books written by Western and indigenous authors, it becomes easier to uncover signs of domination that perpetuate unequal power distribution among nations (Ashcroft, Griffiths, and Tiffin, 1995a).

I have limited myself to West African experiences because Africa is a vast continent with varied cultural practices. Also, I am more familiar with some of the cultural practices that exist in that part of the continent because I was born and raised in Cameroon, a country in West Africa. Cameroon, like most West African countries, has villages, towns, and cities, as well as a variety of socioethnic cultural practices.

Identifying Children's Books

Fifty children's books set in West Africa were identified using Khorana's (1994) *Africa in Literature for Children and Young Adults*. I examined books written after 1960 because this is the era when most African nations won their independence and left colonialism. Also, this era is when "the history of literature written and published specifically for African children began" (Khorana, 1994, p. xxix).

I focused on K–12 fiction set in West Africa because fiction captures an author's version of what really is, what used to be, and what ought to be. I included fiction by African, African American, and White authors in order to understand what these authors believe are the significant and authentic African cultural experiences worth sharing with their audiences.

When looking at each book, I first examined the settings and the characters. Since West Africa is composed of several countries and ethnic groups whose colonial histories overlap or differ at times, I paid attention to the socioeconomic practices of the characters. For example, I read to find out if the setting was rural, urban, or semi-urban/rural. Such elements as the kind of houses/huts that dominate the setting, the economic and cultural activities in the community, and the surrounding environment were crucial in my interpretation of setting. I also read texts and pictures to determine the main characters. If the main characters were human beings, I looked at age and gender to understand what or whose experience was important to the different authors. I considered the different themes in a storyline and examined any dialogue between characters. Knowing that the dialogue generally could not be authentic since most was rendered in English, a foreign language, I searched for the meaning behind the ideas and messages these characters communicated to each other. In this chapter, I limit my discussion to thirteen books randomly selected from the different analytical categories that emerged out of the data on the fifty books.

I found children's books published after 1960 continue to represent West Africa as either primitive/barbaric or natural/romantic. These images have also been used to define other cultures that underwent the colonial experience. Tugend (1997) observed that Africans, Indians, and Chinese are portrayed as "savages" in British children's literature (p. A12). Even in the United States, Native Americans are constantly defined through this colonial lens (Slapin & Seale, 1992). With this trend in children's books, it is necessary to raise issues of cultural authenticity and to identify the colonial markers that negate non-Western cultures.

West Africa as Primitive/Barbaric

As in popular media, one recurrent image in these books is that of Africa as a primitive/barbaric place, an image that is neocolonial. The stories are set in either the jungle or a village and depict West Africa as barbaric with people whose survival methods seem ridiculous and primitive. The "natives" fight with animals in a capricious jungle for their basic needs, and the "nonnatives" live in constant fear of being attacked by animals and barbaric natives.

Barbaric Images

In Ekwensi's *Juju Rock* (1966), fifteen-year-old Rikku goes with European gold seekers in an attempt to win a scholarship to a British university.

As they approach their destination, a remote village, he must risk his life for them and so shaves his hair to look like a "primitive" villager. Rikku manifests a neocolonial attitude when he describes West Africans as having unusual hairstyles and tribal marks that make them look and act in frightening ways. Rikku remarks, "We were regarded as spies, intruders to be sacrificed" (p. 68). Like a typical loyal servant, he plans to save his White masters from West African savages, even though he is aware that these White men have plans to dispose of him after the gold mine expedition.

Ekwensi, a Nigerian, depicts West Africans as barbaric and dangerous. According to Osa (1995), Ekwensi later revised *Juju Rock* because of its overt similarity to adventure stories written by European colonialists. Osa (1995) also comments that *Juju Rock* was "primarily a book of entertainment rather than moral value" (p. 20). To me, the novel oppresses as it entertains.

Ridiculous Survival Methods

Gray's *A Country Far Away* (1989) and Olaleye's *Bitter Bananas* (1994) explore the hardship of life in West Africa. Gray compares the life of an African boy living in a village to that of a White boy growing up in a town. Although the text explores the universals of working, eating, and playing, it is evident that the White world is much better. Gray constantly compares the hardship of the African boy's life in a remote village to the comfort of the White boy's modern urban world. The author's depiction of the hard life in West Africa makes it an unpleasant alternative to life in the West.

The story opens: "Today was an ordinary day. I stayed at home" (unpaged). This text is flanked by two illustrations—one of a West African village and one of a Western suburban town. The great disparity in the two boys' lifestyles is immediately evident and continues throughout the book. The West African boy works hard in the fields as a goat herder, whereas the White boy washes a car in their driveway. Washing a car is work, no doubt, but it is trivial compared to herding goats in the wilderness. The West African boy carries items on his shoulders, climbs a coconut tree to tap palm wine, and rides a donkey home from school. The White boy vacuums the carpet, pushes dirt in a wheelbarrow, and rides a bus home from school.

Gray highlights these differences through illustrations that communicate the material deprivation prevalent in the West African boy's lifestyle (Khorana,1994). Afolayan, Kuntz, and Naze (1992) support this critique but suggest that "this book means well" (p. 421). Though it may mean well, the author inadvertently equates materialism with superiority. From a postcolonial perspective, Gray flaunts the superior ways of Western civilization over African "primitive" ways of survival. A fair comparison would have been to compare urban life and children from similar socioeconomic backgrounds in both regions. Instead, the story perpetuates colonization by depicting Africa as a primitive place.

Olaleye's picture book *Bitter Bananas* (1994) goes one step further by perpetuating the stereotype of Africans fighting for space and food with animals. The author, although writing from an insider's perspective as a Nigerian, depicts a hero who spends too much physical and mental energy chasing baboons off his "palm sap." Through hard work and ingenuity, Yusuf finally figures out a way to outsmart the baboons.

This picture book reminds me of movies like *The Gods Must be Crazy* (1986) and *Congo* (1995). Africans are reduced to objects of entertainment—primitive people who must struggle to live and whose survival methods look ridiculous. According to these texts, to labor in West Africa is to work for little material reward.

Africa as a Capricious Jungle

Zimelman's *Treed by a Pride of Irate Lions* (1990) captures the image of Africa as a capricious jungle. The father, a White man, goes to Africa to see if wild animals will appreciate him, because he believes that domestic animals are "too refined for a man like me" (unpaged). He is rejected violently by the wild animals in West Africa. Father needs to control something and sees his opportunity in West Africa, a body of land that has a history of colonial domination. Throughout his stay in West Africa, he does not interact with any human being. Africa then is stereotyped as a jungle populated by wild animals, a place of violence and danger.

This image is also echoed in Steig's *Doctor De Soto Goes to Africa* (1992). Doctor De Soto, a dentist, accepts an invitation to help an elephant with a tooth problem in Africa. In West Africa, a baboon that "emigrated" from India and that resents the elephant for calling him a "moron" kidnaps Doctor De Soto. This is an interesting twist that reflects a colonial lens. Although the main character survives this experience, he returns home with an image of Africa as a dangerous place. "Doctor De Soto lay on his back, saying his wife's name over and over and wishing he'd never seen Africa, never even heard of it" (unpaged).

These two books communicate the image of Africa as being dangerous to foreigners. To render professional services to West Africa is to put one's life in jeopardy.

Insider Stereotypes of West Africa as Barbaric

The books that portray West Africa as barbaric perpetuate West Africa's supposed inferiority related to the West through characters and settings that are primitive, harsh, and dangerous. These books, two of which are written by West Africans, depict West Africa as a place where people fight for space and food with animals as they struggle to survive in a materially deprived environment.

There are explanations as to why insiders, particularly those who have lived through colonial experiences, would inadvertently perpetuate stereotypes of their culture. Zipes (1993) notes that because writers are part of our society, their works are not free from the hegemony that perpetuates dominant ideological practices. Both Ekwensi and Olaleye have other texts that are not neocolonial.

These shifts among West African writers may indicate their internal struggles with the ideologies of empowerment, oppression, and liberation. Postcolonial theory acknowledges this struggle, but emphasizes the need to identify overt and subtle signs of domination that keep an individual from completely liberating himself or herself from the bondage and cycle of oppression. As Fee (1995) notes, "Rewriting the dominant ideology is not easy" (p. 245); however, it is my hope that West African authors will not give up their attempts at depicting our multiple realities.

West Africa as Romantic

The other dominant image of Africa, nature and romance, comes through the works of Black (African and American) authors and those of White authors. I have decided to divide this discussion into two subcategories because this image is interpreted differently in the works of these two groups of writers. The Black authors glorify their *cultural heritage and past traditions*, whereas their White counterparts emphasize the *exotic* nature of West African cultural practices and the *universal truths* of human experience.

Black Authors' Romantic Images of West Africa

Black authors depict a romantic image through Afrocentric literature that promotes racial solidarity/liberation and cultural pride and treats Africans as subjects. These stories are set in precolonial, contemporary, or implied West African villages. Advocates of this view consider the communal life in the village to be superior to the individualistic quest for materialism that is pervasive in towns (Asante, 1985; Chinweizu, Onwuchekwa, & Madubuike, 1983).

The authors depict cultural experiences that affirm Africans as brave warriors who take pride in their ancestral past; as people who were/are actively involved in cultural practices, which was/is more worthy because it emphasizes communal living over individualist quest for material goods; and as people who should not tolerate any form of injustice within their village community. The plots rotate around West African traditional village cultural practices, and the themes include cultural pride, injustice, and industry.

Traditional Village Cultural Practices as the Standard

Mendez's *The Black Snowman* (1989) explores the struggle of being Black and poor in a White, plentiful society. Jacob hates being Black and poor. His faith in himself and his people is restored when a Black snowman takes him to an imaginary Ghanaian kingdom to show him what his African ancestors contributed to world civilization. The snowman tells him, "These are strong, brave Africans from whom you descend, Black people who should make you proud of your heritage," and encourages him to "believe in your strength" (unpaged). Although Black children need these words of wisdom, Mendez stereotypes West Africa as a romantic precolonial village with thriving kingdoms and brave warriors.

Franklin's *The Old, Old Man and the Very Little Boy* (1992) emphasizes village cultural pride through an intergenerational link between the elderly and the young, who are torn between the old and new ways of doing things. Using an oral storytelling technique with an old man as the storyteller, Franklin describes the accomplishments of great West African warriors of the past. The young boy prepares himself for his future role as a brave warrior through these stories by recognizing the role and cultural practices of the African male within a village setting. The hunting culture is handed down to a new generation of young men who are being prepared for their roles as protectors of the village. As good as this may be, hunting alone can no longer sustain life in contemporary villages, especially with the new awareness of animal preservation.

Communal Life

Easmon's *Bisi and the Golden Disc* (1990) explores marriage within a royal kingdom in a precolonial village. Although Bisi is in love with Akin, her father (the king) wants her to marry a magician who will make him more powerful. The village community is involved in the courtship as Bisi's attendants help locate Akin. Easmon emphasizes communal lifestyles in her depiction of the marriage ritual within this village community. Because she is writing from an Afrocentric perspective, she portrays life in a precolonial village as being harmonious, with the rich living happily together with the not-so-rich. This peace is briefly disturbed by the use of magic and greed. Nonetheless, things work out well in the end.

Power relations in this community are glossed over quickly. Thus even though Bisi is a princess, her "six attendants were like sisters to her" (unpaged). Bisi, however, does not hesitate to treat them as servants when the need arises. Although precolonial communal cultural practices were good, they were not necessarily free from oppression.

Ekeh's *How Tables Came to Umu Madu* (1989) parodies the uncritical attachment of Africans to material things introduced by White folks. The author becomes didactic as he shows how this obsession with material goods destroys an otherwise harmonious community. All is peaceful in the precolonial West African village until a White man, No Skin, appears and donates one table to the entire community. Envy and pride enter the village as "those who ate at the table stuck up their noses in the air and looked down on those who ate on the ground" (p. 15). Even when the table is destroyed, individual villagers never return to eating on the ground.

No Skin's introduction of a material culture into the village where communal cultural practices had been going on for decades makes the villagers materialistic and individualistic. "Young men refused to yield to their elders. Young women became very haughty and refused to get married" (p. 55). Ekeh contrasts the harmony that pervaded the precolonial village with the turbulence of the colonial and postcolonial era. In doing so, he reduces the cultural experience to the popular stereotype of villagers having no differences of opinion with one another.

From a postcolonial stance, these books communicate that West African Blacks are guaranteed a peaceful existence only if they adhere to the traditional practices of long ago. For spiritual strength to face the challenge of living in an unjust society, the characters in these stories must adopt West African village cultural practices. Unfortunately, present-day problems are not that easy to define.

White Authors' Romantic Images of West Africa

White authors capture the dominant image of nature and romance through literature that I categorize as postcolonial Western literature.

This literature continues to colonize by dominating others in a subtle manner as it affirms a particular cultural experience. On the one hand, such literature acknowledges the existence of West African cultural experiences, but it simultaneously maintains a tone of skepticism as to the qualitative value of such cultural experience. It connotes what Sims (1983) describes as the culture being " a half-empty cup" (p. 651), meaning the culture lacks substance. The setting for this type of literature is predominantly rural or semi-rural.

Universal "Truths"

Appiah's adolescent novel, *The Gift of the Mmoatia* (1972), explores the friendship between two girls—one English and the other Ghanaian. They seem to have many things in common, including a belief in mmoatia or fairies. The characters move back and forth between urban and rural communities in both England and Ghana. When these two girls first meet, what strikes them most is each other's color. Anne Marie sees Abena as "very dark—almost black" with "short curly black hair like a boy's" (p. 7). Abena notices that Anne Marie is "very fair and has blue eyes, and is the same age as me" (p. 11). Both girls come from traditional families with affectionate grandmothers who know about the "little people" who live in the bushes. The story seeks to reassure the children that "it doesn't matter if you are black or white."

Subtle forms of colonial domination manifest themselves in this text. For example, Abena's mmoatias are "little people" who are "dark like me or red coloured" (p. 23). Anne Marie's fairies are simply "little men" with "small wrinkled faces full of smiles" (p. 89). While waiting for her mother to be cured in a hospital in England, and staying with Anne Marie's grandmother, Abena is enthralled by the beauty and abundance of the English garden flowers. Appiah confirms her ignorance and enchantment, stating, "English flowers did not do well in Ghana and most gardens only had only a few kinds. Others were either burnt up by the hot sun or broken down by the torrential rains" (p. 62). My reading of this is that although Ghana is fine as a country, its harsh climate deters nature's beauty.

Even though Appiah tries to make the friendship equal, it is the Ghanaian family that profits materially and culturally from the relationship. Yes, White people can be friends with Africans, but Black people end up becoming the White man's burden. They can also benefit more from the superior cultural environment that the West provides.

Grifalconi's *Osa's Pride* (1990) explores the universal experience of being proud. Told in the first person, Osa is viewed as stubborn in her belief that her father who had participated in the "big war" will return home. Her stubbornness leads her to become full of "foolish pride" and to lose her friends. All ends well when her grandmother brings her attention to her behavior. Osa's voice throughout the book sounds more like that of a child from the United States than a Cameroon girl.

Although Grifalconi's illustrations are exquisite, her theme of universal truth results in the book lacking a storyline. It is a story about generic human experiences being passed off as a story about West Africa. Because of its focus on the universal theme of "foolish pride," the story could be set anywhere, and so indigenous West African cultural practices are overlooked. From a postcolonial stance, I believe that it renders West African culture invisible and so maintains Grifalconi's superiority as a Western writer over the subject she chooses to write about.

Ashcroft, Griffiths, & Triffin (1995b) argue that universalism and the notion of a unitary and homogenous human nature serve to marginalize and exclude. When authors capture the universal experience of humankind in children's literature, they try to show that African children have the same needs as children from other cultures. Such stories create the feeling of sameness, which is good; however, what they do not emphasize is our differences. These differences usually define the roles to which West Africans can aspire in a world culture that is marked by prejudice. If all children share the same fears and concerns, why do African children continue to be portrayed in rural settings, whereas White, Western children have the freedom to choose their world and activities? Western children are free to move in between worlds, are free to reject one world in favor of another, and can even walk barefoot without being depicted as uncivilized.

Williams's *When Africa Was Home* (1991), set in South Africa, splendidly illustrates this point. Peter, the White hero, has to choose between an overcrowded modern city in the United States, and a sparse, underdeveloped rural community in Africa. He chooses the African village for its simplicity, but is fully aware that he can always leave his African playmates in their "natural" habitat and return to the modern city. Africa then becomes "home" for those White Westerners who want a change in lifestyle.

Exotic and Mysterious Culture

In *Flyaway Girl* (1992), Grifalconi captures a young girl's rite of passage from childhood into a responsible lifestyle as her mother awaits the coming of a new baby. Grifalconi depicts the exotic aspects of this experience as she creates a spooky background through her illustrations. According to Yulisa Amadu Maddy, a Sierra Leonean novelist who has taught in three African countries, Grifalconi "captures the African spirit, but the mistakes in the text confuse Western and Eastern Africa. The Masai of East Africa cannot be associated with the Benin mask that is shown in the illustrations" (qtd. in MacCann & Richard, 1995, p. 42). Nonetheless, Grifalconi exploits these cultural artifacts to maximize the exotic appeal of the book.

Clifford's *Salah of Sierra Leone* (1975) tells the story of a youth who must do the right thing in the face of political upheavals in Sierra Leone. Clifford presents the indigenous Africans as corrupt and cruel in contrast to their political opponents, the Freetown Creoles, who are more capable of running the country. Through these Creoles, the Western superior ways are preferred over the African ways of doing things. Their familiarity with how the West does things legitimizes their positions as the natural leaders of Sierra Leone, a country they were shipped back to when the British began having a conscience about slavery.

Clifford's main character, Salah, is an indigenous West African. His inferior status is contrasted from the beginning to his friend Luke's superior position in society. He is a Black African from "up country," while Luke is of mixed race, and from an elite Creole family. Salah lives in a local house, but his friend lives in a big colonial house on a hill. "The space and the number of rooms in this house astonished an up country boy who had grown up in a one-room thatch hut" (p. 9). When the story ends, Salah is made to do the "right" thing and betray his father's political party. Only civilized Creoles familiar with the Western ways of doing things should rule Sierra Leone; not his father's type—the "up country people in the bush" (p. 80).

These White authors find West African culture exotic and fascinating, but also wanting. West Africans are viewed as human beings with needs similar to those of the rest of the human race, but, unlike Westerners, they are uncivilized.

The Dominant Image of Nature and Romance

The dominant image of nature and romance maintains the power relationship that exists between Africa and the West. This image can reinforce the inferiority of Blackness that historically was constructed through slavery, imperialism, and colonialism (Du Bois, 1996; Irele, 1995), and can lead Black children in the West to reject the continent their ancestors once inhabited.

To White children in the West, this dominant image of Africa as natural and romantic can confirm their feelings of superiority and encourage them to rationalize the intervention in, and exploitation of, the African continent and its people. They may continue to invent "needs" for West Africans, "which goes hand in hand with the compulsion to help the needy, a noble and self-gratifying task that also renders the helper's service indispensable"(Minh-ha, 1995, p. 267). This subtle form of oppression continues to prevail among well-intentioned Westerners eager to assist developing countries whose differences they interpret as awkwardness or incompleteness.

These culturally inauthentic images are a concern because "what we see about ourselves often influences what we do about ourselves, [and] the role of image and the control of the mind is more important now in a media-saturated society than ever before in history" (Clarke, 1991, p. 329). Clarke goes on to say that "in an indirect way the image we accept of ourselves determines what we think of ourselves and what we do for ourselves" (p. 343). This seems to be a predicament for Africans in the modern world. Perhaps creating a dominant image of West Africa as natural and romantic is an easy way to escape the responsibility of addressing the complex nature of West Africa and West Africans in a world that seeks to continue casting them as simple and dependent. On the other hand, perhaps it is all that the publishers are willing to produce as they target the Western audiences who have the purchasing power (Altbach, 1995; Khorana, 1994).

To Black authors, Africa continues to be home, a romantic place that is fondly remembered for its past glories and rich cultural practices. This ideology is embedded within the historical events that led to the forced migration of African Blacks now living in the diaspora. By refusing to acknowledge the existence of contemporary Africa, these authors are in a way depriving West Africa of its potential to evolve as a contemporary home for its current inhabitants.

Literature that insists on describing West Africa only in terms of its past accomplishments and ancient civilization ignores present-day West Africa, its complexities, and the challenges of modernization. Zipes (1993) interprets this persistence as social conditioning by the dominant ideology that inadvertently shapes the thinking of Blacks in the diaspora. Hanging on to an Africa that no longer is, as a way of dealing with White, capitalistic oppression, serves the interest of White people in the sense that these Western Blacks may transmit the White, Western ideology of Western superiority that perpetuates African Blacks' inferiority status. By doing this they may also communicate a sense of their own superiority over other Blacks and may be oblivious to the subordinate position they occupy in the White, Western world that continues to serve as their home.

Complexity of Life in West Africa

Contemporary Africa is extremely complex. Neither completely traditional nor postcolonial (free from colonial domination) in practice, it continues to accommodate varied cultural practices. It is besieged by modern and traditional problems.

For example, Tutuola's *Ajaiyi and His Inherited Poverty* (1967), set in precolonial Nigeria, and Mwangi's *Kill Me Quick* (1973), set in contemporary Nigeria, explore the themes of poverty and survival. In Tutuola's novel, Ajaiyi raises money for his parents' funeral by pawning himself to a pawnbroker. After giving his parents a befitting burial, he works hard until his debts are paid. Life is not easy but he eventually makes it and returns home in better material condition. Meja, Mwangi's hero, on the other hand, renders his services to a White plantation owner who employs him for a weekly wage. Despite this, Meja is still unable to raise enough money to feed himself in postcolonial Nigeria. He is exploited, but remains poor. He can smell the good life, but hard as he tries, he can never partake of it. Meja is sent to jail, returns home, and then flees back to the city to look for any job to assist his parents in raising his younger siblings. Meja is unable to explain to them the reality of the city and so he returns to his homeless state. These two novels capture similar African youth experiences set in different time periods. They provide evidence that strategies which used to be effective in traditional Africa do not necessarily work in contemporary Africa.

To many White, Western authors, West African culture is "incomplete" (Minh-ha, 1995), but to many Black authors, the culture remains "pure" and untainted. Either way, West African identity remains to be defined in culturally authentic ways within children's literature.

Stereotypical Images and Projects of Possibility

Pointing out stereotypes and issues of authenticity in children's books does not mean I am advocating censorship. Instead, as a teacher, a mother, and a reader from West Africa who is socially responsible, I suggest critical literacy as one way in which teachers and parents can join others in projects of possibility (Simon, 1992; Peirce, 1992). Critical literacy demands that individuals from across cultures be socially responsible for the establishment of a just and equal society (Shannon, 1995). The ability to question signs and meanings embedded in texts empowers readers with skills that enable them to construct new knowledge by subverting these signs and the dominant messages they are expected to retrieve. Teaching children to "consciously subvert signs" (Myers, 1995, p. 582) enables them to read varying kinds of books in an empowering manner. Rather than accept these signs as absolute truths, children ask questions to uncover the different layers of meanings that are undergirded by specific ideologies.

Children should also realize that because society is complex, there is no formula for portraying life in Africa in texts. It then becomes each reader's social responsibility to negotiate personal meanings from existing texts, as well as other meanings that would make social change possible in our immediate and global communities.

References

Adam, I., & Tiffin, H. (1990). Introduction. In I. Adam & H. Tiffin (Eds.), *Past the last post: Theorizing post-colonialism and post-modernism* (pp. vii–xvi). Calgary, Canada: University of Calgary Press.

Afolayan, M., Kuntz, P., & Naze, B. (1992). Sub-Saharan Africa. In L. Miller-Lachmann (Ed.), *Our family, our friends, our world: An annotated guide to significant multicultural books for children and teenagers* (pp. 417–43). New Providence, NJ: R. R. Bowker.

Altbach, P. (1995). Literary colonialism: Books in the third world. In B. Ashcroft, G. Griffiths, & H. Tiffin (Eds.), *The post-colonial studies reader* (pp. 485–90). London: Routledge.

Asante, M. (1985). Afrocentricity and culture. In M. K. Asante & K. Asante-Welsh (Eds.), *African culture: The rhythms of unity* (pp. 3–12). Westport, CT: Greenwood.

Ashcroft, B., Griffiths, G., & Tiffin, H. (1995a). General Introduction. In B. Ashcroft, G. Griffiths, & H. Tiffin (Eds.), *The post-colonial studies reader* (pp. 1–4). London: Routledge.

Ashcroft, B., Griffiths, G., & Tiffin, H. (1995b). Introduction. In B. Ashcroft, G. Griffiths, & H. Tiffin (Eds.), *The post-colonial studies reader* (pp. 55–56). London: Routledge.

Ashcroft, B., Griffiths, G., & Tiffin, H. (1995c). *The post-colonial studies reader.* London: Routledge.

Chinweizu, Onwuchekwa, J., & Madubuike, I. (1983). *Toward the decolonization of African literature,* Vol. 1. Washington, DC: Howard University Press.

Clarke, J. H. (1991). *Africans at the crossroads: Notes for an African world revolution*. Trenton, NJ: African World Press.

Congo (1995). Paramount Pictures. The Kennedy Marshall Production.

Du Bois, W. E. B. (1996). *The world and Africa: An inquiry into the part which Africa has played in world history*. New York: International Publishers.

Fee, M. (1995). Who can write as other? In B. Ashcroft, G. Griffiths, & H. Tiffin (Eds.), *The post-colonial studies reader* (pp. 242–45). London: Routledge.

Giroux, H. A. (1992). Paulo Freire and the politics of postcolonialism. *Journal of Advanced Composition, 12*(1), 15–25.

The Gods must be crazy. (1986). Twentieth Century Fox. A C.A.T. Films Production.

hooks, b. (1992). *Black looks: Race and representation*. Boston: South End Press.

hooks, b. (1994). *Outlaw culture: Resisting representations*. New York: Routledge.

Irele, A. (1995). Dimensions of African discourse. In K. Myrsiades & J. McGuire (Eds.), *Order and partialities* (pp. 15–34). Albany: State University of New York Press.

Khorana, M. (1994). *Africa in literature for children and young adults: An annotated bibliography of English-language books*. Westport, CT: Greenwood.

King Solomon's Mines. (1937). Voyager.

MacCann, D., & Richard, O. (June 1995). Through African eyes: An interview about recent picture books with Yulisa Amadu Maddy. *Wilson Library Bulletin, 69*(10), 41–45; 141.

Minh-ha, T. (1995). Writing postcoloniality and feminism. In B. Ashcroft, G. Griffiths, & H. Tiffin (Eds.), *The post-colonial studies reader* (pp. 264–68). London: Routledge.

Myers, J. (1995). The value-laden assumptions of our interpretive practices. *Reading Research Quarterly, 30*(3), 582–87.

Osa, O. (1995). *African children's and youth literature*. New York: Twayne.

Out of Africa. (1986). Universal Pictures. New York: Mirage Enterprise Production.

Peirce, B. N. (1992). Toward a pedagogy of possibility in the teaching of English internationally: People's English in South Africa. In P. Shannon (Ed.) *Becoming political: Readings and writings in the politics of literacy education* (pp. 155–70). Portsmouth, NH: Heinemann.

Shannon, P. (1995). *Text, lies, and videotape: Stories about life, literacy, and learning*. Portsmouth, NH: Heinemann.

Simon, R. (1992). Empowerment as a pedagogy of possibility. In P. Shannon (Ed.), *Becoming political: Readings and writings in the politics of literacy education* (pp. 139–51). Portsmouth, NH: Heinemann.

Sims, R. (May 1983). What has happened to the "All-White" world of children's books? *Phi Delta Kappan, 64(9),* 650–53.

Slapin, B., & Seale, D. (1992). *Through Indian eyes: The native experience in books for children.* Philadelphia: New Society Publishers.

Spivak, G. (1990). *The post-colonial critic: Interviews, strategies, dialogues.* New York: Routledge.

Tugend, A. (1997). A scholar examines colonial images in British children's literature. *The Chronicle of Higher Education, XLIII(20),* A12, A14.

Ungar, S. J. (1986). *Africa: The people and politics of an emerging continent.* New York: Simon & Schuster.

Zipes, J. D. (1993). *The trials and tribulations of Little Red Riding Hood* (2nd ed.) London: Routledge.

Children's Books Cited

Appiah, P. (1972). *Gift of the mmoatia.* Tema: Ghana.

Clifford, M. L. (1975). *Salah of Sierra Leone.* New York: Crowell.

Easmon, C. (1990). *Bisi and the golden disc.* New York: Crocodile.

Ekeh, E. (1989). *How tables came to Umu Madu: The fabulous history of an unknown continent.* Trenton, NJ: Africa World Press.

Ekwensi, C. (1966). *Juju rock.* Lagos, Nigeria: African University Press.

Franklin, K. L. (1992). *The old, old man and the very little boy* (T. D. Shaffer, Illus.). New York: Atheneum.

Gray, N. (1989). *A country far away* (P. Dupasquier, Illus.). New York: Orchard.

Grifalconi, A. (1990). *Osa's pride.* Boston: Little, Brown.

Grifalconi, A. (1992). *Flyaway girl.* Boston: Little, Brown.

Mendez, P. (1989). *The black snowman* (C. M. Byard, Illus.). New York: Scholastic.

Mwangi, M. (1973). *Kill me quick.* London: Heinemann.

Olaleye, I. (1994). *Bitter bananas* (E. Young, Illus). Honesdale, PA: Boyds Mills.

Steig, W. (1992). *Doctor De Soto goes to Africa.* New York: HarperCollins.

Tutuola, A. (1967). *Ajaiyi and his inherited poverty.* London: Faber.

Williams, K. L. (1991). *When Africa was home* (F. Cooper, Illus). New York: Orchard.

Zimelman, N. (1990). *Treed by a pride of irate lions.* Boston: Little, Brown.

19 The Use of Spanish in Latino Children's Literature in English: What Makes for Cultural Authenticity?

Rosalinda B. Barrera and Ruth E. Quiroa

Spanish words and phrases are often found in English-language editions of Latino children's books published in the United States. These elements appear to have come into greater use in recent years in Latino fiction and nonfiction as well as in poetry for young readers (Barrera, Quiroa, & West-Williams, 1999; Barrera, Thompson, & Dressman, 1997). In the fictional narratives that make up the bulk of Latino children's literature, Spanish words and phrases hold considerable potential for enhancing the realism and cultural authenticity of English-based text, specifically by creating powerful bilingual images of characters, settings, and themes. But in order for their potential to be realized, authors must use these elements strategically and skillfully, and with cultural sensitivity. Historically in English-based text, Spanish words and phrases often have been added only for cultural flavor, or, worse yet, to stereotype and disparage Latino peoples and cultures (Burciaga, 1996; Council on Interracial Books for Children, 1974, 1975).

In a recent interview with Francisco Jiménez, author of the semi-autobiographical books *The Circuit* (1997), *La Mariposa* (1998), *The Christmas Gift / El Regalo de Navidad* (2000), and *Breaking Through* (2001), Rosalinda asked what governed his use of Spanish words within the English editions of these narratives. His remarks included mention that some events in his life were not originally experienced in English, and that particular meanings and emotions could only be conveyed in Spanish. He summed up his reasons for using Spanish in his English writings with the following statement: "I simply use the language because it comes naturally to me, and there's no translation for it" (Barrera, 2003, p. 5).

Jiménez's response offers valuable insight into what makes for effective use of secondary language elements within Latino children's books in particular, and English-based multicultural children's literature in general. In many in-print and out-of-print English editions of Latino children's books, the use of Spanish terms is far from natural and genuine, advancing neither the cultural authenticity of the text nor, in some cases, its structure. To date, professional examination of this use has focused on misspelled words, typographical errors, and grammatical inconsistencies, with relatively little systematic attention from a literary perspective. Although some have called attention to the relationship between Spanish usage and cultural authenticity, an important but contested concept within multicultural children's literature (Duran, 1979; Reséndez, 1985; Nieto, 1992), this connection has not been probed systematically.

In this chapter, we address this void by looking at Spanish words and phrases in relation to the cultural authenticity of English-based Latino children's fiction, specifically picture storybooks. It almost goes without saying that the use of secondary language elements per se does not make for cultural authenticity in English-based literary text. In fact, it has been duly noted that "the borderline between the view from within and the view from without is thin. The cliché and the authentic do not always exclude each other but can overlap" (Rudin, 1996, p. 181). Thus, we seek to examine the complex and differential text effects of selected Spanish terms, with a focus on how they help or hinder a culturally authentic perspective, that is, a "view from within." We do likewise for translation methods employed to convey the meaning of secondary language elements.

The Use of Spanish in Literary Text

Spanish words and phrases in English-based text differ along a number of dimensions (Rudin, 1996), among them size, frequency, typography, grammatical/syntactical form, placement within the text, and semantic field. Additionally, they may differ in purpose (e.g., to evoke reality, to experiment with language) and function (e.g., humor, suspense, parody). Another difference is degree of accessibility for the monolingual reader; some terms may be relatively familiar (e.g., loanwords, clichés, cognates), and others may be quite unfamiliar. Moreover, their meaning may be conveyed in the text in varying ways (e.g., literally, nonliterally, contextually, or not at all) and also apart from the text in a glossary. It is fair to say that all the preceding characteristics make the use of Spanish a highly variable phenomenon likely to have differential effects on the cultural authenticity of Latino-themed text.

Another important notion is that the use of Spanish words and phrases within literary text in English constitutes "literary bilingualism," a phenomenon distinct from societal bilingualism (Keller, 1979, 1984; Keller & Keller, 1993; Rudin, 1996). This means literary bilingual techniques—among them literary code-switching (more prominent in poetry than in prose) as well as the use of secondary language elements—do not necessarily have to mirror their societal or community counterparts. In literature, an aesthetic canon is obeyed, not a social, communicative one. Literary bilingual techniques, like the use of a secondary dialect in English-language literature (Holton, 1984), need only suggest social reality, not reproduce it exactly, even in realist prose. Nonetheless, although literary bilingualism and societal bilingualism may overlap, the latter does not determine the former. Thus the "vernacular authenticity" of Latino realist prose must be examined and judged with this notion in mind, in direct speech and in narrative passages alike.

The potential reader/audience for English-based Latino text must also be considered. This includes monolingual (English) as well as bilingual (Spanish-English) readers, both of whom must be factored by the author into the process of word selection and integration. The author of English-based text must strike a fine balance of sorts in the text, providing the monolingual reader with the necessary information to discern the meaning of unfamiliar Spanish terms while holding to a minimum of information that might be unnecessary or redundant for the bilingual reader already familiar with those terms. Ideally, the author who chooses to incorporate Spanish words and phrases into English-based text must do so in a manner that enhances the literary merits of the story and makes it comprehensible and engaging to both monolingual and bilingual readers, without slighting the language and literary interests of either.

Textual Effects of Spanish in Latino Picture Storybooks

In this section, we examine textual effects first according to selected words from three frequent semantic fields—family, food, and physical environment—and then according to translation methods, although these aspects are interrelated in actual use. Our text examples are drawn from a corpus of Latino picture storybooks (English editions) published in the United States between 1995 and 2000, which we are presently analyzing in a larger study of Spanish usage. We examine Spanish usage only within English-language editions, rather than English-based text in bilingual editions, because of the potentially larger readership for the former. We include narratives set in this country as well as in other countries of origin for U.S. Latinos.

The Use of Kinship Terms in Spanish

Given the centrality of the family to Latino life and culture (and to the young audiences for picture storybooks), it is not surprising that many words related to family members are expressed in Spanish in English-based children's texts. In general, the function of Spanish kinship terms is to capture and convey the emotional closeness between Latino family members. However, these words often are formulaic in nature, capable of being easily "replaced by the corresponding English expressions, if it were not for the advantage that they bring an instant Hispanic flavor" to an English-based text (Rudin, 1996, p. 118). When used as terms of address in characters' direct speech, they can be inserted at the beginning or end of phrases without obstructing story meaning for the monolingual reader.

Probably the most frequent Spanish kinship terms are those spoken by Latino child protagonists/narrators in reference to their parents and grandparents: *mamá, papá, abuela,* and *abuelo,* as well as the more endearing or diminutive forms *mami, papi, abuelito,* and *abuelita.* Mamá and Papá are especially accessible for monolingual readers because of visual similarity to their English counterparts. *Tía* and *tío* also show up in Latino child speech and narration. Conversely, Latino parent/caregiver speech in these books often includes a variety of forms for *hijo* and *hija,* among them, *hijito(a), mi hija(o), mijo(a), m'ija(o), mi'jo(a), mi'jita(o).* The frequent appearance of this last group of terms in present-day Latino children's books attests to their formulaic nature.

Insights into the relationship between Spanish kinship terms and story authenticity can be gained by examining the use of the ubiquitous word *mamá* and a variant, *mami,* in two recent storybooks, *The Rainbow Tulip* (Mora, 1999) and *Get Set! Swim!* (Atkins, 1998). *The Rainbow Tulip* is a first-person account by a young girl of Mexican heritage that incorporates a total of fourteen different Spanish terms. The use of the word *mamá* serves a thematic function by highlighting the language difference that exists between the mother of the child protagonist and the mothers of her first grade classmates. The word *mamá* first appears on the second text page as a term of address:

> At home I'm Estelita. At school my name is Stella. My / mother walks me to school. She likes to hold my hand.
>   I say, "*Mamá*, I can walk to school by myself. I am big now. I / am in first grade."
>   "*Si, si, Estelita*," my mother says, but she holds my hand / tighter.
>   My mother is not like the other mothers. Our neighbors all / speak English. They do not speak Spanish like my mother. . . .

A pattern is laid in this excerpt that is maintained throughout the entire text: the word *mamá* is used consistently in the direct speech of the child narrator-protagonist, while its English correlate "mother" appears consistently in the narrative. This proves to be an effective literary strategy for underscoring the language difference between the parent and child and the home and school that is central to the story. In effect, *mamá* is the more intimate term reserved for the child's dialogue with her mother, which we can infer occurs in Spanish; its English equivalent is a more public form for communicating with the reader and pointing to the girl's developing bilingualism.

In the succeeding pages, the characterization of the mother is developed through details and dialogue—she wears quiet colors, has a quiet demeanor, helps her husband maintain a quiet house, and always has a smile for her daughter. All the mother's dialogue in the first few pages is in Spanish. The word *mamá* is used for the second time in another moment of defiance by the young girl who does not want to be like her mother, especially in her manner of dress. She proclaims to her that when she grows up, she will have dresses of all colors in her closet.

Then in observance of May Day, she and her classmates are required to dress up for the school parade, with the girls wearing tulip costumes. The young girl requests a unique multi-colored tulip costume to wear, and her mother turns to an extended family member, an aunt, to help fashion the special dress. At the parade, friends, teacher, and spectators are pleased with the girl's costume, and she becomes appreciative of her mother's caring ways.

Altogether, the word *mamá* appears in the story six times, always as a term of address, and "mother" (specifically in reference to the girl's mother) appears thirty-four times, always in the narration. On the last text page, where it appears twice, the girl's language interactions with her mother remain the same, but she has gained new understanding of her parent. Her use of the word *mamá* now signals a different tone and attitude, as she tells her mother how both gratifying and difficult it was to be the only rainbow tulip and makes a very different request of her: "*Mamá*, tell me again about our family."

Kinship terms in Spanish tend to be used less well in the narrative passages of stories told from a third-person perspective. In this textual context, a particular kinship term used in dialogue may sound more like a proper name, coming from a relatively unknown narrator, than a child-rendered term for a parent. This seems to be the case in *Get Set! Swim!* (Atkins, 1998), a third-person account about a young Puerto Rican girl and her equally supportive mother, which uses a total of four different Spanish terms. In the opening of the story, the young protagonist, who is heading off to a swimming competition, addresses her mother as *Mami*, a more tender, child-like variant of *mamá*:

> Jessenia's ponytail swished as she skipped downstairs. "Hurry, / Mami," she called. This was Jessenia's first year on the swim / team, her first meet at a rival team's pool. At the door Mami tucked / a box into her purse and pinched her scarf together against the cold.
> Jessenia raced her brother Luis down the street.
> "Watch where you're going!" Mami said. "Stick together."

Rather than invoking tenderness, the potential emotional impact of the word *mami* is diminished for a number of reasons already discernible in the excerpt above: First, *mami* is used almost exclusively in the narrative portions of the text, not in the direct speech of the protagonist. In fact, the young girl uses it to address her mother only on the opening page, as if simply to introduce the term. From then on, it appears only in dialogue carriers or in narration.

Second, there are points in the text when the term would be appropriately used in the dialogue but does not appear. For example, prior to the girl's race, the mother tells her *"te amo,"* and the girl replies, "I love you, too." Later, after winning the competition, the girl likewise tells her mother *"te amo,"* and the mother responds, "I love you, too." In each instance, the addition of *mami* as a term of address in the girl's dialogue would have made for more natural, child-like, and tender speech.

Third, there is monotonous treatment of *mami* as name until almost the end of the story when its English correlate is used. Altogether, *mami* occurs in the narration eighteen times (as *Mami*) and only once in direct speech. Even on the penultimate text page, *mami* continues to be used as a name and not a term of address, though when it would be suitable preceding or following Jessica's statement of *"Gracias"* to her mother. This is another missed opportunity to have the protagonist's speech sound more natural and authentic.

Throughout the story, the mother is defined mostly by recurring recollections of her homeland, Puerto Rico, which she shares perhaps all too frequently with her daughter and son. Little is said, however, about how long she has been gone from there and living in the United States. The characters' Puerto Rican heritage also figures into the story on the penultimate text page, where a stereotypical reference is made that the young girl "danced a little salsa" to shake the earrings her mother had given her. This reference only serves to underscore the text's shortcomings in the use of Spanish.

The Use of Culinary Terms in Spanish

Food terms in Spanish signal in a rather obvious way that their referents are part of Latino life and culture; they are called for especially when there are no English correlates. As markers of difference, they are often used to denote the "other" in anthropological, or objectified, fashion (i.e., from the outside), or even stereotypically. Significantly, Spanish culinary terms used in a skillful, symbolic manner go beyond local color and flavor to capture and convey powerful nuances of Latino experience. Food names in Spanish are so common in English-based Latino picture storybooks that we discuss them here separately from the larger overarching category of ethnographic terms that will be examined in the next section.

Among the most frequent Spanish food names in English-based Latino picture storybooks are *tortilla(s), salsa, chile(s), tamales,* and *mole.* Also appearing frequently are *frijoles (negros/refritos), guacamole, bischochitos, empanadas, pan dulce,* and *arroz.* It should be noted that a sizable portion of these words are loanwords, incorporated into the mainstream lexicon to varying degrees, from universally to regionally. Many are of Mexican origin, reflecting the predominance of this ethnic group within the Latino population and representation in Latino children's literature. The growing popularity and commercialization of Latino cuisine and food products within the dominant culture increases the likelihood that some of these terms will already be familiar to monolingual English readers as loanwords and thus easily accessible during the reading process.

The use of food terms as symbolic and evocative elements rather than as clichés (either formulas or stereotypes) is well illustrated in *Pedrito's Day* (Garay, 1997), a third-person narrative about a young boy living somewhere in Central America, which makes use of six different Spanish terms. Two food items, *tortillas* and *tamales,* are central to this story, representing an important means of livelihood for the young protagonist's family, temporarily composed of only his mother and grandmother while the father is away working in the "North." The daily, pervasive presence of these foods in the life of the young boy is emphasized early on in the story:

> Though it was early when Mama and Pedrito rose to / work in the market, the sun was already cutting through the / cracks of the shutters, and the *flap flap* of Abuela's hands as she / shaped tortillas rang from the patio.
> Every day Mama sold Abuela's tortillas and tamales, and Pedrito shined shoes. . . .

Reference to the flap-flap sound of *tortillas* being made brings in an auditory element that is complemented by the highly visual reference to the grandmother's hands, symbols for hard work and love. Reference to the shaping of the *tortillas*, which requires skill earned over long hours of practice—these are obviously not tool-pressed or machine-made *tortillas*—also suggests an "insider" perspective. Later mention of the look of the finished tortillas (i.e., a golden heap in the basket) plus details on how they are displayed for sale further conveys an insider's knowledge.

The end of the story hints strongly that the making and selling of *tortillas* and *tamales* will continue as usual for the protagonist's family, making demands on them but also giving back and ensuring their survival:

> Finally the long afternoon passed. Pedrito and Mama walked home. There were no tamales or tortillas in Mama's basket, but she carried corn flour she had bought and a length of cloth for a new shirt.

A nuanced, inside view of another widely popular Latino food is found in *Snapshots from the Wedding* (Soto, 1997), a first-person narrative about a Mexican American family wedding, which incorporates fifteen different Spanish terms. This story provides a humorous albeit realistic look at the messy but tasty nature of the Mexican chocolate-and-chile combination, *mole*, cooked with chicken. The young female narrator-protagonist provides a convincing child perspective on this food:

> Then we line up for *pollo con mole*, / *Arroz y frijoles*, / Then some soda or beer.
> I splatter some *mole* on my dress. / I get some on my white anklet socks. / It is so good when you smear some on a *tortilla*. . .
> .

The messiness of *mole* is reinforced by the artwork, which shows a picture of the young protagonist's dress with a dark stain on its lacy bodice, and two pages later, a picture of her socked feet also showing a *mole* stain on the sock's lace. In the text, this is juxtaposed with the tastiness of *mole*. The closing page of the book has the protagonist coming back to the topic of *mole*, which is again served by the artwork.

> And this is me, asleep in the car.
> If you look closely you can see some *mole* /
> on my chin, a little taste I woke up to / The next morning.

In contrast to the credible treatments in these two storybooks, a troublesome treatment of Latino foods, among other problems, appears in *Hurray for Three Kings' Day* (Carlson, 1999), a first-person narrative set in an unnamed locale that resembles modern-day New Mexico, with flat-roofed adobe houses and adobe fences. There is a hint of the trouble to come in the Author's Note in which the author states she has "combined observances of several communities, so that the story appeals to the various groups that celebrate the holiday." From a culinary perspective, the result is a contrived, inauthentic smorgasbord of Spanish-named foods that only serves to raise a "red flag" on the questionable pan-Latino treatment in this book.

In the first half of the book, the young female protagonist and her two older brothers dressed as the Magi visit people in the neighborhood on the evening of January 5. In the second half of the book, in a little over three pages, the young girl recounts the foods her family enjoys on January 6:

> Later, in our house, we eat delicious feast-day foods— / *albóndigas, papas,* and *pavo*—that my parents, aunts, uncles, / and grandma have prepared for this Twelfth Night, twelve days / after Christmas.
> Afterward comes honey cake—*rosca de Reyes*—crispy, / sweet. And there is even more: *chocolate* and *piña, atoles* and / *piñones.* We eat until our stomachs ache.
> As the plate of *postre* passes, each of us takes one big slice / of almond-decorated cake. . . .

This exotic array of traditional holiday fare from several places of origin, among them Mexico (e.g., *atoles, chocolate, rosca de Reyes*) and Puerto Rico (*piña, piñones*), raises questions about the background of the family members participating. Do the people pictured represent different Latino ethnic heritages? Is that why a variety of Latino dishes have been assembled? And where in the United States does this family live?

Some of the terms have multiple food referents, e.g., in Puerto Rico, *piñones* denotes a type of small banana, but in New Mexico where the story appears to be set, it is a type of nut. At best, this food scene leaves young readers guessing about Latino families and this holiday. At worst, it exacerbates the simplistic notion that Latinos are all alike because they share a common language heritage—and perhaps a common (or interchangeable) cuisine.

The Use of Ethnographic Terms for Place and Surroundings

This is a broad category of Spanish words and phrases used to represent or describe Latino culture and "its material tokens, values, surroundings, flora and fauna" (Rudin, 1996, p. 152). Terms of this nature often serve solely as markers of difference, without any other literary function. While readily accessible to monolingual English readers, some ethnographic terms may convey stereotypical views of Latino life and culture. Commonly used ethnographic terms in Latino children's picture storybooks are *piñata*, *burro*, *patio*, and *fiesta*. Others include *siesta*, *plaza*, *adobe*, *coyote*, *barrio*, *sombrero*, *jaguar*, and *sarape*.

We focus on two Spanish terms for place and surroundings, specifically *pueblo* and *adobe*, that appear in two narratives told from a third-person perspective, *The Farolitos of Christmas* (Anaya, 1995) and *The Magic Maguey* (Johnston, 1996), which treat them rather differently. In *The Farolitos of Christmas*, *pueblo* appears in the first line, and, over the next few lines, it is differentiated from what is typically its English counterpart, village:

> Luz hurried down the dirt road toward the *pueblo* where / her friend Reina lived. . . .
>
> Luz lived in the village of San Juan in northern New Mexico. / Across the road lay the pueblo where Reina lived.
>
> Except for a few children on their way to school, the streets of / the village were empty. Smoke rose from the chimneys into the / cold December air.
>
> Luz crossed the road and entered the pueblo. Reina stood waiting in front of her adobe house. . . .

The distinction is between *pueblo* and village not only as different places but also as different cultural worlds. The *pueblo* is where Reina, a Pueblo Indian child, lives; the village of San Juan is where Mexican American Luz lives. This makes for an interesting contrast since the term *pueblo* itself is of Spanish origin and was imposed on the native peoples of New Mexico by Spanish colonizers. However, friendship and harmony between the contemporary *pueblo* and village are

symbolized through Luz and Reina's friendship. This relationship between the two communities is made explicit the third and last time the
word *pueblo* is used, when the narrator explains that the people of the
village went to visit their Indian neighbors.

Two different meanings for *pueblo* are revealed in this book. One
meaning is that of *pueblo* as a geographically bounded place. The other
is of *pueblo* as the people who make up that community, thus akin to a
mass noun, and an authentic use (e.g., "On Christmas morning, the
pueblo will dance the Deer Dance").

Adobe is used three times in *The Farolitos of Christmas,* once to name
the building material for Reina's house and twice to name the building
material for exterior walls: "on top of the *adobe* wall" and "the top of
Abuelo's *adobe* wall." Its function overall appears to be to convey the
southwestern U.S. setting of the story, specifically New Mexico, where
adobe is used to build various types of structures.

In contrast, in *The Magic Maguey, adobe* is used in a rare way that
will not sound authentic to many readers, and *pueblo* has less connota-
tive breadth and depth than in *The Farolitos of Christmas.* These words
first appear in the opening paragraph, where the narrator uses them to
convey the Mexican nature of the setting and the child protagonist's
world:

> Once long ago a boy named Miguel lived in a pueblo in / Mexico.
> Miguel lived with his mother and father in a small adobe / house.
> He had helped his father make the adobe bricks of clay and /
> water and straw.

However, by the middle of the book, when *pueblo* and *adobe* appear together again in a highly objectified description of a Mexican
Christmas, *adobe* changes from being a modifier for house to a noun
substitute for it (e.g., Miguel and his family decorated their adobe), while
the use of *pueblo* remains consistent. This singular use of *adobe* by the
narrator sounds more like what we would describe as "vernacular
Southwest Anglo English" rather than the usage of a Southwest Spanish-English bilingual.

This rare use of *adobe* is repeated several times more in *The Magic
Maguey:* (a) "He had climbed to the top of their adobe." (b) "Mother lit
candles inside the adobe." (c) "On Christmas Eve his mother lit the
candles in the adobe." For the bilingual reader, especially one from the
Southwest, this use of adobe will probably sound doubly strange because it is not common in either English or Spanish. When used alone
in either language, the term typically refers to the building material and
not the structure. What this suggests is that even with ethnographic

terms that have entered the mainstream lexicon, the potential for questionable treatment is always present.

Translation Methods for Conveying the Meaning of Spanish

The way in which an author chooses to convey the meaning of secondary language elements has potential for advancing or thwarting the cultural authenticity of English-based text. According to Rudin (1996), each new Spanish term in the text can be translated in a number of ways for the benefit of the monolingual English reader, or left untranslated. In *literal* translation, the exact (word-for-word) English counterpart of a Spanish word, expression, or phrase is provided. A *nonliteral* translation, which can be a paraphrase, explanation, or summary, is used "whenever there is no literal English translation of a Spanish expression or idiom available" (p. 134). *Contextual* translation is described as the most complex method, not easily defined because context is an ever-present phenomenon that "works for all the words in a text, not only foreign language entries" (pp. 140–41). If a glossary is provided, then the author does not have to convey word meanings in the text and might gain some stylistic freedom textually as a result.

When Spanish words are translated literally too often and/or overtranslated, the result can be textual redundancy for the bilingual reader, as well as a disjointed text with inauthentic speech or narration. The latter can also signal inefficient use of the glossary, if one is included. A book's overall translation pattern can reveal much about its *implied* reader/audience (Iser, 1974), that is, "the imaginary reader a text suggests that it expects" (Nodelman, 1996, p. 292). This makes it possible to assess in part whose literary and linguistic interests are likely to be served by the usage of Spanish elements in a particular English-based text—monolingual English and/or bilingual readers. In some cases, the implied audience is far less inclusive than the *potential* audience claimed for a particular book.

Problematic use of translation methods can be found in two storybooks that make relatively extensive use of Spanish, *Abuelita's Heart* (Córdova, 1997) and *Isla* (Dorros, 1995), each a first-person narrative by a granddaughter-protagonist whose grandmother is the other major character. The former incorporates thirty-five different Spanish terms and is glossary-less; the latter, thirty-eight, with a glossary. In *Abuelita's Heart*, the author translates more than 90 percent of the single- and multiple-word Spanish elements, almost all of them literally. Many of these are *direct* literal translations, with the Spanish term immediately preceding or following its English equivalent. Regrettably, the majority of translations occur in characters' speech, primarily in talk by the grandmother, resulting in a strange, if not inauthentic, bilingual speaker who often repeats what she says in one language in the other language, creating concurrent or "double talk." Sometimes, she speaks first in Spanish, followed by its English equivalent; other times, it is English first, followed by its Spanish equivalent. Because English is the primary text language, the latter comes across as an attempt to teach Spanish.

The grandmother's double talk begins in the opening paragraph of the story with a statement in English (i.e., "The earth is enchanted here."), followed immediately by its Spanish equivalent (i.e., "La tierra está encantada aquí."). Unfortunately, the speech of the granddaughter-narrator also reflects a similarly distracting pattern of direct translation, worsened by the use of back-to-back Spanish terms. More successive Spanish and English sequences by the grandmother follow, threatening to impede the flow of the narrative for the bilingual reader who must alternately stop and start while making his or her way through the text for several lines at a time. Below is an example of multiple direct translations that cut across the granddaughter's narration and the grandmother's talk (a broken line indicates the Spanish term because no highlighting is used in this book, and a wavy line its English equivalent):

> Abuelita tells stories / of the healing plants, her remedios, that
> grow everywhere around us.
> "Mira, look, Corazoncito. We call these that grow near the arroyo, the /stream, yerba buena, the good herb." Their fragrant
> leaves make a tasty / mint tea to cure the stomachaches.

There is even repeated translation in *Abuelita's Heart* in a subsequent occurrence of double talk by the grandmother that rejuxtaposes *remedios* and healing plants, this time with the Spanish term first and then the English one. Overall, the text of *Abuelita's Heart* reflects an overreliance on literal translation for conveying the meaning of Spanish words, an approach that slights the language knowledge of the bilingual reader, who will find all secondary-language items explained in a simplistic, overt way that distorts bilingual speech patterns, in particular, code switching.

Abundant translations in more diverse forms are evident in *Isla*, in which more than 80 percent of the Spanish terms are translated literally or near-literally despite inclusion of a glossary, making this resource seem like an afterthought. As in *Abuelita's Heart*, the bulk of the redundant translations in *Isla* occur in characters' speech and only a few in the narrative portions of the text. The speech segments are all spoken by the Puerto Rican grandmother, who, in contrast to the bilingual grandmother in *Abuelita's Heart*, appears to speak only Spanish. However, unlike *Abuelita's Heart*, which makes heavy use of direct literal translation, *Isla* tends to rely more on *disjoined* literal translation in which the Spanish item and its English correlate are separated by intervening words (e.g., "*Hay mucho más que ver*," Abuela says, taking off. <u>There is much more for us to see</u>.), yielding prose that is more aesthetically pleasing but nonetheless redundant for the bilingual reader.

In a number of other instances of literal translation, the granddaughter-narrator provides very *explicit* translations of her grandmother's Spanish talk, introduced by forms of the verbs "tell" and "say," (e.g., [a] "'*¡Qué pescado!*' Abuela says, telling me <u>what a fish</u> it was." [b] "'*Nos cantan.*' Abuela says <u>they are singing to us</u>."). Not only is this information redundant for the bilingual reader, but it also reveals an overly obtrusive narrator. At several points in the text the grandmother also speaks in partial sentences or phrases that then are expanded by the granddaughter-narrator into complete statements (e.g., [a] "'*Pájaros grandes jugando,*' Abuela says and laughs. We are like <u>big birds playing</u>." [b] "'*De todo el mundo,*' Abuela tells me. They come <u>from all over the world</u>."). Although technically these are contextual translations, these expanded statements offer the bilingual reader almost literal information, as our underscoring of the English equivalents in the preceding examples shows.

In *Isla*, the combined effect of frequent literal and near-literal translations, beyond creating unnatural speech patterns and disrupting the flow of the text, is to create almost parallel texts for the bilingual reader. The account in Spanish by the grandmother runs alongside an English explanation by the granddaughter-narrator of the Spanish account. The text strongly suggests that the monolingual reader is of utmost concern here, and the fact that these methods are used in the presence of a glossary only strengthens that suggestion.

Effective use of translation methods is demonstrated in *La Mariposa* (Jiménez, 1998), a third-person realistic narrative about a young Mexican immigrant boy whose family becomes migrant workers in California. This book incorporates a total of fifteen different Spanish words, of which two-thirds are not translated in the text at all, suggesting that the monolingual may have to consult the glossary for their meanings. Three terms are translated contextually and only two are translated literally. It should be noted that the title's prominent use of untranslated Spanish helps to advance the story's theme of language differences and having to learn a new language, English.

In the text itself, the author's use of Spanish occurs mostly in dialogue. The first instance is in the second paragraph and involves contextual translation, followed by an untranslated term that is likely to
be a known word:

> *"Quítatela en la clase,"* his older brother, Roberto, / warned him,
> for he had been to school before and / knew it was bad manners
> to wear a hat in class.
> 　*"Gracias,"* Francisco told him, taking it off. But after his break-
> fast and just before heading out, he decided to wear the cap. . . .

Because neither of the preceding terms is translated literally or
nonliterally, the bilingual reader does not encounter superfluous information that gets in the way of the flow of the text. Instead, there are
contextual cues that signal the general meaning of the Spanish terms,
and a glossary as resource for the reader unfamiliar with these secondary language elements. The overall effect is natural use of Spanish, with
the longer phrase likely to be unfamiliar to some readers, and the second single-word entry familiar to more readers. The next three Spanish
terms on the subsequent text page are translated contextually or not at
all:

> *"Adiós,* Mamá," Francisco and Roberto called as / they headed
> out to catch the school bus.
> 　*"Adios, hijos,"* she answered, *"Que Dios los bendiga."* Papa had
> already left to thin lettuce, the only work he could find in late
> January. . . .

The dialogue above between the young protagonist and his brother with
their mother has a ring of authenticity, especially the mother's religious
blessing, which follows two uses of Spanish bound to be accessible to
monolingual English readers.

　The author-narrator's use of Spanish also enhances the temporal
authenticity of this autobiographical story that is set not in the recent
past but in the 1950s. The author-narrator conveys a sense of his cultural heritage and childhood era through the word *corridos,* used and
translated in a disjoined manner about midway through the book, plac-
ing himself within the Mexican/Mexican American tradition. Also, on
the same page, the names of two deceased Mexican celebrities, Jorge
Negrete and Pedro Infante, function as symbols of a past era and of the
boy's Mexican roots. These names may not be evocative for children
today, even children of Mexican origin, although they are likely to be
familiar to their parents, grandparents, and great-grandparents.

　Spanish usage on the last two text pages involves an interjection
(*"¡Qué hermosa!"*) and a phrase (*"'es tuyo' en inglés"*), both of which are

translated in a literal but disjoined manner where the English translation is used naturally in the next sentence or statement as *corridos* was translated in the previous excerpt. The English equivalents in these cases are quite harmonious and plausible with their Spanish counterparts. The linguistic and literary needs of both readers, bilingual and monolingual, are likely to be met through these translation means.

Conclusion

Latino literature in English that makes use of Spanish has been described as a "contact zone of literature and bilingualism" (Rudin, 1996). We have presented a number of examples from this zone that provide selected insights into the relationship between Spanish usage and cultural authenticity. One salient insight from our analysis is that literary realism and cultural authenticity, or a view from within, can be advanced in English-based Latino children's literature through a modest number of carefully selected Spanish terms that are well integrated rather than by a large number of ill-selected words and phrases translated simplistically. As such, the monolingual English reader is not overwhelmed by the sheer quantity of the unfamiliar terms introduced, nor is the bilingual Spanish-English reader confronted with redundant and unnecessary information.

For example, in a text with a modest number of secondary language elements, such as *The Rainbow Tulip*, one kinship term, *mamá*, goes a long way toward advancing authenticity because it is used at opportune times in the dialogue as a term of address, adding to the depth of characterization and theme, rather than as a mere "name" in the narration. In a text with an even lower number of Spanish terms, *Pedrito's Day*, two Spanish food terms, *tortillas* and *tamales*, used mostly in the narration but accompanied by nuanced details, are highly evocative of a particular way of life and of human effort and resilience. In other texts, these same words might be nothing more than clichés, but in these two particular books, they serve multiple literary functions and contribute to cultural authenticity.

Another insight from our analysis is that judicious selection of Spanish terms requires a certain level of cultural and linguistic knowledge on the part of the author. Not to possess that sophistication is to risk using Spanish terms superficially or in token-like ways rather than as powerful devices for literary effect. For example, when a mix-and-match stance is taken toward Spanish words and phrases, as with food terms in *Hurray for Three Kings' Day*, it is not surprising that lack of authenticity is the result. Likewise, when the use of Spanish terms points to missed opportunities rather than opportune use, as in *Get Set! Swim!*, where the term *mami* is used monotonously, it is no wonder that authenticity is hampered.

At the same time, many current authors, even those with insider knowledge, are not fully exploiting Spanish words and phrases for maximum literary impact. In general, present usage in the corpus of picture storybooks we examined tends toward formulaic and safe uses of Spanish that will not overly tax monolingual readers. Along with repetitive themes and content across titles (e.g., certain holiday books, certain childhood experiences, and so forth), there appear to be repeated, or formulaic, uses of Spanish (e.g., the overuse of particular kinship and food terms). Such uniformity does not appear to invite bilingual readers to expand their worlds, or to use their dual-language experiences to construct and reconstruct the text. In other words, although the use of Spanish may be aimed at realistic effect, this does not necessarily guarantee creative effect (Rudin, 1996).

A final insight is that translation methods do matter—they affect a text's cultural authenticity. The heavy use of literal and near-literal translations in characters' dialogue in some books, such as *Abuelita's Heart* and *Isla,* makes for questionable bilingual speech that renders the Latino characters unconvincing and unrealistic. Moreover, the extensive use of these types of translations throughout the text (both dialogue and narrative sections) disrupts the unfolding of the stories overall and creates highly redundant text for the bilingual reader. At the same time, overreliance on literal and near-literal translations usurps or undermines the possible role of the glossary, as in *Isla.* From a bilingual perspective, translation methods in English-based texts require as much authorial thought and skill as does Spanish word choice.

In sum, given the immense literary potential of secondary language elements to evoke powerful bilingual images, teachers and librarians should look critically at both the actual Spanish words incorporated into the written texts of English-based children's books and the specific methods for integrating them into the text. Regrettably, questionable findings in either area imply an author (or editor) who is unskilled or unwilling to incorporate secondary language elements in a more thoughtful and credible manner that will serve the linguistic and literary interests of both monolingual and bilingual readers. Ultimately, such usage ought to preserve the integrity and authenticity of the text for all potential readers.

References

Barrera, R. B. (2003). Authors and illustrators: A conversation with Francisco Jiménez. *The New Advocate, 16*(1), 1–8.

Barrera, R. B., Quiroa, R. E., & West-Williams, C. (1999). "Poco a Poco": The continuing development of Mexican American children's literature in the 1990s. *The New Advocate, 12*(4), 315–30.

Barrera, R. B., Thompson, V. D., & Dressman, M. (Eds.). (1997). *Kaleidoscope: A multicultural booklist for grades K–8* (2nd ed.). Urbana, IL: National Council of Teachers of English.

Burciaga, J. A. (1996). Spanish words in Anglo-American literature: A Chicano perspective. In F. R. González (Ed.), *Spanish loanwords in the English language: A tendency towards hegemony reversal* (pp. 213–30). Berlin, Germany: Mouton de Gruyter.

Council on Interracial Books for Children (1974). Special issue on Puerto Rican children's literature and materials. *Interracial Books for Children Bulletin, 4*(1/2).

Council on Interracial Books for Children (1975). Special issue on Chicano children's literature and materials. *Interracial Books for Children Bulletin, 5*(7/8).

Duran, D. F. (1979). *Latino materials: A multimedia guide for children and young adults.* New York: Neal-Schuman.

Holton, S. W. (1984). *Down home and uptown: The representation of Black speech in American fiction.* Rutherford, NJ: Fairleigh Dickinson University Press.

Iser, W. (1974). *The implied reader: Patterns of communication in prose fiction from Bunyan to Beckett.* Baltimore: Johns Hopkins University Press.

Keller, G. D. (1979). The literary strategems available to the bilingual Chicano writer. In F. Jiménez (Ed.), *The identification and analysis of Chicano literature* (pp. 263–316). New York: Bilingual Press/Editorial Bilingüe.

Keller, G. D. (1984). How Chicano authors use bilingual techniques for literary effect. In E. E. García, F. A. Lomelí, & I. D. Ortiz (Eds.). *Chicano studies: A multidisciplinary approach* (pp. 171–92). New York: Teachers College Press.

Keller, G. D., & Keller, R. G. (1993). The literary language of United States Hispanics. In F. Lomelí, N. Kanellos, & C. Estava-Fabregat (Eds.), *Handbook of Hispanic cultures in the United States: Literature and art* (pp. 163–91). Houston, TX: Arte Público Press.

Nieto, S. (1992). We have stories to tell: A case study of Puerto Ricans in children's books. In V. J. Harris (Ed.), *Teaching multicultural literature in grades K–8* (pp. 173–201). Norwood, MA: Christopher-Gordon.

Nodelman, P. (1996). *The pleasures of children's literature* (2nd ed.). White Plains, NY: Longman.

Reséndez, G. A. (1985). Chicano children's literature. In J. A. Martínez & F. A. Lomelí (Eds.), *Chicano literature: A reference guide* (pp. 107–21). Westport, CT: Greenwood Press.

Rudin, E. (1996). *Tender accents of sounds: Spanish in the Chicano novel in English.* Tempe, AZ: Bilingual Press.

Children's Books Cited

Anaya, R. A. (1995). *The farolitos of Christmas.* New York: Hyperion.

Atkins, J. (1998). *Get set! Swim!* New York: Lee & Low.

Carlson, L. M. (1999). *Hurray for Three Kings' Day!* New York: Morrow Junior.

Córdova, A. (1997). *Abuelita's heart.* New York: Simon & Schuster.

Dorros, A. (1995). *Isla.* New York: Dutton.

Garay, L. (1997). *Pedrito's day.* New York: Orchard.

Jiménez, F. (1997). *The circuit: Stories from the life of a migrant child.* Boston: Houghton Mifflin.

Jiménez, F. (1998). *La mariposa.* Boston: Houghton Mifflin.

Jiménez, F. (2000). *The Christmas gift/El regalo de navidad.* Boston: Houghton Mifflin.

Jiménez, F. (2001). *Breaking through.* Boston: Houghton Mifflin.

Johnston, T. (1996). *The magic maguey.* San Diego: Harcourt Brace.

Mora, P. (1999). *The rainbow tulip.* New York: Viking.

Soto, G. (1997). *Snapshots from the wedding.* New York: Putnam.

V Connecting Cultural Authenticity to the Classroom

20 Multiple Definitions of Multicultural Literature: Is the Debate Really Just "Ivory Tower" Bickering?

Mingshui Cai

There has been an inordinate amount of discussion among educators about the meaning of the term "multicultural literature." Levy (1995) observes that the term seems to "have taken on a life of its own, meaning different things to different people. To some, it's all inclusive. To others, it's all exclusive. Us against them. To still others, it's simply confusing" (p. 11). This debate over definition is not just bickering over terminology in the ivory tower of academia, but rather is concerned with fundamental sociopolitical issues. We should not underestimate the power of naming, "for the notion of giving something a name is the vastest generative idea that ever was conceived" (Langer, 1957, p. 140).

Like a signpost, the definition of multicultural literature points to a direction for choosing and using multicultural literature. Each definition reflects a different stance behind a different course of action. While it is unlikely we will achieve consensus on a single definition, clarifying the concepts may help us better understand different perspectives and positions on multicultural issues. In this chapter, I first argue that the controversy over the definition focuses on how many cultures should be covered in multicultural literature. Then I discuss three problematic views on how to define multicultural literature. Finally, I explain the implications of the controversy for teachers and teacher educators.

The Focal Point of the Controversy

Many definitions of multicultural literature have been offered, varying in their extent of inclusion, from "works that focus on 'people of color'"

This chapter is a revised version of an essay that originally appeared in *The New Advocate*, 1998, *11*(4), 311–24. Reprinted with permission.

(Horning & Kruse, 1991, p. vii), to "literature about racial or ethnic minority groups" outside the mainstream culture of the United States (Norton, 1995, p. 531), to "books that feature people of color, the elderly, gays and lesbians, religious minorities, language minorities, people with disabilities, gender issues, and concerns about class" (Harris, 1994a, p. 117).

Bullard (1991) comments on the difficulty of defining the parameters of the prefix *multi:* "Educators disagree, first, over which groups should be included in multicultural plans—racial and ethnic groups, certainly, but what about regional, social class, gender, disability, religious, language, and sexual orientation groupings?" (p. 5). It is obvious that the focal point of the controversy is often how many cultures are included in multicultural literature.

Smith (1993) provides a historical perspective by tracing the origins of the term "multicultural" to the 1940s. In a 1941 *Herald Tribune* book review, William Safire (cited in Smith, 1993) argued that "a multicultural way of life" was held out as an antidote to "nationalism, national prejudice and behavior"(p. 341). Used in this sense, the term meant a broad representation of diverse cultures. Just as the term "minority" was not used to designate America's ethnic groups until the 1930s, the term "multicultural" was not limited to ethnic cultures in the 1940s.

In the 1980s, when the dominant status of Western civilization was more widely challenged, the term became more inclusive: "a college curriculum code word for 'not dominated by whites'" (Smith, 1993, p. 341). Multiculturalism encompassed the major ethnic groups in the United States that were politically and socially disenfranchised: African Americans, Hispanic Americans, Asian Americans, and Native Americans. Later, as American society continued to recognize the needs of various cultures, "multicultural" again assumed a broader representation, including people with disabilities, gays and lesbians, and, "in short, any persons whose lifestyle . . . distinguishes them as identifiable members of a group other than the 'mainstream'" (p. 341).

Historically, the prefix *multi* varied in its inclusiveness based on the sociopolitical concerns of the time. At present, defining multicultural literature is still a matter of determining the parameters of *multi.* At one end of the wide range of definitions, multicultural literature is "books by and about people of color"; at the opposite end, it is all-inclusive— "all literature is multicultural" (Fishman, 1995, p. 79). The trend is toward all-inclusiveness.

Three Views on the Definition of Multicultural Literature

I believe that the trend toward inclusiveness has led to three problematic views on how to define multicultural literature. The first view holds that multiple + cultures = multiculturalism. Therefore, multicultural literature should include as many cultures as possible, with no distinction between the dominant and the dominated. The second view focuses on racial and ethnic issues in multicultural literature. The third view maintains that every human being is multicultural (e.g., an Asian American who is female, middle class, Buddhist, and disabled) and all literature is multicultural (Fishman, 1995).

"Multiple + Culture = Multiculturalism"

Some argue that multiculturalism means inclusion of multiple cultures and therefore multicultural literature is the literature of multiple cultures. They believe that the more cultures covered, the more diverse the literature, and that both underrepresented and mainstream cultures should be included. I believe that this view is inconsistent with the fundamental assumptions of multiculturalism.

Multiculturalism is about diversity and inclusion, but more important, it is about power structures and struggle. Its goal is not just to help people understand, accept, and appreciate cultural differences, but also to ultimately transform the existing social order to ensure greater voice and authority to marginalized cultures and to achieve social equality and justice between all cultures so that people of different cultural backgrounds can live peacefully together in a truly democratic world (Banks & Banks, 1997). This is an ideal embodied in the founding documents of the nation. However, before the ideal is realized, it is, paradoxically, imperative for marginalized cultures to empower themselves.

If the issues of inequality, discrimination, oppression, and exploitation are excluded from consideration when we define multicultural literature, there is a danger of diluting, or even deconstructing, the sociopolitical goals that underlie the term. When culture is used as a broad concept in the definition of multicultural literature, it incorporates nationality, ethnicity, class, gender, religion, disability, age, sexual orientation, family status, geographic difference, linguistic variation, and the list goes on. In each of these categories there are subcategories of differences. In religion, for example, how many different faiths and denominations are there in the world? Christianity, Judaism, Islam, Buddhism, Hinduism, Shintoism, to name just the major faiths. Within each of these faiths there are various denominations. A multitude of cultures exists in the world. Are we to include them all in our multicultural list?

Multiculturalism does not mean the sum of multiple diverse cultures. The thrust of its conception is to decentralize the power of the mainstream culture. "Diversity must be framed within a politics of cultural criticism and a commitment to social justice" (Estrada & McLaren, 1993, p. 31). Instead of embracing the literature of any culture, a definition of multicultural literature should draw a demarcation line between the literature of the dominant mainstream culture and that of marginalized cultures. If multicultural literature includes all cultures, the term loses its meaning. In other words, the concept is deconstructed when its opposition to the literature of mainstream culture is dissolved. Without the binary opposition, what is the point of using a different name? All-inclusiveness reduces multicultural literature to just literature (Bishop, 1994).

The view that multiple + cultures = multiculturalism amounts to a "tourist's conception of multiculturalism" (Hade, 1997, p. 236). It assumes that the mainstream culture in which we live is essentially fair and suggests that we "travel" to as many cultures as possible to learn from them. We'll overcome ignorance and bigotry when we return and are more aware of cultural differences and respectful of other cultural groups.

From this perspective, a hierarchy of cultures is nonexistent and issues of social justice and social change are not primary concerns. This tourist's view of multiculturalism is idealistic at best and deceptive at worst, glossing over the grim reality of conflicts between races, classes, genders, and other social groups. This equal treatment of different cultures recalls the insightful remarks of former U.S. Supreme Court Chief Justice Oliver Wendell Holmes when he said, "There is nothing as unequal as the equal treatment of unequals" (cited in Cortes, 1994, p. 30).

"Multiculturalism Should Not Focus on People of Color"

Whether multicultural literature should focus on people of color has been discussed and debated intermittently for some time. Patrick Shannon (1994), Rudine Sims Bishop (1994), and Violet Harris (1994b) engaged in a heated exchange over this issue in the *Journal of Children's Literature*. While acknowledging the multiple dimensions of cultural difference, some educators contend that we should focus on racial issues. Harris (1992) believes that we should "concentrate on those who are most excluded and marginalized, people of color" (p. xvi). Bishop (1994) also argues for a focus on people of color in selecting multicultural literature: "This is not an attempt to exclude other groups from the body of multicultural literature. It is to call attention to the voices that have been traditionally omitted from the canon[,] . . . the part of the picture that needs most to be filled in" (p. 7). Others (Horning & Kruse, 1991) simply define multicultural literature as books about people of color. They believe the issues of race are so critical that they should be the focus of multicultural literature.

In actual use within schools and libraries, the term "multicultural literature" is usually treated as equivalent to multiethnic literature. Teachers and librarians do not typically classify books dealing with class, gender, and other differences as multicultural literature.

This concentration on people of color has been criticized for reducing multiculturalism to a racial essentialism that excludes many cultures from the concept of multiculturalism. "Such treatment," Shannon (1994) comments, allows most teachers and students "to stand apart from multiculturalism, as if it were only about The Other and not about themselves" (p. 2). Since the majority of teachers and students in his institution are white, Shannon says, they find multiculturalism irrelevant or even an imposition when limited to issues of race. In this book, Rochman (1993) argues vehemently against emphasizing racial issues: "Multiculturalism means across cultures, against borders and multiculturalism doesn't mean only people of color" (p. 9).

Everyone does seem to agree with the goal of multiculturalism as stated by Shannon (1994), i.e., "changing the definition and reality of America until they stand for equality, freedom, and justice" (p. 5). To achieve the goal of multiculturalism, in Shannon's view, all teachers and students should be involved in talking about multiculturalism and acknowledge cultural biases by "making issues of culture problematic" (p. 2) in *all* the books we read. Shannon argues that instead of focusing on literature about people of color we should discover and discuss the cultural aspects of any children's literature which itself "demonstrates the complexity of multiculturalism" (p. 3).

One of the examples Shannon uses to illustrate his point is the animal fantasy book *Farmer Duck* (Waddell, 1992), which is about farm animals revolting against a farmer who makes Farmer Duck toil for him. The "multiracial," "multilingual" animals form a united front against the common class enemy. This book normally would not be classified as multicultural literature, but Shannon touts it as "a multicultural book at its best" (p. 3) because it has the "potential for serious discussion of economic class and the injustices of capitalism" (p. 3) as well as issues of gender, race, and language difference.

In his argument, I believe, Shannon sets up a false dichotomy between reading all books multiculturally (Hade, 1997) and reading books about the Other. These two approaches are mutually complementary. To read books by and about people of color does not exclude whites from the discussion of multiculturalism. Books about people of color may not directly reflect the lives of white teachers and students, but they definitely expose them to racial issues that they will inevitably confront at some point in their lives. Exposure to these books may help them become aware of racial discrimination and oppression.

Roll of Thunder, Hear My Cry (Taylor, 1976), for example, depicts the sufferings of an African American family under racist oppression during the Depression years, definitely a book about the Other. But how can any white readers rightfully say that it has nothing to do with them? If they recognize the fact that whites have contributed to the oppression of people of color, how can they feel that reading the book is irrelevant to their lives or an imposition? A book like *Roll of Thunder, Hear My Cry* concerns everyone regardless of ethnic background. While its text is mainly about African American experiences, the book presents an opportunity for every reader to ponder the racial issues that have plagued the United States. In this sense, this book is "about all of us."

Emphasizing issues of race and ethnicity does not exclude whites from the discussion of multiculturalism; instead it calls attention to a critical aspect of multiculturalism that concerns everyone—we live in a racialized society (Morrison, 1992; West, 1993). People of color have been discriminated against, oppressed, and exploited throughout our nation's history. They still experience varying degrees of inequality and injustice today. While progress has been made, American society is unfortunately still torn apart along racial lines. Anyone who recognizes the urgency of the racial issues would not "fear, demonize, and dismiss an ideology that attempts to redress historic and on-going inequalities and institutionalized racism" (Harris, 1994b, p. 9).

"All Literature Is Multicultural Literature"

Shannon (1994) makes a valid point about implementing multiculturalism through exploration of all children's books. His argument, however, suggests that we should not have a separate category of literature called multicultural literature, because the separation would make general literature appear as the norm and multicultural literature as alien. Shannon's argument about the multicultural nature of literature is shared by Andrea Fishman (1995), who explicitly states that "all literature is multicultural" (p. 79). Different from the first view that multicultural literature is multiple plus literature, this view denies the necessity of creating a type of literature about various specific cultures, whether it be dominant or dominated cultures.

The view that all literature is multicultural has the merit of expanding our understanding of literature from a multicultural perspective. We should try to read any piece of literature multiculturally to discover and deal with the cultural issues in it, but we need books directly dealing with cultural issues to make a concentrated study of underrepresented cultures. Multicultural literature is still a much-needed separate category of literature, for its existence poses a challenge to the domination of all-white literature.

Whether multicultural literature is alien or exotic is not inherent in the literature itself, but rather lies in the perception of the reader. From the perspective of marginalized ethnic groups, this new category of literature is not alien or exotic at all. Instead, it represents their world, reflecting their images and voices. When it is incorporated into the curriculum, children find characters to identify with in books they read in school. Think of the all-white world of children's literature that Nancy Larrick described in 1965 where only 6.7 percent of children's books published between 1962 and 1964 included African Americans in text or illustration. That is a really exotic world for children from marginalized cultures.

If we argue that multicultural literature should be integrated into the curriculum instead of being excluded and treated as something added on like an appendix, that is another matter. In some standard children's literature textbooks, such as Huck et al. (1997) and Norton (1995), there is a chapter or a section that deals exclusively with multicultural literature. This treatment of multicultural literature does not necessarily make it appear as alien if the same attitude also permeates the discussion of children's literature in general. Norton (1995) notes:

> This chapter is not intended to isolate the literature and contributions of racial and ethnic minorities from other literature discussed in this book. Instead, it tries to place multicultural literature in a context helpful to librarians, teachers, and parents who wish to select and share such materials with children or develop multicultural literature programs. (p. 560)

The integration of multicultural literature into the curriculum does not and should not entail the abandonment of multicultural literature as a category of literature deserving special attention.

To exclude multicultural literature because it might possibly set up barriers between "them" and us may contribute to the demise of multicultural literature. Historically marginalized cultures are still underrepresented in children's literature. Books by and about people of color, for example, are still disproportionate to the population of people of color (Bishop, 1997). Nieto (1997) is apprehensive that the conservative agenda may bring books portraying the Puerto Rican experience to "an abrupt halt" in the 1990s (p. 69). Horning, Kruse, and Schliesman (1997) are worried that "the collective span of Americans is beginning to move away from multicultural literature." They stress that "it is critical that multicultural literature be viewed as a substantial component of children's book publishing, rather than a passing fad" (p. 10). Obviously, what is especially at stake is literature about ethnic minorities, not multicultural literature broadly defined.

Historically, protest against a virtually all-white world of children's literature played an important role in bringing about multicultural literature. To keep this fledgling literature alive, educators, librarians, parents, and students again need to raise their voices to demand its publication. That will not happen if they are confused or misled by the controversy over the definition of multicultural literature.

Implications for Teachers and Teacher Educators

The debate over the definition of multicultural literature has great implications for teachers and teacher educators. It raises general questions about upholding and pursuing the goals of multicultural education and specific questions about incorporating multicultural literature into the curriculum. Three key issues that concern me are the relationships between diversity and equity, between informing and empowering, and between reading multiculturally and reading multicultural literature.

Diversity and Equity

Multicultural literature is an important tool in achieving the goal of diversity and equity within the multicultural education movement. The view that multiple + culture = multiculturalism emphasizes diversity without distinguishing between dominated and dominant cultures. If educators accept this view, they aim at teaching diverse cultures more than addressing issues of equity. When considering multicultural infusion in the curriculum, they require the curriculum to represent all the diverse cultures that constitute the vast demographic web of the United States.

I do not support this perspective, because the dominated cultures have been and are still underrepresented in the curriculum. We should focus on the disenfranchised cultures rather than on all cultures. In including every culture, the curriculum would not only be unmanageably big but also miss the ultimate goal of multiculturalism. For example, in an instructional unit on the Revolutionary War, we cannot and should not try to cover every cultural group. Rather, we should include literature on underrepresented groups such as African Americans and women since their perspectives and contributions are not included in textbook interpretations of this historical event.

It is not my contention that we should exclude books about mainstream cultures. In instructional activities that compare and contrast different cultures in order to show human commonalities, books about the dominated groups are usually used along with books about European cultures. But if the historically underrepresented groups are not included in thematic units, attempts to affirm diversity and address equity will not be successful.

Using or implying that a Eurocentric perspective is the standard of measure can be counterproductive. When students compare different variants of the Cinderella story, a popular activity in school, they learn about different cultures but may still "subconsciously" be presented with "a message of European American cultural superiority. Even though a Chinese tale about Yeh Shen is believed to be the earliest of the so-called Cinderella tales, discussion is unlikely to be about the variations of 'Yeh Shen tales' but rather about 'Cinderella tales'" (Yamate, 1997, p. 122). To affirm diversity is to ultimately achieve equity. Diversity without equity is not the goal of multiculturalism.

A multicultural activity aimed at diversity can backfire and generate prejudice if we do not teach equity at the same time. Glenn-Paul (1997) notes that during some "multicultural days" in a school "children were cruel to others because their contributions didn't meet the level of expectation or the children placed valued judgment on the dish and culture" (p. 269).

If diversity is presented with little respect for the less known culture, a multicultural activity may build, instead of break down, cultural barriers. Lee (1995) reports that on a field trip to a cemetery to celebrate the Chinese Clear Brightness festival, a teacher encouraged her students to tour the cemetery and make rubbings of the tombstones. The Chinese families who were cleaning the graves and making offerings to their ancestors were offended by the intruders. For the Chinese, this festival is a solemn occasion on which to pay respect to their ancestors and ask for blessings from them. The ceremonial meal they eat at the graveside is not a family picnic, as the teacher thought. The teacher might have been well intentioned in organizing the activity, but due to insensitivity her efforts at diversity were counterproductive.

Informing and Empowering

Many activities aimed at diversity follow an information-driven approach that centers on informing students about other cultures but does not tackle issues related to cultural differences. Many of the "multicultural weeks or months" in school and colleges are typical examples of this type of activity. They feature the so-called four *f*'s: food, festival, fashion, and folklore. Some multicultural books facilitate this information-driven approach, such as *Everybody Cooks Rice* (Dooley, 1991), *Hopscotch around the World* (Lankford, 1992), and *This Is the Way We Go to School* (Baer, 1990). They compare and contrast ways of life in different cultures with a view to broadening the reader's vision of cultural diversity. While they are informative and interesting, they do not deal with cultural conflicts, and many of them are somewhat superficial.

To encourage students to empower themselves, issue-driven activities and thought-provoking books are needed to challenge children's thinking about real-life issues. *Empowerment* is a buzzword. Defined in a narrow sense, it means "not only helping students understand and engage with the world around them, but also enabling them to exercise the kind of courage needed to change the social order where necessary" (Mclaren, 1998, pp. 185–86). According to this definition, students can empower themselves if they develop the ability to identify, analyze, and take action on cultural/ethnic issues (Rasinski & Padak, 1990).

Teachers need to create learning experiences that encourage students to empower themselves. For example, interracial relationships are an issue all students have to deal with at some point in their lives. Adopting an issue-driven approach, a teacher may want to do a thematic unit to help students address this issue using picture books such as *Angel Child, Dragon Child* (Surat, 1989), *Chicken Sunday* (Polacco, 1992), and *Smoky Night* (Bunting, 1994). These books begin with interracial tension but end with reconciliation or friendship. They have the potential to

encourage readers to reflect on interracial relationships through thinking about issues such as: What causes the tension in the story? How is
it solved? How is friendship forged? What would you do if you were
faced with the same problems as the characters? After discussing these
issues, students can engage in activities to help them empathize with
the characters and gain deeper insights. An activity for *Angel Child,
Dragon Child,* in which an immigrant girl from Vietnam is teased because
her dress is different, may be talking about their own unpleasant experiences of being teased because they were different from others in some
way, such as having a different hairstyle, dress, habit, etc. Students may
also role-play the Vietnamese girl and keep a diary of her experience in
the new school. Then they may move on to action-oriented activities,
for example, doing something to help new immigrants in their district.

   If we subscribe to a tourist view of multiculturalism, we will not
move from informing to empowering in our curricular experiences.
Unless students empower themselves to deal with issues of social equity and justice, multicultural education stops short of its ultimate goal.

Reading Multiculturally and Reading Multicultural Literature

The view that all literature is multicultural and should be read
multiculturally does open up new channels for multicultural education.
Reading multiculturally enhances our multicultural awareness and
helps us see multicultural issues that are not readily apparent. Hade
(1997) uses the children's classic *The Secret Garden* (Burnett, 1911/1987)
as an example of reading multiculturally. According to Hade, this book
can be interpreted as a subversive story in that children triumph over
adults. A multicultural reading, however, reveals a different meaning:

> The poor and women, though apparently each with more sense
> than rich males, have been put on earth to serve rich males. The
> working-class people in *The Secret Garden* exist for the upper class.
> . . . A romantic view of class pervades the book. The poor are
> noble savages. They don't need modern medicine or money, just
> fresh air and starchy food. They are uncorrupted by wealth, in-
> nocently happy in their destitution. (Hade, 1997, p. 245)

   A reader who reads *The Secret Garden* this way takes a multicultural stance—"one that seeks to understand how race, class, and gender mean in a story" (Hade, 1997, p. 245)—and interprets the cultural
implications of the book. A multicultural stance provides the reader with
an instrument, a magnifier, to expose assumptions about race, class, and
gender hidden in a story. We can adopt this stance toward many other
classics, such as *The Adventures of Huckleberry Finn* and *The Merchant of*

Venice and traditional folktales such as "Cinderella" and "Little Red Riding Hood" and find similar problems of race, class, and gender. College courses in children's and young adult literature should help students develop this stance and learn to analyze the cultural issues implicit in the books they read.

While we should read any literary work multiculturally, we also need to read multicultural literature that concentrates on oppressed groups, especially ethnic groups. In *Farmer Duck* or *The Secret Garden*, race is not a central issue. If a reader wants to learn about the history and reality of racial issues in the United States, what books can provide the information and perspectives? *Farmer Duck*, or books about people of color like *Tar Beach* and *Roll of Thunder, Hear My Cry*? The latter, obviously. Teachers and librarians need to help children find and engage with these books. As Bishop (1994) points out, "White students and their teachers will find *Farmer Duck*. . . . But will they find Jacob Lawrence or Lulu Delacre or Shonto Begay or Yoshiko Uchida on their own? And if they do, will they turn away because they think it represents something and someone alien to them?" (p. 7)

Some mainstream students may find it hard to engage with multicultural literature because this literature does not reflect their experiences. The role of educators is to help them find ways into these books. Shannon (1994) and Fishman (1995) both believe that a reader's "multiple cultural identities" may provide ways into literature that seems owned by Others. They have a valid point. Shannon demonstrates this possibility with *Tar Beach* (Ringgold, 1991), which depicts an African American girl's imaginary flight over New York City. In her imagination, she and her family are free of the bondage of discrimination and poverty. Although "this book is about race and racism in America," (p. 2), Shannon points out that the racial issues are situated "within a complex social context which cuts across other social groups" (p. 3). There are other cultural markers such as class and gender in the book with which all readers can identify. They may not belong to the same ethnic group of the characters in the story, but they may share the same socioeconomic status or have other connections with the characters. These connections enable them to engage in the story and empathize with the characters. Teachers who listened to Shannon read this book, for example, have subsequently written about devastating experiences of their spouses or parents being laid off and about their desires to move from working- to middle-class experiences.

However, if the response and discussion stops at seeking out the common experiences with the characters and does not examine closely the social inequality and injustice caused by racism as reflected in *Tar Beach,* the point of reading about the Other is missed.

To see commonalities between cultures is important, but to study the differences is equally or more important. Through discussion of differences while reading *Tar Beach,* white students may become aware of their privilege and power over African Americans and also their bias against them. Some of Shannon's students revealed their bias when they snickered at the menu of fried chicken, watermelon, and beer at the picnic of the black family. How these students developed this negative response to images of African Americans should be given serious attention (Bishop, 1994). If the issue is not addressed in their discussion of the book, the reading of the book is largely counterproductive even if they can relate to the story, because instead of removing the negative stereotype, the literary encounter perpetuates it. For all readers, reading various cultural messages in a book about people of color should not end with narcissistic self-reflection but should eventually lead to a change of perspective on the Other.

Multicultural literature embodies a dream of equity for oppressed groups. We should hold fast to this dream (Reimer, 1992). Since its inception, multicultural literature has gained some ground but is still far from permeating the curriculum. To make multiculturalism the core of education, we need more, not less, multicultural literature.

References

Banks, J. A., & Banks, C. (Eds.). (1997). *Multicultural education: Issues and perspectives.* Boston: Allyn and Bacon.

Bishop, R. S. (1994). A reply to Shannon the canon. *Journal of Children's Literature, 20*(1), 6–8.

Bishop, R. S. (1997). Selecting literature for a multicultural curriculum. In V. J. Harris (Ed.), *Using multiethnic literature in the K–8 classroom* (pp. 1–20). Norwood, MA: Christopher-Gordon.

Bullard, S. (1991). Sorting through the multicultural rhetoric. *Educational Leadership, 49*(4), 4–7.

Cortes, C. E. (1994). Multiculturation: An educational model for a culturally and linguistically diverse society. In K. Spangenberg-Urbschat & R. H. Pritchard (Eds.) *Kids come in all languages: Reading instruction for ESL students* (pp. 22–35). Newark, DE: International Reading Association.

Estrada, K., &. McLaren, P. (1993). A dialogue on multiculturalism and democratic culture. *Educational Researcher, 22*(3), 27–33.

Fishman, A. R. (1995). Finding ways in: Redefining multicultural literature. *English Journal, 84*(6), 73–79.

Glenn-Paul, D. (1997). Toward developing a multicultural perspective. In V. J. Harris (Ed.), *Using multiethnic literature in the K–8 classroom* (pp. 257–76). Norwood, MA: Christopher-Gordon.

Hade, D. D. (1997). Reading multiculturally. In V. J. Harris (Ed.), *Using multiethnic literature in the K–8 classroom* (pp. 233–56). Norwood, MA: Christopher-Gordon.

Harris, V. J. (Ed.). (1992). *Teaching multicultural literature: In grades K–8.* Norwood, MA: Christopher-Gordon.

Harris, V. (1994a). Review of *Against borders: Promoting books for a multicultural world* by Hazel Rochman. *Journal of Reading Behavior, 26*(1), 117–20.

Harris, V. (1994b). No invitation required to share multicultural literature. *Journal of Children's Literature, 20*(1), 9–13.

Horning, K. T., & Kruse, G. M. (1991). Looking into the mirror: Considerations behind the reflections. In M. V. Lindgren (Ed.), *The multicolored mirror: Cultural substance in literature for children and young adults* (pp. 1–13). Fort Atkinson, WI: Highsmith Press.

Horning, K. T., Kruse, G. M., & Schliesman, M. (1997). *CCBC Choices 1996.* Madison: University of Wisconsin Press.

Huck, C. S., Hepler, S., Hickman, J., & Loefer, B. Z. (1997). *Children's literature in the elementary school* (6th ed.). Madison, WI: Brown & Benchmark.

Langer, S. (1957). *Philosophy in a new key: A study in the symbolism of reason, rite, and art.* Cambridge, MA: Harvard University Press.

Larrick, N. (1965, September 11). The all-white world of children's books. *Saturday Review,* 63–65.

Lee, M. (1995, March). Building bridges or barriers? *The Horn Book Magazine,* 233–36.

Levy, M. (1995). Reflections on multiculturalism and the tower of psychobabble. *The ALAN Review, 22*(3), 11–15.

McLaren, P. (1998). *Life in schools: An introduction to critical pedagogy in the foundations of education* (3rd ed.). New York: Longman.

Morrison, T. (1992). *Playing in the dark: Whiteness and the literary imagination.* Cambridge, MA: Harvard University Press.

Nieto, S. (1997). We have stories to tell: Puerto Ricans in children's books. In V. J. Harris (Ed.), *Using multiethnic literature in the K–8 classroom* (pp. 59–94). Norwood, MA: Christopher-Gordon.

Norton, D. E. (1995). *Through the eyes of a child: An introduction to children's literature.* Englewood Cliffs, NJ: Merrill.

Rasinski, T. V., & Padak, N. D. (1990). Multicultural learning through children's literature. *Language Arts, 67,* 576–80.

Reimer, K. M. (1992). Multiethnic literature: Holding fast to dreams. *Language Arts, 69,* 14–21.

Rochman, H. (1993). *Against borders: Promoting books for a multicultural world.* Chicago: ALA Editions and Booklist Publications.

Rochman, H. (2003). Beyond political correctness. In D. L. Fox & K. G. Short (Eds.), *Stories matter: The complexity of cultural authenticity in children's literature* (pp. 101–15). Urbana, IL: National Council of Teachers of English.

Shannon, P. (1994). I am the canon: Finding ourselves in multiculturalism. *Journal of Children's Literature, 20*(1), 1–5.

Smith, K. P. (1993). The multicultural ethic and connections to literature for children and young adults. *Library Trends, 41*(3), 340–53.

West, C. (1993). *Race matters.* Boston: Beacon.

Yamate, S. S. (1997). Asian Pacific American children's literature: Expanding perceptions about who Americans are. In V. J. Harris (Ed.), *Using multiethnic literature in the K–8 classroom* (pp. 95–128). Norwood, MA: Christopher-Gordon.

Children's Books Cited

Baer, E. (1990). *This is the way we go to school: A book about children around the world* (S. Bjorkman, Illus.). New York: Scholastic.

Bunting, E. (1994). *Smoky night* (D. Diaz, Illus.). San Diego: Harcourt Brace.

Burnett, F. H. (1987). *The secret garden.* New York: Bantam. (Original work published 1911)

Dooley, N. (1991). *Everybody cooks rice* (P. Thornton, Illus.). Minneapolis, MN: Carolrhoda.

Lankford, M. D. (1992). *Hopscotch around the world* (K. Milone, Illus.). New York: Morrow Junior.

Polacco, P. (1992). *Chicken Sunday.* New York: Philomel.

Ringgold, F. (1991). *Tar Beach.* New York: Scholastic.

Surat, M. M. (1989). *Angel child, dragon child* (V.-D. Mai, Illus.). New York: Scholastic.

Taylor, M. D. (1976). *Roll of thunder, hear my cry.* New York: Dial.

Waddell, M. (1992). *Farmer duck.* Cambridge, MA: Candlewick Press.

21 The Trivialization and Misuse of Multicultural Literature: Issues of Representation and Communication

Zhihui Fang, Danling Fu, and Linda Leonard Lamme

New state and national educational standards now place greater emphasis than ever before on higher levels of literacy (Allington, 2001). Increasingly, children need to develop critical thinking and analytical skills beyond the "basics" and to acquire a more tolerant disposition toward the complexity of our pluralistic world. Ironically, many school districts are adopting systematic skills-based approaches that actually work against these standards. We believe that a literature-based curriculum—with its emphasis on multicultural literature—is a pedagogy that can achieve today's educational goals.

While a literature-based curriculum has become a viable vehicle for revamping classroom climate and instruction (Young, Campbell, & Oda, 1995), it has, in practice, also created a paradoxical situation in which multicultural literature runs the risk of being trivialized and misused. In this chapter, we provide a critique of the representation of minorities within multicultural literature and of the use of these books within the literature-based context. We argue for a reconceptualization of literacy beyond narrowly defined basic skills and suggest that literacy pedagogy should give greater attention to the communicative process of literature and integrate social, cultural, critical, and literary theories. Because Asian American literature is rarely referenced in the professional literacy discourse, we draw examples primarily from this marginalized body of literature in our discussion.

This chapter is a revised version of an essay that originally appeared in *The New Advocate*, 1999, *12*(3), 259–76. Reprinted with permission.

Problematizing Multicultural Literature: The Issue of Representation

The term "multicultural literature" has been defined in various ways (Cai, 2003b; Cai & Bishop, 1994; Sims, 1982). Most literacy educators in the United States use it to refer to literature by and about people belonging to the various self-identified ethnic, racial, religious, and regional groups in American society. Multicultural literature is supposed to accurately present the historical, cultural, political, sociological, economical, and educational contributions of various ethnic and cultural groups that reside in the United States (Banks, 1993). Therefore, it is considered appropriate not only for developing a more tolerant and positive disposition toward our multicultural society, but also for contextualizing the practice of literacy skills as well as teaching content-area knowledge.

While there is much to be applauded in the current interest among literacy educators in multicultural literature, there are causes for concern. At the forefront of such concern is the issue of representation. The proliferation of multicultural literature in the past decade can be seen as part of the democratic process that aims at giving minority cultures a voice in the larger social and cultural hegemony. However, as Marx (1889) pointed out more than a century ago, these minorities often do not have the economic or political power to represent themselves and, as a result, they have to be represented by others (i.e., the dominant culture) who imitate and simulate their cultural voices. In fact, multicultural books about minorities are written predominantly by European American authors from an outsider's perspective (Reimer, 1992). We recently surveyed a collection of more than ninety children's picture books depicting Chinese and Chinese Americans that were listed in Cai (1994) and Zhang, Lamme, and Fang (1999). We found that over two-thirds of these books were by authors of non-Chinese heritage. While it might be expected that minority cultures are represented by outsiders, this percentage seems much too high.

One challenge confronting writers who present a culture of which they are not a part is the difficulty of dealing with dialects and cultural authenticity (Spivak & Gunew, 1993). For example, a white male author who decides to write a fictional account that depicts a Japanese American girl as the main character may struggle with authenticity because he has no lived experiences to rely on as he creates his story. He is neither Japanese American nor female. His central character is outside his lived experience. Furthermore, if that author is unwilling to research the historical events (e.g., internment camps in the United States during World War II) that have shaped the culture he is depicting, his representation will likely reflect mainstream cultural rationales for past injustice and current silence rather than historical authenticity. A case in point can be seen in Cai's (2003a) contrastive critique of *Footprints of the Dragon* (Oakes, 1949) and *Dragon's Gate* (Yep, 1993), both depicting the trials and tribulations of the Chinese workers during the construction of American railroads at the turn of the twentieth century.

Issues of authenticity are complex in that racial, ethnic, religious, and gender identities do not always ensure that writers will accurately portray their own group cultures and outsiders can write sympathetic and historically accurate fictional stories. However, Yokota (1993) argues that the further writers are removed from the experience or heritage of the object culture they are depicting, the harder they have to work in order to attain cultural authenticity. Writers who step beyond their lived experiences need to carefully research and explore the cultural group they portray in order to avoid using stereotypical images and erroneous cultural information. As Dynak (1995) aptly observes, "Cultural stereotypes derive from a lack of intimacy" (p. 369).

Hoffman (1996) and Lim and Ling (1992) suggest that multicultural literature written from a European American perspective tends to be shaped by the dominant cultural frame, and therefore these books often reflect the institutional power relations by heightening the discourse of European American domination within society. Scholars such as Mingshui Cai, Violet Harris, Sonia Nieto, and Rudine Sims Bishop have argued that a disproportionate percentage of the so-called multicultural books are imprinted with dominant Eurocentric ideologies and values. Fang (1998) examined three picture storybooks written by European Americans depicting Chinese and Chinese Americans: *The Journey of Meng* (Rappaport, 1991), *The River Dragon* (Pattison, 1991), and *Pie-biter* (McCunn, 1983). He found that these so-called multicultural books are influenced by Western ideologies and imbued with orientalism and ahistoricism, all of which are forms of postcolonial discourse reflective of an imperialist mentality (Said, 1978, 1993).

Doreen Rappaport's *The Journey of Meng* (1991) is a contemporary U.S. picture book retelling of a Chinese folktale. The original story reflects the Chinese attitude toward fidelity in marriage; it tells of a woman in search of her enslaved husband and ends when her heartbreaking cries over his death tumble the Great Wall. The tale was originally meant to commend a married woman's fidelity to her husband and to emphasize her moral and ethical integrity (Chin, Center, & Ross, 1989). However,

The Journey of Meng virtually transforms the original folktale into a quest story that readily fits within Western literary traditions. The woman leaves home to look for her husband, learns of his death, and, once her mourning causes the Great Wall to tumble, the emperor demands that she marry him as a reprisal.

Contrary to the original story's emphasis on the moral and ethical virtues of marriage, this retelling depicts Meng as a symbol of courage and defiance against male tyranny. In the original Chinese tale, Meng is an ordinary countrywoman whose faithfulness to her husband fits the traditional social expectations and cultural values placed on women and marriage. Her strength is in this simple act. She is not battling a sexual oppressor. In contrast, Rappaport depicts Meng as a sexual object and has her kill herself rather than betray her loyalty to her dead husband. Rappaport seems to not understand that exploration of sexuality is extremely rare in Chinese children's literature and is assiduously avoided in classic Chinese folktales because such discussion, it is believed, endangers the true significance of male-female relations. Viewed with an understanding of Chinese cultural and literary traditions, *The Journey of Meng* is an example of the Western pattern of ultrafeminization, which in this case means the fetishizing of Chinese women as "the embodiment of perfect womanhood" (Wong, 1992, p. 112).

Despite their inaccuracies, many multicultural books are nonetheless favorably reviewed and touted as authentic renditions of certain ethnic, cultural, and literary heritages. These naive reaffirmations of cultural inauthenticity reflect a more troubling facet of a society tied to capitalist economy. Kim (1982) notes that books by Anglo-Americans about Asians are often preferred over those written by Asian Americans themselves because American publishers, critics, and readers seem better attuned to "morbid or comical stereotypes created by Anglo-American writers" (p. 22). The pressure to meet the demands of a market-driven economy has even led some insiders to succumb to the public readership's taste, failing to represent their subjects accurately. Ma (1998) laments that there is a tendency among some Chinese American writers to "orientalize" their Chinese subjects in order to cater to expectations of otherness and exoticism by mainstream American readers.

In the end, the publication and circulation of these pseudo-multicultural books perpetuates the dominant power structure in American society. On the one hand, these books privilege the established stereotypical representations of intercultural relations by creating positive images of imperialism. On the other hand, they substantiate support for maintaining the recognized conditions of a minority culture within contemporary U.S. political and social systems by making the minority culture less significant as an exotic other. As Gunew (1985) points out, "The textual production of marginal minorities exists to confirm hegemonic textualities" (p. 142).

The Communication of Multicultural Literature

To understand the consequences of cultural inauthenticity for children's literacy, it is necessary to look closely at how messages in literature are communicated in our society. Hall (1993) offers a compelling account of how messages in mass media are produced and disseminated. He criticizes the traditional communication model for its focus on the linear level of message exchange (i.e., sender-message-receiver), suggesting that it does not reflect the complex relationships that occur in the different moments of communication. He uses a sociosemiotic paradigm to argue that the process of communication is "a complex structure in dominance" produced and sustained through production, circulation, distribution/consumption, and reproduction.

Each of these four stages is relatively autonomous but also inextricably interrelated in that they reflect different moments within the whole of the social relations of the communication process. The encoding of a message at the production phase tends to be framed by the dominant discursive form, with its often institutionalized ideologies, practices, values, and beliefs. This dominant discursive code gets reinforced and sustained in each of the subsequent stages of the communication process because they too are influenced and controlled by the dominant political, cultural, and economic order of society. Further, any society tends to privilege certain ways of reading texts, and these "preferred readings" are themselves imprinted with the institutionalized ideological order. This means that while there is always room for a message to be understood somewhat against its intended grain, it is not open to interpretation. From this perspective, television and mass media (including literature) in general become vehicles for reproducing the dominant social order of mainstream culture.

Hall's communication theory provides a framework for explaining why many multicultural books become a powerful, yet often unrecognized, force for reinforcing dominant ideologies and stereotypes. Because mainstream American culture is often used, intentionally or unwittingly, as the frame of reference by European American and other writers in their depiction of minority cultures, the resulting "multicultural" books will most likely embody such Eurocentrism. The

---

Share Ruthanne McCunn's (1983) *Pie-biter* with class (read aloud).

Discuss the characters, setting, problems, and resolution (story grammar worksheet).

Write key vocabulary words and review with students, decode the words, look for word families or patterns, and discuss the meanings of words (vocabulary worksheet).

Distribute student copies of the book and pair up students to read to one another (partner reading).

Present spelling words from the story on board. Decode together and use orally in sentences (phonics worksheet).

Figure 1. A second-grade lesson plan.

discourses of power and dominance that have been written into the literature are sustained and oftentimes heightened through the communication process, particularly when readers are not encouraged to engage in a critical reading of these books to identify this dominant discourse.

To demonstrate this point within the context of literacy education, we next focus our discussion on the uses of multicultural literature within a literature-based classroom. We hope to show how contemporary pedagogical practices are, ironically, defeating the very ideals they seek to advance and, at the same time, promoting the very ideology they seek to overthrow.

The Misuse of Multicultural Literature in Classrooms

Literature-based instruction has posed new challenges for teachers who do not have experience in identifying hidden messages in multicultural literature. In fact, many elementary teachers and teacher education programs do not have "either an instructional philosophy for the teaching of literature or a well-developed practical scheme for integrating it within the elementary education" (Walmsley, 1992, p. 509). Consequently, several problems have emerged in classroom practices involving the use of multicultural literature.

One problem is that some teachers treat multicultural books as disembodied texts to use as a springboard for contextualizing the teaching of isolated reading/writing skills. For example, a second-grade teacher planned the following morning lesson for a literature unit on China (see Figure 1).

In this schedule, literature is used as a vehicle for teaching reading and language arts skills (e.g., decoding, spelling, vocabulary, story grammar, comprehension). The lesson moves directly from shared reading to a worksheet exercise on story grammar and then to vocabulary and phonics activities. There is no time allotted for a literary discussion of the story's sociocultural attributes, even though the book is replete with cultural inaccuracies, stereotypes, and colonial discourse (Fang, 1998). Sharing literature for personal interpretation and reflection is not incorporated, and there is no discussion of the artistry of writing or illustration, the author's role in constructing the text, or cultural authenticity. The teacher seems to assume that children will understand the cultural messages in this book simply by reading the story on their own. Controlled by a time schedule that suggests completing a list of predetermined worksheet tasks is more important than the story itself, the teacher did not allow time for reflective, critical, or literary explorations (Freire & Macedo, 1987; Hoffman, 1996; May, 1995; Purves; 1993b; Rosenblatt, 1983).

A second problem with current literature-based instruction has to do with the fact that many elementary school teachers have not explored the critical traditions of cultural studies and literary analysis in their teacher education programs. As a consequence, they are not likely to detect inconsistencies, inaccuracies, and false notes in multicultural literature. As Moore-Kruse (cited in Madigan, 1993) has suggested, because most of the adults involved in creating and promoting children's books and linking them with children are European Americans, they are more likely to interpret literature from the dominant Eurocentric perspective. Thus, the hidden messages (i.e., power relations, cultural stereotypes) encoded in multicultural literature are seldom recognized, not to mention challenged, during its sharing in the classroom.

For example, students are often taught to look at culture through the lens of categories, a practice that results in reinforcing stereotypes and does little to create a real space for understanding of self and other (Hoffman, 1996). One third-grade teacher's discussion of Darcy Pattison's (1991) *The River Dragon* epitomizes this practice. The teacher (T) tries to activate students' (S) prior knowledge about the Chinese culture before reading the book:

> *T:* Boys and girls, today we are going to read a book about the Chinese culture. The book is called *The River Dragon* by Darcy Pattison. Who can tell me what you know about China?
>
> *S:* Fortune cookies.

T: Good, anything else?

S: Orange chicken.

S: Kongbao chicken.

S: Chao-mei.

T: Good! You all seem to have known a lot about the Chinese culture. Where did you learn all these?

Ss: In the Chinese restaurant.

T: Do you like Chinese food?

Ss: (nod their heads)

S: My parents like it, but I don't.

T: Is there anything else you know about the Chinese culture besides Chinese food?

S: Chinese New Year!

T: What do you know about the Chinese New Year?

(The whole class is silent.)

T: Okay, I am going to read the book to you. This is a story about the Chinese people and culture. Listen carefully. After the reading, I will ask you what you have learned from the book about the Chinese culture.

During reading, the teacher tries to draw her students' attention to the elements that she thinks they should notice:

T: (starts to read) *Once there were . . . , Ying Shao . . .* excuse me, boys and girls, Chinese names are hard to pronounce. I want you to repeat after me:
/i-ñ sh-ao/.

Ss: /i-ñ sh-ao/, /i-ñ sh-ao/, . . .

(The teacher continues reading and stops on page 3, pointing to the picture.)

T: Now, boys and girls, look at this picture. What kind of outfit does this man wear? Is it the same as ours?

Ss: (loudly) No.

T: (continues reading and stops on p. 5, pointing to the picture) Look at what he wears on his head. Does it look like the hats we wear in this country?

S: No. But my Chinese friend . . . Wong never wears that kind of hat.

T: Do you think the Chinese wear this type of hat in China?

S: I don't know. Maybe.

T: (continues reading and stops on p. 6, pointing to the picture) What do you see in this picture?

S: Chinese food.

S: I saw fortune cookies.

S: They look like kongbao chicken.

T: Don't they look delicious? Let's see what they are. (continues reading) *The servants brought in the main dish: swallows in delicate curry sauce . . .*

Ss: Oh . . . , swallows in curry sauce, yuk . . . how can they eat that?

T: How do you know it is not good? Have you ever tried it? Maybe it tastes good.

Ss: (shake their heads and mumble) I will never eat that!

T: (The teacher continues reading and stops on pp. 11–12, pointing to the picture of a dragon.) Now, let's look at this picture. Does anyone know what this animal is called?

Ss: Dragon.

T: What does it look like?

S: An alligator.

S: His head is like a monster.

S: His claws are like an eagle's.

T: Good job!

The teacher continues reading and stops intermittently to ask similar questions. After reading, the teacher reviews with students what they have learned from the book:

T: Boys and girls, what have you learned about the Chinese culture?

S: They eat swallows in curry sauce.

S: The dragon.

T: What about the dragon?

S: It likes to eat swallows.

S: It's afraid of centipedes. . . .

S: (interrupts) and a scarf of five colors.

T: Good for you! You've obviously learned a lot about the dragon. Is a dragon a good animal or a bad one?

Ss: Bad.

T: How bad is it?

S: It's scary.

S: It wants to eat people.

S: Don't they have a dragon dance on Chinese New Year?

T: Yep, I heard that too. It seems that the Chinese people love dragons. . . .(looks at her watch) Okay, boys and girls, we are going to do a few projects related to the book. I want you to draw a dragon and write about what you now know about the dragon. We will make a big dragon and try out a dragon dance tomorrow.

S: Could we have some Chinese food, too? I like kongbao chicken.

T: That sounds like a good idea. We will probably order some Chinese food for tomorrow.

The teacher initially tried to activate the children's background knowledge about Chinese culture through the lens of categories such as food and holidays. They were allowed to voice stereotypes without expansion or clarification. Furthermore, students were set up to take an efferent stance (i.e., what can you learn about the Chinese culture?) more than an aesthetic stance (i.e., what are you experiencing, thinking, and feeling?) toward the folktale. They were also not encouraged to take a critical perspective, even though the story is filled with cultural inaccuracies and stereotypes (Fang, 1998). During shared reading, rather than expanding on children's cultural knowledge and broadening their views of an ethnic culture, the teacher reinforced the children's misconceptions by drawing their attention only to dress, food, and dragons. At times, even when the children voiced their curiosity or challenged the depiction of storybook characters, their questions were ignored by the teacher and not further explored.

Overall, this classroom discourse features IRE (initiation-response-evaluation) sessions (Cazden, 1988). There was no discussion about the theme of the story, the values and traditions of the Chinese culture, or the symbolism of dragons. The after-reading discussion supported students' cultural misunderstandings and stereotypes, and the activities of drawing a dragon, making a dragon, performing a dragon dance, and tasting a Chinese dish reinforced the children's narrow and stereotypical view of Chinese culture. In the end, their knowledge about Chinese culture remains superficial and distorted.

This type of approach to literature does more harm than good. It accomplishes little toward helping children learn about others. It ridicules and distances others rather than opening up the children's minds and cultivating their respect for and appreciation of other cultures. The teacher and children not only know very little about Chinese culture, but they also have a narrow view of culture. By way of comparison, if a teacher in another country took this narrow view, she would introduce American culture by mentioning only McDonalds hamburgers, Thanksgiving, Halloween, and so on and say nothing about the democratic values and self-reliant spirit of the American people.

A third and corollary problem is that multicultural education is often defined in oversimplified terms in the curriculum as the teaching of cultural differences, celebration of a particular ethnic holiday (e.g., Kwanzaa, Chinese New Year), memorization of historical and geographical facts, examination of art and artifacts from different countries, and the experiencing of culinary diversity (Wurzel, 1988). While these activities can increase students' *awareness* of cultural differences and diversity, they are superficial. Their scope emphasizes mainstream history and values as the perspective for looking at "different" peoples. Such practices narrow the educational potential which diversity offers and run the risk of perpetuating separateness and reinforcing negative cultural stereotypes.

The fourth problem in literature-based instruction concerns the lack of diversity in the teaching force in contrast to the tremendous diversity of students (Ducharme & Ducharme, 1993). For example, of total 1989 enrollment in teacher education, 86.5 percent are European Americans, 6.8 percent African Americans, 2.7 percent Latino/Latina Americans, and less than 1 percent Asian Americans (AACTE, 1990). While the situation has improved somewhat over the past decade, the gross underrepresentation of minorities in the teaching force remains. This lack of diversity *incidentally* creates a school culture that does not facilitate dialogue and power sharing between white teachers and minority teachers. It perpetuates dominant social power structures in schools and silences minority voices (Delpit, 1995). Thus, the school reproduces the dominant social order found in society. This structural relationship between school and society creates a pedagogical context that limits possibilities for sharing divergent viewpoints and critical interpretations of literature. Such a school culture is likely to foster literacy practices that indoctrinate students to think in the same way and to interpret literature almost invariably from the dominant perspective. Students often couch their responses to fit the teacher's expectations (Purves, 1993b). There seems to be a proper/preferred way to think and be aware in the classroom, with the overall effect of ideological conformity (Hoffman, 1996).

These pedagogical practices, taken together, fail to deal with the hidden curriculum in school. By treating inherently sociopolitical and aesthetic literary work as disembodied text, teachers are not only trivializing multicultural literature but inflicting violence on it as well. They contribute to perpetuating and legitimating the dominance of mainstream values in literature. These practices, Pearson (1994) warned, run the risk of doing injustice to particular cultures and of creating new stereotypes, because they foster a distorted view of the world and of our relationships to it and other human beings. In the end, what began as a benevolent movement in literacy education (i.e., literature-based instruction) has, beyond its well-intended rhetoric, served to reinforce white supremacy, cultural hegemony, and social fragmentation.

Toward a Critical Literacy Pedagogy

We have painted a somewhat less than wholesome picture of literature-based instruction in many elementary school classrooms. Our intent here is not to ridicule the current pedagogical movement, nor to engage in teacher bashing. Rather, our purpose is to reflect, albeit painfully, on the nature and unexamined assumptions of contemporary literacy discourse and practice. Teachers and teacher educators need to heighten their awareness of the limitations and potentialities of multicultural literature and to exercise due caution in their uses of these books. A new direction is needed in literature-based instruction, both to promote more productive use of children's literature and to nurture a new generation of more critical and thoughtful readers.

Most important of all, literacy educators need to reconceptualize what it means to "read" in an increasingly pluralistic, multimodal, and complex society. We believe that reading means not only the skill to identify and decode written words, but also the capacity to put them into a creative relation with other cultural and symbolic signs. As Allen (1992) has stated, genuine understanding of literature requires knowledge of the contexts in which it was originally written and has since been read by others. For example, a true understanding of Rappaport's *The Journey of Meng* (1991) requires that readers not only know the words in the actual text being created but also, and more important, attend to its original Chinese source text, the texts to which it stands in relation (e.g., other versions of the same story or similar Chinese and American folktales), and the otherness it both embodies and delineates. In this connection, it is important that literacy educators recognize the relationship between reading ability—as traditionally defined—and literary knowledge. Meaningful experiences with literature should not only help students develop the skills typically taught in the reading/language arts program (e.g., phonics, vocabulary, comprehension), but also teach students strategies for reflectively and critically interpreting the texts they read (Walmsley, 1992).

We believe that the ultimate goal of literacy instruction should look beyond extending students' reading/writing skills to helping them attain "a new mental and emotional consciousness that enables individuals to negotiate more readily new formations of reality" in the texts they read (Wurzel, 1998, p. 10). Multicultural literature cannot serve as the handmaiden to skill-and-drill methodology. Although we agree that skills need be taught, they are best taught in response to student questions or to an observed need, especially *after* students have had the opportunity to personally and critically respond to a text.

One feasible way to integrate skills instruction with multicultural literature is to use a whole-part-whole approach (Trachtenburg, 1990). Using this approach, the teacher first engages students in reading, comprehending, critiquing, and enjoying a literature selection. Then the teacher provides explicit instruction on certain skills or strategies based on student needs by drawing from or extending that literature. Later on, the teacher encourages students to apply these skills when they read and enjoy another literature selection.

We want to emphasize that multicultural books are not just instructional products; they are also aesthetic representations of specific ethnic and cultural beliefs and values. Therefore, they should not be viewed as disembodied texts solely for the purpose of contextualizing students' practice of traditional literacy skills. They should be considered sociocultural and political texts for fostering students' understanding of the social and historical forces underpinning the construction of cultural identities (Taxel, 1992).

Accordingly, the curriculum must move beyond an emphasis on narrowly defined literacy skills and be expanded to integrate social, cultural, critical, and literary theories (Corcoran, Hayhoe, & Pradl, 1994; May, 1995; Purves, 1993a). Students should be encouraged to adopt what Hall (1993) calls negotiated and oppositional positions in their reading of multicultural texts. An oppositional stance involves a reader in considering multiple interpretations of a book, both from a dominant mainstream perspective and from alternative frames of reference. The reader understands the literal and implied meanings of the book but decides to be an uncooperative, subversive reader who considers other, "globally contrary" interpretations. From a negotiated stance, the reader acknowledges the legitimacy of the dominant code but at the same time reserves the right to make his or her own ground rules. In this sense, the reader makes adaptations of the message according to his or her experiences, knowledge, beliefs, and values.

We believe that, ultimately, students should have opportunities to discuss and reflect on multicultural stories as literary texts, to participate in a deeper study of diverse cultures across the curriculum, and to come to the understanding that others also have identities constructed across many registers (Wurzel, 1988). Teachers should help students understand that learning is a continuous process involving learning about others by listening to new story patterns, analyzing why they are different and what makes these patterns important, and reflecting on their personal preferences.

To give an example of what we believe is a good lesson framework for using literature, we suggest that teachers introduce literature by first encouraging students to share their knowledge and experiences in relation to the story's topic, genre, and author/illustrator. They should also discuss the context in which the story was produced. If the book contains an explanation by the author of how and why the book was written—including the source of a folktale or the process by which research was undertaken—such information should be shared and discussed before and/or after reading. Next, the literature selection can be read using different modes of reading, such as read-aloud, shared reading, guided reading, partner reading, or independent reading.

After reading, students should have time to talk and/or write about their personal reactions to the story. They can share particularly meaningful personal responses and explore themes, issues, genre, and writing style in more depth. It is important that literature discussion groups be flexible and heterogeneous so as to capitalize on the experience and knowledge of all students in the class. Teachers should sometimes participate as members of a group, sharing their opinions, knowledge, or ideas but rarely asking questions. A question-and-answer session, even if the questions are open-ended, is not a discussion and rarely taps students' genuine feelings or deeper thoughts.

As more knowledgeable others and discussion facilitators, teachers should have already critically read the selection and understood its potential for historical and cultural discrepancies and inaccurate interpretations. Once students have shared their own responses and issues, teachers can introduce significant issues that have not been raised. For example, they can urge students to consider certain social issues (e.g., gender, poverty, race, and culture), to discuss whether a story is a lived experience of the author or whether the author is an outsider to the culture depicted in the book, or to explore the craft of writing. Looking closely at the story provides strong clues as to the authenticity of the work and the perspective presented to the reader. It nearly always precipitates a more critical and analytical reading of a text and more thoughtful interpretations of and discussions about the reading.

The following excerpts from a discussion of Pattison's *The River Dragon* (1991) by a group of fifth graders during literature circle time in a class that had critically read literature all year illustrates the kind of thoughtful reading that we believe critical readers should be engaging in. In this literature circle, a group of five students (S) were responding to Darcy Pattison's *The River Dragon*. The teacher (T) functioned as facilitator during the small-group discussion.

> S: Gee, I really liked that folktale. I liked the pattern of three times Ying Shao goes to dinner and faces the dragon and the humor in the fortune cookies. I like how he outwits the dragon. But I wonder—aren't fortune cookies an American thing?
>
> S: You get them at Chinese restaurants.
>
> S: I got one about finding riches, but I never did.
>
> S: Yeah—well, the author says she researched dragons, but did she research Chinese culture as well? Is there a tradition of three meals with the bride's family? Do people leave dishes of rice for the river dragon and things like that?
>
> T: The author states that this is an original folktale—what does that mean?
>
> S: It is not retold through the centuries—she just wrote it?
>
> S: Yeah, but if she wrote it about the Chinese it should be an accurate picture of their culture.
>
> S: Arranged marriages were a Chinese tradition.
>
> S: I wonder how it would be to marry someone you don't really know. Arranged marriages sound horrible.
>
> S: Uh huh, and I wonder why the father objected to the marriage if it was an arranged marriage in the first place. Why would a blacksmith not be a good job?
>
> T: When do you suppose marriages are arranged? Maybe it is when the children are young and before they have decided upon their careers.
>
> S: Do you think the father was trying to test the groom? Do you think he purposely had swallows for each dish to trick the young man or to test him?
>
> S: I think it was a test and I think the daughter knew that and that is why she planted the clues in the fortune cookies.

S: That couldn't have been a coincidence.

T: So then you rather like the tale but think it may misrepresent Chinese culture?

S: Right.

S: Yes—I wonder how a Chinese person would respond to reading it.

T: Maybe we could ask a Chinese native to interpret it from her perspective?

Ss: Yes, let's do.

Activities such as conducting further research or inviting someone knowledgeable about the culture to add to the discussion can validate the importance of thoughtful critique of literature. Teachers can also guide students to connect the current piece of literature to other similar stories by author, genre, and/or topic. These related stories can support further reading and discussion so that students' understandings are extended. Teachers can also provide explicit instruction and practice in particular skills and strategies by drawing examples from related literature or encourage students to write about what they have learned from reading and responding to these stories.

Conclusion

In closing, we wish to emphasize that teachers themselves need experience as analytically critical readers of multicultural texts so that they can engage children in dynamic discussions about important issues and ideas. We acknowledge that it is not possible for teachers to know everything about every culture. However, what is more important is for teachers to cultivate the habit of approaching literature from a questioning and wondering stance. A critical pedagogy starts with teachers thoughtfully engaging in literature and then sharing similar processes with their students. Along with their students, teachers can question the perspective of the author and the purpose for writing the book. They can wonder about issues of gender, race, culture, and socioeconomic status, asking, for example, how the book would be received had the author been of a different race, culture, or gender. There are many sources of information about authors, illustrators, and children's books on the Internet and in professional print publications. A questioning and wondering stance invites further investigation into the books that teachers share with children.

Admittedly, such a pedagogy will not transform classroom practices overnight. It may even run counter to the accountability culture of schooling and the competency performance culture of teacher preparation. However difficult, uncertain, and complex their task, teachers should by no means resort to what Dudley-Marling (2003) refers to as "pedagogical arrest," in which teachers do nothing for fear of making mistakes or being criticized. To realize the potential of literacy and multicultural education in a literature-based classroom, we need alternative pedagogies that foster a literate community of thoughtful, analytical, and critical readers and writers.

Authors' Note

After the first author, the second and third authors contributed equally to this essay and are therefore listed alphabetically. We would like to thank Jill May for reading and reacting to an earlier version of this work. We also want to thank the editors and reviewers for their invaluable comments. However, we are solely responsible for the statements made herein.

References

Allen, P. G. (1992). "Border" studies: The intersection of gender and color. In J. Gibaldi (Ed.), *Introduction to scholarship in modern languages and literatures* (2nd ed., pp. 303–19). New York: Modern Language Association.

Allington, R. L. (2001). *What really matters for struggling readers: Designing research-based programs.* New York: Longman.

American Association of Colleges for Teacher Education (AACTE). (1990). *Teacher education pipeline II: Schools, colleges and departments of education enrollments by race and ethnicity.* Washington, DC: Author.

Banks, J. A. (1993). Approaches to multicultural curriculum reform. In J. A. Banks & C. A. Banks (Eds.), *Multicultural education: Issues and perspectives* (2nd ed., pp. 195–214). Boston: Allyn and Bacon.

Cai, M. (1994). Images of Chinese and Chinese Americans mirrored in picture books. *Children's Literature in Education, 25*(3), 169–91.

Cai, M. (2003a). Can we fly across cultural gaps on the wings of imagination? Ethnicity, experience, and cultural authenticity. In D. L. Fox & K. G. Short (Eds.), *Stories matter: The complexity of cultural authenticity in children's literature* (pp. 167–81). Urbana, IL: National Council of Teachers of English.

Cai, M. (2003b). Multiple definitions of multicultural literature: Is the debate really just "Ivory Tower" bickering? In D. L. Fox & K. G. Short (Eds.),

Stories matter: The complexity of cultural authenticity in children's literature (pp. 269–83). Urbana, IL: National Council of Teachers of English.

Cai, M., & Bishop, R. S. (1994). Multicultural literature for children: Towards a clarification of the concept. In A. H. Dyson & C. Genishi (Eds.), *The need for story: Cultural diversity in classroom and community* (pp. 57–71). Urbana, IL: National Council of Teachers of English.

Cazden, C. B. (1988). *Classroom discourse: The language of teaching and learning.* Portsmouth, NH: Heinemann.

Chin, Y. C., Center, Y. S., & Ross, M. (1989). *Traditional Chinese folktales.* Armonk, NY: M. E. Sharpe.

Corcoran, B., Hayhoe, M., & Pradl G. M. (1994). *Knowledge in the making: Challenging the text in the classroom.* Portsmouth, NH: Boynton/Cook Heinemann.

Delpit, L. D. (1995). *Other people's children: Cultural conflict in the classroom.* New York: New Press.

Ducharme, E. D., & Ducharme, M. K. (1993). Editorial: Primary issues and the first issue. *Journal of Teacher Education, 44*(1), 2–3.

Dudley-Marling, C. (2003). "I'm not from Pakistan": Multicultural literature and the problem of representation. In D. L. Fox & K. G. Short (Eds.), *Stories matter: The complexity of cultural authenticity in children's literature* (pp. 304–18). Urbana, IL: National Council of Teachers of English.

Dynak, D. (1995). First things first: A foreword to the themed issue on multicultural education in the language arts. *Reading Horizons, 35*(5), 369–74.

Fang, Z. (1998, November). *Exploring cultural perspectives on reading.* Paper presented at the 88th annual meeting of the National Council of Teachers of English, Nashville, Tennessee.

Freire, P., & Macedo, D. P. (1987). *Literacy: Reading the word and the world.* South Hadley, MA: Bergin & Garvey.

Gunew, S. (1985). Framing marginalia: Distinguishing the textual politics of the marginal voice. *Southern Review, 10,* 142–56.

Hall, S. (1993). Encoding, decoding. In S. During (Ed.), *The cultural studies reader* (pp. 90–103). New York: Routledge.

Hoffman, D. M. (1996). Culture and self in multicultural education: Reflections on discourse, text, and practice. *American Educational Research Journal, 33*(3), 545–69.

Kim, E. H. (1982). *Asian American literature: An introduction to the writings and their social context.* Philadelphia: Temple University Press.

Lim, S., & Ling, A. (1992). *Reading the literatures of Asian America.* Philadelphia: Temple University Press.

Ma, S. M. (1998). *Immigrant subjectivities in Asian American and Asian diaspora literatures.* Albany: State University of New York Press.

Madigan, D. (1993). The politics of multicultural literature for children and adolescents: Combining perspectives and conversations. *Language Arts, 70,* 168–76.

Marx, K. (1889). *Capital: A critical analysis of capitalist production* (S. Moore & E. Aveling, Trans., F. Engels, Ed.). New York: Appleton.

May, J. P. (1995). *Children's literature and critical theory: Reading and writing for understanding.* New York: Oxford University Press.

McCunn, R. L. (1983). *Pie-biter* (Y. Tang, Illus.). San Francisco: Design Enterprises of San Francisco.

Oakes, V. A. (1949). *Footprints of the dragon: A story of the Chinese and Pacific railways.* Philadelphia: Winston.

Pattison, D. (1991). *The river dragon* (J. Tseng & M. S. Tseng, Illus.). New York: Lothrop, Lee & Shepard.

Pearson, P. D. (1994). Integrated language arts: Sources of controversy and seeds of consensus. In L. M. Morrow, J. K. Smith, & L. C. Wilkinson (Eds.), *Integrated language arts: Controversy to consensus* (pp. 11–32). Boston: Allyn and Bacon.

Purves, A. (1993a). Making space: Perspectives on writing policy. The ideology of canons and cultural concerns in the literature curriculum. In S. M. Miller & B. McCaskill (Eds.), *Multicultural literature and literacies: Making space for difference* (pp. 105–27). Albany: State University of New York Press.

Purves, A. C. (1993b). Toward a reevaluation of reader response and school literature. *Language Arts, 70*(5), 348–61.

Rappaport, D. (1991). *The journey of Meng: A Chinese legend* (M. Y. Yang, Illus.). New York: Dial.

Reimer, K. M. (1992). Multiethnic literature: Holding fast to dreams. *Language Arts, 69*(1), 14–21.

Rosenblatt, L. M. (1983). *Literature as exploration* (4th ed.). New York: Modern Language Association.

Said, E. W. (1978). *Orientalism.* New York: Pantheon.

Said, E. W. (1993). *Culture and imperialism.* New York: Knopf.

Sims, R. (1982). *Shadow and substance: Afro-American experience in contemporary children's fiction.* Urbana, IL: National Council of Teachers of English.

Spivak, G., & Gunew, S. (1993). Questions of multiculturalism. In S. During (Ed.), *The cultural studies reader* (pp. 193–202). New York: Routledge.

Taxel, J. (1992). The politics of children's literature: Reflections on multiculturalism, political correctness, and Christopher Columbus. In V. J. Harris (Ed.), *Teaching multicultural literature in grades K–8* (pp. 1–36). Norwood, MA: Christopher-Gordon.

Trachtenburg, P. (1990). Using children's literature to enhance phonics instruction. *The Reading Teacher, 43*(9), 648–54.

Walmsley, S. A. (1992). Reflections on the state of elementary literature instruction. *Language Arts, 69*(7), 508–14.

Wong, S. C. (1992). Ethnicizing gender: An exploration of sexuality as sign in Chinese immigrant literature. In S. G. Lim & A. Ling (Eds.), *Reading the literatures of Asian America* (pp. 111–30). Philadelphia: Temple University Press.

Wurzel, J. S. (1988). Multiculturalism and multicultural education. In J. S. Wurzel (Ed.), *Toward multiculturalism* (pp. 1–14). Yarmouth, ME: Intercultural Press.

Yep, L. (1993). *Dragon's gate.* New York: HarperCollins.

Yokota, J. (1993). Issues in selecting multicultural children's literature. *Language Arts, 70*(3), 156–67.

Young, T. A., Campbell, L. C., & Oda, L. K. (1995). Multicultural literature for children and young adults: A rationale and resources. *Reading Horizons, 35*(5), 375–93.

Zhang, G., Lamme, L., & Fang, Z. (1999). Moral themes in Chinese folktales retold in English picture books. *TELLing Stories, 3*(1), 12–21.

22 "I'm Not from Pakistan": Multicultural Literature and the Problem of Representation

Curt Dudley-Marling

When I took a leave from my duties at York University to teach third grade, I hadn't taught children in thirteen years, and I was anxious to renew my teaching experience. The Toronto-area school in which I taught is located in a neighborhood that is ethnically, economically, racially, linguistically, and culturally diverse, and my classroom mirrored the diversity of the community. Four of my twenty-four students were born outside of Canada. Eight others had parents who had immigrated to Canada. Two of my third graders were African Canadians and one an Asian Canadian. Greek, Portuguese, Cantonese, Arabic, Farsi, and Urdu were spoken in my students' homes, and several parents spoke little English. One-fourth of my students were Muslim, the others Christian. Almost all my students came from working-class homes, although several families received some form of public assistance.

This incredible diversity led me to seek multicultural literatures—which I understood to be books for and about people who fell outside the narrow conception of Canadians as White, middle-class, English-(or French-) speaking Protestants of British descent (a profile which applies to less than half the people living in Toronto)—as a means of creating a language arts curriculum that affirmed the range of social and cultural influences on my students' lives.

In this chapter, I share some of the uncertainties, ambiguities, and contradictions that emerged in my own practice when I attempted to use multicultural literature as a means of enacting a multicultural cur-

This chapter is a revised version of an essay that originally appeared in *The New Advocate*, 1997, *10*(2), 123–34. Reprinted with permission.

riculum. I begin by providing a brief overview of the theoretical frame that informed my examination of multicultural practices in my third-grade classroom and, to a lesser degree, my formulation of those practices when I was teaching.

Multiculturalism and Multicultural Literature

Multicultural literature has been described as "literature that represents any distinct cultural group through accurate portrayal and rich detail" (Yokota, 1993, p. 157). More often, however, the term "multicultural literature" refers to "literature by and about people who are members of groups considered to be outside the socio-political mainstream" (Bishop, 1992, p. 39). It was this latter definition that guided my own practice when I was teaching third grade. I hoped that multicultural literature by and about people outside the sociopolitical mainstream could play an important role in creating space for the range of social, cultural, linguistic, and racial experiences my students brought with them to school. Specifically, I wished to create *opportunities for students to see themselves in the curriculum.*

Colleen Russell, a second-grade teacher who worked in a racially and culturally diverse school, told me that her students often complained that the characters in the books they read didn't "look like them." Annette Henry (1994) recalls, "My school lessons never enabled me to make sense of my Blackness in positive, affirming ways. . . . [Teachers] selected lessons from an educational menu that rendered me emotionally and spiritually invisible" (pp. 298–99). Arguably, any students who are "members of groups outside the political mainstream" (Bishop, 1992) have been—and continue to be—slighted by dominant curricular practices that often render them invisible (Reimer, 1992).

If the people who appear in the trade books or textbooks that students read don't "look like them," or if students are exposed to negative or stereotypic representations of the groups to which they belong, they may come to feel that they aren't worthy of positive regard (Bishop, 1992; Taxel, 1992). As Adrienne Rich (1986) put it: "What happens when someone with the authority of a teacher [describes our society] and you're not in it?" (p. 199).

Conversely, the thoughtful integration of multicultural literature "can be used as an important tool in helping all students develop a healthy self-concept, one that depends upon a knowledge of and a sense of pride in family and educational background" (Walker-Dalhouse, 1992, p. 417). My own experience and my reading of the research tells me that children will prefer and engage more with books related to their personal experiences and cultural backgrounds (Allen, 1995; Harris, 1993), which we might expect to have a positive effect on students' reading ability and academic achievement.

I also imagined that literature had the power to *promote intercultural understanding* by transforming students' attitudes and values (Eeds & Hudelson, 1995). Multicultural literature can help students grow in their understanding of themselves and others (Norton, 1990) and, by learning more about each other, develop an appreciation of other cultures (Rasinski & Padak, 1990). Certainly, the increased availability of books by and about girls and women and people of color had the potential to diversify my students' experiences and change their "ideas of time and life and birth and relationship and memory" (Greene, 1993, p. 191). Multicultural literature also offered a way for my students and I to share in the diverse *lives and feelings* of literary characters rather than dealing only with "facts" which may or may not accurately portray the lives of others (Bieger, 1995).

Still, it is unlikely that presenting my students with "accurate" and "authentic" representations of particular cultures would be sufficient to challenge existing relations of power in which certain groups possess a disproportionate share of society's social and economic goods (Britzman, Santiago-Válles, Jiménez-Munoz, & Lamash, 1993). As Sonia Nieto (1996) makes clear, if multicultural education is limited to "lessons in human relations and sensitivity training, units about ethnic holidays, . . . or food festivals . . . the potential for substantive change in schools is severely diminished" (p. 306).

Literature may, however, *provide a ready means for gaining insights into relations of power* as well as an opportunity to critique and challenge the way social and economic power works. Either implicitly or explicitly, literature "provides statements about a host of critically important social and political questions: what it means to be human; the relative worth of boys and girls, men and women, and people from various racial, ethnic, and religious communities; the value of particular kinds of action; how we relate to one another, and about the nature of community, and so forth" (Taxel, 1992, p. 11). Literature written by and for people from marginalized groups can provide to students from more privileged backgrounds a sense of the lived experience of people who suffer the effects of poverty and discrimination. Literature offers all students an opportunity to talk about the meaning of difference, to imagine how the world could be different, and to consider how to challenge practices that diminish the lives of our fellow citizens.

Colleen Russell (1995), for example, responded to her students' concern that the illustrations in the books they were reading didn't "look like them" by engaging her second-grade class in a study of the way children's picture books portray females and people of color as a means of challenging racist and sexist practices in their classroom, the school, and the world beyond the school. Similarly, Karen Smith (1995) encouraged political discussions between her students by sharing articles by critics who disapproved of particular books because of doubtful cultural accuracy or authenticity, and she asked students for their comments on points raised by the critics. With older students, literature can provide a context for examining issues of systemic racism or sexism (Britzman, 1991; Weiler, 1988) even if students resist discussions that challenge social and economic hierarchies in which they themselves may benefit (Britzman et al., 1993).

Another benefit of multicultural literature is that it *provides an antidote to monoculturalism* (May, 1993). School curricula, including much available children's literature, assume there is a national culture that we all share or, perhaps, should share. In general, schooling is a reflection of the culture and experience of White, Protestant, middle- and upper-class students. The reality, however, is that America is not a monocultural society and never has been (Takaki, 1993). Diversity of culture, language, race, and ethnicity is the hallmark of the American experience. Multicultural curricula reflect the multitude of children's backgrounds (Yokota, 1993) and help students entertain multiple ways of understanding and being in the world (Smith, 1995). A monocultural curriculum, however, excludes the social and cultural identities of significant numbers of students in our classrooms and is, therefore, profoundly undemocratic.

Multicultural literature and multicultural education are not unproblematic, however. Multicultural education has its share of critics from both the right and the left of the political spectrum. Conservative critics, for example,

> worry that a multicultural approach to education is too "political" and simply panders to minorities, while also detracting from the "basics" of education. Radical critics . . . think it is not political enough and see it merely as an attempt to placate minorities while leaving unchanged the wider social issues . . . that continue to disadvantage them, both in schools and society. (May, 1993, p. 365)

From this perspective, multicultural education must be part of a pervasive process of school reform involving "changes in the total school environment in order to create equal educational opportunities for all students" (Banks, 1993, p. 11). As Nieto (1996) puts it: "Multicultural education is a philosophy, a way of looking at the world, not simply a program or a class or a teacher" (p. 315). This way of looking at the world, because it challenges the culture of the school as well as mainstream tenets and assumptions dominant in the school, will not always be welcomed (Banks, 1993).

Another critique of multiculturalism comes from those who worry about the tendency of multicultural education to essentialize people's identities by privileging "one social marker, such as race, at the cost of another, such as sex" (Britzman et al., 1993, p. 192). Multicultural education that reduces students' identities to essential qualities like race, for example, ignores the complicated ways that class, gender, sex, language, ethnicity, and so on affect the lived experience of our students. As will become apparent, this is one of the more serious problems with the kind of multicultural curriculum I enacted in my third-grade classroom.

"I'm Not from Pakistan": A Folktale Study

Early in the school year, I began a folktale study and, over the next three months, I read and discussed more than fifty folktales with students. I chose to study folktales in the hope that these texts would engage students' interests, invite more reading and writing, and expand the ways students thought and talked about literature. The availability of multicultural folktales also provided an opportunity to use folktales as a means of exposing students to a range of cultural stories, customs, and traditions.

It's important to note that this multicultural agenda was secondary to my interest in exposing students to a range of folktales. I did not set out to use folktales as a means of taking up issues of multicultural and antiracist education, and the degree to which the folktale unit enabled me to address these issues was the result of serendipity more than a deliberate strategy. It was, however, within this broader effort to offer students a diversity of literary experiences that it occurred to me that I might focus on folktales that *matched* their ethnic, racial, cultural, and religious backgrounds. For the benefit of Ali, whose family had immigrated to Canada from Egypt, for example, I read Egyptian folktales such as *The Egyptian Cinderella* (Climo & Heller, 1989). I also read Persian, West Indian, Portuguese, Greek, Chinese, Scottish, Indian, and African folktales in an attempt to acknowledge the cultural heritage of students whose families had emigrated from those places.

I am well aware that there isn't such a thing as an "African" folktale as much as there are folktales associated with various ethnic, linguistic, and cultural groups such as the Vai, Ashanti, Ouadai, Zulu, and so on. However, many librarians and authors make no effort to make these distinctions beyond identifying regional differentiations (e.g., West African), thereby effacing differences among various people residing in Africa. In this context, representing "Egyptian" as distinct from "African" is particularly troubling.

Additionally, I drew on both literature and expository texts to acknowledge various religious observances important to students. When I discovered that some students were fasting for Ramadan, for example, I read several poems about Ramadan and Iyds, and I invited my Muslim students to talk about how their families observed these traditions. A couple of weeks later, in order to acknowledge the religious heritage of Christian students, we read about Christian religious practices surrounding the observance of Good Friday and Easter.

I was generally pleased with my efforts to use literature to acknowledge students' cultural and religious heritage until I rediscovered an episode in my field notes where I had grossly misrepresented the background of a student I believed was Pakistani:

> Today we read a Pakistani folktale, *The Talking Parrot* (Chia, 1976) and I made a point of singling out Nader [I was led to believe he was from Pakistan]. When I made the connection between the Pakistani folktale and Nader, he protested, "I'm not from Pakistan." (Field notes, December 2, 1991)

Since, as it turned out, Nader was from Afghanistan, not Pakistan (his family spent a year in a Pakistani refugee camp to escape the war in Afghanistan), my effort to acknowledge his cultural heritage clearly missed the mark. However, I have come to doubt that I was any more successful in using multicultural literature as a means of representing the cultural backgrounds of Roya, Shyrose, Fatima, Razika, Ali, or any other student in my class whose families had immigrated to Canada.

First of all, it was unreasonable for me to have assumed that a piece of literature could speak to the culture and experience of *all* people from a particular continent, region, or country. Roya's family, for example, was from Iran and therefore shared a common history with other Iranians. However, her family's upper-middle-class status—they were wealthy enough to buy their way out of Iran—set them apart from the vast majority of people living in Iran. Her family's status as secular Muslims also distinguished them from the fundamentalist Muslims who now run the country. It is unlikely that Roya and her family shared a cultural experience common to all Iranians. It is even less likely that Connie, an ethnic Chinese girl whose parents had immigrated to Canada from Vietnam, shared a common cultural heritage with the mainland Chinese—themselves a diverse mix of cultures and languages—depicted in much Asian literature. And it is almost certain that Shyrose, whose family had migrated to East Africa several generations earlier from India, did not share a common cultural bond with many Black Africans.

The reality is that Africa and Asia are culturally, ethnically, linguistically, and racially diverse places. "African" or "Asian" literature cannot represent the cultural backgrounds of all students of African or Asian descent since there isn't an African or Asian culture as much as there are African and Asian cultures.

If literature from Africa cannot speak to the heritage of all Africans, what can be said about the relationship of nonimmigrant Black children to African literature? I would like to distance myself from claims that the "African" folktales I read to my class somehow affirmed the cultural heritage of the African Canadian students, but I cannot deny that I read African folktales with these students in mind. I imagined that these folktales would somehow speak to African Canadian students as if a homogeneous African culture existed. The fact that the only student in my class who was actually from Africa was of East Indian descent gives an indication of how complicated questions of African identity and culture really are. It is also doubtful that I represented the cultural heritage of Black students any more accurately when I read Caribbean folktales since, although these students' parents grew up in the West Indies, there is clearly not a Caribbean culture either. One Black student did, however, have a strong attachment to Virginia Hamilton's (1985) anthology of Black American folktales, *The People Could Fly,* because his mother read them to him at home.

My efforts to acknowledge the religious heritage of Muslim students by sharing literature and expository texts about Ramadan were also based on a tacit assumption that these students shared a *common* (i.e., identical) religious experience. Our whole-class discussions indicated, however, that there were significant differences in how my Muslim students lived Islam. Unfortunately, I effaced these differences by reading texts that presented a unitary description of Islam. My efforts to recognize Christian holidays fared no better since our readings and discussions did not acknowledge the range of ways the Christian students lived their traditions either.

It is one thing to offer students diverse literary experiences as a means of exposing them to various cultural practices and literary traditions. It is quite another matter to use multicultural literature as part of an explicit effort to affirm or celebrate the cultural heritage of individual children or groups of children, as I attempted to do in my classroom. Using literature to *represent* students' cultural and religious heritages assumed an essential homogeneity in people's cultural heritage that clearly does not exist. People's cultural and religious identities are complicated by factors like race, class, language, socioeconomic status, gender, and so on. The ways in which Roya's family lived Iranian culture, for example, were complicated by their economic privilege and religious practices.

My attempts to match literature to students' ethnic backgrounds were based on a homogeneous sense of culture that ignored the complicated ways people construct their cultural identities. Even my goal to improve cultural understanding was undermined by an approach to multicultural education that distorted the complexity of the people I tried to represent (McDermott & Verenne, 1995). It is unlikely that the stereotypes produced by unitary constructions of culture could ever improve intercultural understanding or communication.

A multicultural curriculum that focuses on folktales and religious celebrations, as mine did, also misses the mark by assuming a stability in culture and cultural practices that ignores the complicated ways people go about making and remaking culture in their daily lives. Culture refers not so much to "food and festivals" (Henry, 1994) as to *relationships* between elements in a whole way of life (Williams, 1981). Culture is a process by which people make—and remake—meaning in their lives, and as such it is not something people can put into a container and transport from place to place. Connie's family, for example, didn't pack their culture into a suitcase and carry it with them when they emigrated from Vietnam to Canada. It may appear that immigrants are mainly in the business of preserving their cultures but, in fact, people actively reinvent their cultures in order to make sense of their lives in new geographical, social, and political surroundings.

My tendency to use certain multicultural texts—folktales, for example—to represent the cultural heritage of some students failed to recognize this more dynamic sense of culture. Assuming a direct link between the culture of Connie's family and the culture of China presumed "some mystical pipeline of authenticity from Asian [Canadians] to their 'heritage culture,' ignoring the fact that their experience has been a transforming one" (Wong, 1993, p. 117). A particular Chinese folktale may have been part of the literary heritage of Connie's family but, as a representation of their culture, it ignored the vibrant and complex ways in which Connie and her family live culture in their daily lives. In Connie's case, certain folktales may have acknowledged a Chinese identity, but it's doubtful this identity had much of a relationship to the way Connie and her family actually live their lives. Connie's family and other Chinese Canadians may work to preserve certain cultural forms or symbols, but the meaning of these forms or symbols in the lives of Chinese Canadians is almost certainly different from their meaning for people living in China (Liu, 1995). In some cases, the children of Chinese Canadians or other immigrant groups may resent, or even reject, efforts to link their identities to cultural forms associated with the place from which their families emigrated (Liu, 1995). Perhaps worse, linking the experience of Asian or African Canadians to folklore and traditions in faraway lands as I did, for example, effaced the contributions these groups have made in shaping Canadian culture(s).

"I Didn't Ask You To"

Since I imagined that my use of multicultural literature would affirm and celebrate students' cultural backgrounds, I was disappointed when students failed to respond enthusiastically to my efforts. Ali, for example, behaved so badly before and during the reading of *The Egyptian Cinderella* (Climo & Heller, 1989) that I removed him from the classroom halfway through the story. Perhaps this was Ali's way of indicating his discomfort with having attention drawn to his background, or he may have been unhappy with the way this folktale linked ethnicity and gender. It's hard to be certain about the relationship between Ali's behavior and this particular tale since Ali was often disruptive. Nonetheless, I was angry at his disruption and, further, I was miffed that Ali didn't *appreciate* my efforts to affirm his cultural identity—more accurately, my sense of his cultural identity.

I was even more upset a few weeks later when Ali disrupted a discussion of the religious significance of Good Friday. When I pointed out that "the other students were considerate when I read about his religious traditions," he responded, "I didn't ask you to" (Field notes, April 10, 1992). At the time I attributed his remark to rudeness. However, I might have at least considered the possibility that Ali may have been telling me something about his interpretation of my efforts to represent *his* cultural identity.

More often, the children for whom I read the multicultural literature responded with silence. Roya, for example, had nothing to say about the Persian folktale. Nor did Connie comment on any of the Chinese folktales we read. Razika and Shyrose actually refused to help me with the pronunciation of certain words when I read about Ramadan. Conversely, the Christian students were not at all hesitant about discussing Christian traditions such as Good Friday and Easter.

From my perspective, the use of multicultural literature was an explicit way to acknowledge my students' ethnic, racial, and religious backgrounds. I imagined these efforts would lead to understanding and pride. As my experience with Ali suggests, this may not have been how the students who were singled out by these practices saw it. Associating Connie, Nader, Charles, Denise, Razika, Shyrose, Roya, and Fatima with exotic cultures and faraway lands marked them as different from "ordinary" Canadians at a time when most of them may have been trying to fit in. Nader, the victim of frequent ethnic slurs and physical abuse, was trying to adopt behaviors that indicated he wasn't different from his peers. However, I was doing my best—through my use of multicultural literature—to say that he *was* different. Similarly, drawing attention to non-Christian students' religious backgrounds through stories about Ramadan and Iyds, for example, may have been an unwelcome intrusion into students' personal lives that also had the effect of marking some students as "different." Ali was an observant Muslim, but it isn't at all clear that he wished me to draw attention to that fact. As he succinctly put it, "he didn't ask me to."

Ali's complaint, "I didn't ask you to," raises what is perhaps the crucial question in interrogating the use of multicultural literature in my third-grade classroom: *Who gets to represent whom and for what purpose?* What counts as an authentic representation of someone else's culture and who decides what's authentic are problems all around. As McCarthy and Crichlow (1993) put it: "issues of identity and representation directly raise questions about who has the power to define whom, and when, and how, . . . [and] often minorities do not have central control over the production of images about themselves in this society" (p. xvi).

When I selected Chinese folktales to celebrate Connie's ethnic heritage, I made assumptions about the relationship between Connie's physical appearance and language and a cultural identity that may have had little to do with the identity Connie and her family imagined for themselves. Similarly, the African and West Indian folktales I chose to acknowledge the racial and cultural heritages of Denise and Charles assumed a Black or African identity they did not choose for themselves and may not have chosen, for all I know.

This isn't simply a matter of selecting more authentic books—that is, books that portray the lives of African Canadians or Asian Canadians instead of the lives of Africans or Asians. A story about a poor African Canadian family living in public housing may be closer to Charles's lived experience than a West African folktale, but it still begs the question: who gets to represent whose experience? And what does it mean for me to decide that Connie is an Asian Canadian when she may think of herself only as a Canadian? I did not, for example, think of Lila as a Portuguese Canadian, Hugh as a Scottish Canadian, or, more to the point, Catherine as a White Canadian. By what right did I assume racialized identities for Connie, Denise, or Charles?

Like it or not, my practice of multiculturalism often assumed that skin color and language were essential identity qualities. Moreover, the practice of essentializing students' identities also had the effect of effacing all the other qualities—class, gender, sex, and so on—that made each student a unique and interesting person (Britzman et al., 1993).

There is another problem with my use of multicultural literature that I want to mention briefly, and it is a dilemma that plagues multicultural education more generally. This is the problem of explicitly taking up the culture of *others* while leaving unmarked the Eurocentric culture underlying most children's literature and school curricula more generally (Wallace, 1993; Wong, 1993). Targeting the culture of nondominant groups for explicit instruction while failing to name the Eurocentric biases in curricular materials tacitly signals the marginality of nondominant groups and leaves unquestioned the status of Eurocentric culture as *the norm* (Norton, 1990). Paradoxically, multicultural education can reinforce the monoculturalism that seeks to deny many of our fellow citizens equal access to our nation's social and economic riches.

Conclusion

I made a range of cultural, ethnic, and racial images available to my students, but this isn't the problem. A diversity of literary experiences permitted students the opportunity to see themselves in curricular materials and exposed them to a range of cultural and ethnic images. Multicultural literature does not, by its mere presence, impose racial or cultural identities on children. The problem is that I tried to *match* texts to the social and cultural identities I imagined for students. I chose to use particular texts to represent the ethnic and religious identities of students without regard to how they themselves might have chosen to represent those identities had they been given the opportunity. However, it wasn't for me to represent students' identities, but rather to create a space where students could represent themselves or at least see themselves represented in the books in our classroom.

My critique of how I used multicultural literature is intended to illustrate some of the pitfalls of multicultural education in general and the use of multicultural literature in particular. This critique should not be used as an excuse to ignore the need to create space in our classrooms for the linguistic, ethnic, cultural, and racial diversity that is America. Nor should the complex issues and the uncertain and incomplete knowledge involved in creating a space congenial to the range of differences our students bring with them to school lead to a sort of pedagogical arrest in which teachers do nothing for fear of making mistakes. This is difficult work, but it must be done.

Despite problems in the way multicultural education was enacted in my classroom, many students did manage to use the spaces for talk in our class and the opportunities to create their own books to infuse their social and cultural identities into our classroom. Roya, for example, often wrote and talked about issues related to her identity as a Muslim and an Iranian. Other students, Razika and Shyrose, for example, resisted my invitations to talk or write about their religious and cultural backgrounds and preferred to write generic stories that betrayed neither their ethnic nor religious heritages. In these situations, students retained the right to control how they would be represented in our classroom. Making available texts in which students could find a range of cultural stories, customs, and traditions enabled them to make their own decisions about their relationship to the stories and characters in those texts.

On the other hand, my deliberate efforts to match texts to my own constructions of students' identities gave students little say in how they were represented. No matter how well intentioned, speaking on behalf of students' cultural and religious identities, instead of letting them speak for themselves, may have had the effect of reinforcing stereotypes that have been used to oppress those I imagined I was speaking for (Alcoff, 1991). Ultimately, representing the experiences of others as we expect them to be cannot lead to either accurate or fair representations or to greater understanding.

Effective multicultural education is also antiracist and antisexist education (Nieto, 1996), and it is unfortunate that I failed to take up multiculturalism in a context in which students are challenged to examine relations of power. Teachers such as Andrew Allen (1995) and

Colleen Russell (1995), for example, demonstrate the possibility of using literature as a means of taking up issues of racism and sexism with children as young as seven and eight years old. Celebrating students' cultural or racial identities and increasing their sensitivities to difference will never be enough to confront systemic racism, sexism, and homophobia that restrict the economic and social opportunities of many of our fellow citizens merely because of who they are and where they are from.

Finally, acknowledging the complexities, uncertainties, and ambiguities of multicultural, antiracist, and antisexist curricula points to the need for teachers to recognize the limitations imposed by their own backgrounds and experiences. The limits of my own knowledge, for example, tell me that I need to participate in a broader discussion of the issues associated with multicultural education with students, colleagues, parents, and the communities in which our schools reside. Only by participating in a conversation that includes a diversity of perspectives and experiences can any of us hope to create a space that is considerate of students' social and cultural identities and that allows teachers and students to be enriched by the diverse ways of being in the world our students bring with them to school each day.

References

Alcoff, L. (1991). The problem of speaking for others. *Cultural Critique 20*, 5–32.

Allen, A. (1995). *Constructing meaning: The responses of emergent readers to Black images in children's picture books.* Unpublished master's thesis, York University, Toronto, Canada.

Banks, J. A. (1993). The canon debate, knowledge construction, and multicultural education. *Educational Researcher, 22*(5), 4–14.

Bieger, E. M. (1995). Promoting multicultural education through a literature-based approach. *The Reading Teacher, 49*, 308–12.

Bishop, R. S. (1992). Multicultural literature for children: Making informed choices. In V. J. Harris (Ed.), *Teaching multicultural literature in grades K–8* (pp. 37–53). Norwood, MA: Christopher-Gordon.

Britzman, D. P. (1991). Decentering discourses in teacher education: Or, the unleashing of unpopular things. *Journal of Education, 173*(3), 60–80.

Britzman, D. P., Santiago-Válles, K., Jiménez-Munoz, G., & Lamash, L. M. (1993). Slips that show and tell: Fashioning multiculture as a problem of representation. In C. McCarthy & W. Crichlow (Eds.), *Race, identity, and representation in education* (pp. 188–200). New York: Routledge.

Chia, H. C. (1976). *The talking parrot: A Pakistani folktale.* Toronto: Dominie.

Climo, S., & Heller, R. (1989). *The Egyptian Cinderella.* New York: Crowell.

Eeds, M., & Hudelson, S. (1995). Literature as a foundation for personal and classroom life. *Primary Voices K–6, 3*(2), 2–7.

Greene, M. (1993). The passions of pluralism: Multiculturalism and the expanding community. In T. Perry & J. W. Fraser (Eds.), *Freedom's plow* (pp. 185–96). New York: Routledge.

Hamilton, V. (1985). *The people could fly: American Black folktales.* New York: Knopf.

Harris, V. J. (1993). African American children's literature: The first one hundred years. In T. Perry & J. W. Fraser (Eds.), *Freedom's plow: Teaching in the multicultural classroom* (pp. 167–83). New York: Routledge.

Henry, A. (1994). The empty shelf and other curricular challenges of teaching for children of African descent: Implications for teacher practice. *Urban Education, 29,* 298–319.

Liu, Y. (1995). *Dragons and chopsticks: When will it end?* Unpublished manuscript, York University, Toronto, Canada.

May, S. A. (1993). Redeeming multicultural education. *Language Arts, 70,* 364–72.

McCarthy, C., & Crichlow, W. (1993). Introduction: Theories of identity, theories of representation, theories of race. In C. McCarthy & W. Crichlow (Eds.), *Race, identity and representation in education* (pp. xiii–xxix). New York: Routledge.

McDermott, R., & Verenne, H. (1995). Culture as disability. *Anthropology and Education Quarterly, 26,* 324–48.

Nieto, S. (1996). *Affirming diversity: The sociopolitical context of multicultural education* (2nd ed.). White Plains, NY: Longman.

Norton, D. E. (1990). Teaching multicultural literature in the reading curriculum. *The Reading Teacher, 44,* 28–40.

Rasinski, T. V., & Padak, N. D. (1990). Multicultural learning through children's literature. *Language Arts, 67,* 576–80.

Reimer, K. M. (1992). Multiethnic literature: Holding fast to dreams. *Language Arts, 69,* 14–21.

Rich, A. C. (1986). *Blood, bread, and poetry: Selected prose, 1979–1985.* New York: Norton.

Russell, C. (1995, November). *Using children's literature to teach anti-discriminatory concepts.* Paper presented at the annual meeting of the National Council of Teachers of English, San Diego, CA.

Smith, K. (1995). Bringing children and literature together in the elementary classroom. *Primary Voices K–6, 3*(2), 22–32.

Takaki, R. T. (1993). *A different mirror: A history of multicultural America.* Boston: Little, Brown.

Taxel, J. (1992). The politics of children's literature: Reflections on multiculturalism, political correctness, and Christopher Columbus. In V. J. Harris (Ed.), *Teaching multicultural literature in grades K–8* (pp. 1–36). Norwood, MA: Christopher-Gordon.

Walker-Dalhouse, D. (1992). Using African-American literature to increase ethnic understanding. *The Reading Teacher, 45,* 416–22.

Wallace, M. (1993). Multiculturalism and oppositionality. In C. McCarthy & W. Crichlow (Eds.), *Race, identity, and representation in education* (pp. 251–61). New York: Routledge.

Weiler, K. (1988). *Women teaching for change: Gender, class and power.* South Hadley, MA: Bergin & Garvey.

Williams, R. (1981). The analysis of culture. In T. Bennett, G. Martin, C. Mercer, & J. Woollacott (Eds.), *Culture, ideology and social process: A reader* (pp. 43–52). London: Open University Press.

Wong, S. C. (1993). Promises, pitfalls, and principles of text selection in curricula diversification: The Asian-American case. In T. Perry & J. W. Fraser (Eds.), *Freedom's plow: Teaching in the multicultural classroom* (pp. 109–20). New York: Routledge.

Yokota, J. (1993). Issues in selecting multicultural children's literature. *Language Arts, 70*(3), 156–67.

Index

Editors

Dana L. Fox currently teaches in the English education and reading, language, and literacy programs in the Department of Middle/Secondary Education and Instructional Technology at Georgia State University, where she also serves as the department's graduate coordinator. Formerly associate professor in language, reading, and culture at the University of Arizona, her research focuses on teacher preparation and professional development in secondary English, teacher beliefs and knowledge, academic writing in graduate education, and gender and literacy. Fox was assistant editor of NCTE's *English Journal* from 1988 to 1990 and coeditor of *The New Advocate* from 1995 to 2000. She has published numerous articles and book chapters and currently serves as coeditor of NCTE's *English Education.*

Kathy G. Short has focused her work on dialogue in literature circles, curriculum as inquiry, and collaborative learning environments for teachers and children. She is professor in language, reading, and culture at the University of Arizona and has worked extensively with teachers to develop curricula that actively involve students as inquirers. She was coeditor of *The New Advocate* from 1995 to 2000 and is current coeditor of NCTE's *Language Arts.* Short has coauthored a number of books, including *Creating Classrooms for Authors and Inquirers* (1996), *Learning Together through Inquiry* (1996), *Literature as a Way of Knowing* (1997), *Talking about Books* (1998), and *Teacher Study Groups* (1998).

Contributors

Marc Aronson is publisher of Book Divisions and vice president of Nonfiction Content Development at Carus Publishing. As an editor, he works with authors and artists, and he developed and ran an imprint devoted to international and multicultural books for teenagers. Aronson is the author of *Art Attack: A Short Cultural History of the Avant-Garde* (1998) and the award-winning *Sir Walter Ralegh and the Quest for El Dorado* (2000). He holds a doctorate in American history, specializing in the history of publishing. Aronson frequently teaches courses on children's and young adult publishing, and he lives in New York with his wife, the author Marina Budhos, and their son Sasha.

Rosalinda B. Barrera is professor in the Department of Curriculum and Instruction at the University of Illinois at Urbana-Champaign, where she teaches graduate and undergraduate courses in multicultural children's literature and early childhood literacy. Her publications include *Kaleidoscope: A Multicultural Booklist for Grades K–8*, Second Edition (1997) and *Multicultural Issues in Literacy and Practice* (2003). She conducts research on Latino/Latina children's literature and the literacy education of Latino/Latina children. Barrera is currently associate director of the Center on Democracy in a Multiracial Society at the University of Illinois.

Rudine Sims Bishop is professor emerita in the Department of Language, Literacy, and Culture at The Ohio State University, where she taught courses in children's literature, including poetry, multicultural literature, and the history of children's literature. Her scholarly interests include the classroom use of children's literature in the context of multicultural education and the effects of cultural identities and other cultural factors on children's responses to literature. She is currently working on a book about the history and development of African American children's literature over the past century and a half.

Mingshui Cai received his Ph.D. from The Ohio State University. He is currently associate professor of education at the University of Northern Iowa, where he teaches courses in children's literature. His research interests include children's literature, multicultural literature, and reader response to literature. Cai has published articles in *Children's Literature in Education, The New Advocate,* and *Journal of Children's Literature,* among others. In addition to journal articles and book chapters, he is author of *Multicultural Literature for Children and Young Adults: Reflections on Critical Issues* (2002).

Curt Dudley-Marling is professor of education in the Lynch School of Education at Boston College, where he teaches courses in language and literacy. His research focuses on struggling readers and writers, parents of struggling learners, and teacher education. Dudley-Marling is the author of numerous articles and books, including *Living with Uncertainty: The Messy Reality of Classroom Practice* (1997), which offers a more thorough examination of data he collected during his year as a third-grade teacher. He is also former coeditor of *Language Arts* and is currently a member of NCTE's Elementary Section Steering Committee.

Zhihui Fang is associate professor in language and literacy in the School of Teaching and Learning at the University of Florida. He has been actively involved in several outreach projects to help teachers design and implement exemplary literacy programs in inclusive elementary classrooms. His research interests include the grammatical and pedagogical construction of literacy, literacy teacher education, and sociolinguistics. Fang's many publications have appeared in several edited volumes and over twenty different refereed journals around the world. He has received formal recognition for his teaching and scholarship from the University of Florida, NCTE, the International Reading Association, and the American Educational Research Association.

Danling Fu is associate professor in language and literacy in the School of Teaching and Learning at the University of Florida. She teaches language arts methods at the undergraduate level and graduate seminars on culture and literacy and composition theory and research. Her research focus is on children's writing development, writing assessment, and literacy education for minority and new immigrant children. Fu has been a literacy consultant since 1997 in New York Chinatown schools, where she also conducts research on the education of new immigrants in both primary and secondary classrooms.

Henry Louis Gates Jr. is the W. E. B. Du Bois Professor of the Humanities, chair of the Department of Afro-American Studies, and director of the W. E. B. Du Bois Institute for Afro-American Research at Harvard University. He is the author of several works of literary criticism, including *Figures in Black: Words, Signs, and the "Racial" Self* (1987); *The Signifying Monkey: A Theory of Afro-American Literary Criticism* (1988), which received the 1989 American Book Award; and *Loose Canons: Notes on the Culture Wars* (1992). He has also authored *Colored People: A Memoir* (1994), which traces his childhood experiences in a small West Virginia town in the 1950s and 1960s; *The Future of the Race* (1996), coauthored with Cornel West; and *Thirteen Ways of Looking at a Black Man* (1997). Gates has edited several anthologies and is coeditor with K. Anthony Appiah of the encyclopedia *Microsoft Encarta Africana* published on CD-ROM (1999) and in book form under the title *Africana: The Encyclopedia of the African and African American Experience*

(1999). He is the author of *Wonders of the African World* (1999), the book companion to the six-hour BBC/PBS television series of the same name.

Susan Guevara is the illustrator of twelve books for children. She was the first recipient of the Tomás Rivera Award and received both the 1995 and 2002 Pura Belpré Awards for the best-illustrated works affirming and celebrating the Latino/Latina cultural experience in outstanding children's books. Some of Guevara's books include *Chato's Kitchen* (1995), *Chato and the Party Animals* (2000), and *My Daughter, My Son, the Eagle, the Dove* (2000), which is also available in a Spanish-language edition. She lives in an old cabin in the Sierras with her cat Bulldozer.

Violet J. Harris is professor of language and literacy in the Department of Curriculum and Instruction at the University of Illinois at Urbana-Champaign, where she was department head from 1998 to 2003. She teaches undergraduate and graduate courses in children's literature and literacy and holds faculty affiliate status with African Studies, the Afro-American Research Program, and the Graduate School of Library and Information Science. Harris's scholarship focuses on literacy and language acquisition and development, the historic development of literacy among Blacks, and literacy materials created specifically for Blacks; literature for children and youth, especially that labeled multicultural; reader response; and analysis of the publishing industry.

Linda Leonard Lamme is professor of language and literacy in the School of Teaching and Learning at the University of Florida. She consults with elementary schools implementing inclusive literacy education practices, and she teaches courses in children's literature, multicultural children's literature, social justice issues in children's literature, and research on children's literature. Author or editor of six books and numerous professional articles, she is coeditor of the historical fiction and picture book chapters in *Adventuring with Books: A Booklist for Pre-K–Grade 6,* Thirteenth Edition (2003). Her current research interest concerns critical multiculturalism in children's literature.

Kathryn Lasky is an award-winning author of more than eighty books, including fiction and nonfiction for children, young adults, and adults. Her books have received such honors as the Parents' Choice Award, the National Jewish Book Award, and a Newbery Honor citation. Many of Lasky's nonfiction books are illustrated with photographs by her husband, Christopher Knight. Some of her recent works include *Vision of Beauty: The Story of Sarah Breedlove Walker* (2000), *The Man Who Made Time Travel* (2003), *A Brilliant Streak: The Making of Mark Twain* (1998), *She's Wearing a Dead Bird on Her Head!* (1995), and *The Emperor's Old Clothes* (1999). She lives in Cambridge, Massachusetts, with her husband and their two children, Max and Meribah.

Weimin Mo is associate professor in the Department of Childhood, Reading, and Language Arts at the University of South Florida at Sarasota/Manatee, where he teaches children's literature and reading/language arts. Born in Shanghai, China, he received his B.A. from Shanghai Institute of Foreign Languages. In China, he taught English as a second language, Chinese, and fine arts, and in 1981 he came to the United States to further his education. Mo's research interests include children's literature, multicultural education, ESOL, and early childhood literacy learning. A trained artist, he is also interested in illustrating picture books.

Judi Moreillon serves as co-librarian at Sabino High School in Tucson, Arizona. She completed her Ph.D. in the Department of Language, Reading, and Culture at the University of Arizona. Her research focus is media and literacy. As a graduate teaching assistant, she taught children's literature to preservice classroom teachers, and as an adjunct professor she teaches a course on electronic literacy offered to graduate library school students. Moreillon has a master's degree in library science and worked for ten years as an elementary school librarian. She maintains a Web site at personal.riverusers.com/~storypower.

W. Nikola-Lisa is professor of education at National-Louis University in Evanston, Illinois, where he works with teachers in a graduate program in interdisciplinary studies. Nikola-Lisa is the author of a number of popular children's books, including *Bein' with You This Way* (1994), *Tangletalk* (1997), *The Year with Grandma Moses* (2000), *Summer Sun Risin'* (2002), and *Shake Dem Halloween Bones* (1997), which recently won the Wisconsin Golden Archer Award. In addition to writing professional articles as well as books for children, Nikola-Lisa regularly visits schools across the nation sharing his love of literature.

Elizabeth Noll is associate professor of language, literacy, and sociocultural studies at the University of New Mexico. Her research interests include children's and young adult literature, the role of local communities in literacy curricula, and alternative representations of research data. She has published articles in journals such as *The New Advocate, Journal of Literacy Research,* and *English Journal* and is currently working on an edited volume about alternative forms of data representation.

Ruth E. Quiroa is a doctoral student in the Department of Curriculum and Instruction at the University of Illinois at Urbana-Champaign specializing in bilingual education and children's literature. She formerly taught bilingual kindergarten and second grade and also served as coordinator for an after-school program at a middle school. In her dissertation study, she is examining the responses of first graders, all Mexican-origin immigrants or children of immigrants, to Mexican American–themed bilingual picture storybooks read aloud in Spanish.

Hazel Rochman is editor of young adult books at *Booklist,* the reviewing journal of the American Library Association. She was born and raised under apartheid in South Africa, where she worked as a journalist. She left there without a passport in 1963 and taught English in Leeds, England, and London, until she moved to Chicago in 1972, where she was librarian at the University of Chicago Laboratory Schools. Rochman came to *Booklist* in 1984. She edited the collection *Somehow Tenderness Survives: Stories of Southern Africa* (1988), and her book *Against Borders: Promoting Books for a Multicultural World* (1993) won the G. K. Hall Award for Library Literature. She was selected to give the Arbuthnot Lecture in 2000, where her subject was "A Stranger Comes to Town."

Thelma Seto is Eurasian of Japanese and European descent, born to Canadian and American parents in Syria and raised in Lebanon and Iran. The cultures and geopolitical realities of her childhood home have informed her development as a writer, especially in Iran, where writers were targeted by the shah and the CIA. Active for two decades in the literary and Nikkei communities of Los Angeles and San Francisco, she currently works on sustainable farms in Appalachian Ohio in a preabolition, mixed-race community on the route of the Underground Railroad. Her poetry, fiction, and essays appear in numerous publications including *Into the Fire: Asian American Prose* (1996), *Premonitions: The Kaya Anthology of New Asian North American Poetry* (1995), and *Two Worlds Walking: Short Stories, Essays and Poetry by Writers with Mixed Heritages* (1994).

Wenju Shen is professor in the Department of Early Childhood and Reading Education at Valdosta State University, where she teaches courses in children's literature and fine arts, curriculum, assessment, and reading methods. Her research interests include multicultural education, integrative curricula for young children, and performance-based assessment in early childhood education. Born in Shanghai, China, Shen received her B.A. in China and her graduate degrees in the United States. She has been collaborating with her husband, Weimin Mo, for many years in the area of children's literature and fine arts.

Laura B. Smolkin is associate professor of elementary education in the University of Virginia's Curry School of Education, where she teaches courses in language and literacy education, including children's literature. Her research has focused on text in a variety of sociocultural contexts. Currently she is studying the influence of genre on classroom trade book read-alouds.

Joseph H. Suina, tribal council member and former governor of his native Cochiti Pueblo, is associate professor of multicultural education at the University of New Mexico. His current research explores indigenous teachers' lives and work histories, examining the sociolinguistic and pedagogical aspects of their personal stories.

Joel Taxel is professor and head of the Department of Language Education at the University of Georgia. A graduate of the University of Wisconsin–Madison, he is best known for his research on the sociocultural, economic, and political dimensions of children's literature. The founding editor of *The New Advocate*, Taxel has published articles in such journals as *Curriculum Inquiry, Interchange,* and *Teachers College Record.* His recent article, "Children's Literature at the Turn of the Century: Toward a Political Economy of the Publishing Industry," appeared in the November 2002 issue of *Research in the Teaching of English.*

Jacqueline Woodson is the author of a number of books for children and young adults, including *If You Come Softly* (1998), *I Hadn't Meant to Tell You This* (1994), *From the Notebooks of Melanin Sun* (1995), and *Miracle's Boys* (2000), which won the 2000 Coretta Scott King Medal and the *Los Angeles Times* Book Prize. Her picture books include *We Had a Picnic This Sunday Past* (1997), *Sweet, Sweet Memory* (2000), *The Other Side* (2001), and *Visiting Day* (2002). She lives in Brooklyn, New York, with her partner and their young daughter.

Vivian Yenika-Agbaw is associate professor of English education at Bloomsburg University, where she teaches courses in children's and young adult literature. She has published articles in *Children's Literature Association Quarterly, The New Advocate, Journal of African Children's Literature,* and *International Review of Education,* among others. In addition, Yenika-Agbaw is a member of the 2003–2004 editorial review board of the *Journal of Adolescent and Adult Literacy.* Her research interests include children's literature, cultural studies, critical literacy, and postcolonial theory.